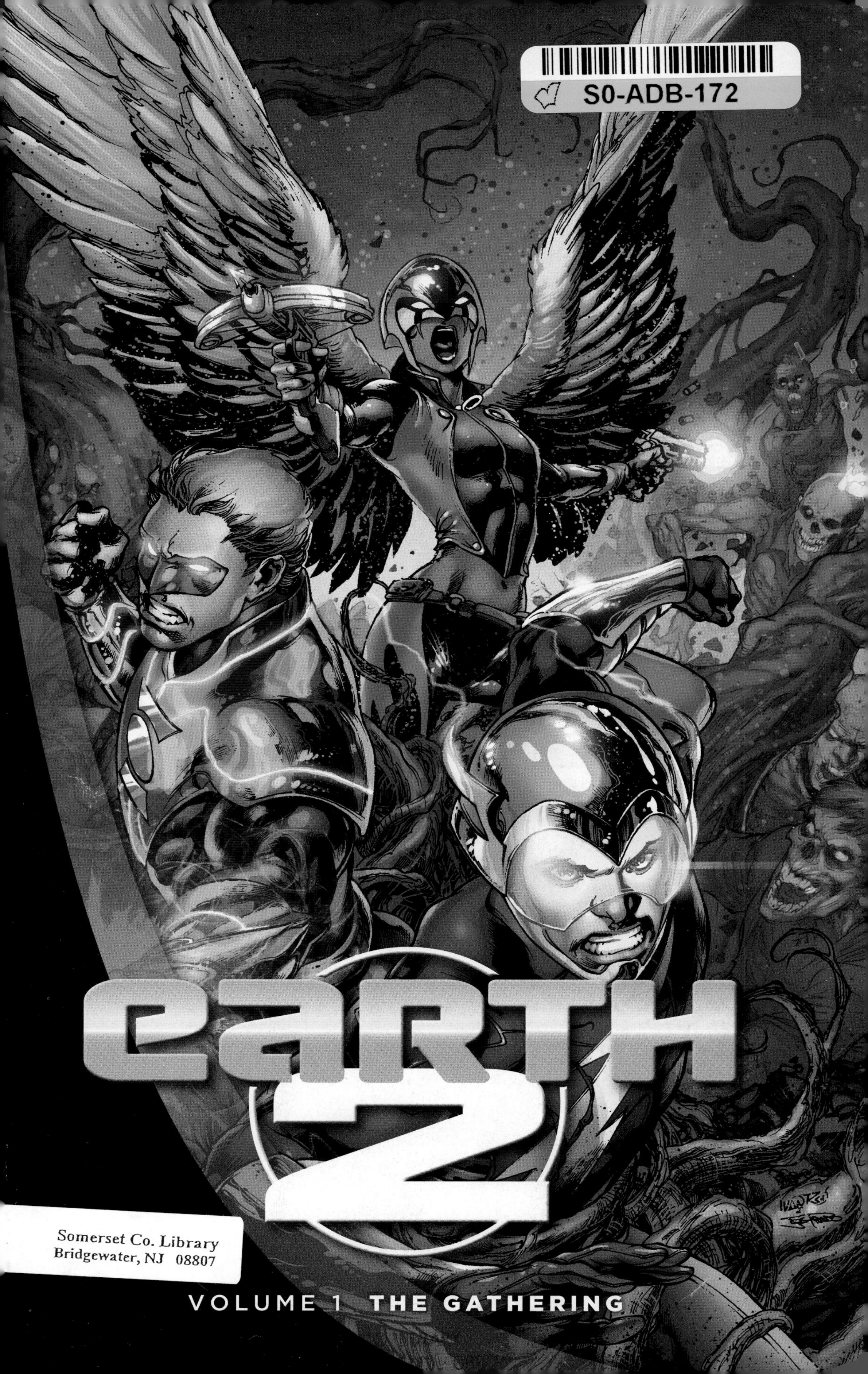

EARTH 2

VOLUME 1 THE GATHERING

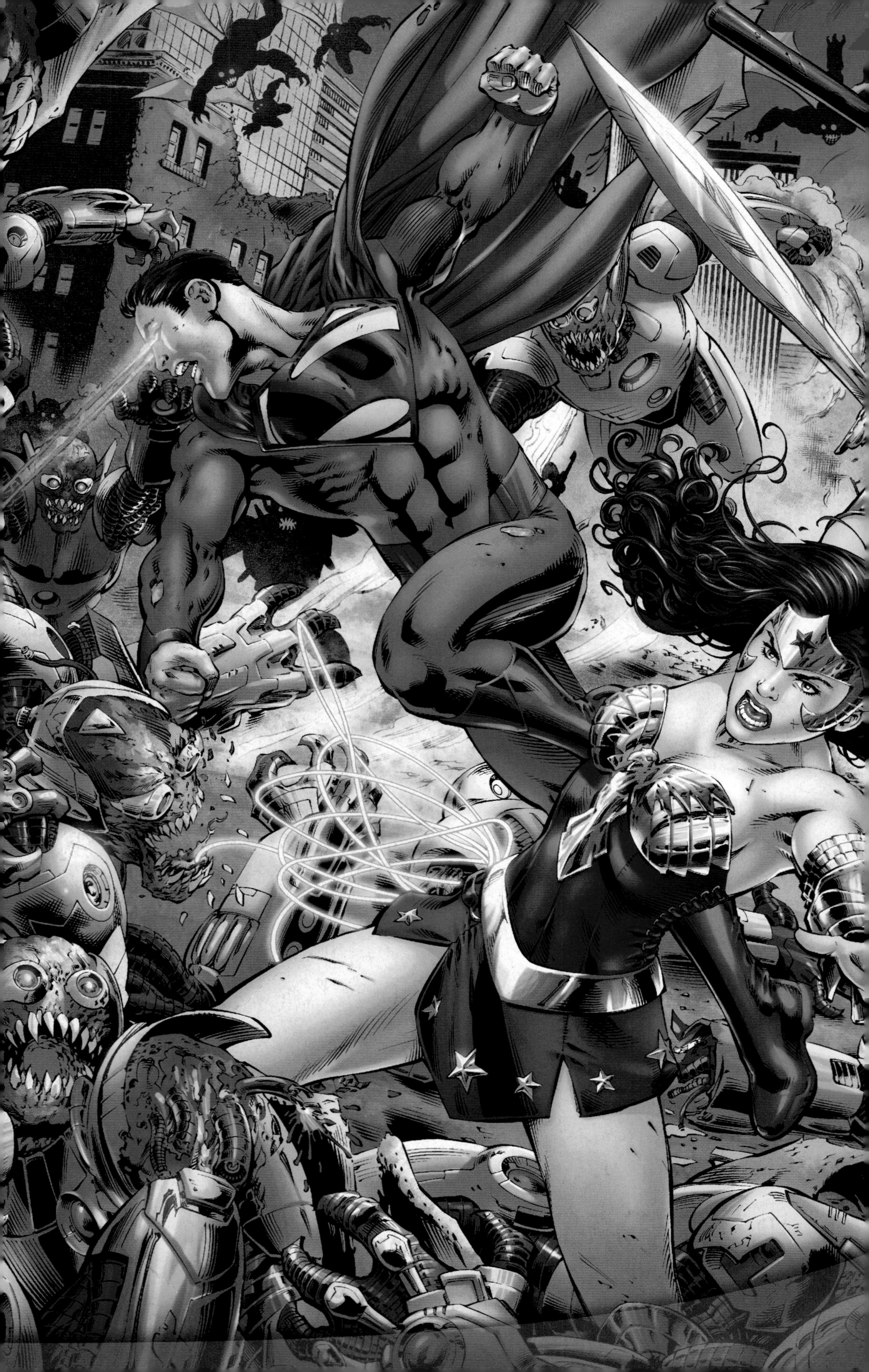

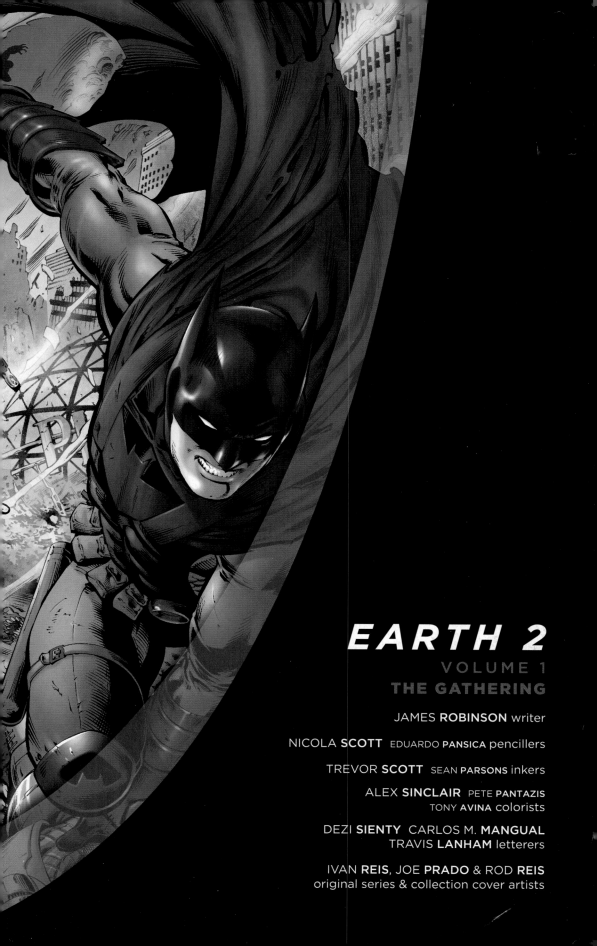

EARTH 2
VOLUME 1
THE GATHERING

JAMES **ROBINSON** writer

NICOLA **SCOTT** EDUARDO **PANSICA** pencillers

TREVOR **SCOTT** SEAN **PARSONS** inkers

ALEX **SINCLAIR** PETE **PANTAZIS**
TONY **AVINA** colorists

DEZI **SIENTY** CARLOS M. **MANGUAL**
TRAVIS **LANHAM** letterers

IVAN **REIS**, JOE **PRADO** & ROD **REIS**
original series & collection cover artists

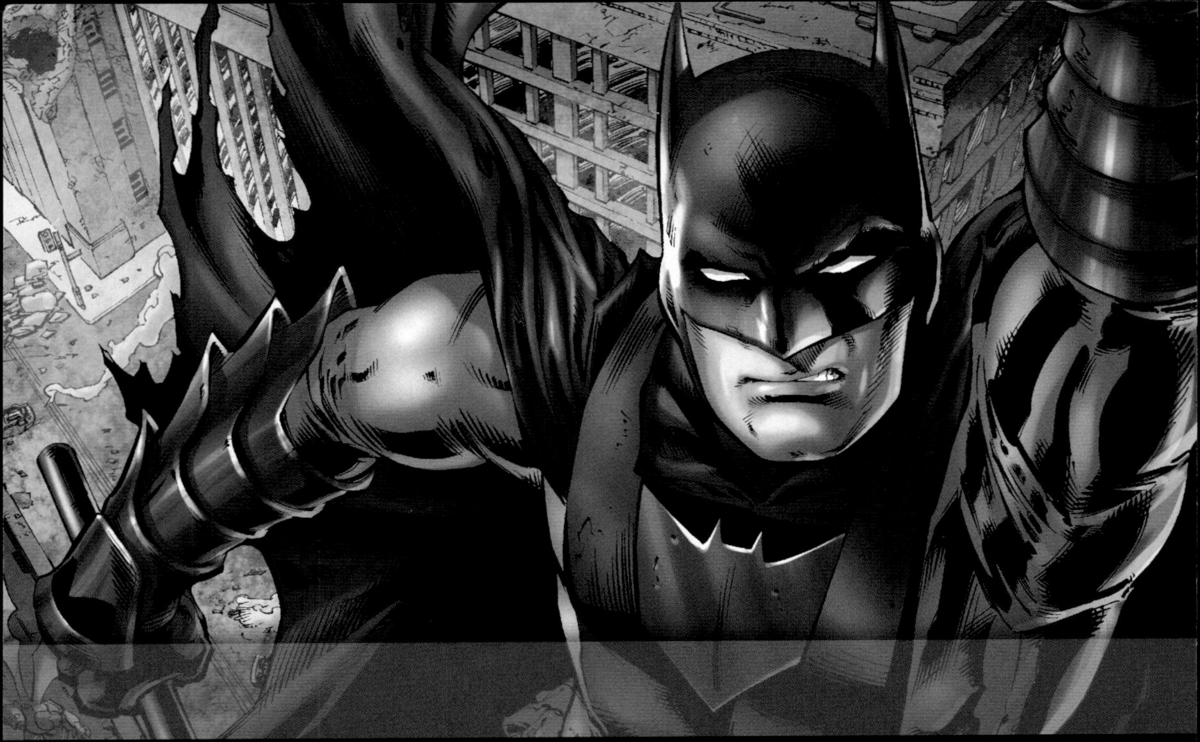

PAT McCALLUM Editor – Original Series SEAN MACKIEWICZ KATE STEWART Assistant Editors – Original Series
PETER HAMBOUSSI Editor ROBBIN BROSTERMAN Design Director – Books
ROBBIE BIEDERMAN Publication Design

BOB HARRAS Senior VP – Editor-in-Chief, DC Comics

DIANE NELSON President DAN DIDIO and JIM LEE Co-Publishers
GEOFF JOHNS Chief Creative Officer
JOHN ROOD Executive VP – Sales, Marketing and Business Development
AMY GENKINS Senior VP – Business and Legal Affairs NAIRI GARDINER Senior VP – Finance
JEFF BOISON VP – Publishing Planning MARK CHIARELLO VP – Art Direction and Design
JOHN CUNNINGHAM VP – Marketing TERRI CUNNINGHAM VP – Editorial Administration
ALISON GILL Senior VP – Manufacturing and Operations HANK KANALZ Senior VP – Vertigo and Integrated Publishing
JAY KOGAN VP – Business and Legal Affairs, Publishing JACK MAHAN VP – Business Affairs, Talent
NICK NAPOLITANO VP – Manufacturing Administration SUE POHJA VP – Book Sales
COURTNEY SIMMONS Senior VP – Publicity BOB WAYNE Senior VP – Sales

EARTH 2 VOLUME 1: THE GATHERING

DC Comics, 1700 Broadway, New York, NY 10019
A Warner Bros. Entertainment Company.
Printed by RR Donnelley, Salem, VA, USA. 8/30/13. First Printing.

ISBN: 978-1-4012-4281-7

Library of Congress Cataloging-in-Publication Data

Robinson, James Dale, author.
Earth 2. Volume 1, The gathering / James Robinson, Nicola Scott, Trevor Scott.
pages cm
"Originally published in single magazine form in Earth 2 1-6."
ISBN 978-1-4012-3774-5
1. Graphic novels. I. Scott, Nicola, illustrator. II. Scott, Trevor, illustrator. III. Title. IV. Title: Gathering.
PN6727.R58E23 2013
741.5'973—dc23
2012046491

SUSTAINABLE FORESTRY INITIATIVE
Certified Chain of Custody
At Least 20% Certified Forest Content
www.sfiprogram.org
SFI-01042
APPLIES TO TEXT STOCK ONLY

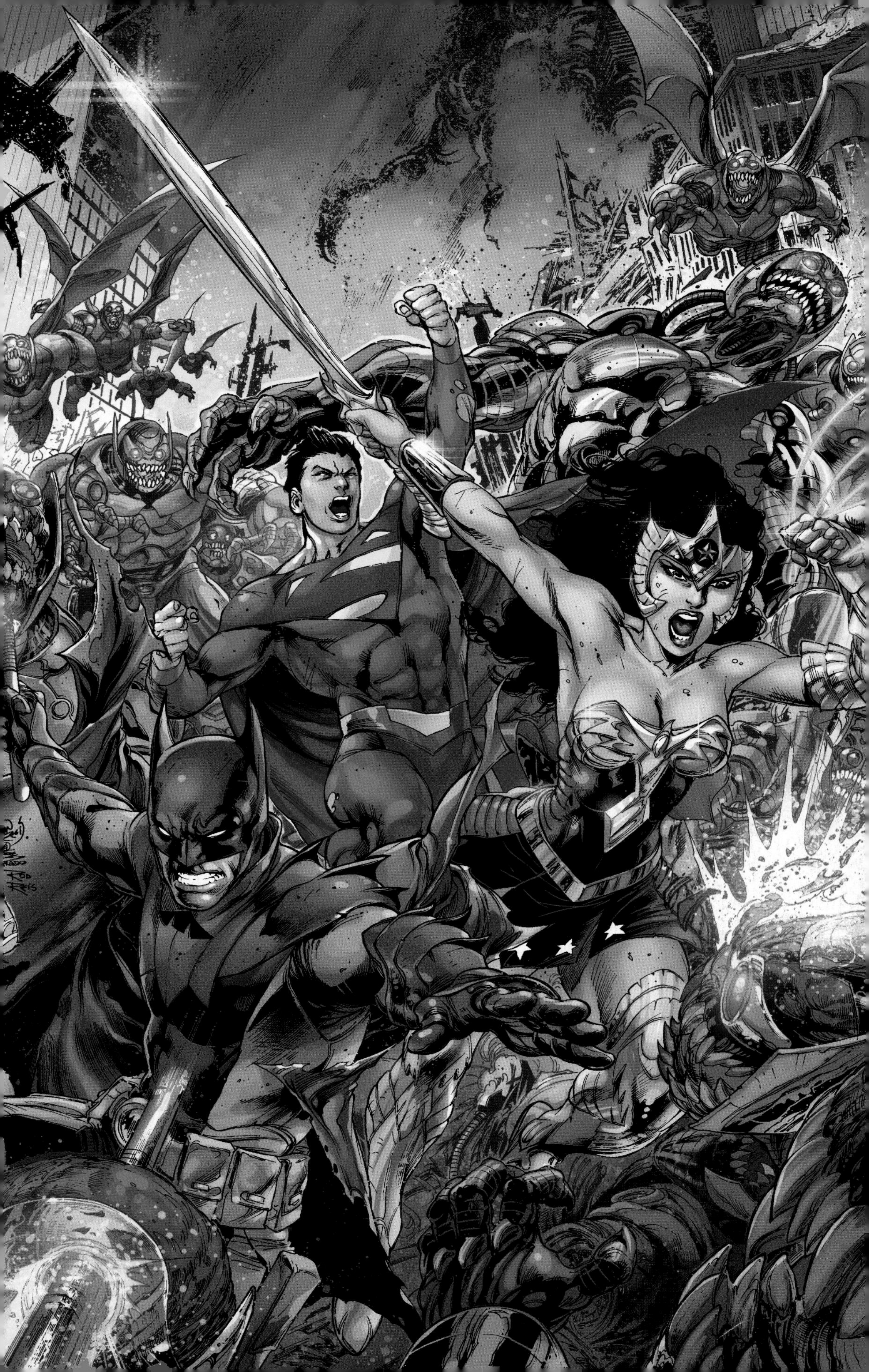

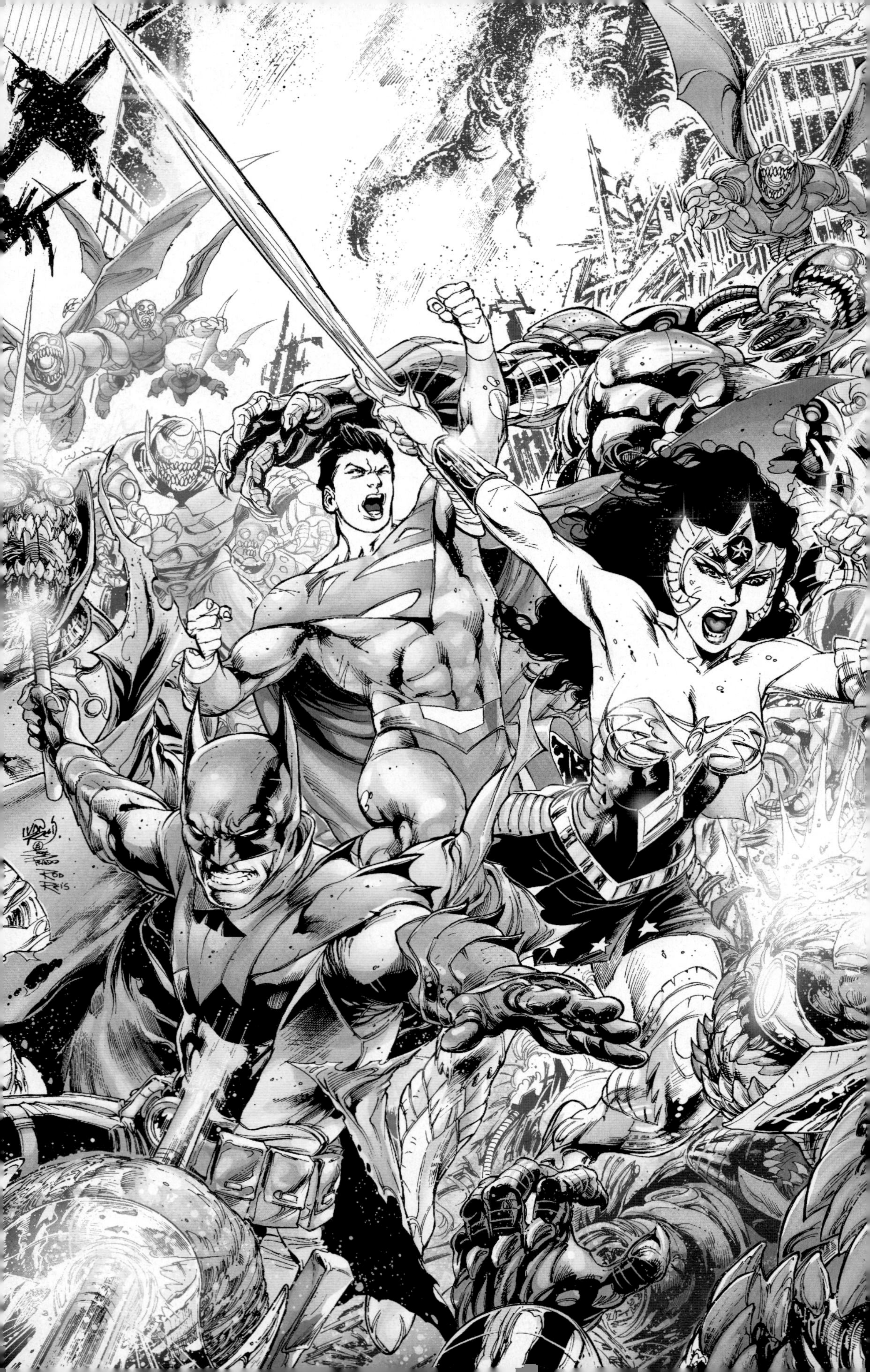
PRADO
ROD REIS

WE ALL KNOW THE FACTS, OF COURSE. WE ALL KNOW WHAT HAPPENED...

HOW THEY APPEARED OUT OF NOWHERE, OR AT LEAST IT SEEMED THAT WAY AT THE TIME...PARADEMONS AS THEY CAME TO BE KNOWN... ATTACKING FROM OUT OF "TUBES" OF ENERGY AND LIGHT.

INVADING EARTH. DESTROYING COUNTRIES, ENSLAVING THEM.

THEIR LEADER, STEPPENWOLF, SEEMINGLY BRILLIANT... UNSTOPPABLE!

AND SO BEGAN THE APOKOLIPS WAR.

WE FOUGHT BACK OF COURSE, SOLDIERS OF THE WORLD UNITED, WE FOUGHT BACK AND KEPT THOSE DEMONS AT BAY.

A BLOODY STALE-MATE THAT SEEMED UNENDING. IT WOULD TAKE A GENIUS TO TURN THE TIDE...

KAL, DIANA, I HAVE THE ANSWER, FINALLY. I KNOW HOW WE CAN END THE WAR.

...BUT LUCKILY WE HAD ONE.

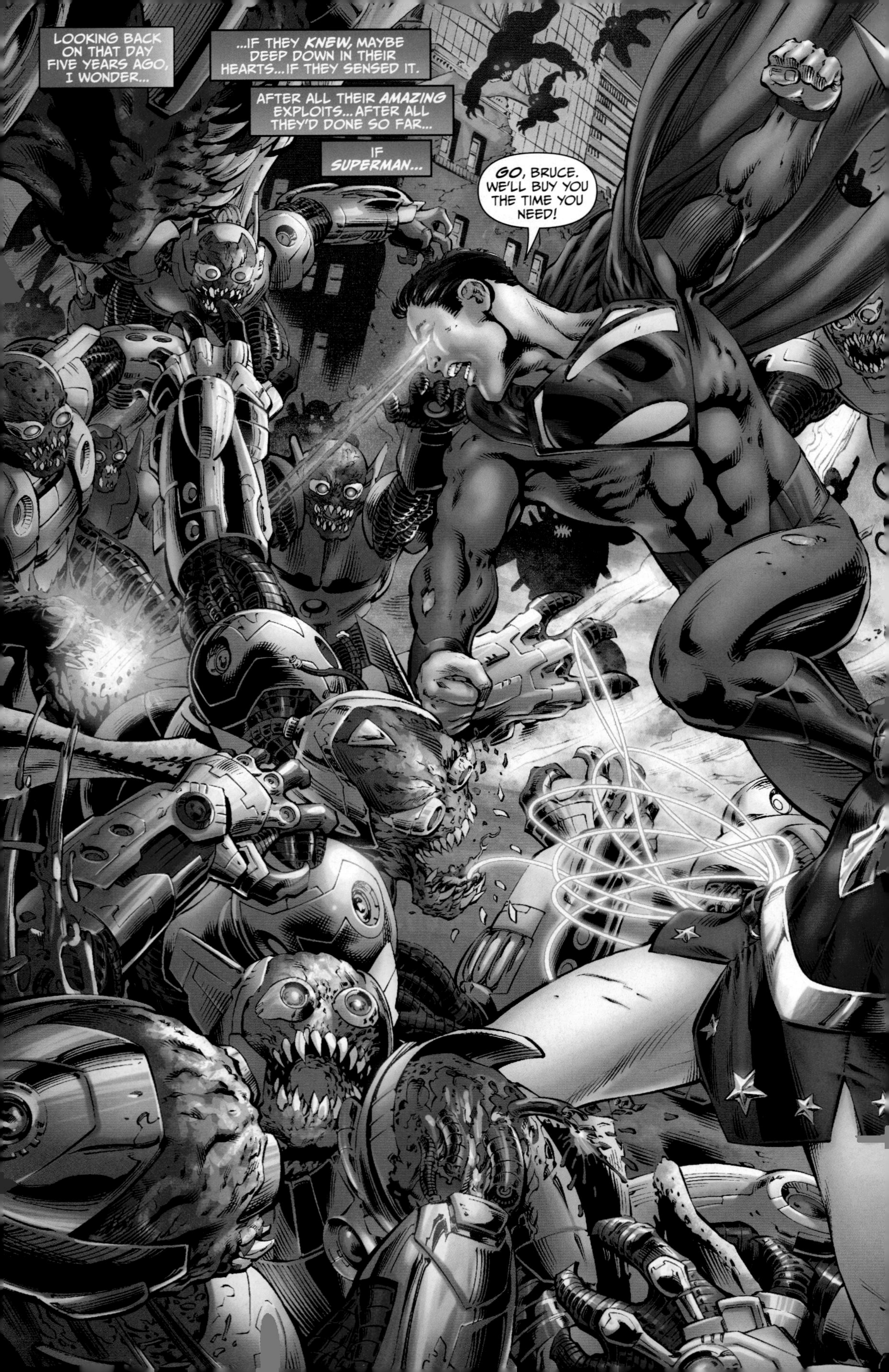
LOOKING BACK ON THAT DAY FIVE YEARS AGO, I WONDER...
...IF THEY KNEW, MAYBE DEEP DOWN IN THEIR HEARTS...IF THEY SENSED IT.
AFTER ALL THEIR AMAZING EXPLOITS...AFTER ALL THEY'D DONE SO FAR...
IF SUPERMAN...
GO, BRUCE. WE'LL BUY YOU THE TIME YOU NEED!

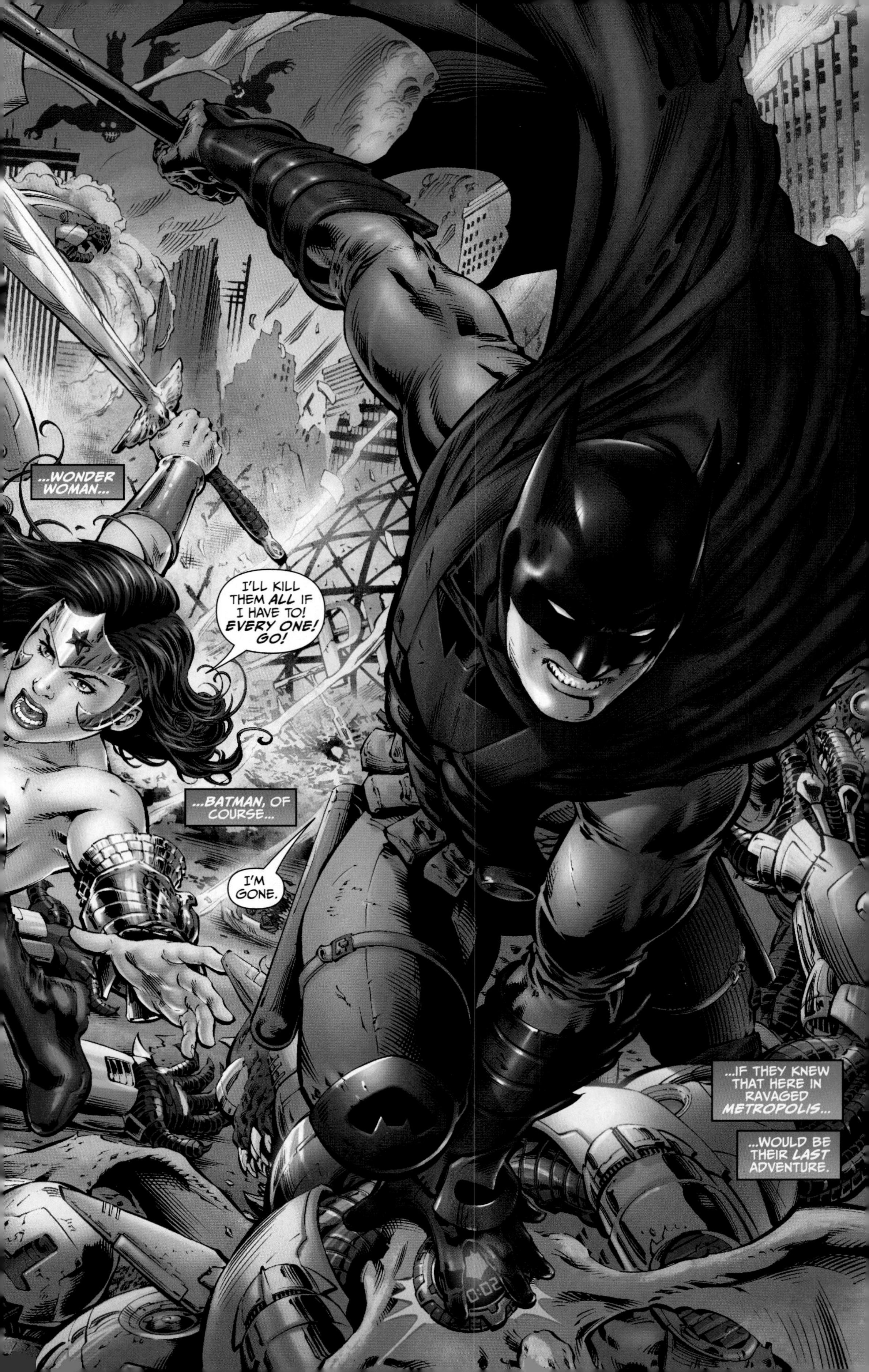
...WONDER WOMAN...
I'LL KILL THEM ALL IF I HAVE TO! EVERY ONE! GO!
...BATMAN, OF COURSE...
I'M GONE.
...IF THEY KNEW THAT HERE IN RAVAGED METROPOLIS...
...WOULD BE THEIR LAST ADVENTURE.

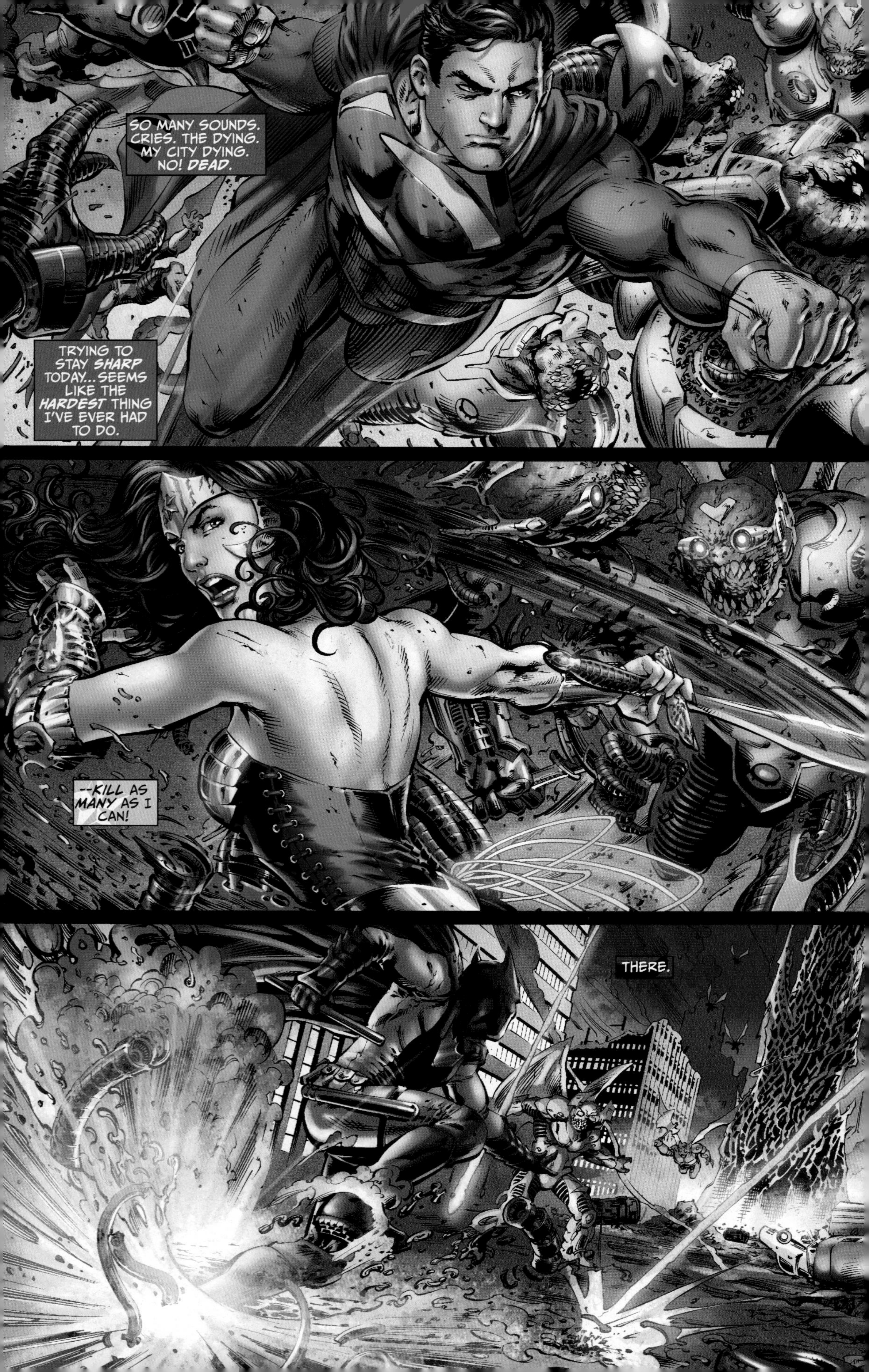
SO MANY SOUNDS. CRIES. THE DYING. MY CITY DYING. NO! DEAD.
TRYING TO STAY SHARP TODAY... SEEMS LIKE THE HARDEST THING I'VE EVER HAD TO DO.
--KILL AS MANY AS I CAN!
THERE.

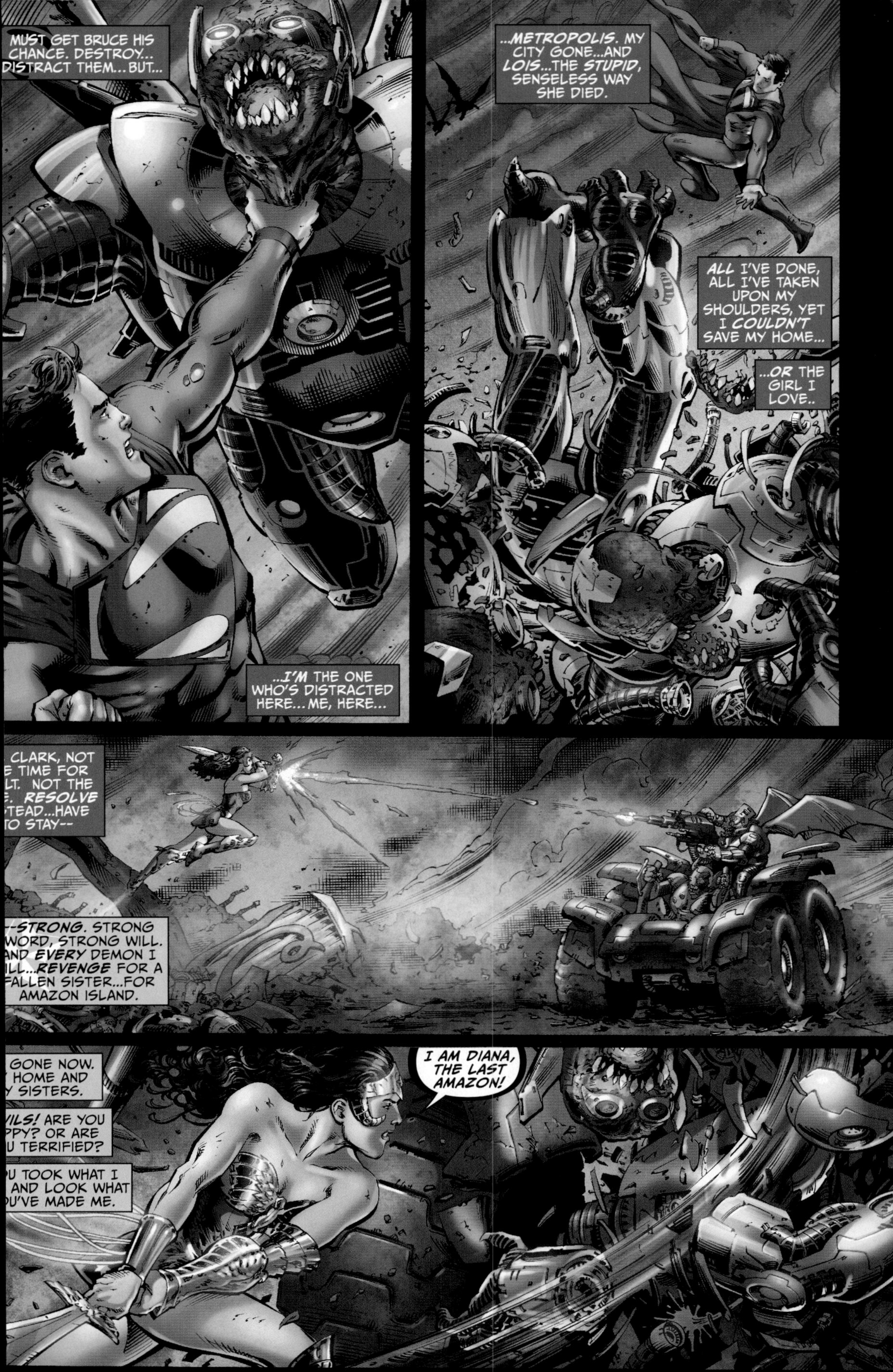
MUST GET BRUCE HIS CHANCE. DESTROY... DISTRACT THEM... BUT...
...I'M THE ONE WHO'S DISTRACTED HERE... ME, HERE...
...METROPOLIS. MY CITY GONE...AND LOIS...THE STUPID, SENSELESS WAY SHE DIED.
ALL I'VE DONE, ALL I'VE TAKEN UPON MY SHOULDERS, YET I COULDN'T SAVE MY HOME...
...OR THE GIRL I LOVE..
CLARK, NOT E TIME FOR LT. NOT THE E. RESOLVE STEAD...HAVE TO STAY--
STRONG. STRONG WORD, STRONG WILL. AND EVERY DEMON I ILL...REVENGE FOR A FALLEN SISTER...FOR AMAZON ISLAND.
GONE NOW. HOME AND SISTERS.
VILS! ARE YOU PPY? OR ARE U TERRIFIED?
U TOOK WHAT I AND LOOK WHAT U'VE MADE ME.
I AM DIANA, THE LAST AMAZON!

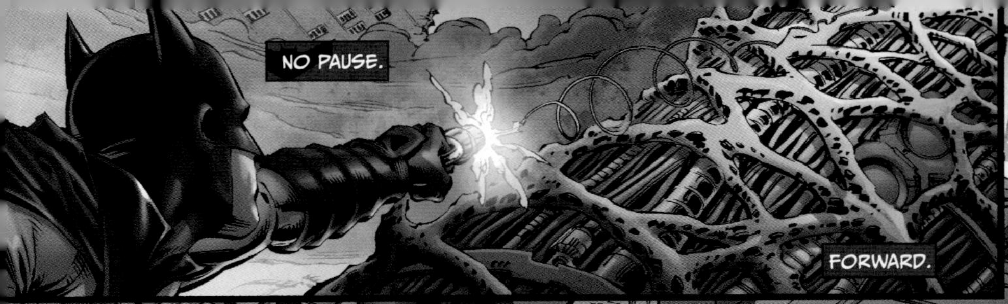
NO PAUSE.
FORWARD.
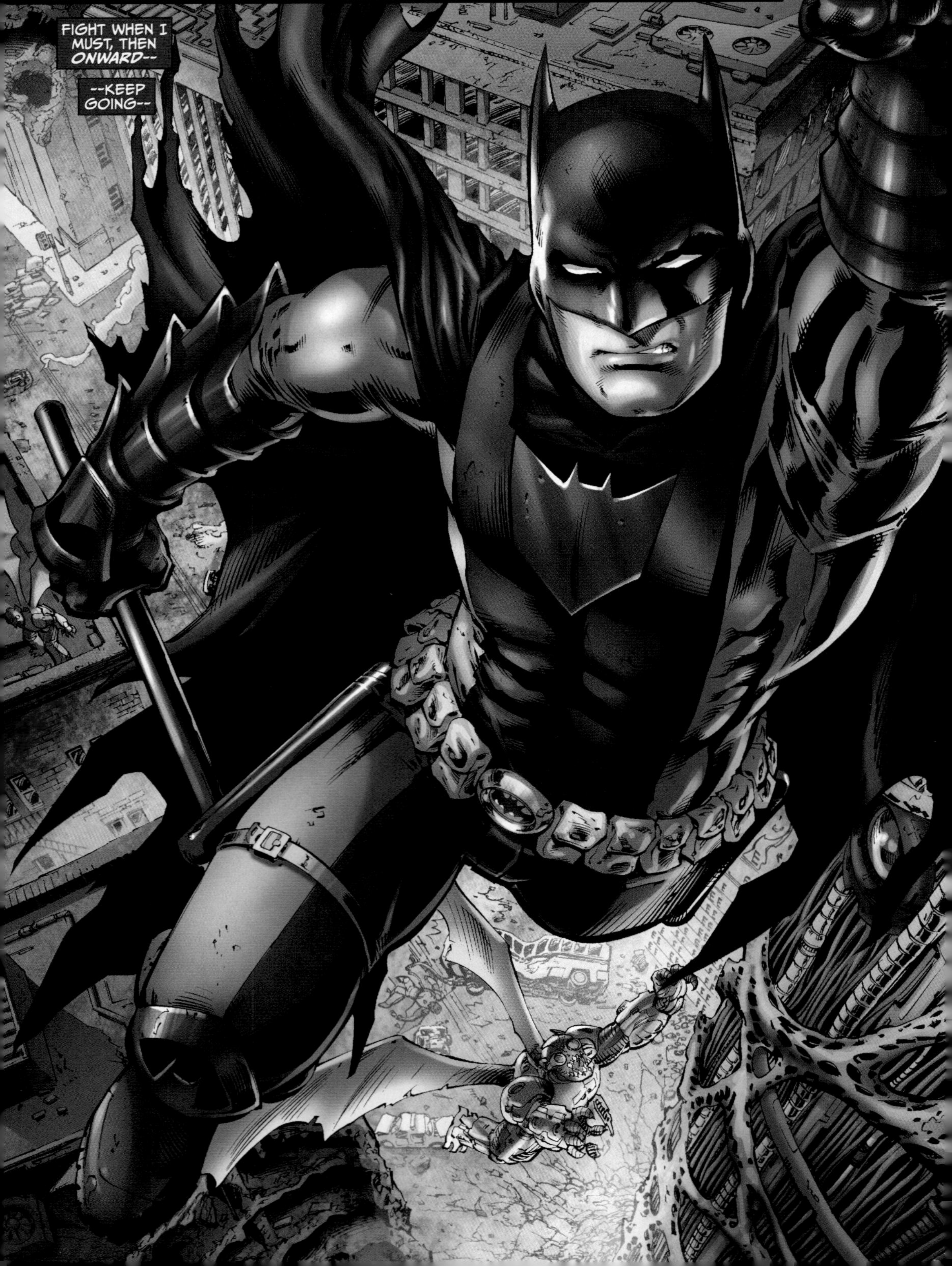
FIGHT WHEN I MUST, THEN *ONWARD*--
--KEEP GOING--

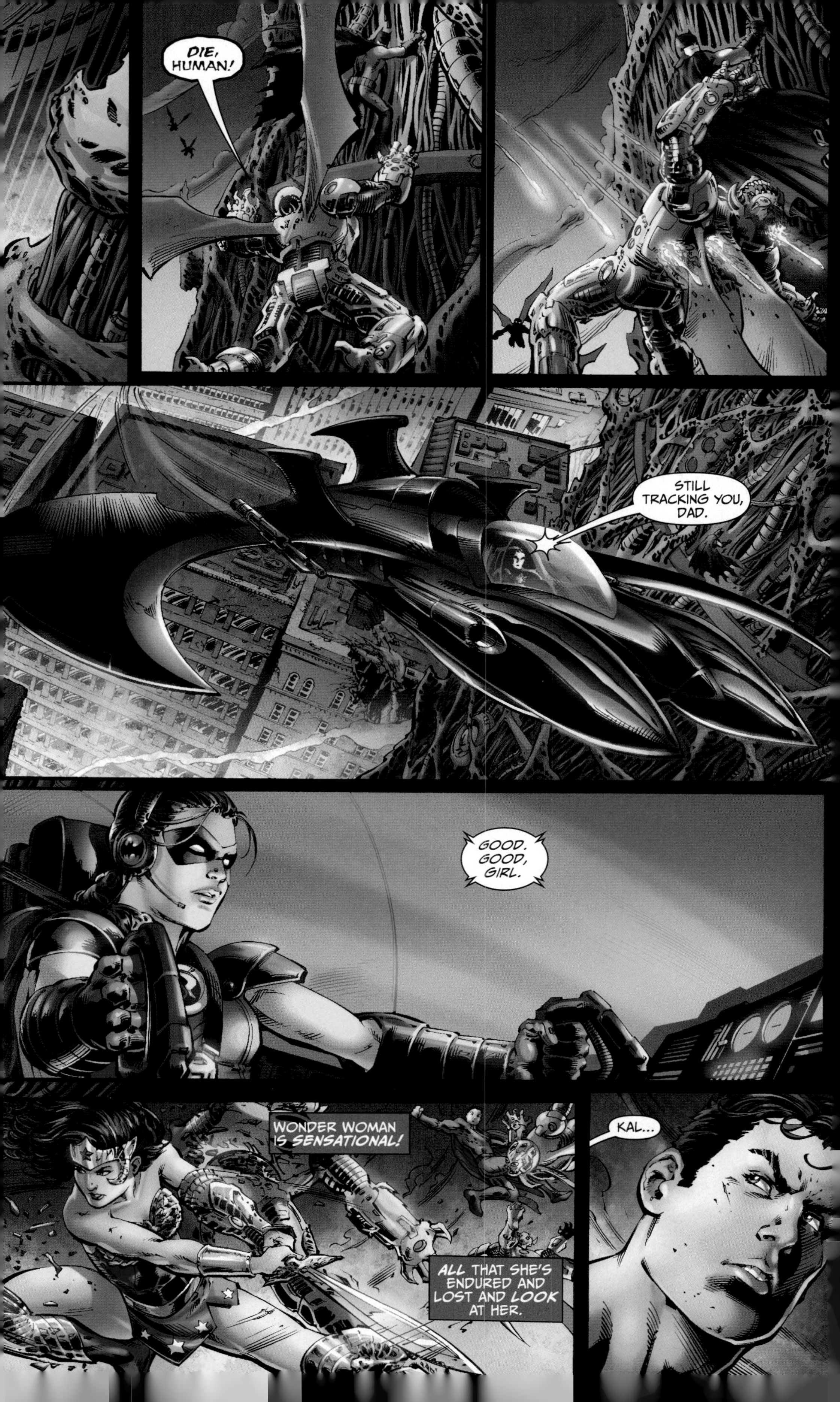
DIE, HUMAN!
STILL TRACKING YOU, DAD.
GOOD. GOOD, GIRL.
WONDER WOMAN IS SENSATIONAL!
ALL THAT SHE'S ENDURED AND LOST AND LOOK AT HER.
KAL...

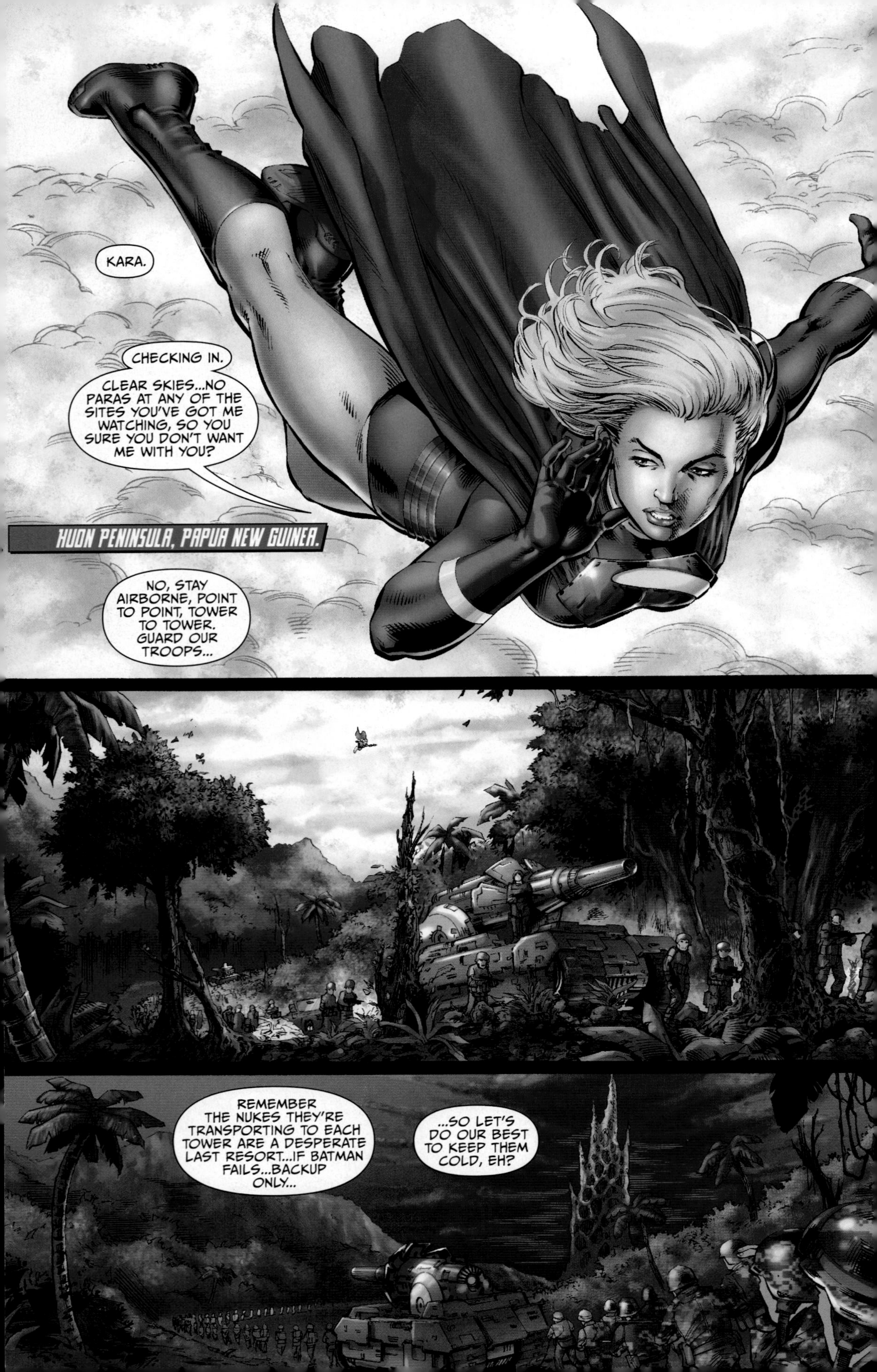
KARA.
CHECKING IN.
CLEAR SKIES...NO PARAS AT ANY OF THE SITES YOU'VE GOT ME WATCHING, SO YOU SURE YOU DON'T WANT ME WITH YOU?
HUON PENINSULA, PAPUA NEW GUINEA.
NO, STAY AIRBORNE, POINT TO POINT, TOWER TO TOWER. GUARD OUR TROOPS...
REMEMBER THE NUKES THEY'RE TRANSPORTING TO EACH TOWER ARE A DESPERATE LAST RESORT...IF BATMAN FAILS...BACKUP ONLY...
...SO LET'S DO OUR BEST TO KEEP THEM COLD, EH?

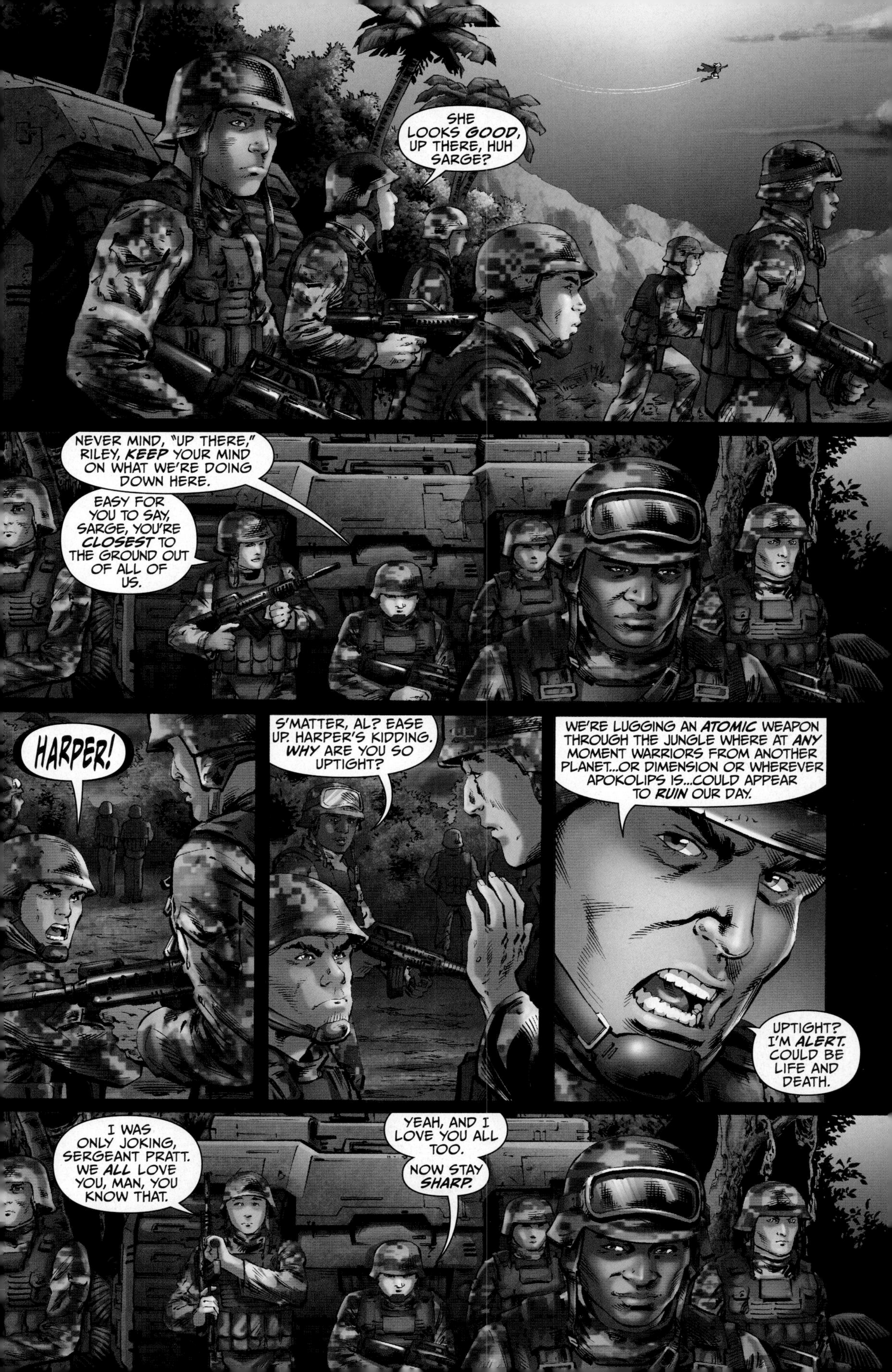
SHE LOOKS GOOD, UP THERE, HUH SARGE?
NEVER MIND, "UP THERE," RILEY, KEEP YOUR MIND ON WHAT WE'RE DOING DOWN HERE.
EASY FOR YOU TO SAY, SARGE, YOU'RE CLOSEST TO THE GROUND OUT OF ALL OF US.
HARPER!
S'MATTER, AL? EASE UP. HARPER'S KIDDING. WHY ARE YOU SO UPTIGHT?
WE'RE LUGGING AN ATOMIC WEAPON THROUGH THE JUNGLE WHERE AT ANY MOMENT WARRIORS FROM ANOTHER PLANET...OR DIMENSION OR WHEREVER APOKOLIPS IS...COULD APPEAR TO RUIN OUR DAY.
UPTIGHT? I'M ALERT. COULD BE LIFE AND DEATH.
I WAS ONLY JOKING, SERGEANT PRATT. WE ALL LOVE YOU, MAN, YOU KNOW THAT.
YEAH, AND I LOVE YOU ALL TOO.
NOW STAY SHARP.

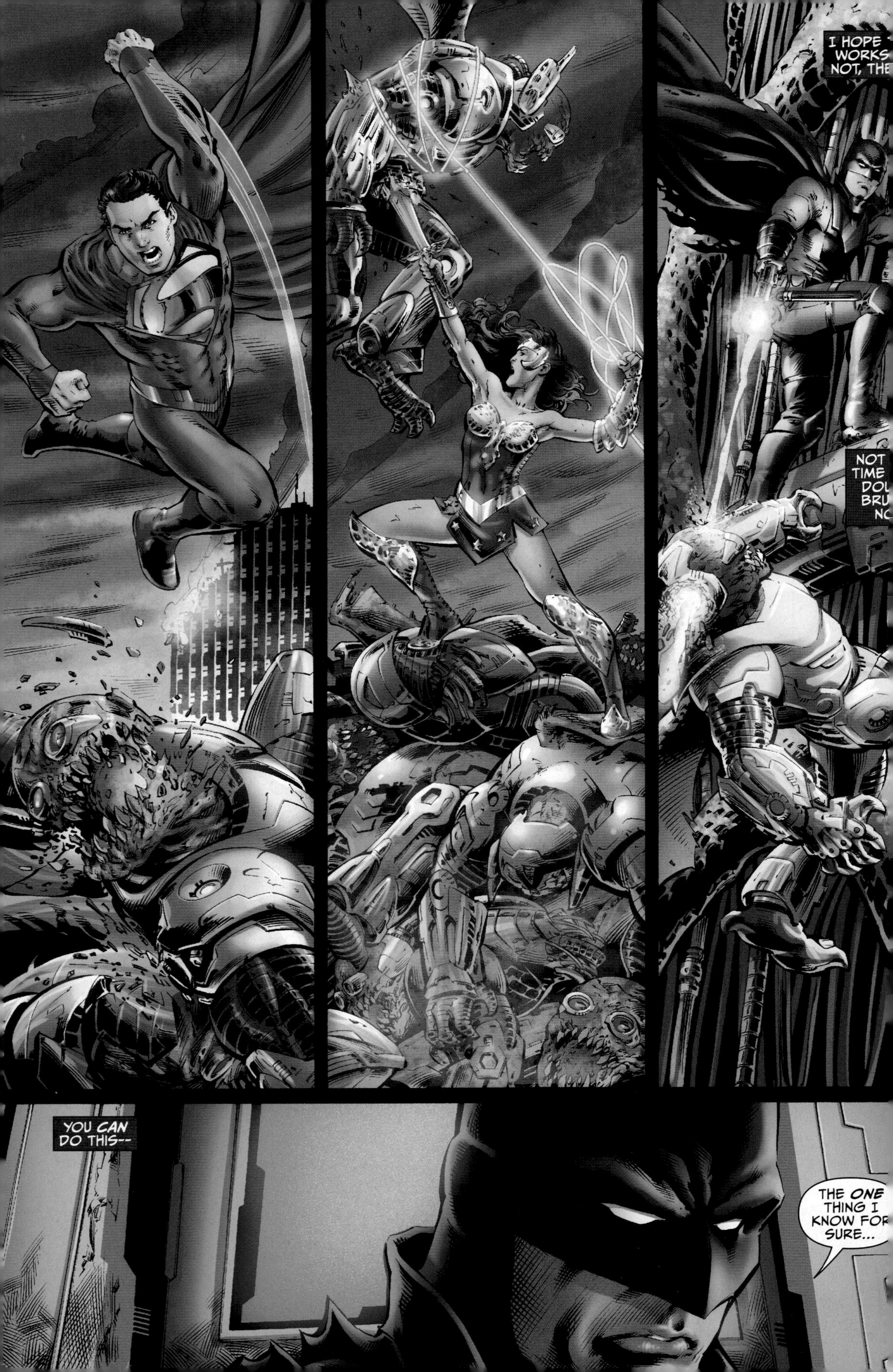
I HOPE WORKS NOT, THE
NOT TIME DOU BRU NO
YOU CAN DO THIS--
THE ONE THING I KNOW FOR SURE...

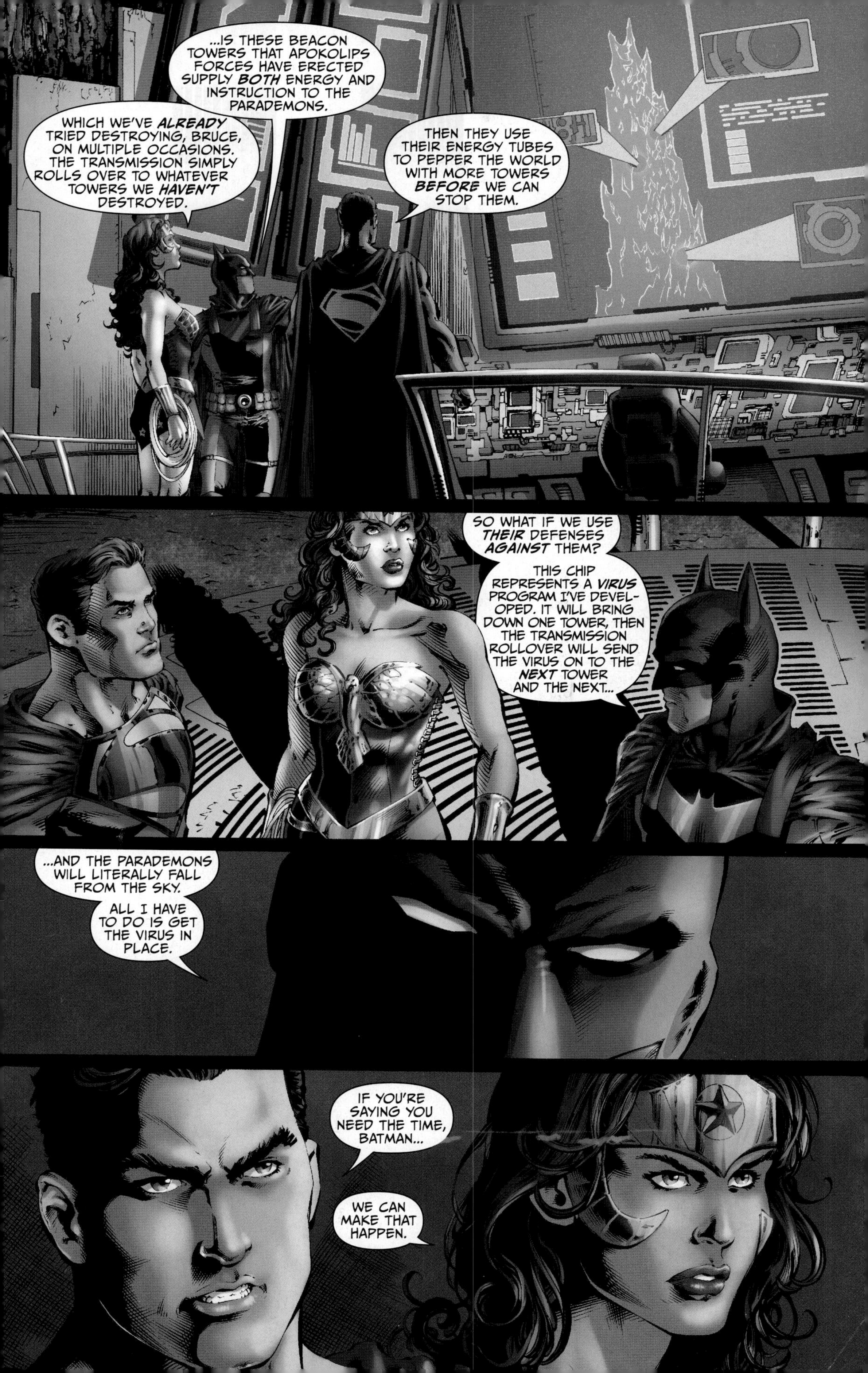
...IS THESE BEACON TOWERS THAT APOKOLIPS FORCES HAVE ERECTED SUPPLY BOTH ENERGY AND INSTRUCTION TO THE PARADEMONS.
WHICH WE'VE ALREADY TRIED DESTROYING, BRUCE, ON MULTIPLE OCCASIONS. THE TRANSMISSION SIMPLY ROLLS OVER TO WHATEVER TOWERS WE HAVEN'T DESTROYED.
THEN THEY USE THEIR ENERGY TUBES TO PEPPER THE WORLD WITH MORE TOWERS BEFORE WE CAN STOP THEM.
SO WHAT IF WE USE THEIR DEFENSES AGAINST THEM?
THIS CHIP REPRESENTS A VIRUS PROGRAM I'VE DEVEL-OPED. IT WILL BRING DOWN ONE TOWER, THEN THE TRANSMISSION ROLLOVER WILL SEND THE VIRUS ON TO THE NEXT TOWER AND THE NEXT...
...AND THE PARADEMONS WILL LITERALLY FALL FROM THE SKY.
ALL I HAVE TO DO IS GET THE VIRUS IN PLACE.
IF YOU'RE SAYING YOU NEED THE TIME, BATMAN...
WE CAN MAKE THAT HAPPEN.

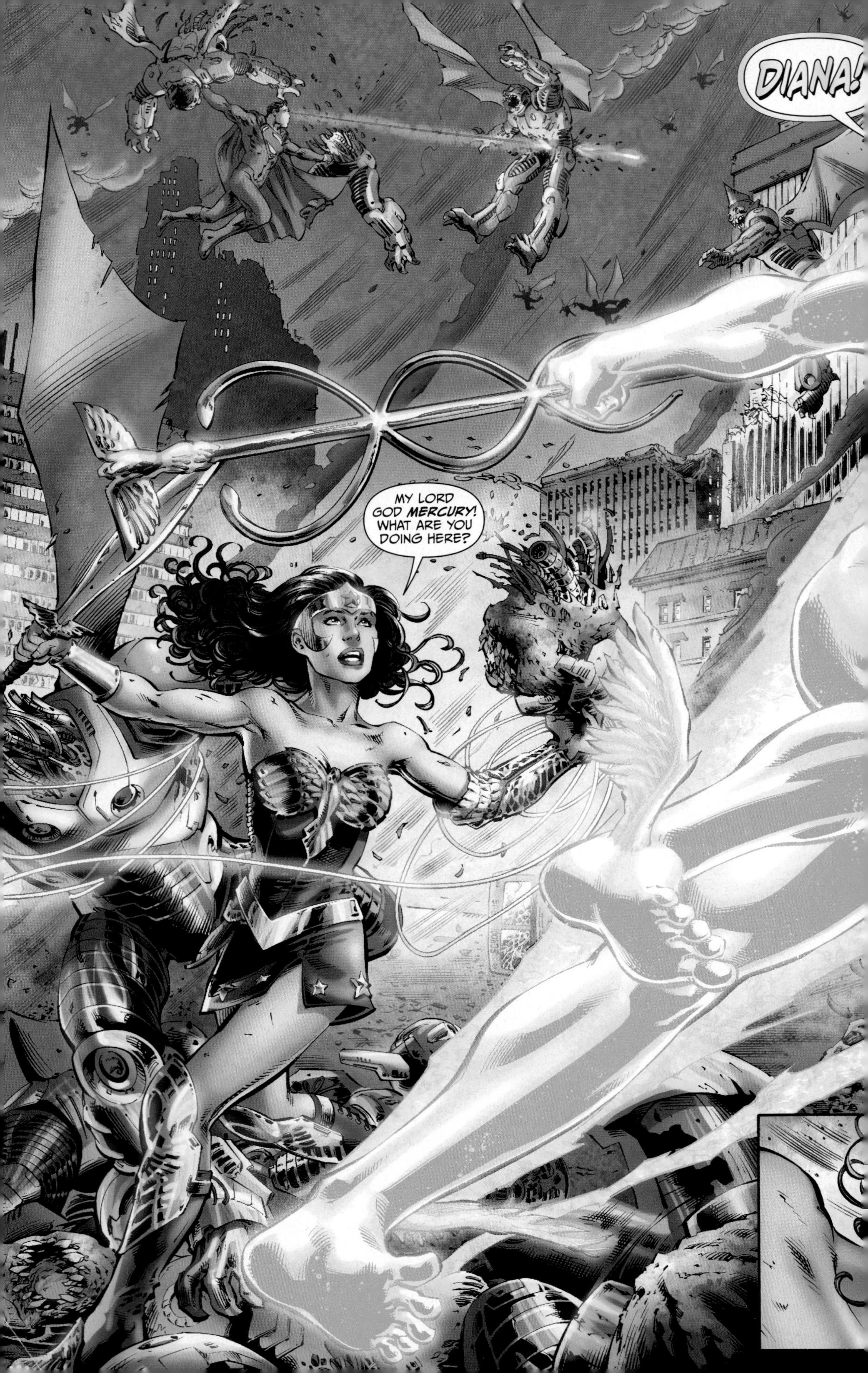
DIANA!
MY LORD GOD MERCURY! WHAT ARE YOU DOING HERE?

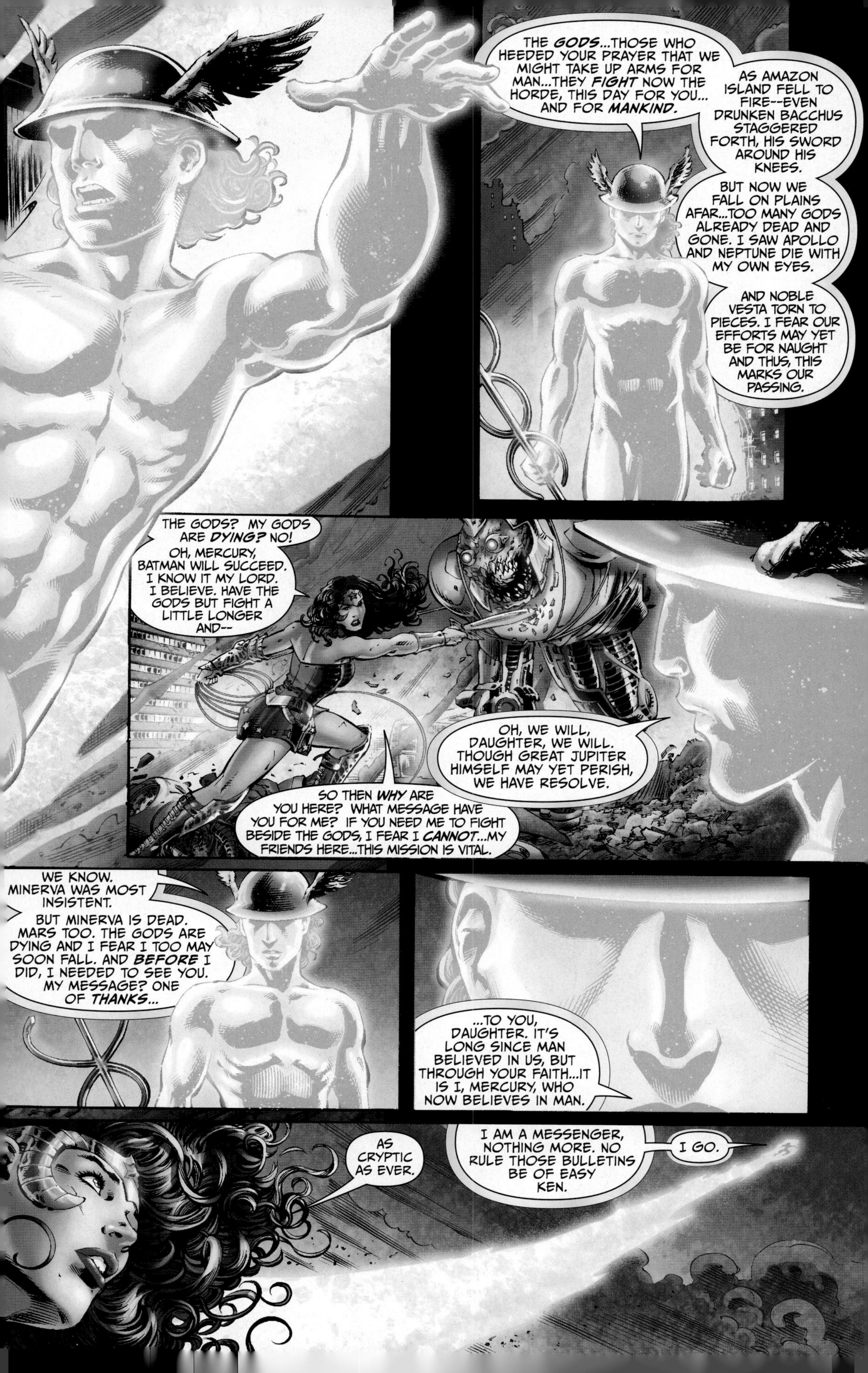
THE GODS...THOSE WHO HEEDED YOUR PRAYER THAT WE MIGHT TAKE UP ARMS FOR MAN...THEY FIGHT NOW THE HORDE, THIS DAY FOR YOU... AND FOR MANKIND.
AS AMAZON ISLAND FELL TO FIRE--EVEN DRUNKEN BACCHUS STAGGERED FORTH, HIS SWORD AROUND HIS KNEES.
BUT NOW WE FALL ON PLAINS AFAR...TOO MANY GODS ALREADY DEAD AND GONE. I SAW APOLLO AND NEPTUNE DIE WITH MY OWN EYES.
AND NOBLE VESTA TORN TO PIECES. I FEAR OUR EFFORTS MAY YET BE FOR NAUGHT AND THUS, THIS MARKS OUR PASSING.
THE GODS? MY GODS ARE DYING? NO!
OH, MERCURY, BATMAN WILL SUCCEED. I KNOW IT MY LORD. I BELIEVE. HAVE THE GODS BUT FIGHT A LITTLE LONGER AND--
OH, WE WILL, DAUGHTER, WE WILL. THOUGH GREAT JUPITER HIMSELF MAY YET PERISH, WE HAVE RESOLVE.
SO THEN WHY ARE YOU HERE? WHAT MESSAGE HAVE YOU FOR ME? IF YOU NEED ME TO FIGHT BESIDE THE GODS, I FEAR I CANNOT...MY FRIENDS HERE...THIS MISSION IS VITAL.
WE KNOW. MINERVA WAS MOST INSISTENT.
BUT MINERVA IS DEAD. MARS TOO. THE GODS ARE DYING AND I FEAR I TOO MAY SOON FALL. AND BEFORE I DID, I NEEDED TO SEE YOU. MY MESSAGE? ONE OF THANKS...
...TO YOU, DAUGHTER. IT'S LONG SINCE MAN BELIEVED IN US, BUT THROUGH YOUR FAITH...IT IS I, MERCURY, WHO NOW BELIEVES IN MAN.
AS CRYPTIC AS EVER.
I AM A MESSENGER, NOTHING MORE. NO RULE THOSE BULLETINS BE OF EASY KEN.
I GO.

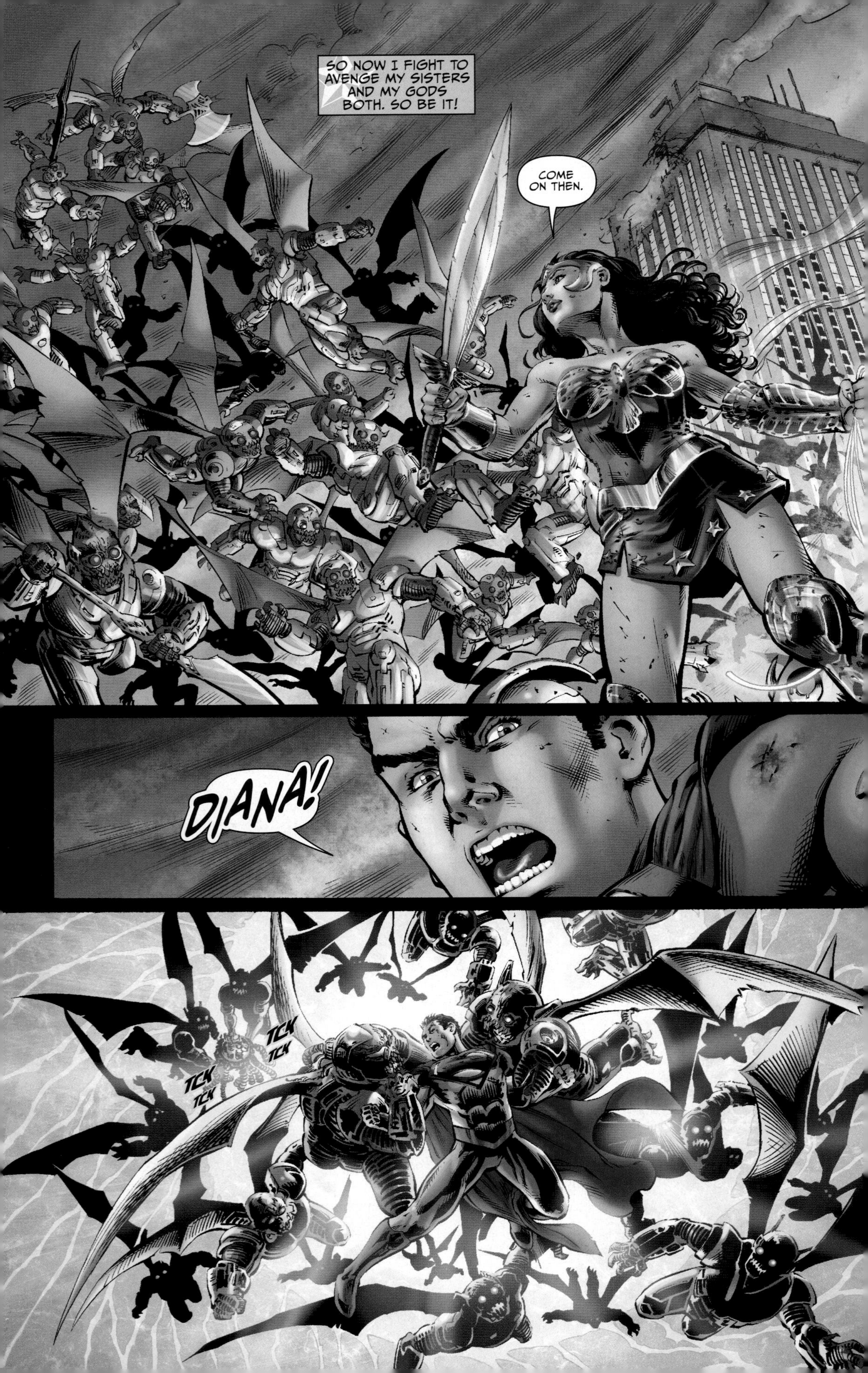
SO NOW I FIGHT TO AVENGE MY SISTERS AND MY GODS BOTH. SO BE IT!
COME ON THEN.
DIANA!
TCK TCK
TCK TCK

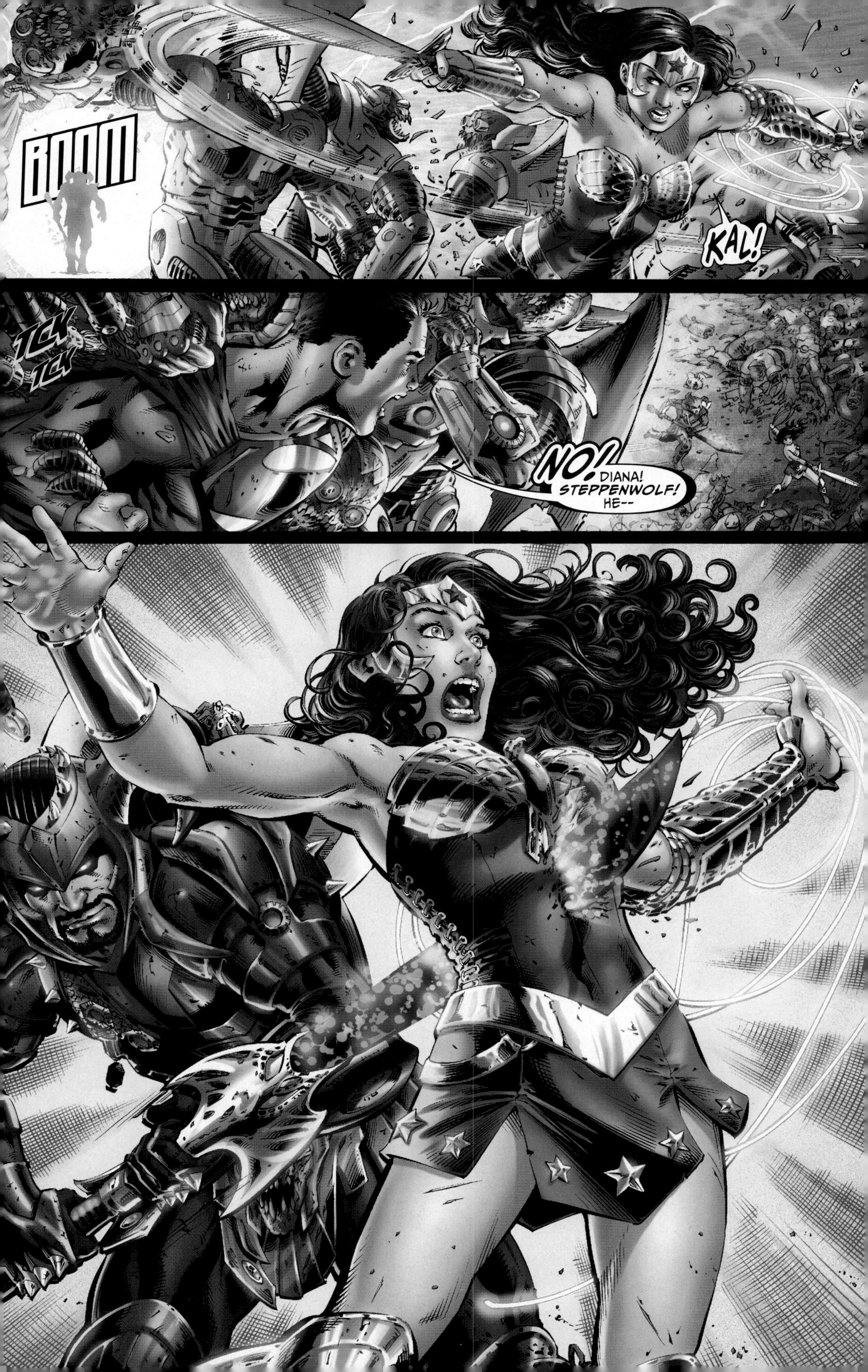
BOOM
KAL!
TCK TCK
NO!
DIANA! STEPPENWOLF! HE--

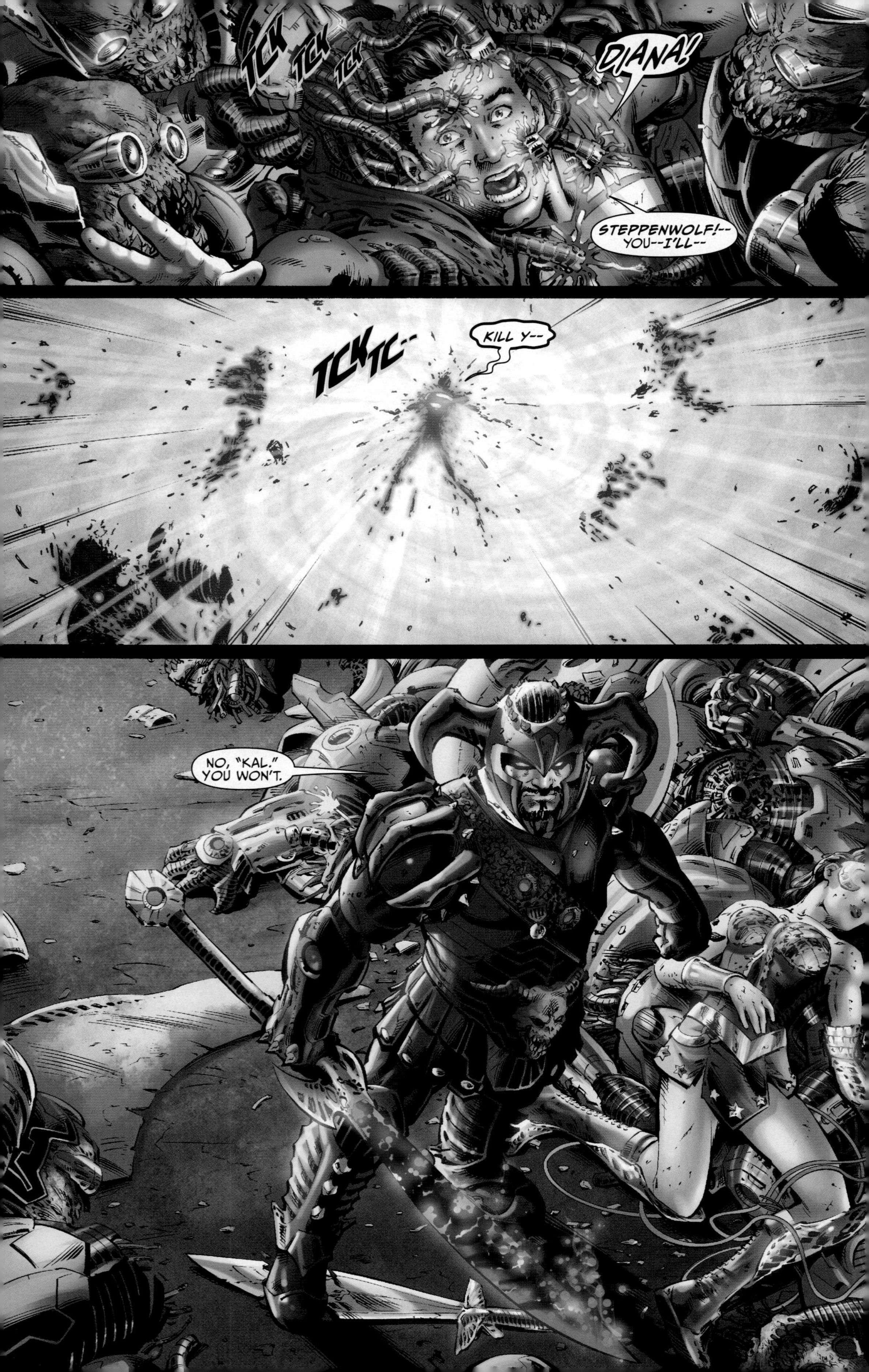
TCK
TCK
TCK
DIANA!
STEPPENWOLF!-- YOU--I'LL--
TCK TC--
KILL Y--
NO, "KAL." YOU WON'T.

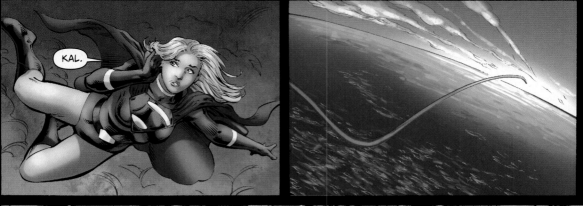

KAL.

PEEDEES ARE CLOSING IN, SARGE.

I GOT EYES.

WHERE'S SUPERGIRL?

SOMEWHERE ELSE.

SO WHAT'D WE DO?

SERGEANT PRATT?! I'M *SCARED*, THEY'RE--

SARGE! OUR SHELLS AREN'T--

STOW IT! ALL O' YOU.

WE'RE SOLDIERS, *AMERICAN* SOLDIERS, YOU HEAR ME? WE *FIGHT!*

WE GET IT *DONE!*

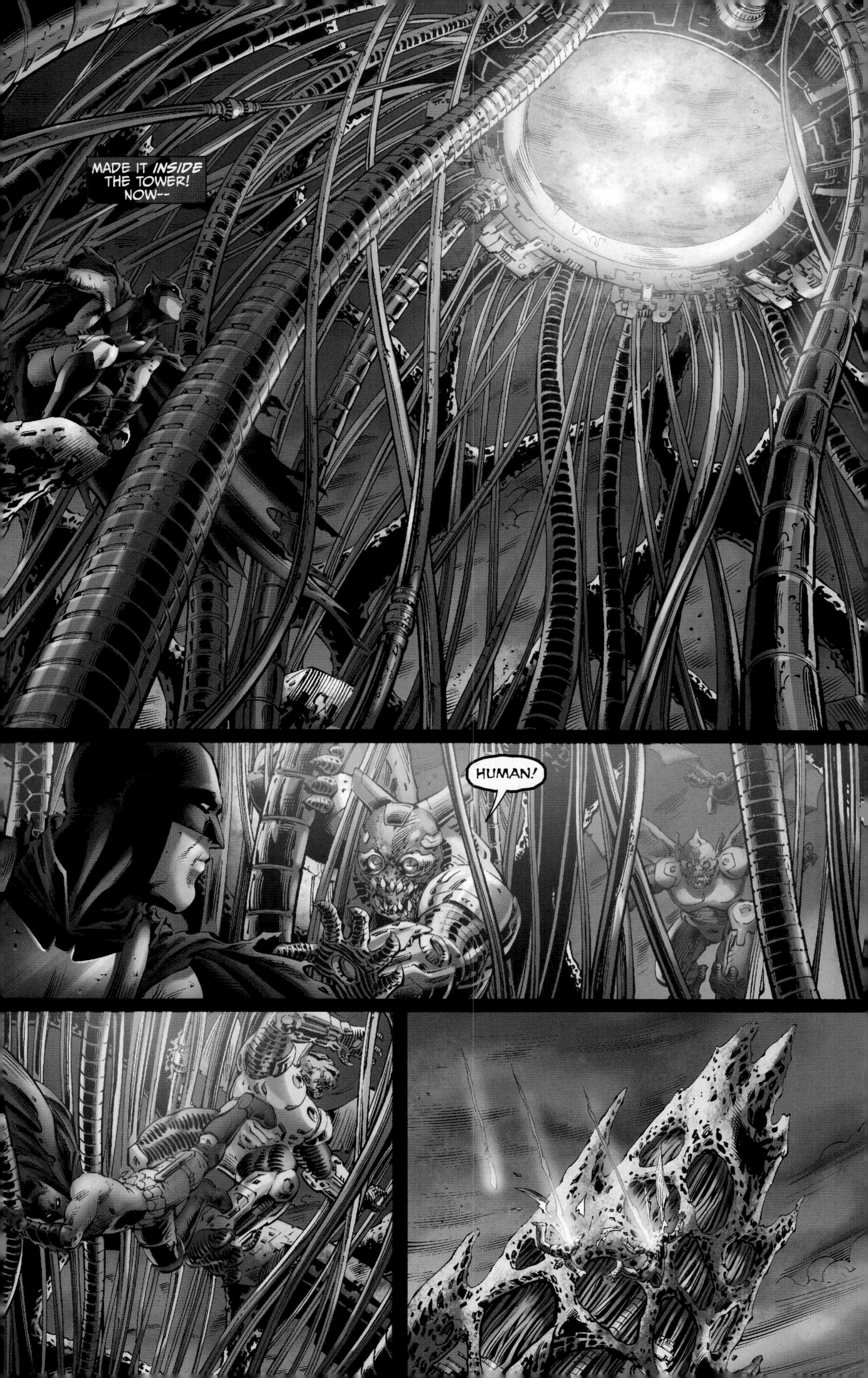
MADE IT *INSIDE* THE TOWER! NOW--
HUMAN!

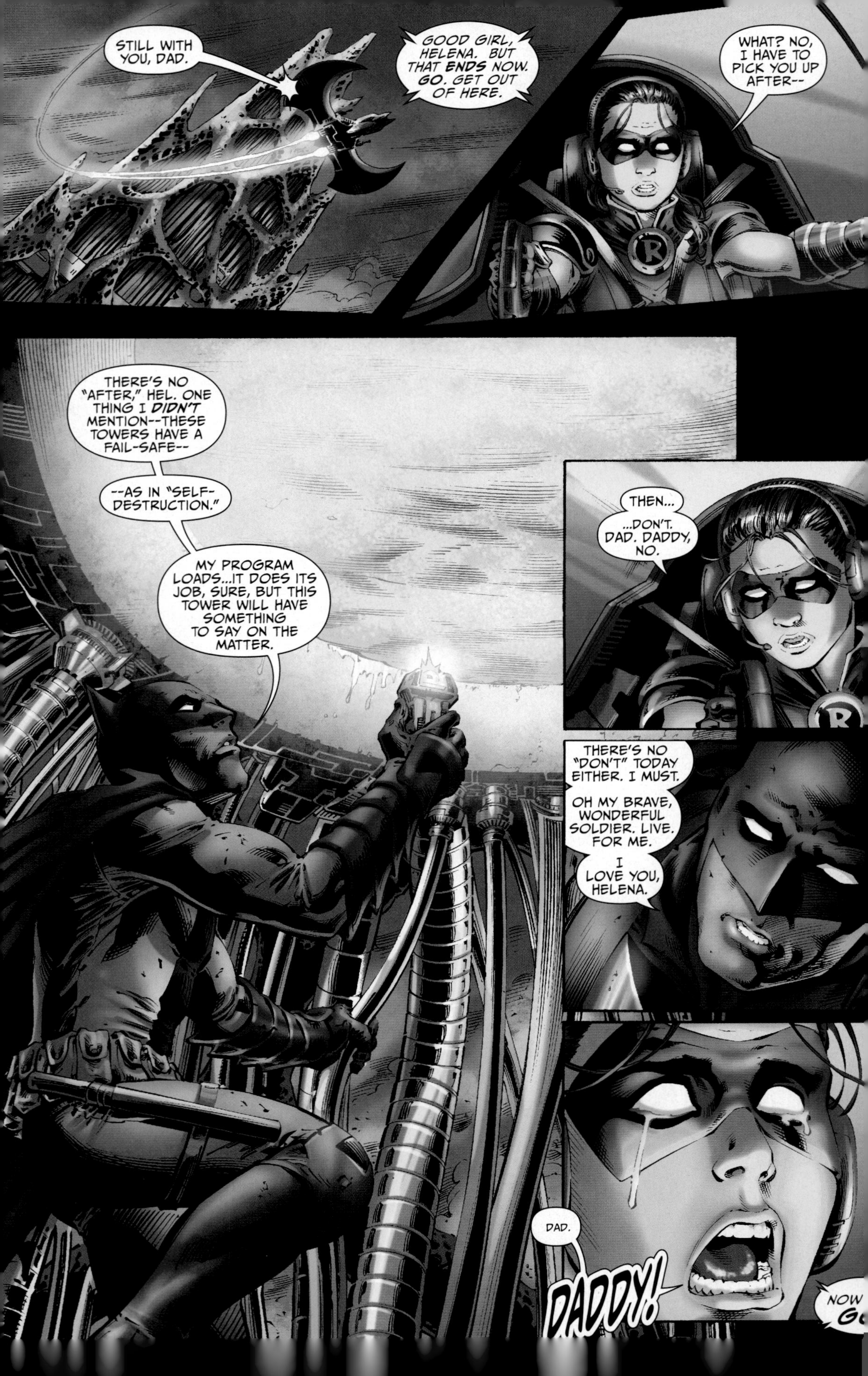

STILL WITH YOU, DAD.
GOOD GIRL, HELENA. BUT THAT **ENDS** NOW. **GO.** GET OUT OF HERE.
WHAT? NO, I HAVE TO PICK YOU UP AFTER--
THERE'S NO "AFTER," HEL. ONE THING I ***DIDN'T*** MENTION--THESE TOWERS HAVE A FAIL-SAFE--
--AS IN "SELF-DESTRUCTION."
MY PROGRAM LOADS...IT DOES ITS JOB, SURE, BUT THIS TOWER WILL HAVE SOMETHING TO SAY ON THE MATTER.
THEN...
...DON'T. DAD. DADDY, NO.
THERE'S NO "DON'T" TODAY EITHER. I MUST.
OH MY BRAVE, WONDERFUL SOLDIER. LIVE. FOR ME.
I LOVE YOU, HELENA.
DAD.
DADDY!
NOW

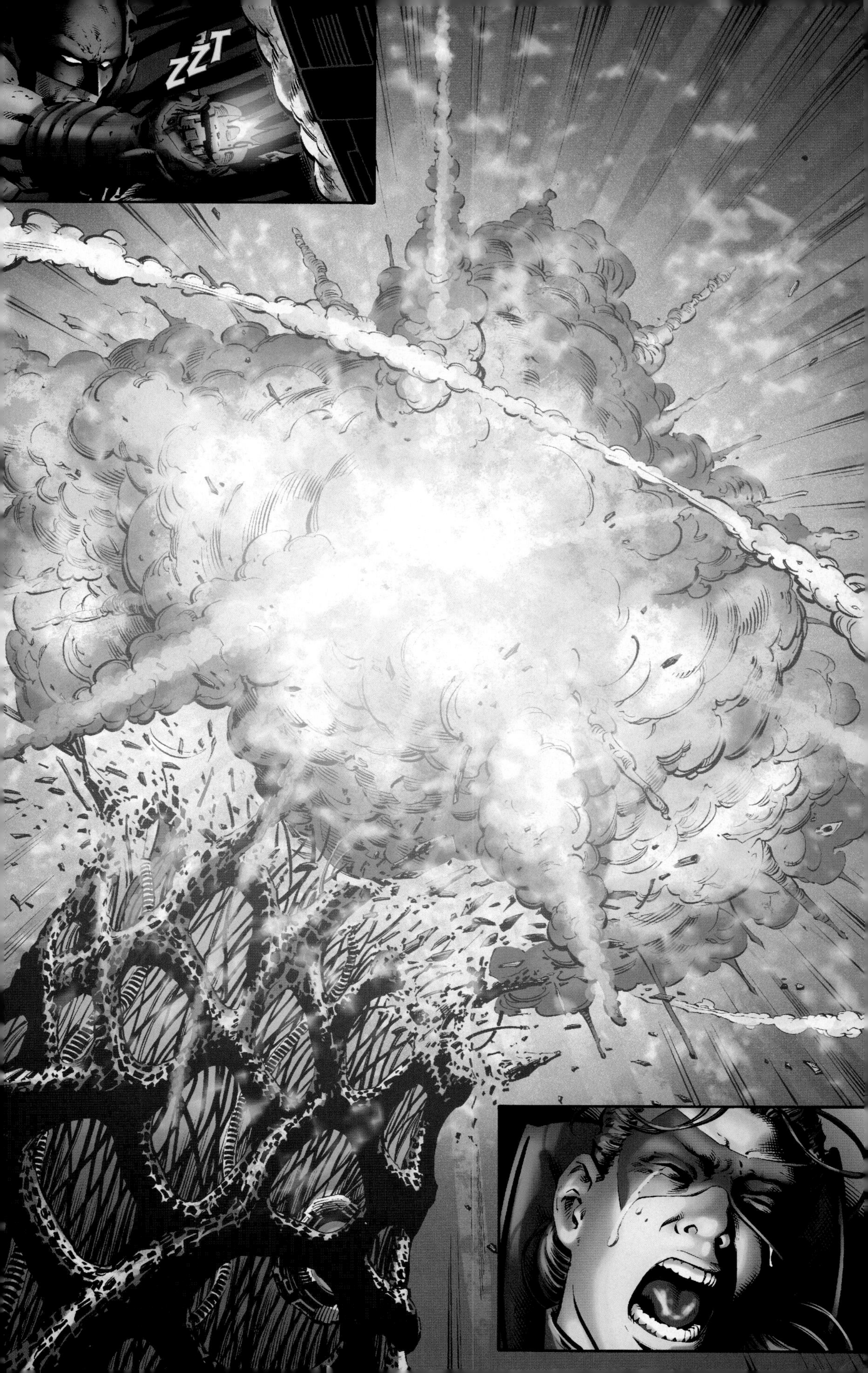
ZZT

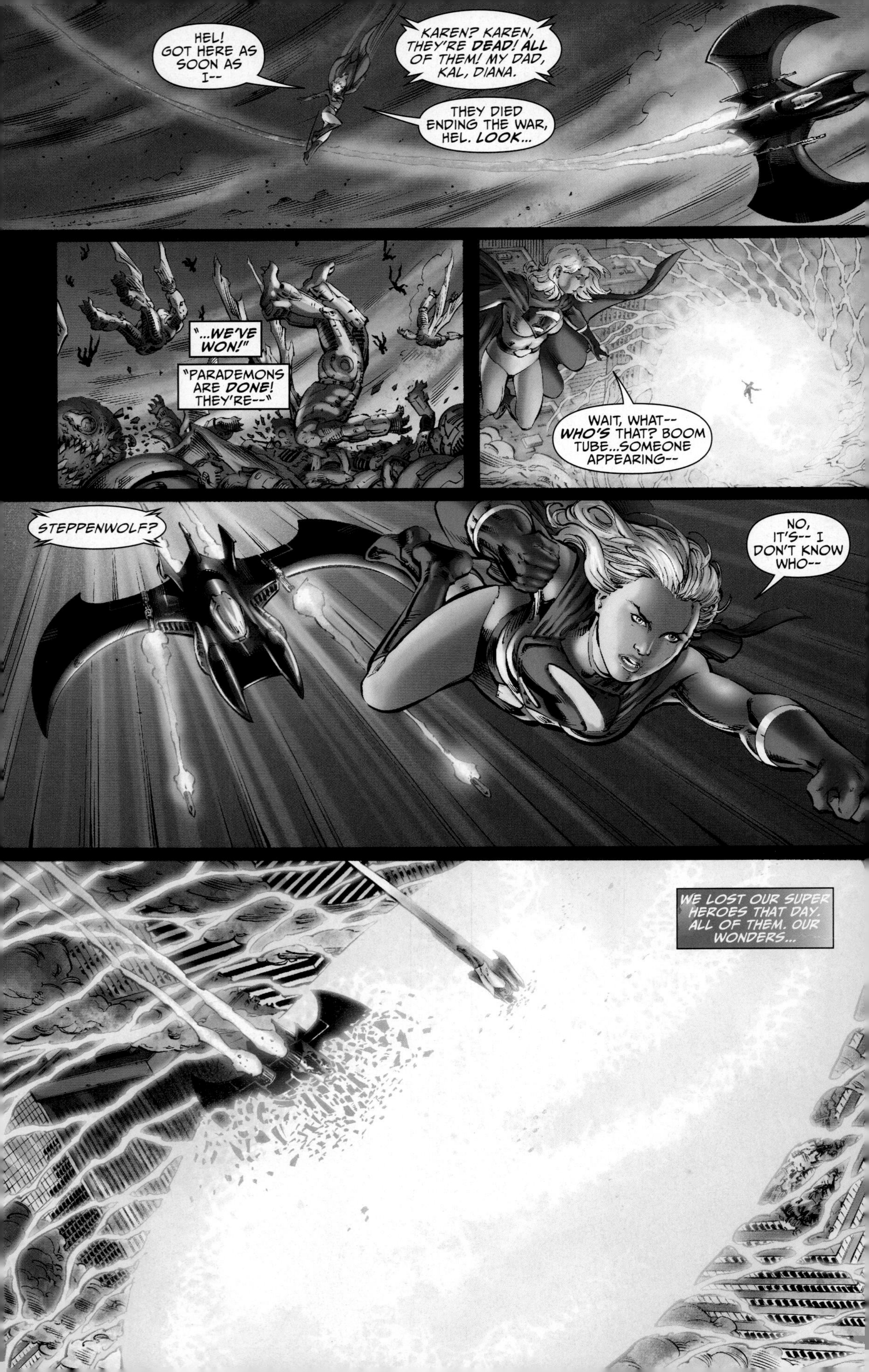
HEL! GOT HERE AS SOON AS I--
KAREN? KAREN, THEY'RE DEAD! ALL OF THEM! MY DAD, KAL, DIANA.
THEY DIED ENDING THE WAR, HEL. LOOK...
"...WE'VE WON!"
"PARADEMONS ARE DONE! THEY'RE--"
WAIT, WHAT-- WHO'S THAT? BOOM TUBE...SOMEONE APPEARING--
STEPPENWOLF?
NO, IT'S-- I DON'T KNOW WHO--
WE LOST OUR SUPER HEROES THAT DAY. ALL OF THEM. OUR WONDERS...

...ALL AS WELL AS COUNTLESS BRAVE SOLDIERS OF THE WORLD.

HEROES ALL.

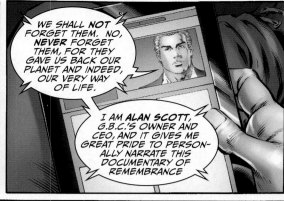

WE SHALL **NOT** FORGET THEM. NO, **NEVER** FORGET THEM, FOR THEY GAVE US BACK OUR PLANET AND INDEED, OUR VERY WAY OF LIFE.

I AM **ALAN SCOTT**, G.B.C.'S OWNER AND CEO, AND IT GIVES ME GREAT PRIDE TO PERSONALLY NARRATE THIS DOCUMENTARY OF REMEMBRANCE

WOW. NOT BAD IF I DO SAY SO MYSELF.

MR. SCOTT?

SURVEYING MY HANDIWORK, SARAH. THE ANNIVERSARY SPECIAL WENT OUT A LITTLE WHILE AGO...I WAS JUST CHECKING I CAME OFF AS SINCERE...

...AND NOT A RAVING EGO MANIAC IN LOVE WITH THE SOUND OF HIS OWN VOICE.

WELL I WATCHED AN EARLY EDIT LAST WEEK AND I THOUGHT IT WAS VERY MOVING. I'LL NEVER UNDERSTAND WHY YOU DIDN'T CHARGE TO DOWNLOAD, BUT--

SOME THINGS ARE TOO IMPORTANT TO PROFIT FROM. AND IF YOU TELL ANYONE I SAID THAT, I'LL KILL YOU. JOKING.

AH, I SEE FROM THE VIEW OUTSIDE WE'RE OVER ITALY.

WHAT'S LEFT OF IT, SURE.

THEN WILL [Y]OU ASK THE PILOT [FO]R E.T.A. TO CHINA? YOU KNOW HOW EAGER I AM TO GET THERE.

[D]ID IT A MOMENT [A]GO, ACTUALLY, MR. SCOTT. A LITTLE UNDER FIVE HOURS...

BOY, LOOK OUT THERE. NEVER CEASES TO TAKE MY BREATH AWAY.

YEAH, MAKES ME THINK HOW SOCIETY **ALWAYS** RECOVERS... REBUILDS...AND SOON THE HORRORS OF A WAR FADE AWAY LIKE THEY NEVER HAPPENED AT ALL.

SEEMS TO ME THIS IS THE ONE TIME...

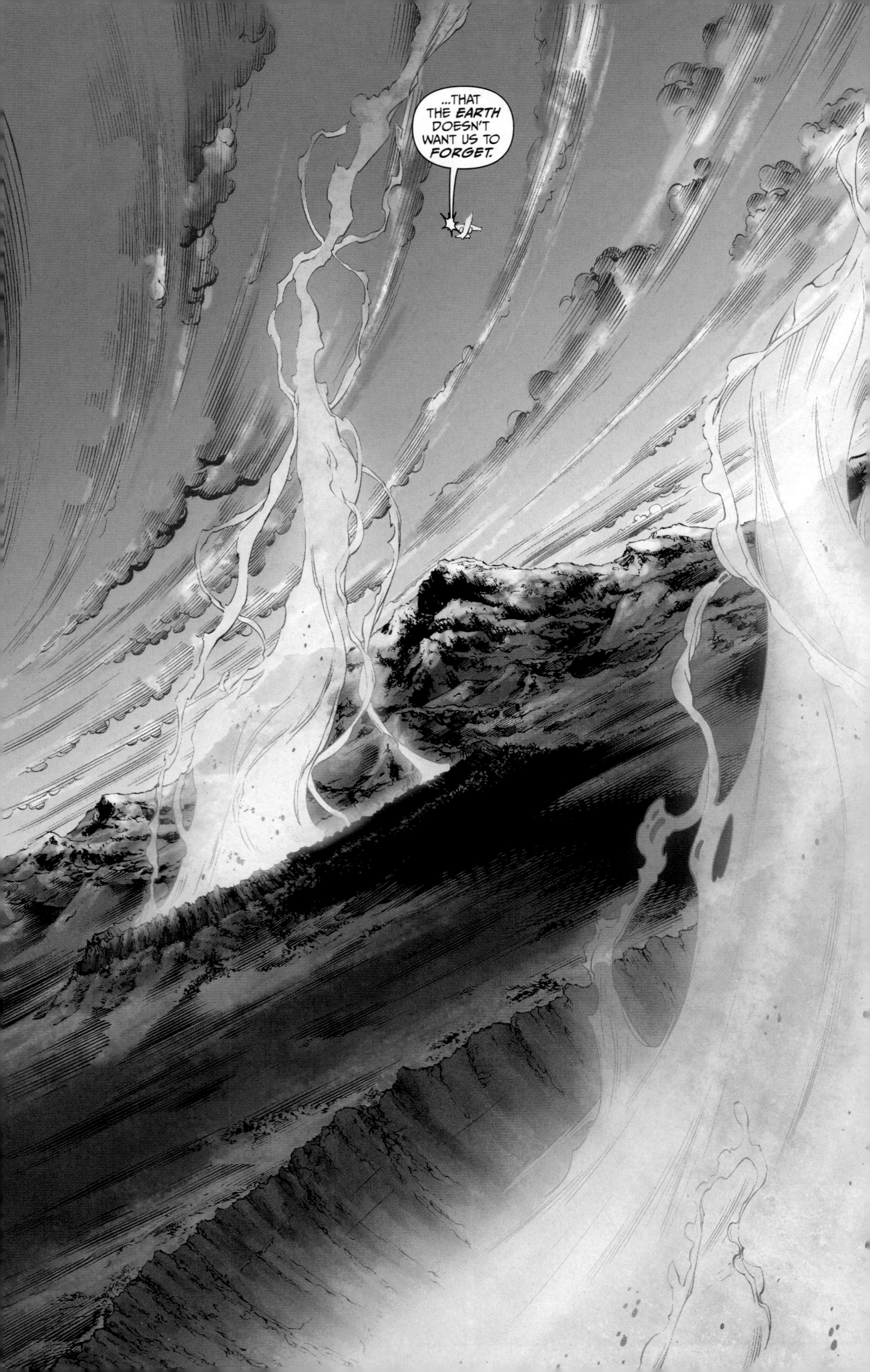
...THAT THE EARTH DOESN'T WANT US TO FORGET.

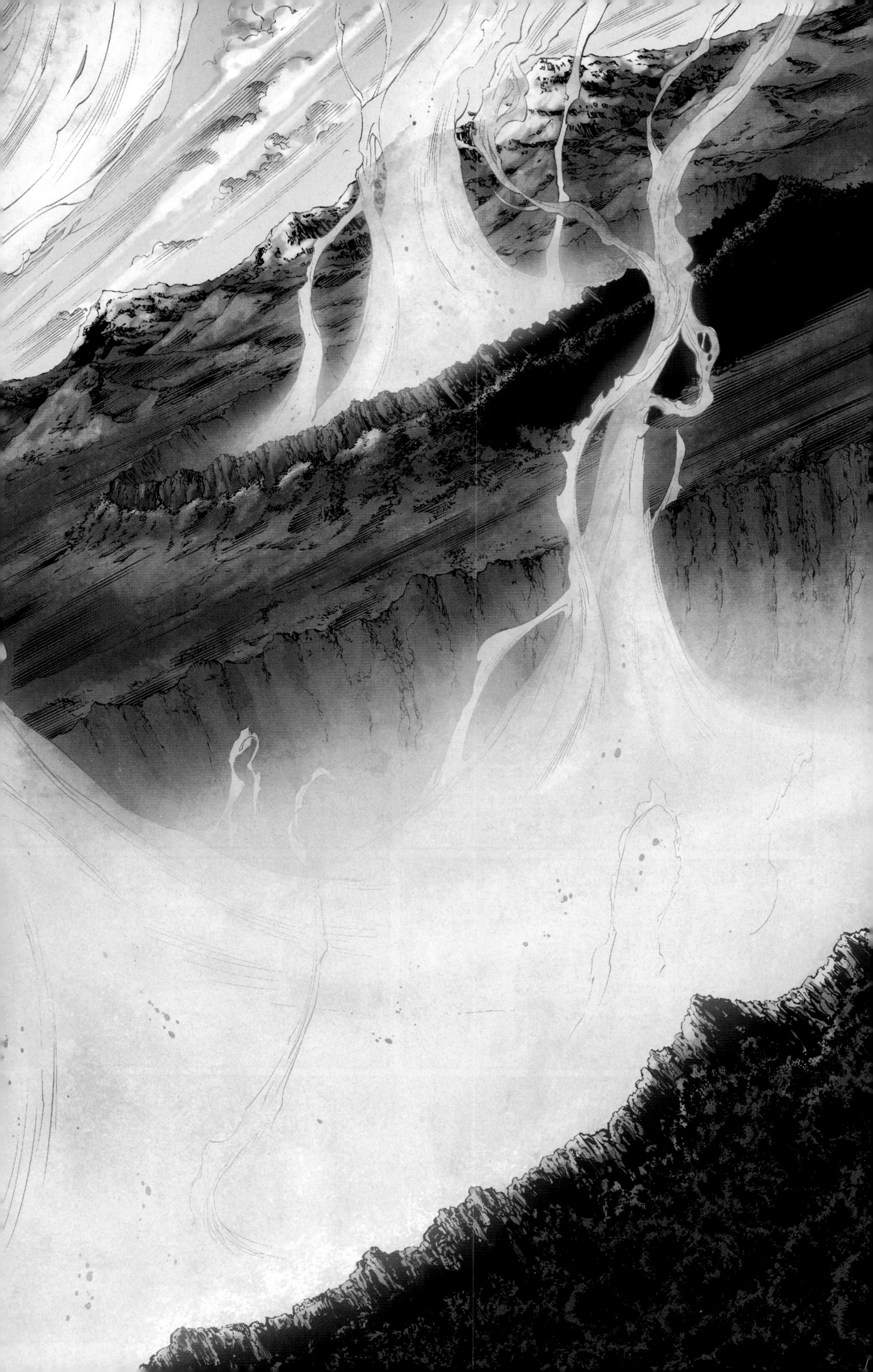

YOU'VE REALLY KIND OF *RUINED* EVERYTHING, JAY, YOU KNOW THAT?

NO, I HAVEN'T. I WANTED TO SAY GOODBYE. IT'S NOT CRAZY I'D WANT TO SEE MY GIRL OFF ON HER GREAT BIG ADVENTURE, IS IT?

FIRSTLY, I'M *NOT* YOUR GIRL, WE'RE *DONE*. CIVILIZED DINNER, BREAK-UP SEX, WE TICKED OFF ALL THE BOXES.

AND THIS ISN'T MY "BIG ADVENTURE," YOU CONDESCENDING JERK, IT'S MY *FUTURE*. GETTING THIS JOB AT TYLER-CHEM IS HUGE FOR ME. WEST COAST. A NEW LIFE, JAY. SO CHANCES WE'LL SEE EACH OTHER AGAIN...SLIM TO NONE.

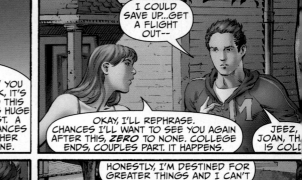

I COULD SAVE UP...GET A FLIGHT OUT--

OKAY, I'LL REPHRASE. CHANCES I'LL WANT TO SEE YOU AGAIN AFTER THIS, *ZERO* TO NONE. COLLEGE ENDS, COUPLES PART. IT HAPPENS.

JEEZ, JOAN, TH IS COL

NO, JAY, *REALISTIC*. YOU WERE FUN TO BE YOUNG WITH, BUT NOW YOU'RE JUST A FEW HAPPY MEMORIES AND SOME PHOTOS IN AN ALBUM THAT I'LL FOB OFF ONE DAY, WHEN MY FUTURE HUSBAND ASKS ME WHO THAT GUY IS NEXT TO ME.

HONESTLY, I'M DESTINED FOR GREATER THINGS AND I CAN'T SAY THE SAME OF YOU.

GOODBYE, JAY.

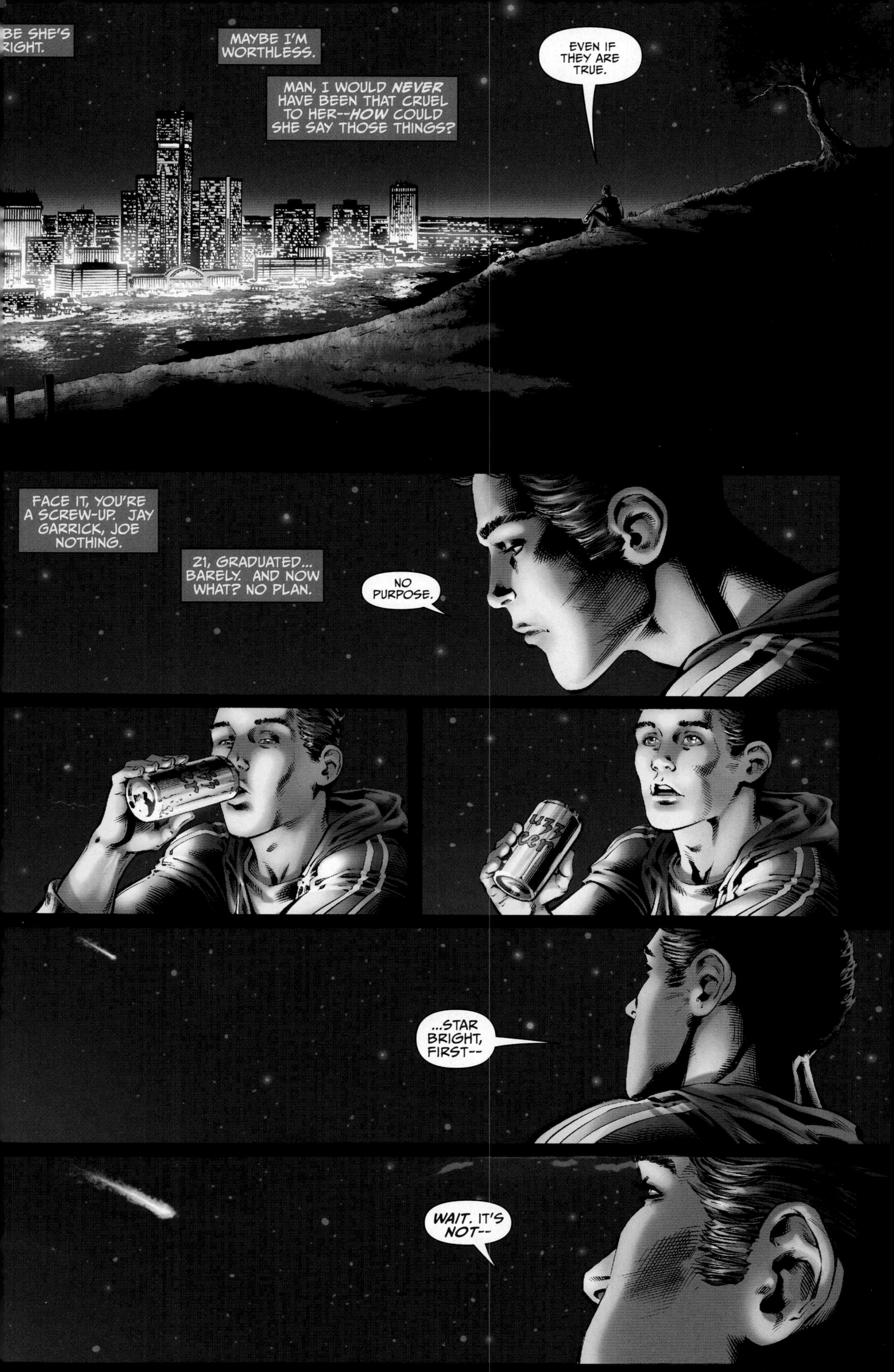
BE SHE'S RIGHT.
MAYBE I'M WORTHLESS.
MAN, I WOULD NEVER HAVE BEEN THAT CRUEL TO HER--HOW COULD SHE SAY THOSE THINGS?
EVEN IF THEY ARE TRUE.
FACE IT, YOU'RE A SCREW-UP. JAY GARRICK, JOE NOTHING.
21, GRADUATED... BARELY. AND NOW WHAT? NO PLAN.
NO PURPOSE.
...STAR BRIGHT, FIRST--
WAIT. IT'S NOT--

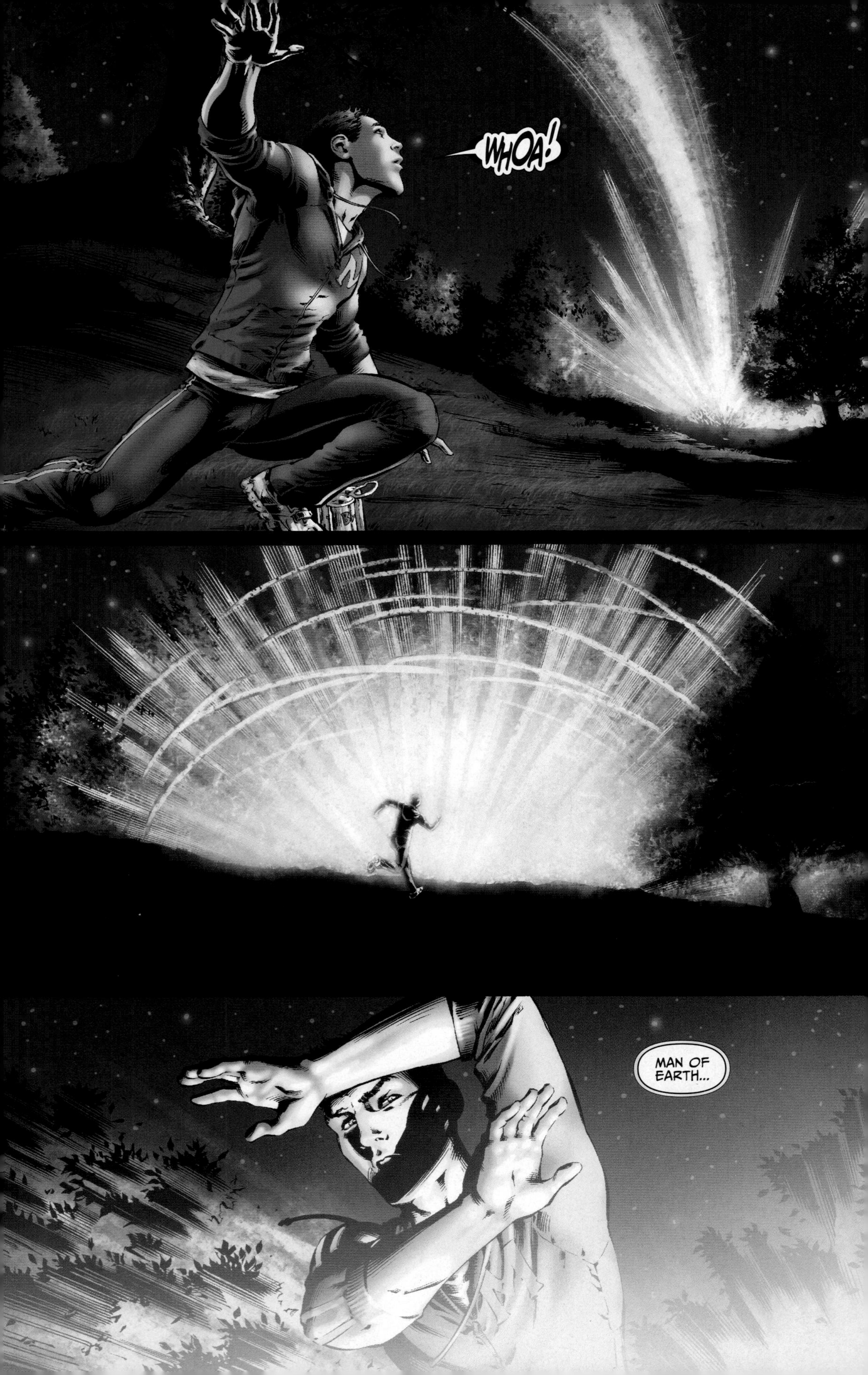
WHOA!
MAN OF EARTH...

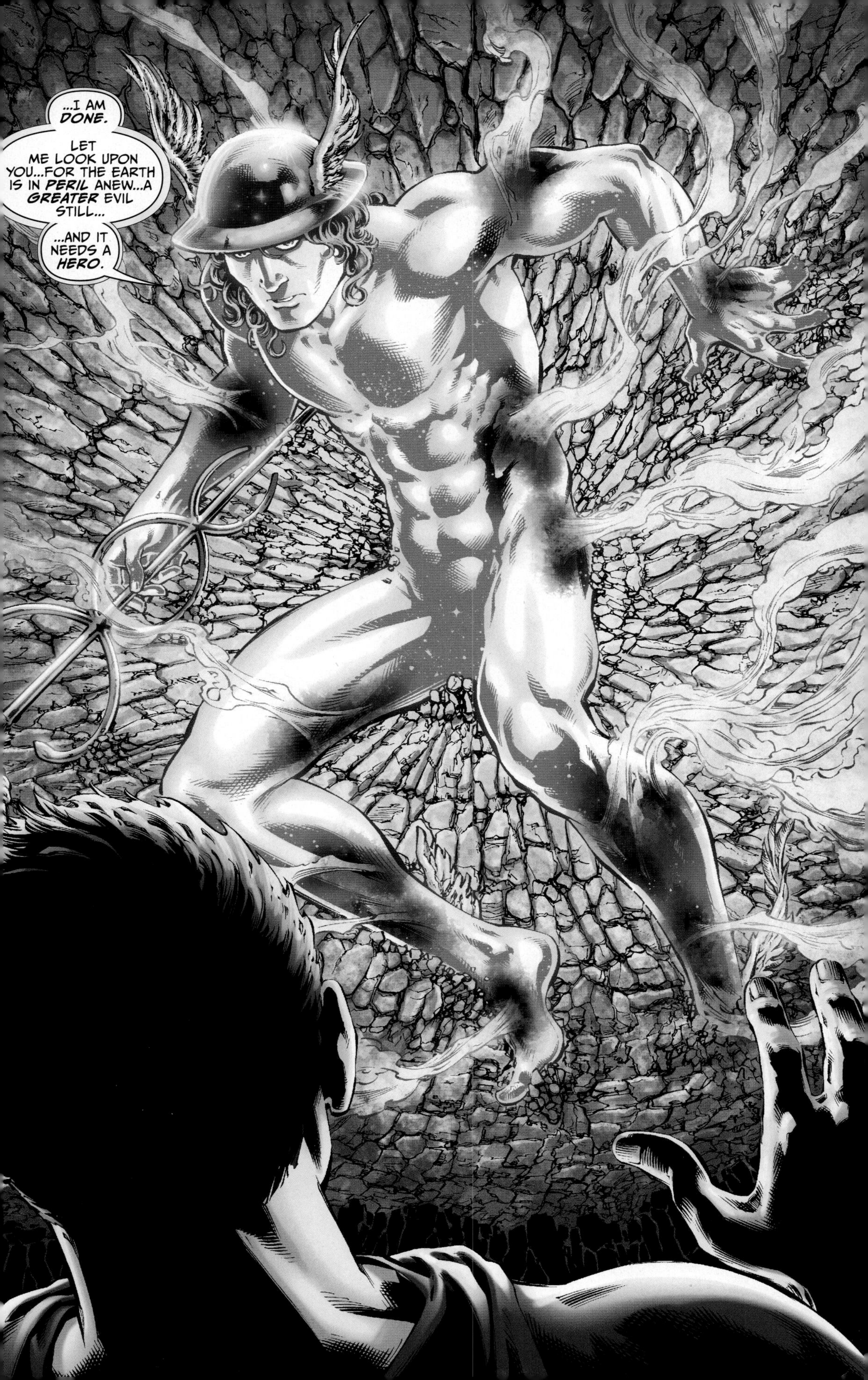
...I AM *DONE.*
LET ME LOOK UPON YOU...FOR THE EARTH IS IN *PERIL* ANEW...A *GREATER* EVIL STILL...
...AND IT NEEDS A *HERO.*

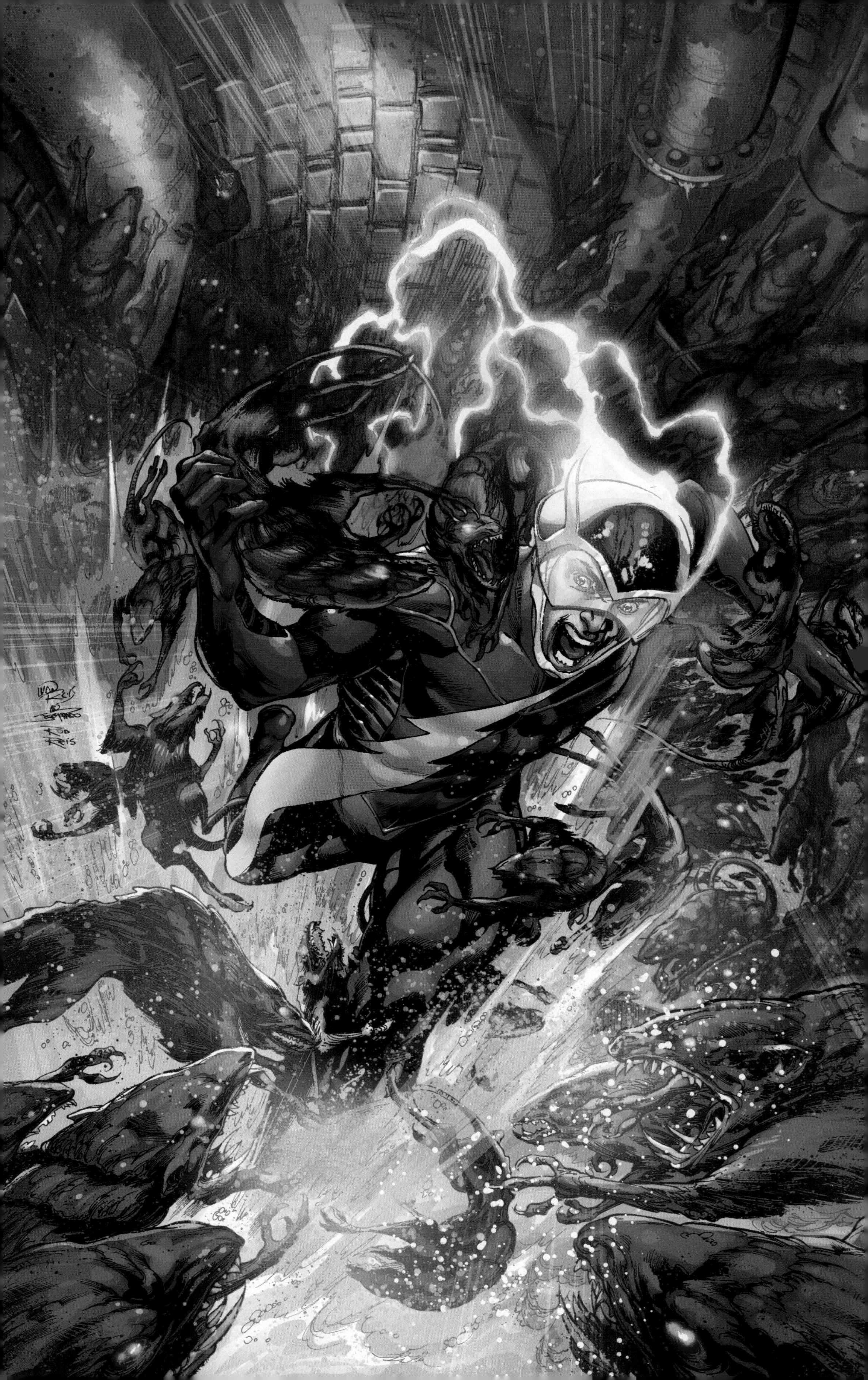

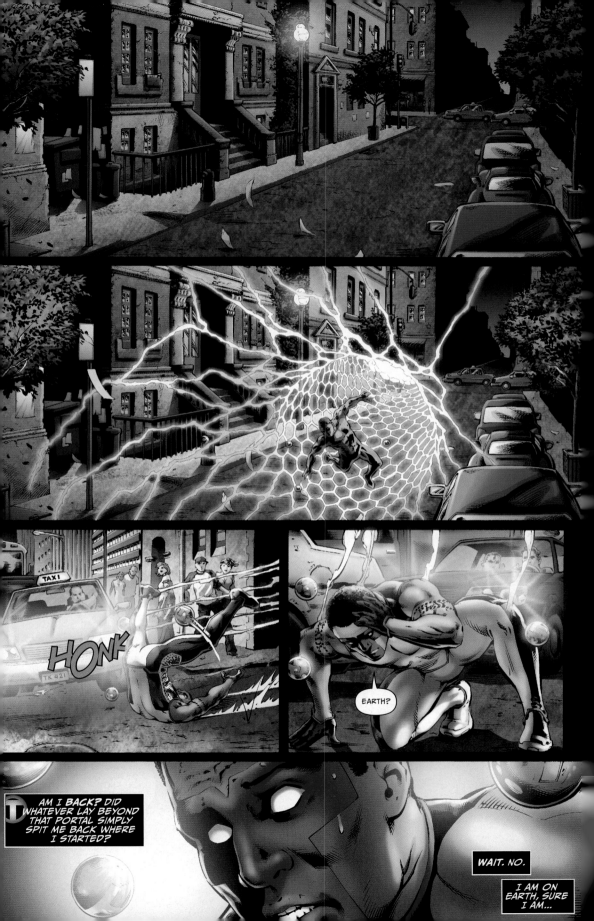

EARTH?

AM I BACK? DID WHATEVER LAY BEYOND THAT PORTAL SIMPLY SPIT ME BACK WHERE I STARTED?

WAIT. NO.

I AM ON EARTH, SURE I AM...

HONK

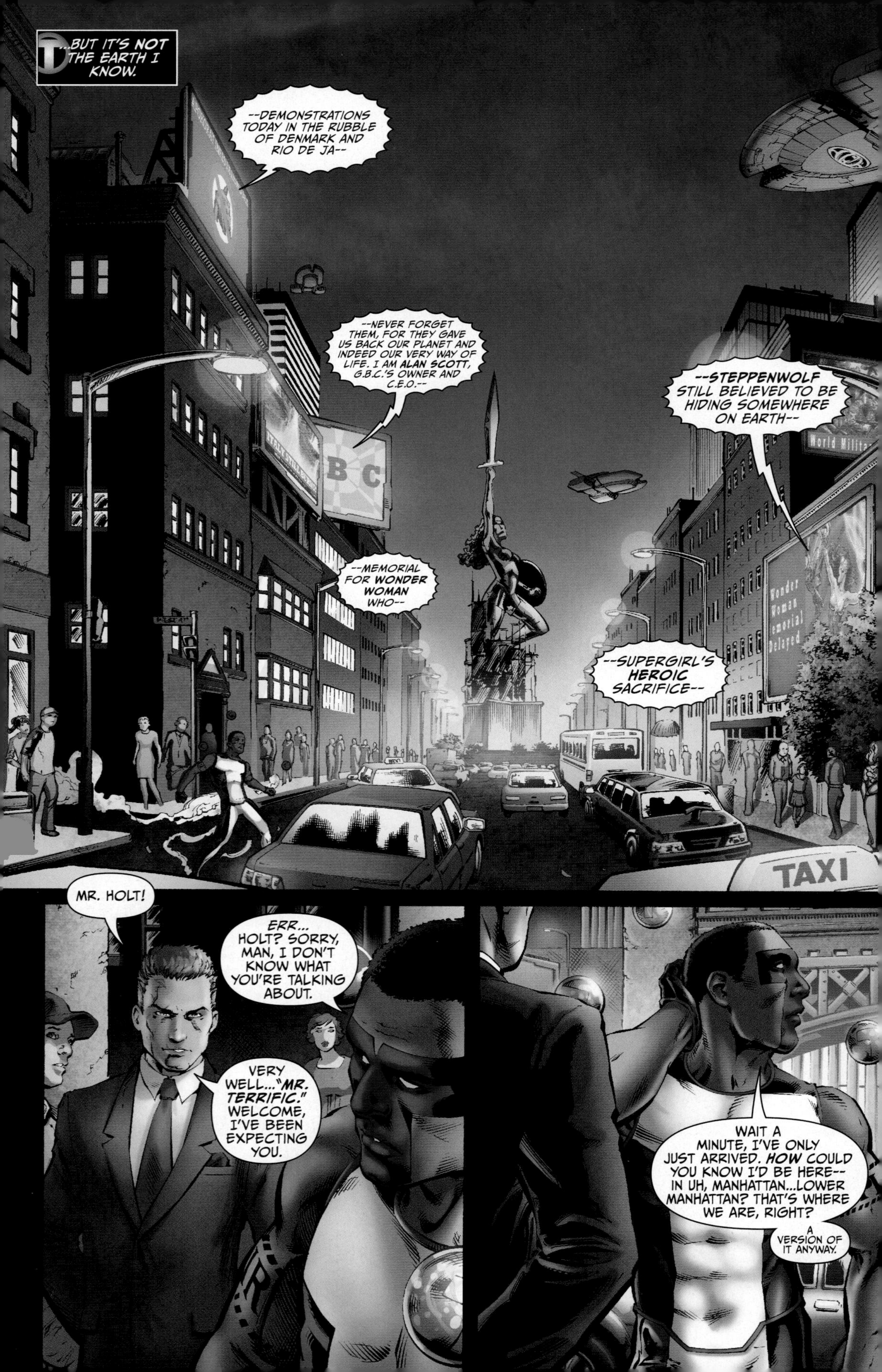
...BUT IT'S NOT THE EARTH I KNOW.
--DEMONSTRATIONS TODAY IN THE RUBBLE OF DENMARK AND RIO DE JA--
--NEVER FORGET THEM, FOR THEY GAVE US BACK OUR PLANET AND INDEED OUR VERY WAY OF LIFE. I AM ALAN SCOTT, G.B.C.'S OWNER AND C.E.O.--
BC
--STEPPENWOLF STILL BELIEVED TO BE HIDING SOMEWHERE ON EARTH--
--MEMORIAL FOR WONDER WOMAN WHO--
Wonder Woman Memorial Delayed
--SUPERGIRL'S HEROIC SACRIFICE--
TAXI
MR. HOLT!
ERR... HOLT? SORRY, MAN, I DON'T KNOW WHAT YOU'RE TALKING ABOUT.
VERY WELL..."MR. TERRIFIC." WELCOME, I'VE BEEN EXPECTING YOU.
WAIT A MINUTE, I'VE ONLY JUST ARRIVED. HOW COULD YOU KNOW I'D BE HERE-- IN UH, MANHATTAN...LOWER MANHATTAN? THAT'S WHERE WE ARE, RIGHT?
A VERSION OF IT ANYWAY.

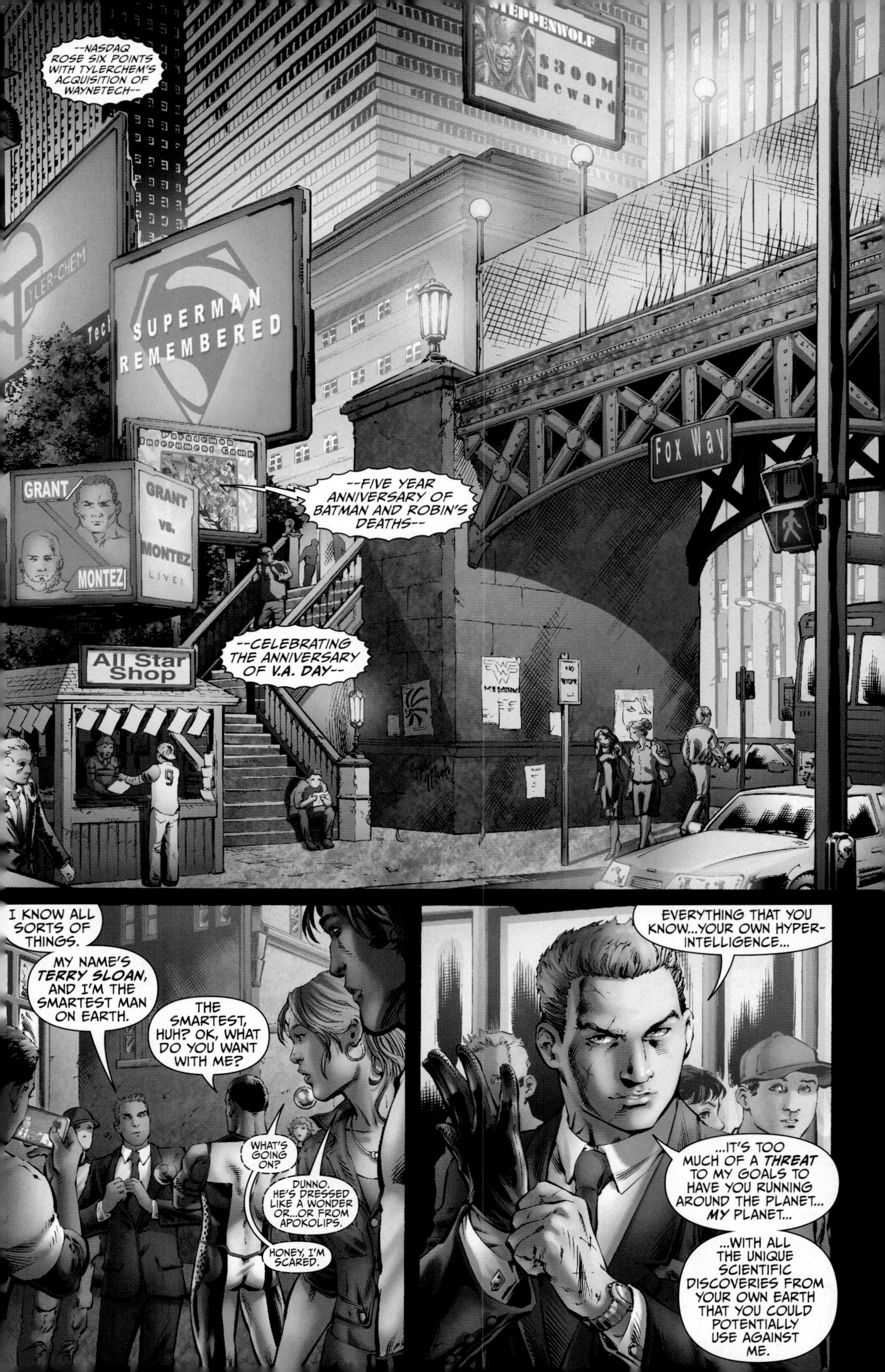
--NASDAQ ROSE SIX POINTS WITH TYLERCHEM'S ACQUISITION OF WAYNETECH--
STEPPENWOLF
$300M Reward
TYLER-CHEM
Tech
SUPERMAN REMEMBERED
GRANT
MONTEZ
GRANT vs. MONTEZ LIVE!
--FIVE YEAR ANNIVERSARY OF BATMAN AND ROBIN'S DEATHS--
Fox Way
--CELEBRATING THE ANNIVERSARY OF V.A. DAY--
All Star Shop
I KNOW ALL SORTS OF THINGS.
MY NAME'S TERRY SLOAN, AND I'M THE SMARTEST MAN ON EARTH.
THE SMARTEST, HUH? OK, WHAT DO YOU WANT WITH ME?
WHAT'S GOING ON?
DUNNO. HE'S DRESSED LIKE A WONDER OR...OR FROM APOKOLIPS.
HONEY, I'M SCARED.
EVERYTHING THAT YOU KNOW...YOUR OWN HYPER-INTELLIGENCE...
...IT'S TOO MUCH OF A THREAT TO MY GOALS TO HAVE YOU RUNNING AROUND THE PLANET... MY PLANET...
...WITH ALL THE UNIQUE SCIENTIFIC DISCOVERIES FROM YOUR OWN EARTH THAT YOU COULD POTENTIALLY USE AGAINST ME.

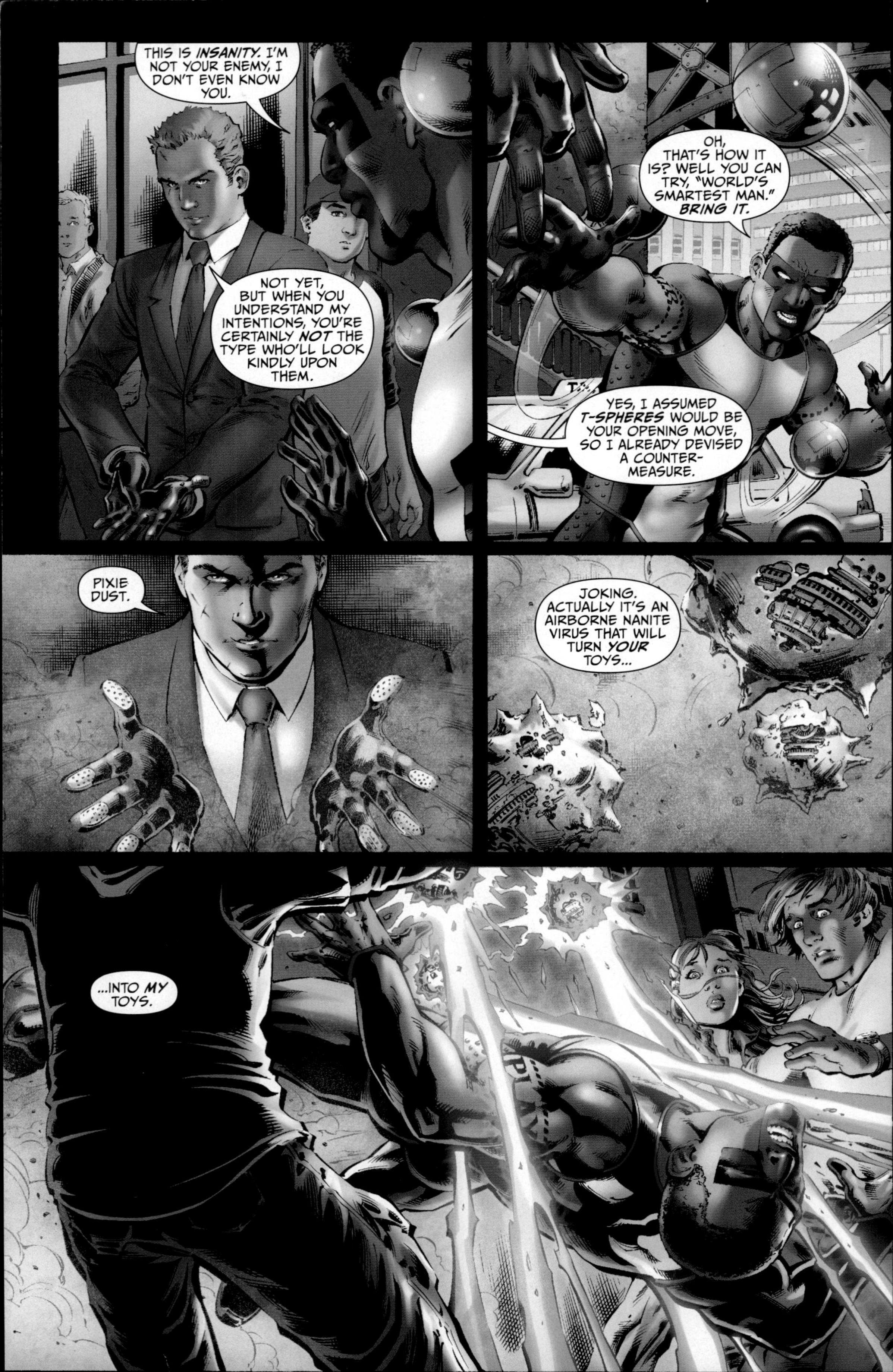
THIS IS INSANITY. I'M NOT YOUR ENEMY, I DON'T EVEN KNOW YOU.
NOT YET, BUT WHEN YOU UNDERSTAND MY INTENTIONS, YOU'RE CERTAINLY NOT THE TYPE WHO'LL LOOK KINDLY UPON THEM.
OH, THAT'S HOW IT IS? WELL YOU CAN TRY, "WORLD'S SMARTEST MAN." BRING IT.
YES, I ASSUMED T-SPHERES WOULD BE YOUR OPENING MOVE, SO I ALREADY DEVISED A COUNTER-MEASURE.
PIXIE DUST.
JOKING. ACTUALLY IT'S AN AIRBORNE NANITE VIRUS THAT WILL TURN YOUR TOYS...
...INTO MY TOYS.

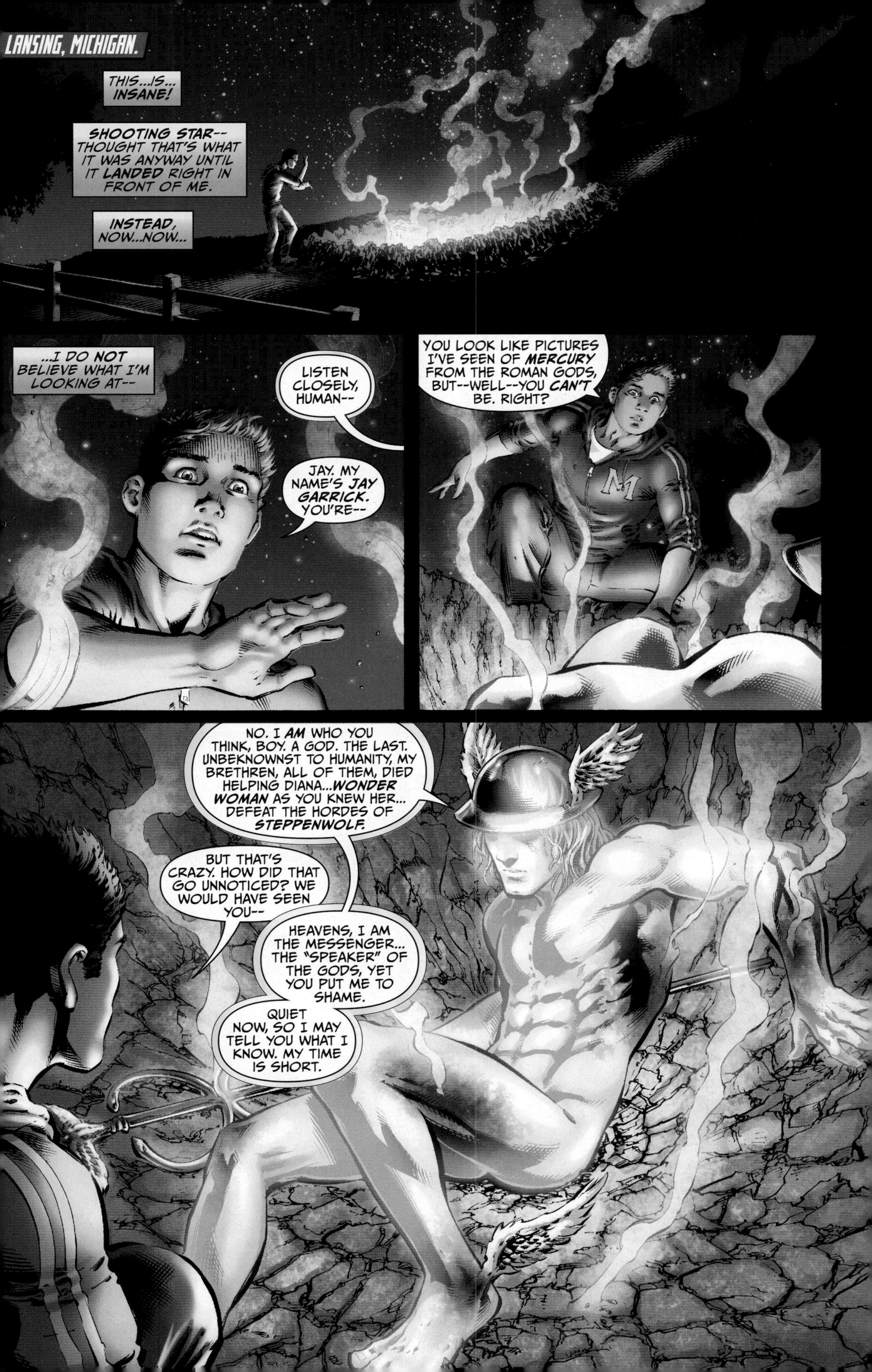
LANSING, MICHIGAN.
THIS...IS... INSANE!
SHOOTING STAR-- THOUGHT THAT'S WHAT IT WAS ANYWAY UNTIL IT LANDED RIGHT IN FRONT OF ME.
INSTEAD, NOW...NOW...
...I DO NOT BELIEVE WHAT I'M LOOKING AT--
LISTEN CLOSELY, HUMAN--
JAY. MY NAME'S JAY GARRICK. YOU'RE--
YOU LOOK LIKE PICTURES I'VE SEEN OF MERCURY FROM THE ROMAN GODS, BUT--WELL--YOU CAN'T BE. RIGHT?
NO. I AM WHO YOU THINK, BOY. A GOD. THE LAST. UNBEKNOWNST TO HUMANITY, MY BRETHREN, ALL OF THEM, DIED HELPING DIANA...WONDER WOMAN AS YOU KNEW HER... DEFEAT THE HORDES OF STEPPENWOLF.
BUT THAT'S CRAZY. HOW DID THAT GO UNNOTICED? WE WOULD HAVE SEEN YOU--
HEAVENS, I AM THE MESSENGER... THE "SPEAKER" OF THE GODS, YET YOU PUT ME TO SHAME.
QUIET NOW, SO I MAY TELL YOU WHAT I KNOW. MY TIME IS SHORT.

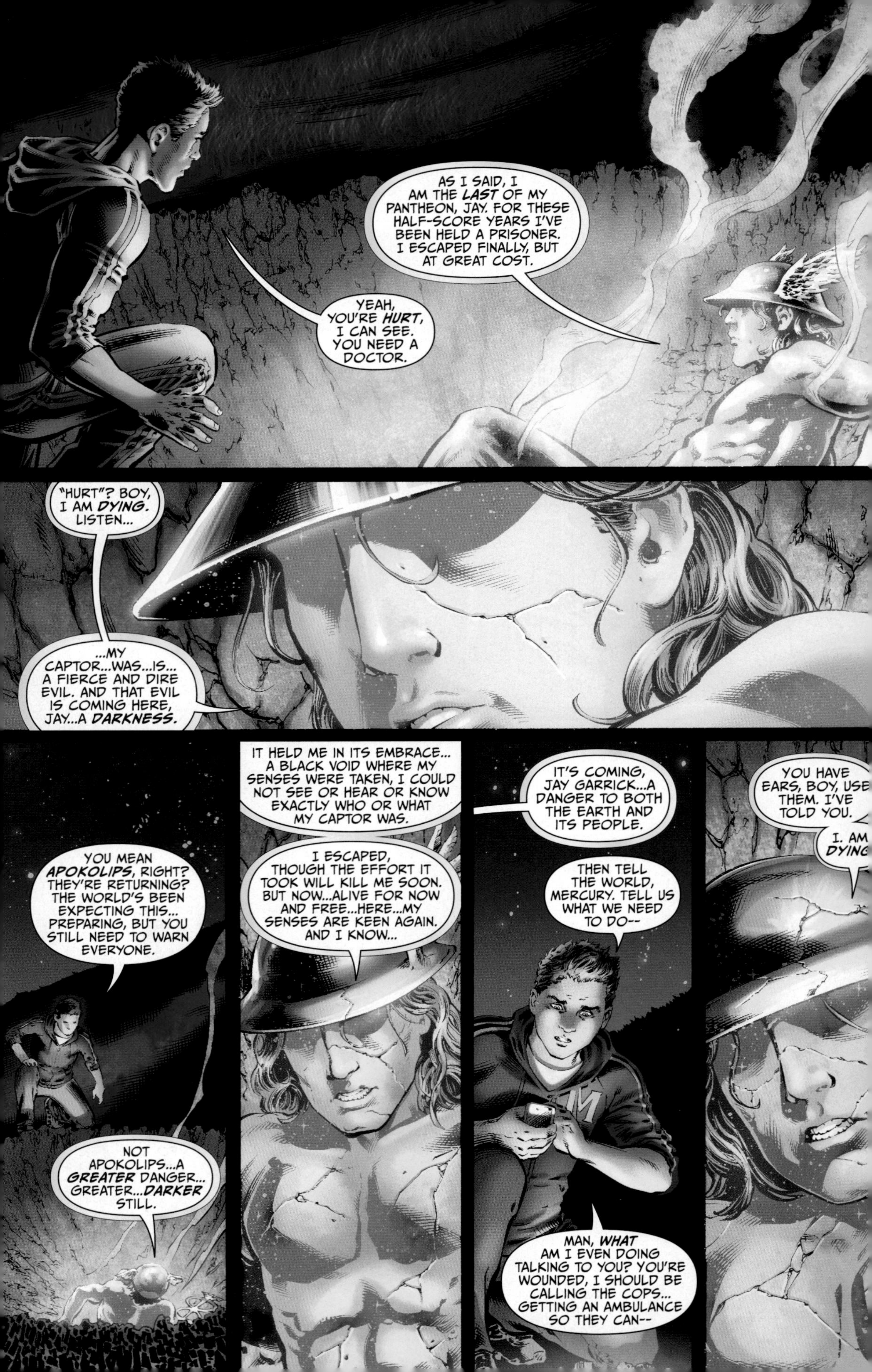
AS I SAID, I AM THE LAST OF MY PANTHEON, JAY. FOR THESE HALF-SCORE YEARS I'VE BEEN HELD A PRISONER. I ESCAPED FINALLY, BUT AT GREAT COST.
YEAH, YOU'RE HURT, I CAN SEE. YOU NEED A DOCTOR.
"HURT"? BOY, I AM DYING. LISTEN...
...MY CAPTOR...WAS...IS... A FIERCE AND DIRE EVIL. AND THAT EVIL IS COMING HERE, JAY...A DARKNESS.
YOU MEAN APOKOLIPS, RIGHT? THEY'RE RETURNING? THE WORLD'S BEEN EXPECTING THIS... PREPARING, BUT YOU STILL NEED TO WARN EVERYONE.
NOT APOKOLIPS...A GREATER DANGER... GREATER...DARKER STILL.
IT HELD ME IN ITS EMBRACE... A BLACK VOID WHERE MY SENSES WERE TAKEN, I COULD NOT SEE OR HEAR OR KNOW EXACTLY WHO OR WHAT MY CAPTOR WAS.
I ESCAPED, THOUGH THE EFFORT IT TOOK WILL KILL ME SOON. BUT NOW...ALIVE FOR NOW AND FREE...HERE...MY SENSES ARE KEEN AGAIN. AND I KNOW...
IT'S COMING, JAY GARRICK...A DANGER TO BOTH THE EARTH AND ITS PEOPLE.
THEN TELL THE WORLD, MERCURY. TELL US WHAT WE NEED TO DO--
MAN, WHAT AM I EVEN DOING TALKING TO YOU? YOU'RE WOUNDED, I SHOULD BE CALLING THE COPS... GETTING AN AMBULANCE SO THEY CAN--
YOU HAVE EARS, BOY, USE THEM. I'VE TOLD YOU.
I. AM DYING

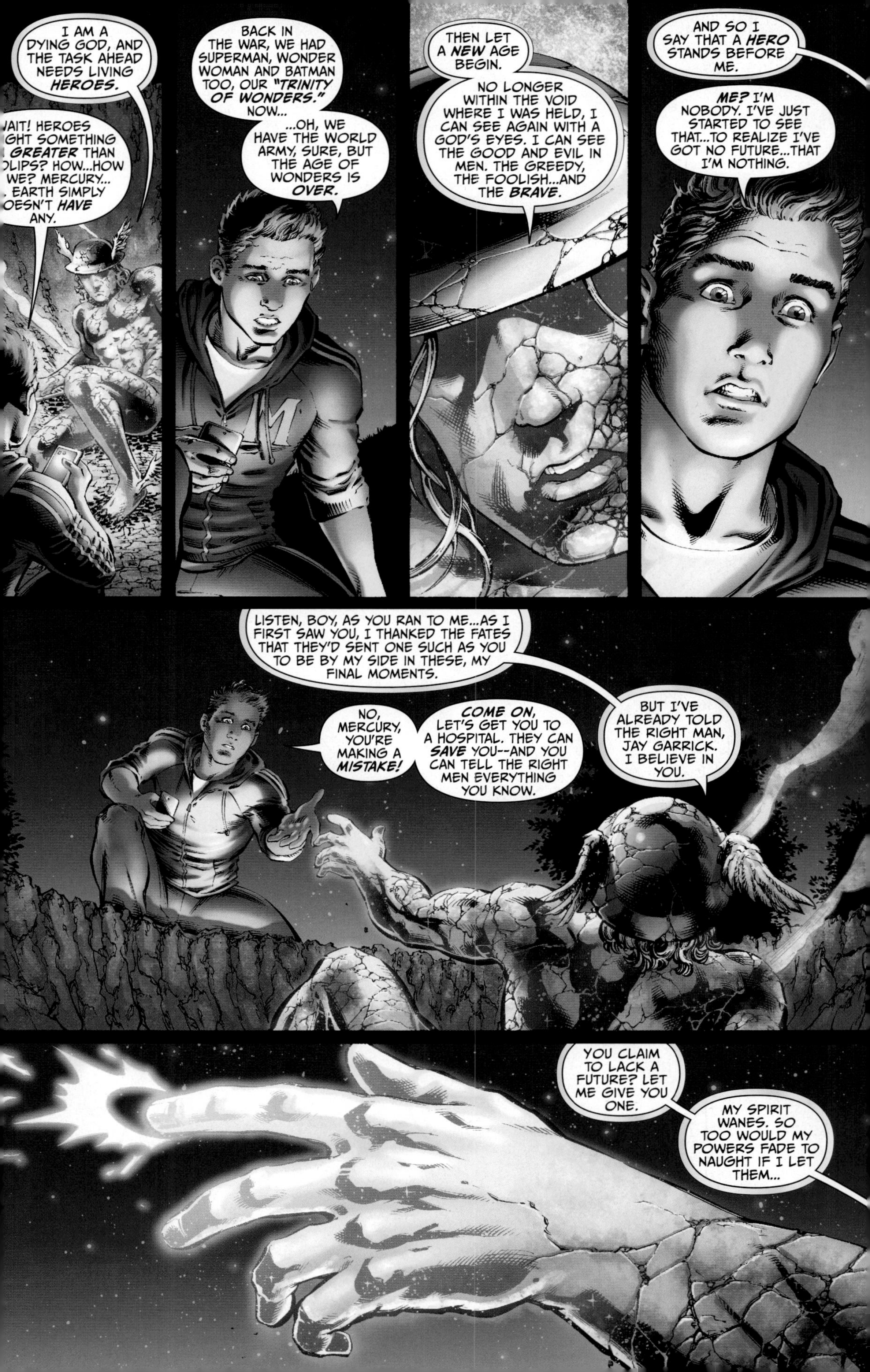
I AM A DYING GOD, AND THE TASK AHEAD NEEDS LIVING HEROES.
HEROES IGHT SOMETHING GREATER THAN OLIPS? HOW...HOW WE? MERCURY... EARTH SIMPLY OESN'T HAVE ANY.
BACK IN THE WAR, WE HAD SUPERMAN, WONDER WOMAN AND BATMAN TOO, OUR "TRINITY OF WONDERS." NOW...
...OH, WE HAVE THE WORLD ARMY, SURE, BUT THE AGE OF WONDERS IS OVER.
THEN LET A NEW AGE BEGIN.
NO LONGER WITHIN THE VOID WHERE I WAS HELD, I CAN SEE AGAIN WITH A GOD'S EYES. I CAN SEE THE GOOD AND EVIL IN MEN. THE GREEDY, THE FOOLISH...AND THE BRAVE.
AND SO I SAY THAT A HERO STANDS BEFORE ME.
ME? I'M NOBODY. I'VE JUST STARTED TO SEE THAT...TO REALIZE I'VE GOT NO FUTURE...THAT I'M NOTHING.
LISTEN, BOY, AS YOU RAN TO ME...AS I FIRST SAW YOU, I THANKED THE FATES THAT THEY'D SENT ONE SUCH AS YOU TO BE BY MY SIDE IN THESE, MY FINAL MOMENTS.
NO, MERCURY, YOU'RE MAKING A MISTAKE!
COME ON, LET'S GET YOU TO A HOSPITAL. THEY CAN SAVE YOU--AND YOU CAN TELL THE RIGHT MEN EVERYTHING YOU KNOW.
BUT I'VE ALREADY TOLD THE RIGHT MAN, JAY GARRICK. I BELIEVE IN YOU.
YOU CLAIM TO LACK A FUTURE? LET ME GIVE YOU ONE.
MY SPIRIT WANES. SO TOO WOULD MY POWERS FADE TO NAUGHT IF I LET THEM...

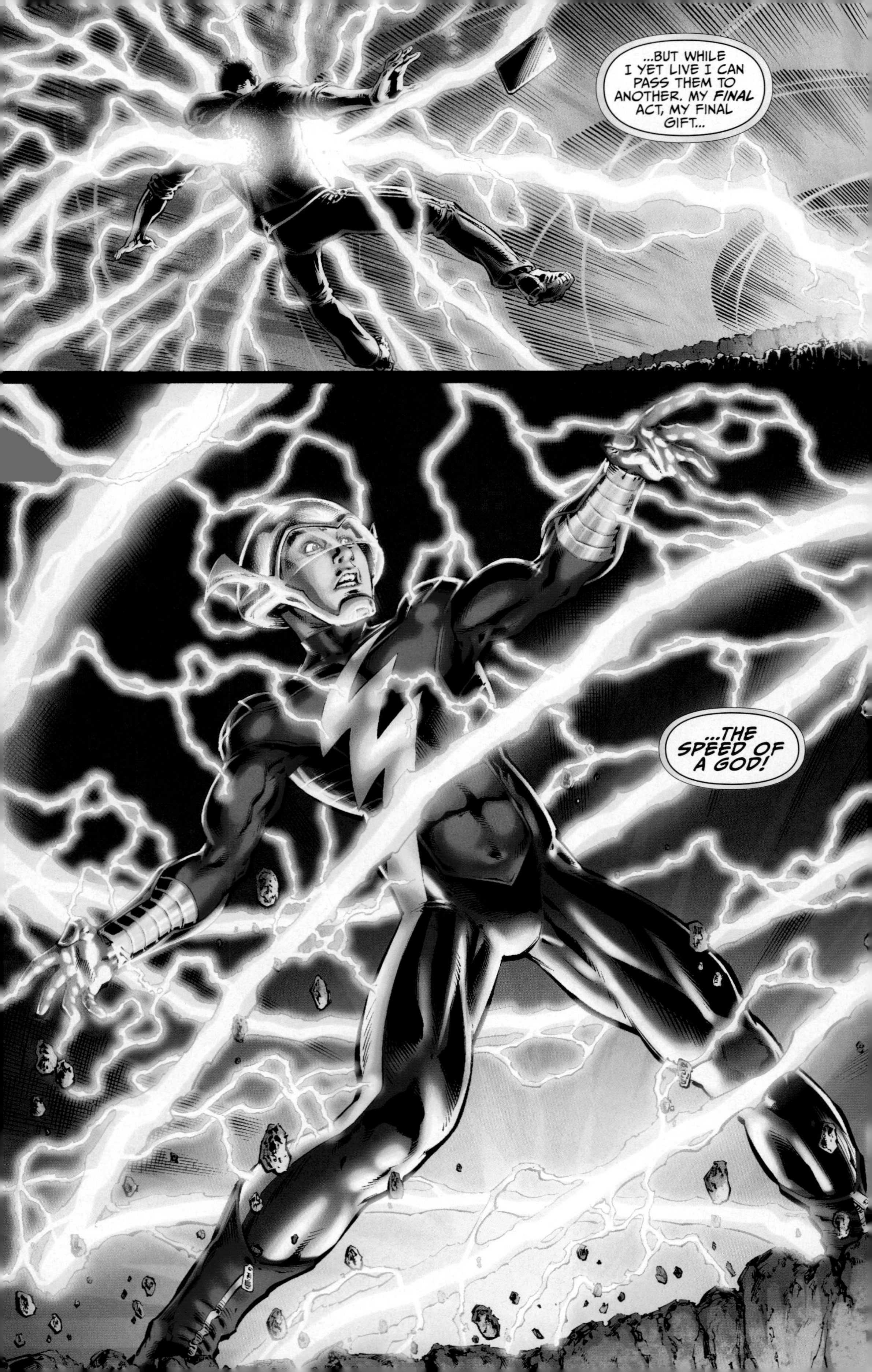
...BUT WHILE I YET LIVE I CAN PASS THEM TO ANOTHER. MY *FINAL* ACT, MY FINAL GIFT...
...THE SPEED OF A GOD!

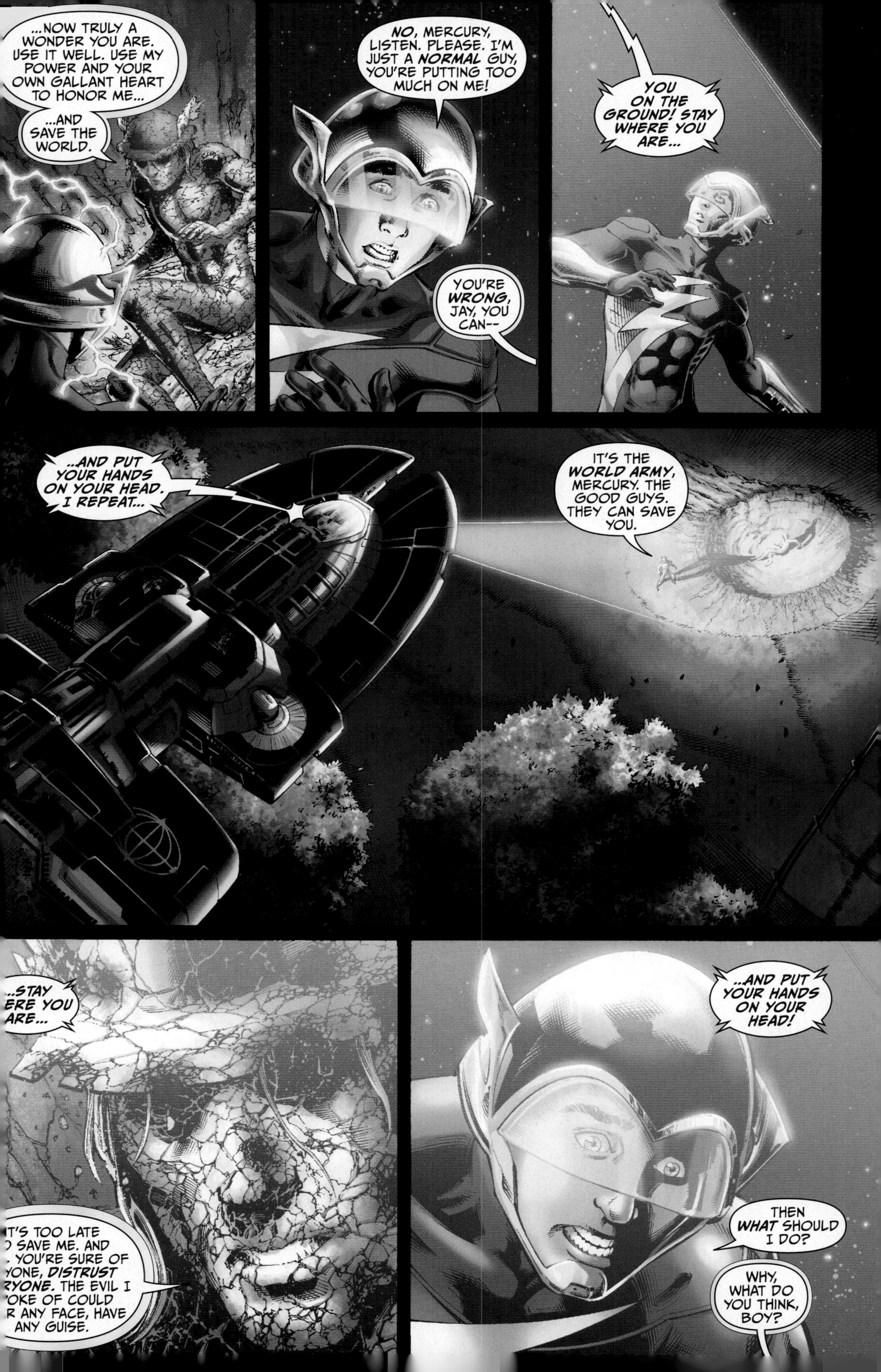
...NOW TRULY A WONDER YOU ARE. USE IT WELL. USE MY POWER AND YOUR OWN GALLANT HEART TO HONOR ME...
...AND SAVE THE WORLD.
NO, MERCURY, LISTEN. PLEASE. I'M JUST A NORMAL GUY, YOU'RE PUTTING TOO MUCH ON ME!
YOU'RE WRONG, JAY, YOU CAN--
YOU ON THE GROUND! STAY WHERE YOU ARE...
...AND PUT YOUR HANDS ON YOUR HEAD. I REPEAT...
IT'S THE WORLD ARMY, MERCURY. THE GOOD GUYS. THEY CAN SAVE YOU.
...STAY
ERE YOU ARE...
T'S TOO LATE
O SAVE ME. AND
. YOU'RE SURE OF
YONE, DISTRUST
RYONE. THE EVIL I
OKE OF COULD
R ANY FACE, HAVE
ANY GUISE.
...AND PUT YOUR HANDS ON YOUR HEAD!
THEN WHAT SHOULD I DO?
WHY, WHAT DO YOU THINK, BOY?

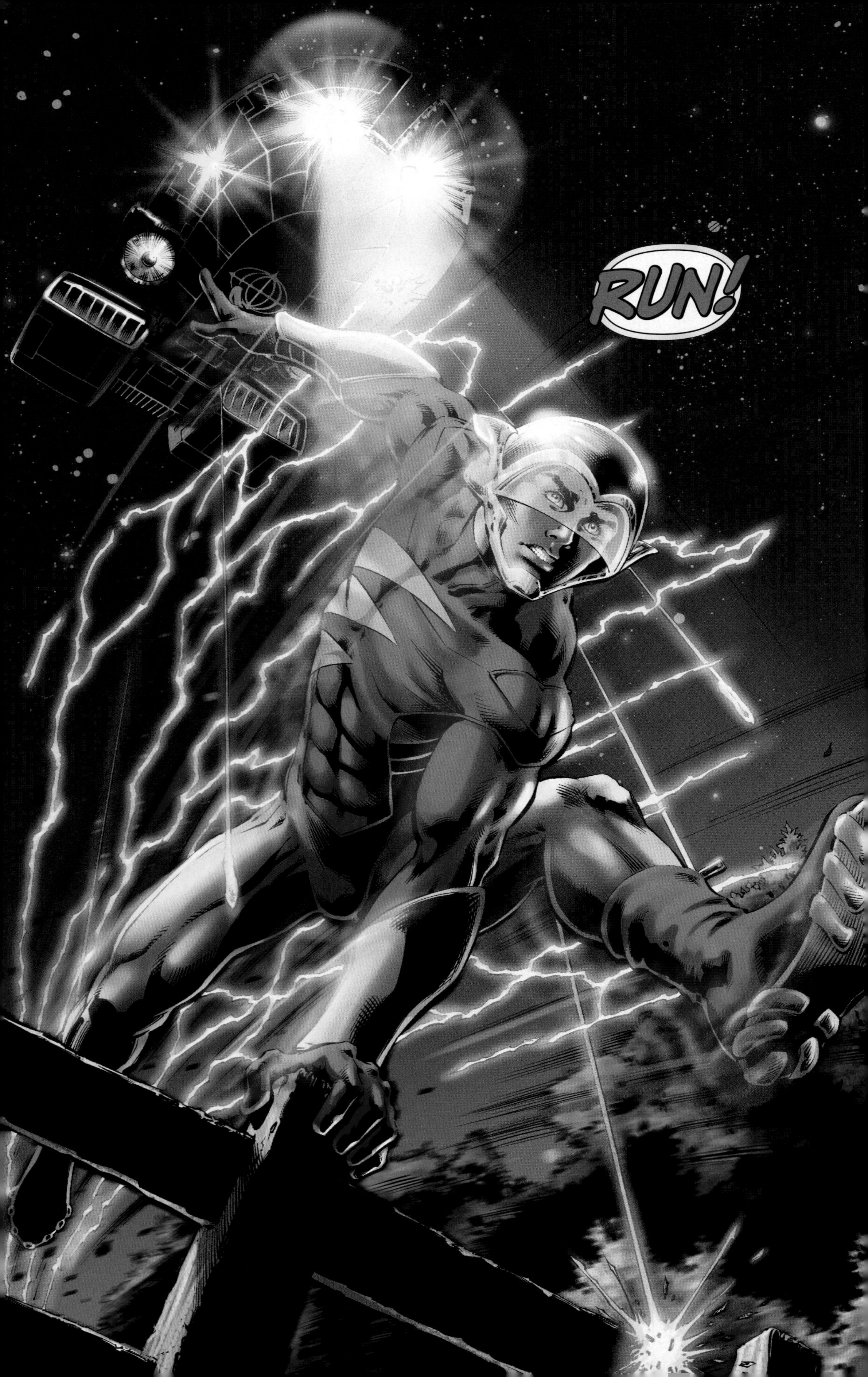
RUN!

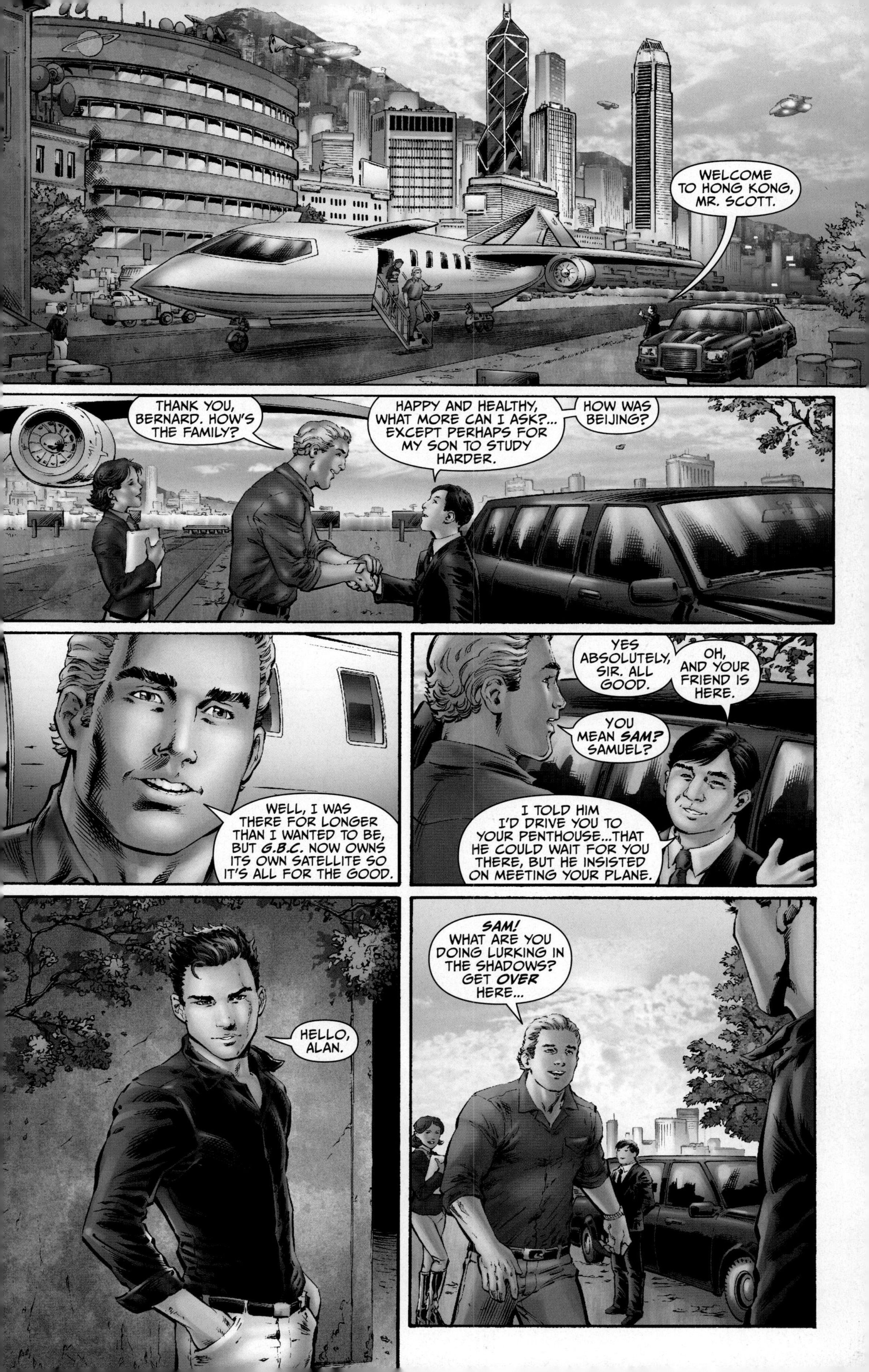
WELCOME TO HONG KONG, MR. SCOTT.
THANK YOU, BERNARD. HOW'S THE FAMILY?
HAPPY AND HEALTHY, WHAT MORE CAN I ASK?... EXCEPT PERHAPS FOR MY SON TO STUDY HARDER.
HOW WAS BEIJING?
WELL, I WAS THERE FOR LONGER THAN I WANTED TO BE, BUT G.B.C. NOW OWNS ITS OWN SATELLITE SO IT'S ALL FOR THE GOOD.
YES ABSOLUTELY, SIR. ALL GOOD.
OH, AND YOUR FRIEND IS HERE.
YOU MEAN SAM? SAMUEL?
I TOLD HIM I'D DRIVE YOU TO YOUR PENTHOUSE...THAT HE COULD WAIT FOR YOU THERE, BUT HE INSISTED ON MEETING YOUR PLANE.
HELLO, ALAN.
SAM! WHAT ARE YOU DOING LURKING IN THE SHADOWS? GET OVER HERE...

"...GOD, I'VE MISSED YOU."

I'M REALLY SORRY, SAM, I DIDN'T THINK I'D BE GONE SO LONG. WHICH IS SOMETHING I WANT TO TALK TO YOU ABOUT, BY THE WAY.

IT'LL KEEP, LOVE. LET'S GET OUT O' HERE.

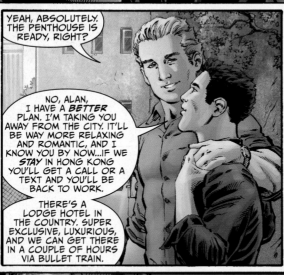

YEAH, ABSOLUTELY. THE PENTHOUSE IS READY, RIGHT?

NO, ALAN, I HAVE A *BETTER* PLAN. I'M TAKING YOU AWAY FROM THE CITY. IT'LL BE WAY MORE RELAXING AND ROMANTIC, AND I KNOW YOU BY NOW...IF WE *STAY* IN HONG KONG YOU'LL GET A CALL OR A TEXT AND YOU'LL BE BACK TO WORK.

THERE'S A LODGE HOTEL IN THE COUNTRY. SUPER EXCLUSIVE, LUXURIOUS, AND WE CAN GET THERE IN A COUPLE OF HOURS VIA BULLET TRAIN.

COME ON, SAY YES. BESIDES YOU OWE ME FOR BEING AWAY AS LONG AS YOU HAVE.

WHY NOT, IT SOUNDS *MAGICAL*...

"...LET'S GO."

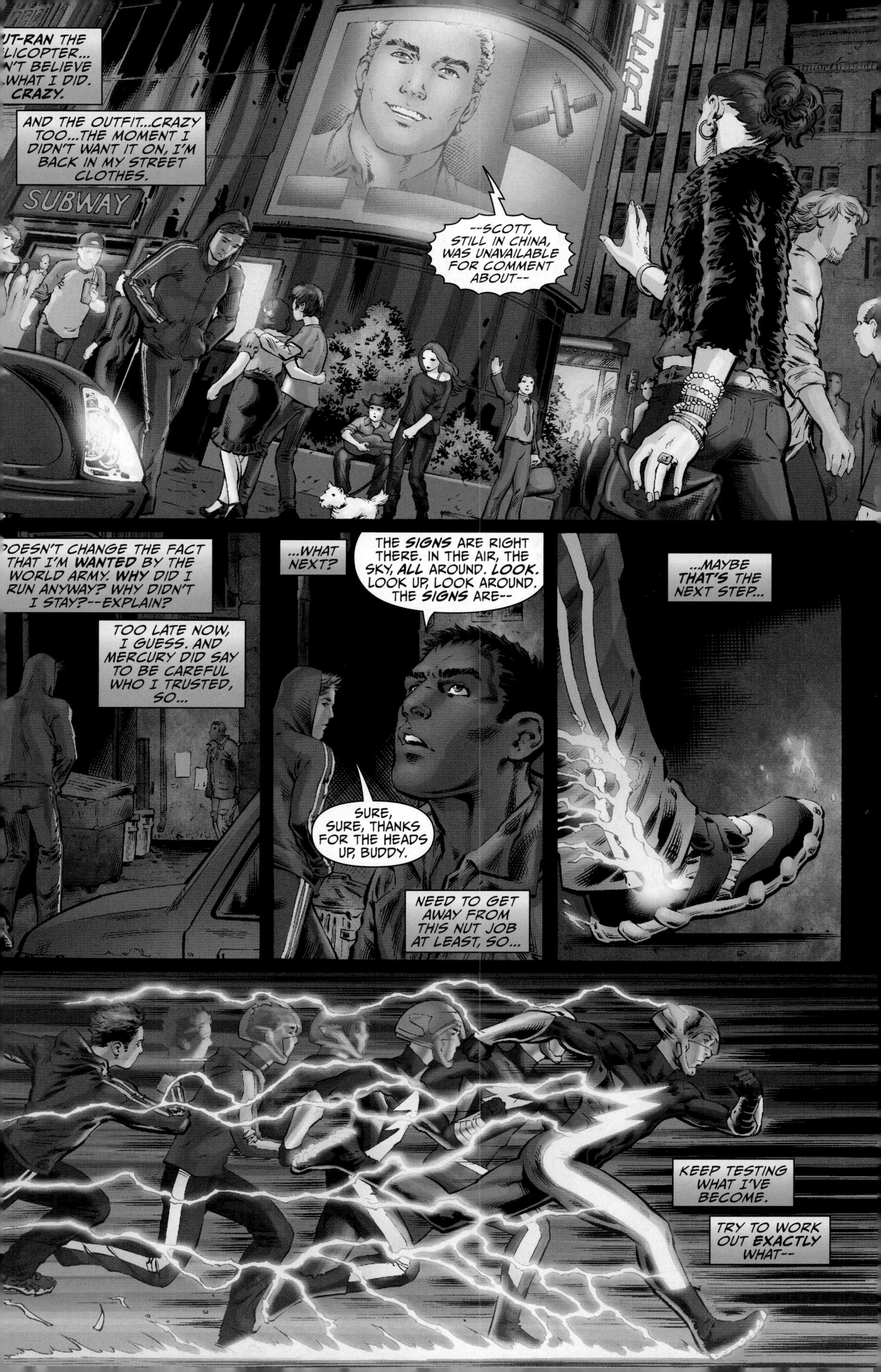
UT-RAN THE ELICOPTER... N'T BELIEVE ..WHAT I DID. CRAZY.
AND THE OUTFIT...CRAZY TOO...THE MOMENT I DIDN'T WANT IT ON, I'M BACK IN MY STREET CLOTHES.
SUBWAY
--SCOTT, STILL IN CHINA, WAS UNAVAILABLE FOR COMMENT ABOUT--
OESN'T CHANGE THE FACT THAT I'M WANTED BY THE WORLD ARMY. WHY DID I RUN ANYWAY? WHY DIDN'T I STAY?--EXPLAIN?
TOO LATE NOW, I GUESS. AND MERCURY DID SAY TO BE CAREFUL WHO I TRUSTED, SO...
...WHAT NEXT?
THE SIGNS ARE RIGHT THERE. IN THE AIR, THE SKY, ALL AROUND. LOOK. LOOK UP, LOOK AROUND. THE SIGNS ARE--
SURE, SURE, THANKS FOR THE HEADS UP, BUDDY.
NEED TO GET AWAY FROM THIS NUT JOB AT LEAST, SO...
...MAYBE THAT'S THE NEXT STEP...
KEEP TESTING WHAT I'VE BECOME.
TRY TO WORK OUT EXACTLY WHAT--

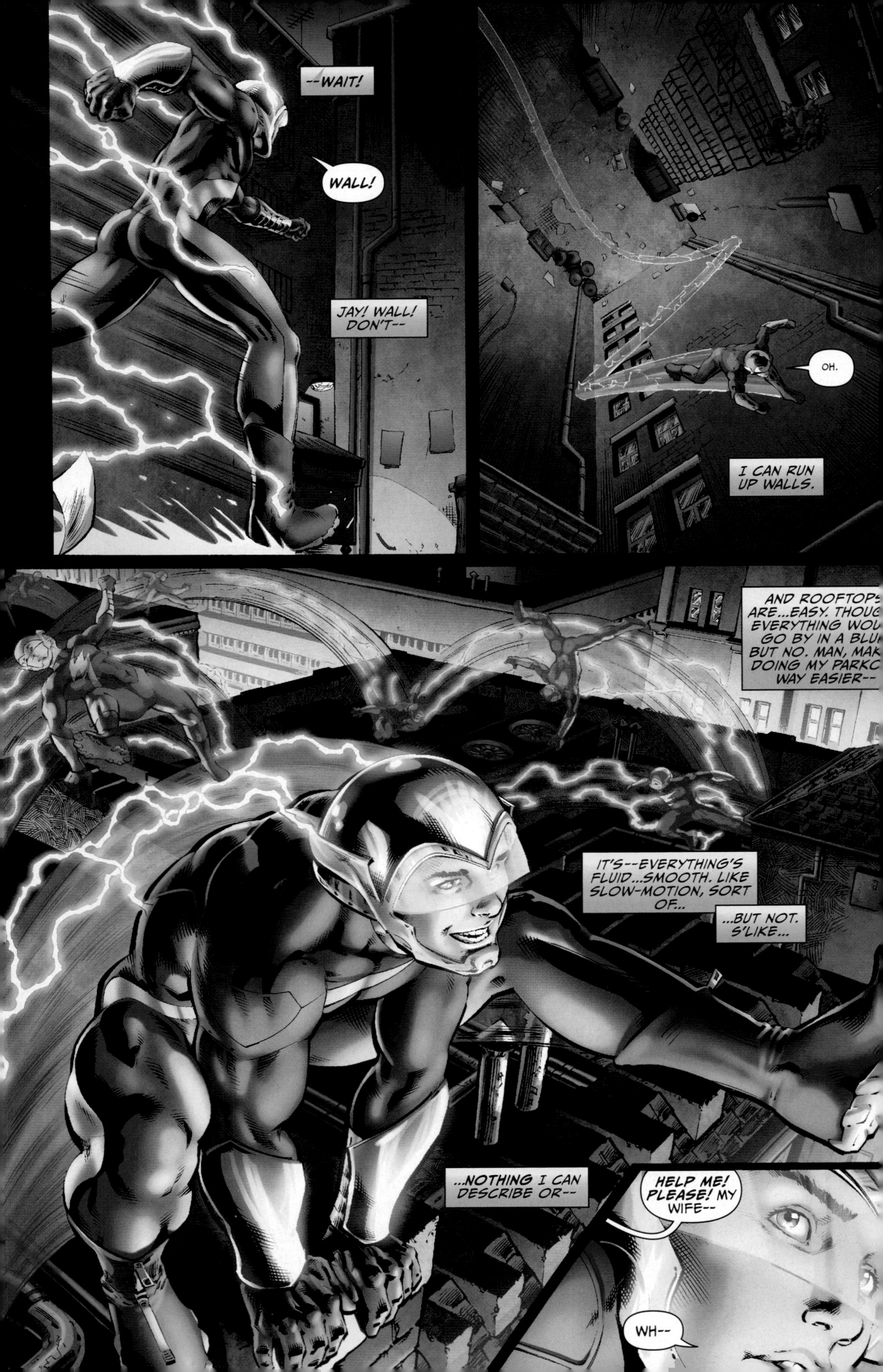
--WAIT!
WALL!
JAY! WALL! DON'T--
OH.
I CAN RUN UP WALLS.
AND ROOFTOPS ARE...EASY. THOUG EVERYTHING WOU GO BY IN A BLU BUT NO. MAN, MAK DOING MY PARKO WAY EASIER--
IT'S--EVERYTHING'S FLUID...SMOOTH. LIKE SLOW-MOTION, SORT OF...
...BUT NOT. S'LIKE...
...NOTHING I CAN DESCRIBE OR--
HELP ME! PLEASE! MY WIFE--
WH--

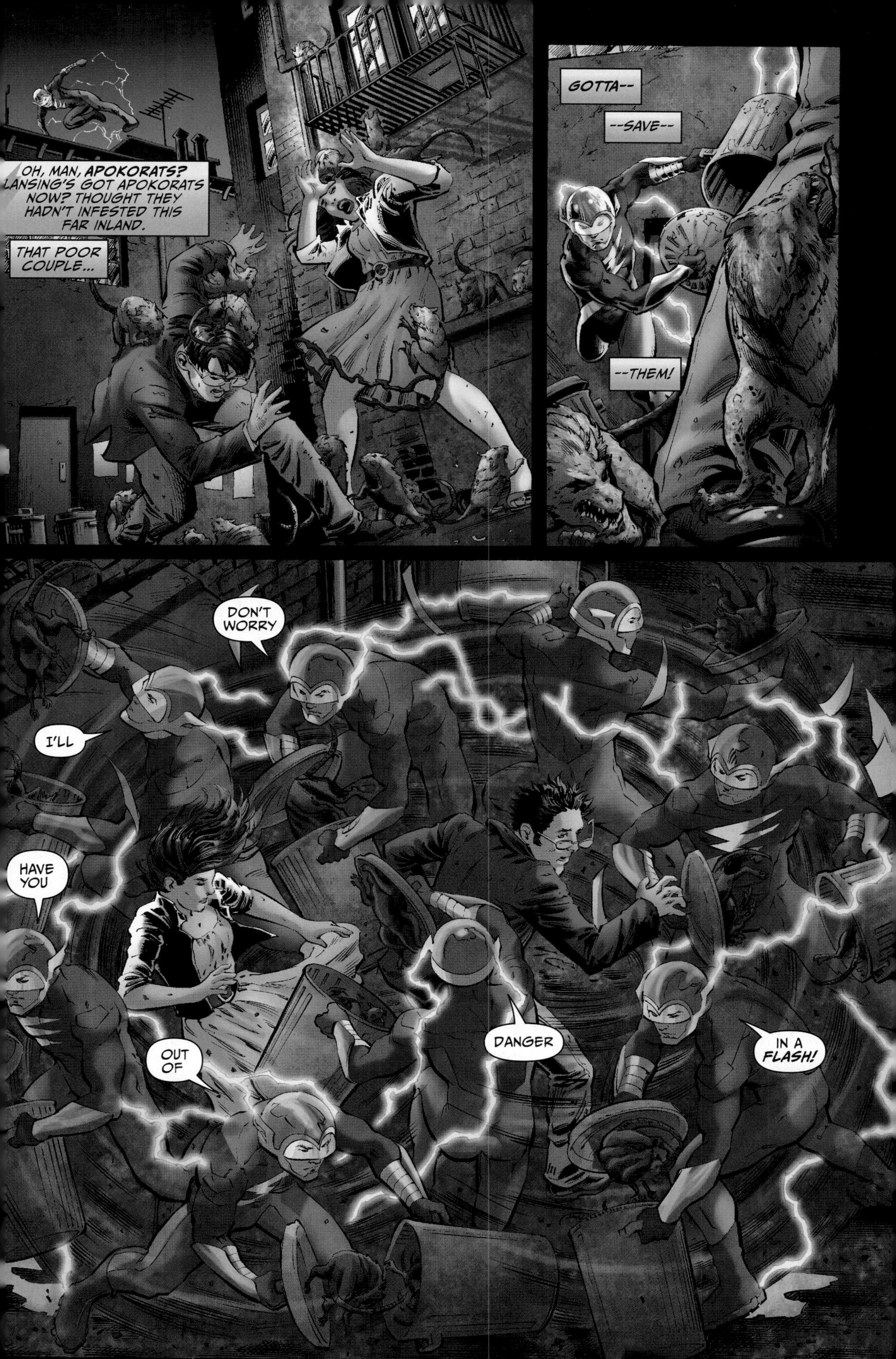
OH, MAN, APOKORATS? LANSING'S GOT APOKORATS NOW? THOUGHT THEY HADN'T INFESTED THIS FAR INLAND.
THAT POOR COUPLE...
GOTTA--
--SAVE--
--THEM!
DON'T WORRY
I'LL
HAVE YOU
OUT OF
DANGER
IN A FLASH!

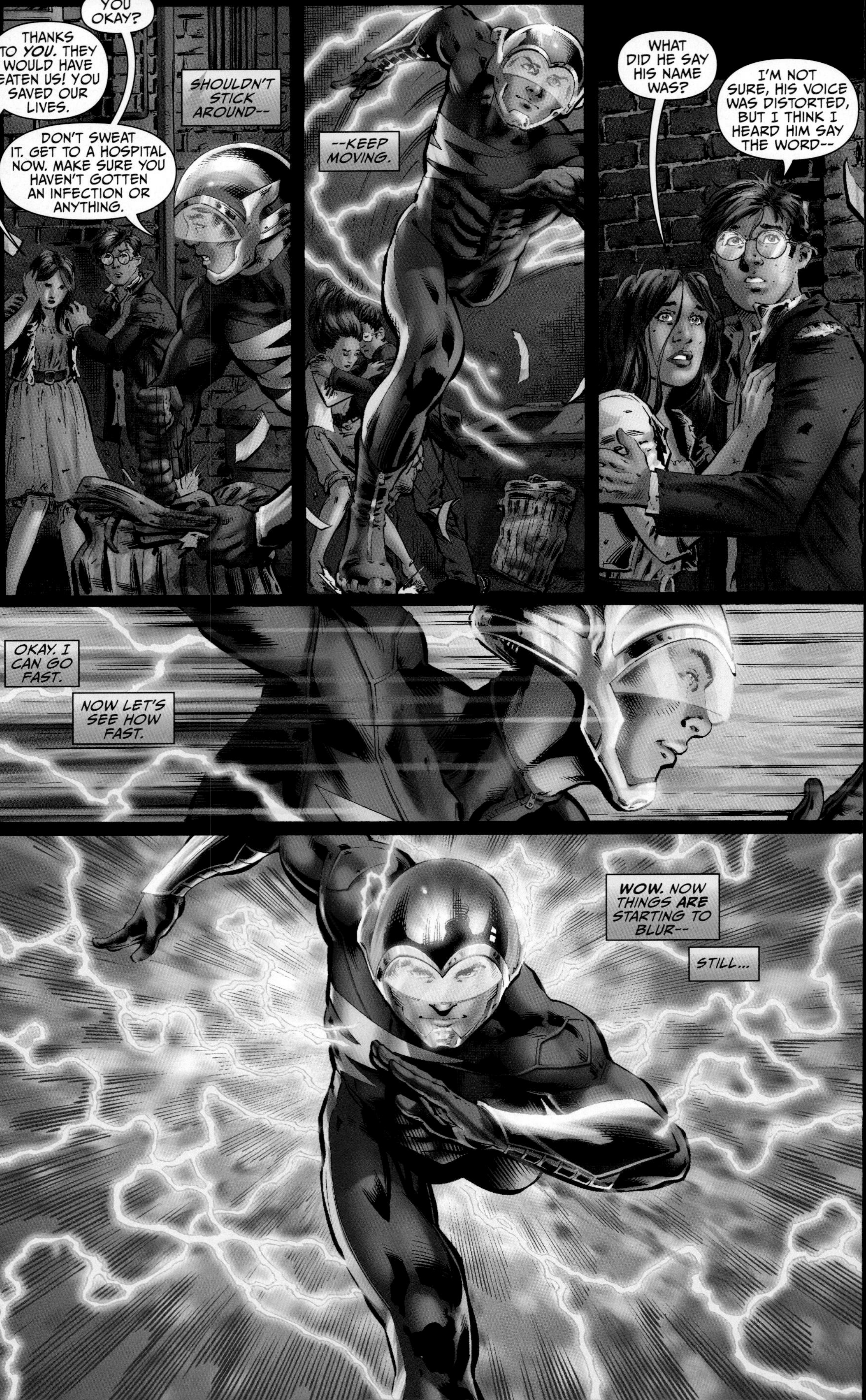
YOU OKAY?
THANKS TO YOU. THEY WOULD HAVE EATEN US! YOU SAVED OUR LIVES.
DON'T SWEAT IT. GET TO A HOSPITAL NOW. MAKE SURE YOU HAVEN'T GOTTEN AN INFECTION OR ANYTHING.
SHOULDN'T STICK AROUND--
--KEEP MOVING.
WHAT DID HE SAY HIS NAME WAS?
I'M NOT SURE, HIS VOICE WAS DISTORTED, BUT I THINK I HEARD HIM SAY THE WORD--
OKAY. I CAN GO FAST.
NOW LET'S SEE HOW FAST.
WOW. NOW THINGS ARE STARTING TO BLUR--
STILL...

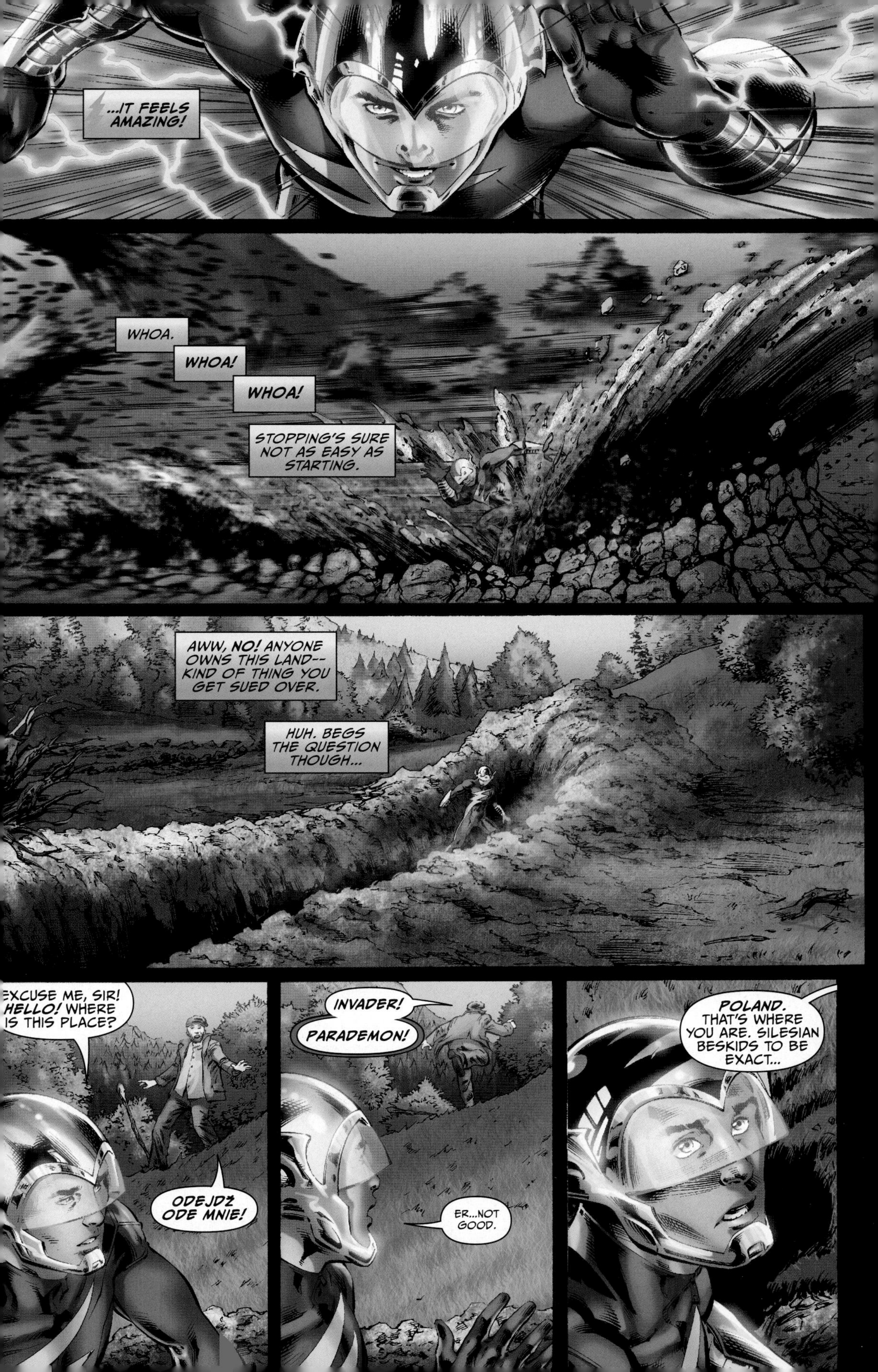

...IT FEELS AMAZING!
WHOA.
WHOA!
WHOA!
STOPPING'S SURE NOT AS EASY AS STARTING.
AWW, NO! ANYONE OWNS THIS LAND-- KIND OF THING YOU GET SUED OVER.
HUH. BEGS THE QUESTION THOUGH...
EXCUSE ME, SIR! HELLO! WHERE IS THIS PLACE?
ODEJDŹ ODE MNIE!
INVADER!
PARADEMON!
ER...NOT GOOD.
POLAND. THAT'S WHERE YOU ARE. SILESIAN BESKIDS TO BE EXACT...

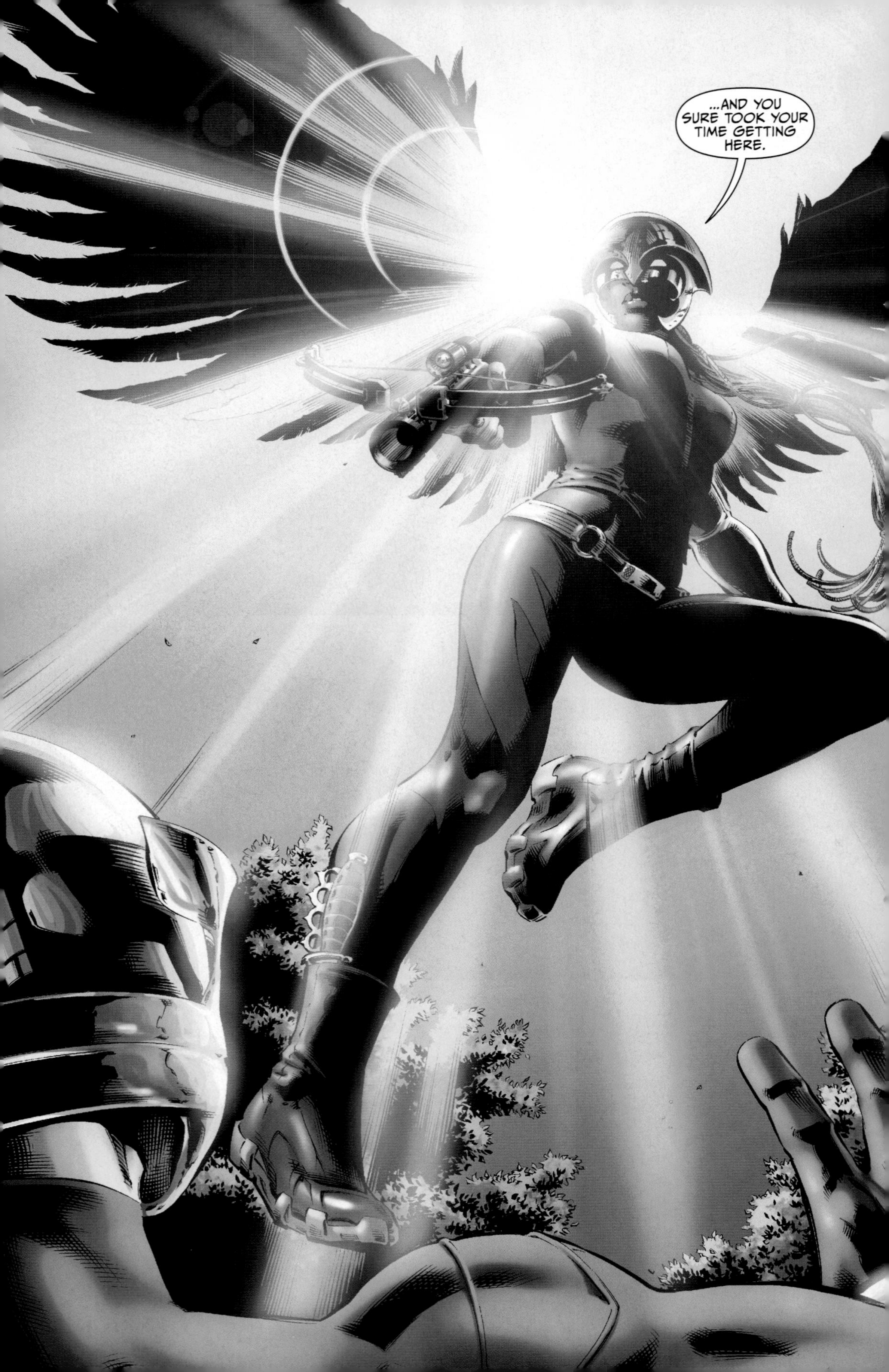
...AND YOU SURE TOOK YOUR TIME GETTING HERE.

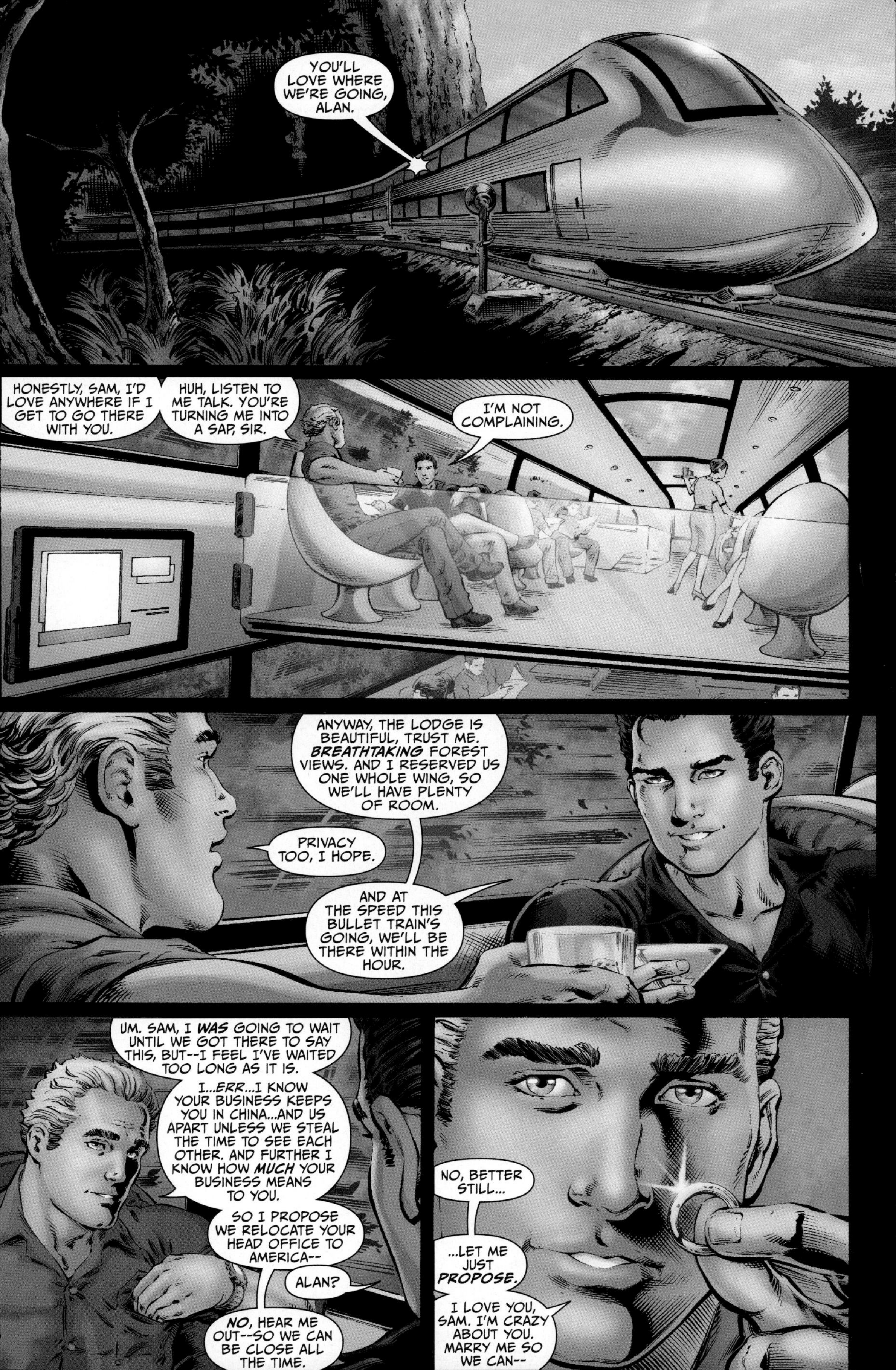
YOU'LL LOVE WHERE WE'RE GOING, ALAN.
HONESTLY, SAM, I'D LOVE ANYWHERE IF I GET TO GO THERE WITH YOU.
HUH, LISTEN TO ME TALK. YOU'RE TURNING ME INTO A SAP, SIR.
I'M NOT COMPLAINING.
ANYWAY, THE LODGE IS BEAUTIFUL, TRUST ME. BREATHTAKING FOREST VIEWS. AND I RESERVED US ONE WHOLE WING, SO WE'LL HAVE PLENTY OF ROOM.
PRIVACY TOO, I HOPE.
AND AT THE SPEED THIS BULLET TRAIN'S GOING, WE'LL BE THERE WITHIN THE HOUR.
UM. SAM, I WAS GOING TO WAIT UNTIL WE GOT THERE TO SAY THIS, BUT--I FEEL I'VE WAITED TOO LONG AS IT IS.
I...ERR...I KNOW YOUR BUSINESS KEEPS YOU IN CHINA...AND US APART UNLESS WE STEAL THE TIME TO SEE EACH OTHER. AND FURTHER I KNOW HOW MUCH YOUR BUSINESS MEANS TO YOU.
SO I PROPOSE WE RELOCATE YOUR HEAD OFFICE TO AMERICA--
ALAN?
NO, HEAR ME OUT--SO WE CAN BE CLOSE ALL THE TIME.
NO, BETTER STILL...
...LET ME JUST PROPOSE.
I LOVE YOU, SAM. I'M CRAZY ABOUT YOU. MARRY ME SO WE CAN--

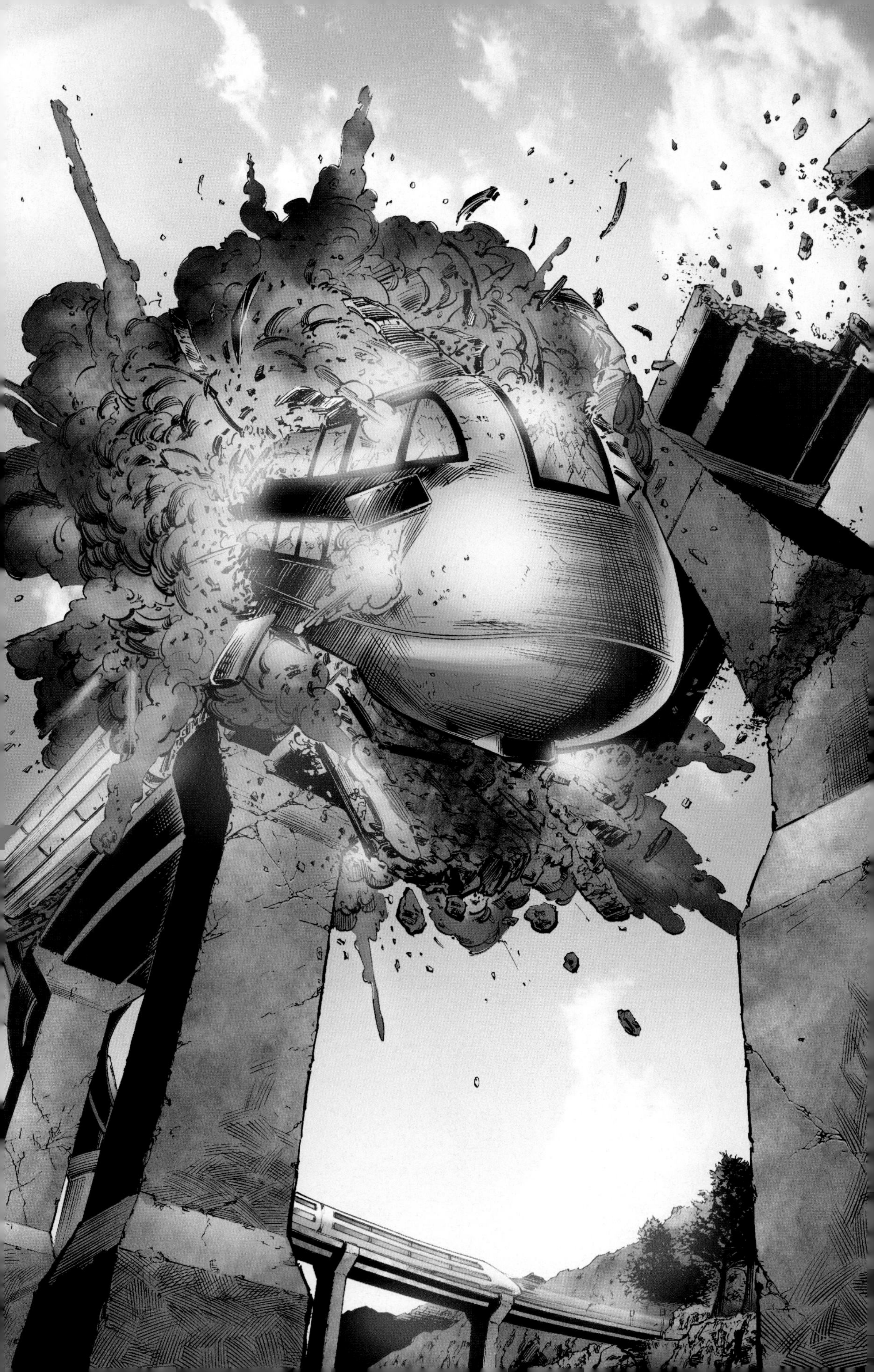

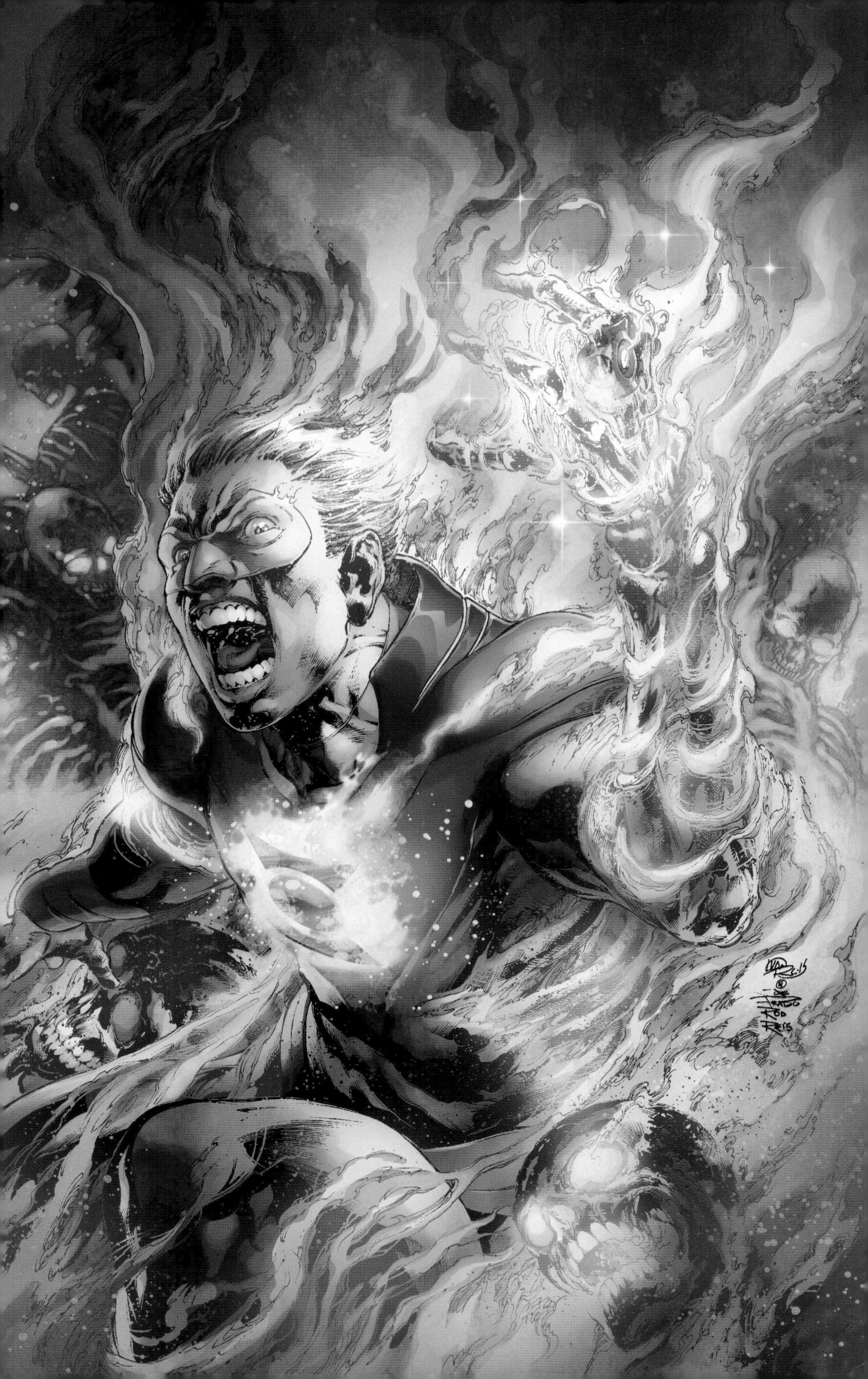

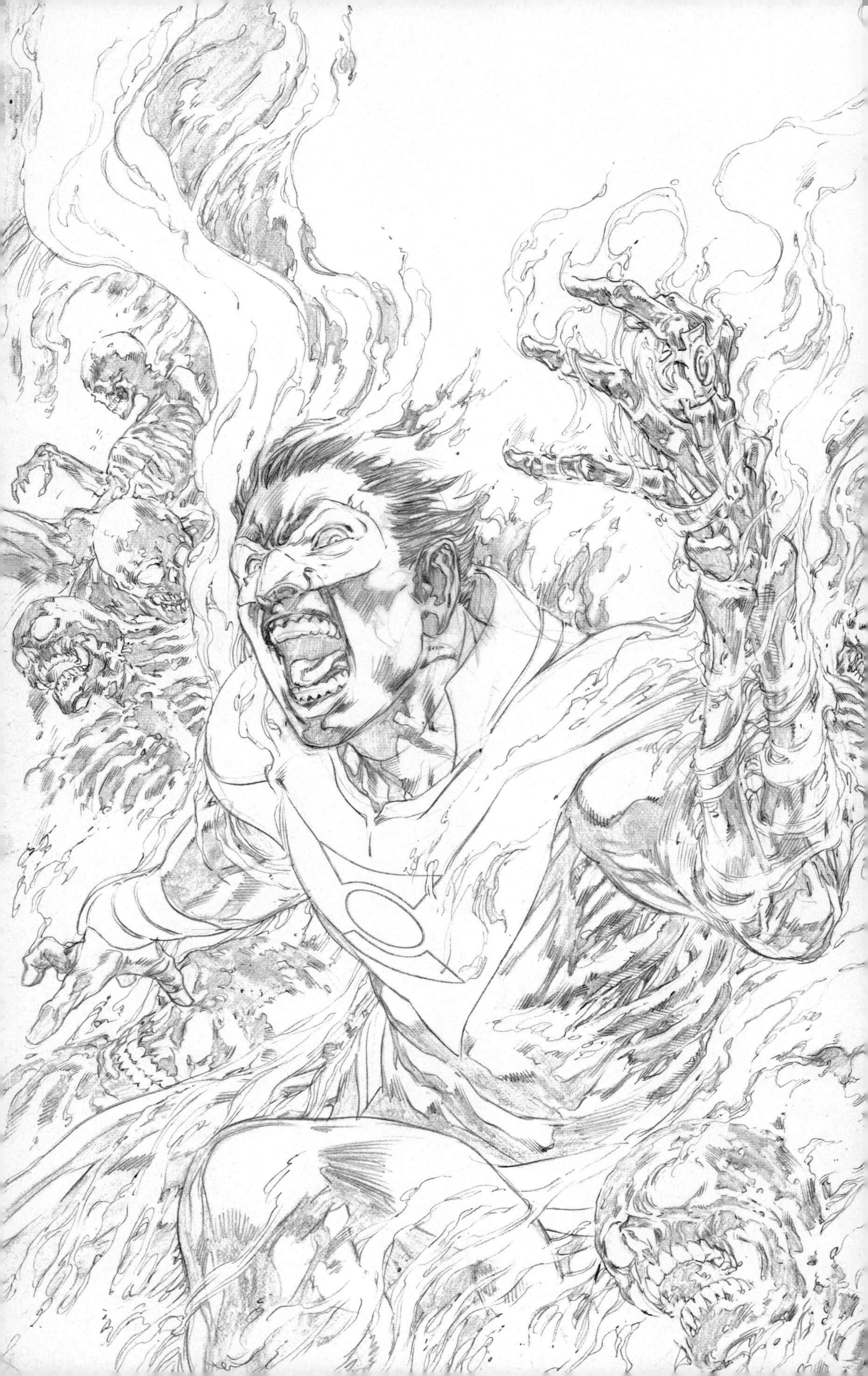

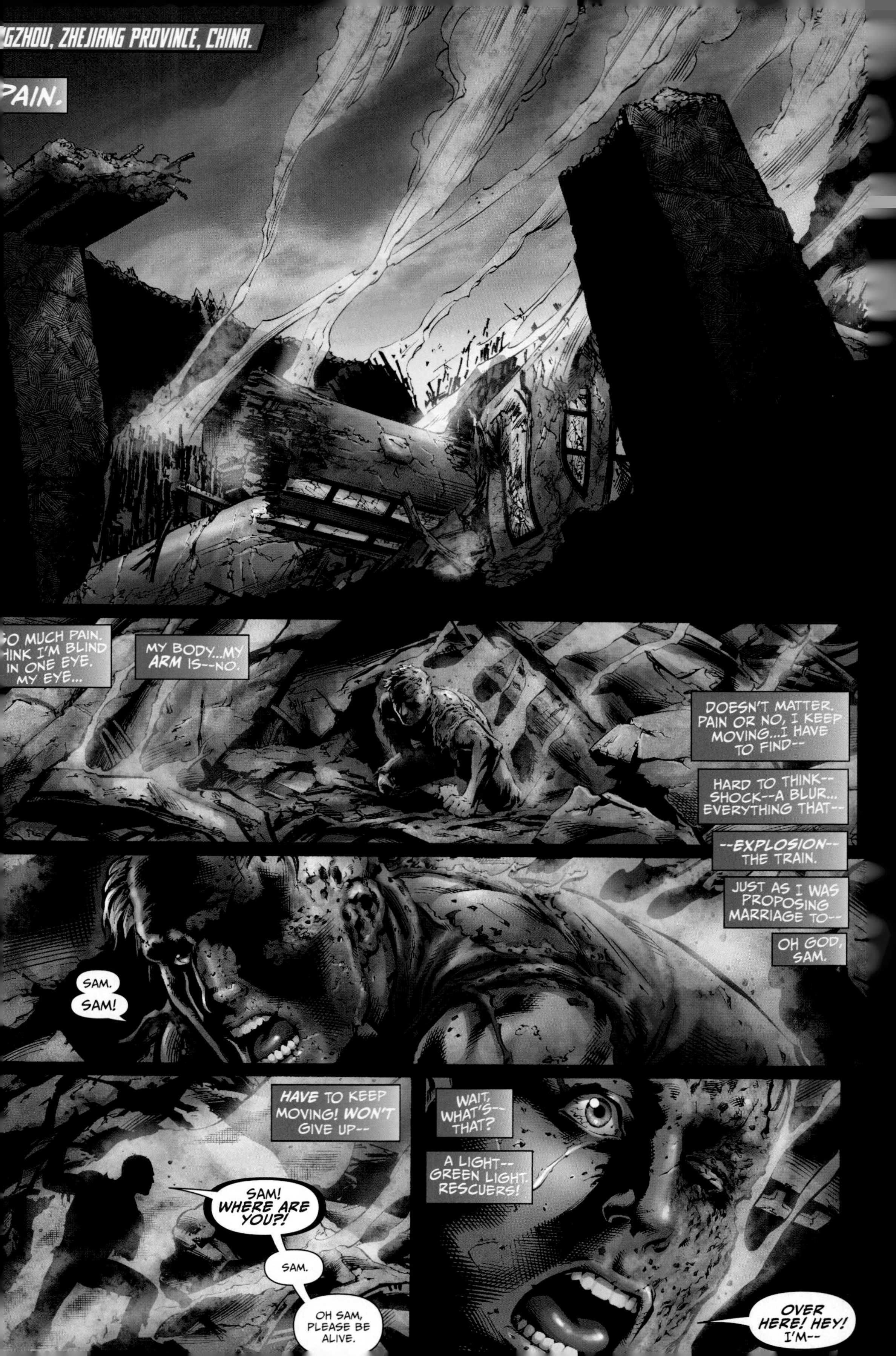

GZHOU, ZHEJIANG PROVINCE, CHINA.
PAIN.
O MUCH PAIN. HINK I'M BLIND IN ONE EYE. MY EYE...
MY BODY...MY ARM IS--NO.
DOESN'T MATTER. PAIN OR NO, I KEEP MOVING...I HAVE TO FIND--
HARD TO THINK--SHOCK--A BLUR... EVERYTHING THAT--
--EXPLOSION--THE TRAIN.
JUST AS I WAS PROPOSING MARRIAGE TO--
OH GOD, SAM.
SAM. SAM!
HAVE TO KEEP MOVING! WON'T GIVE UP--
SAM! WHERE ARE YOU?!
SAM.
OH SAM, PLEASE BE ALIVE.
WAIT, WHAT'S--THAT?
A LIGHT--GREEN LIGHT. RESCUERS!
OVER HERE! HEY! I'M--

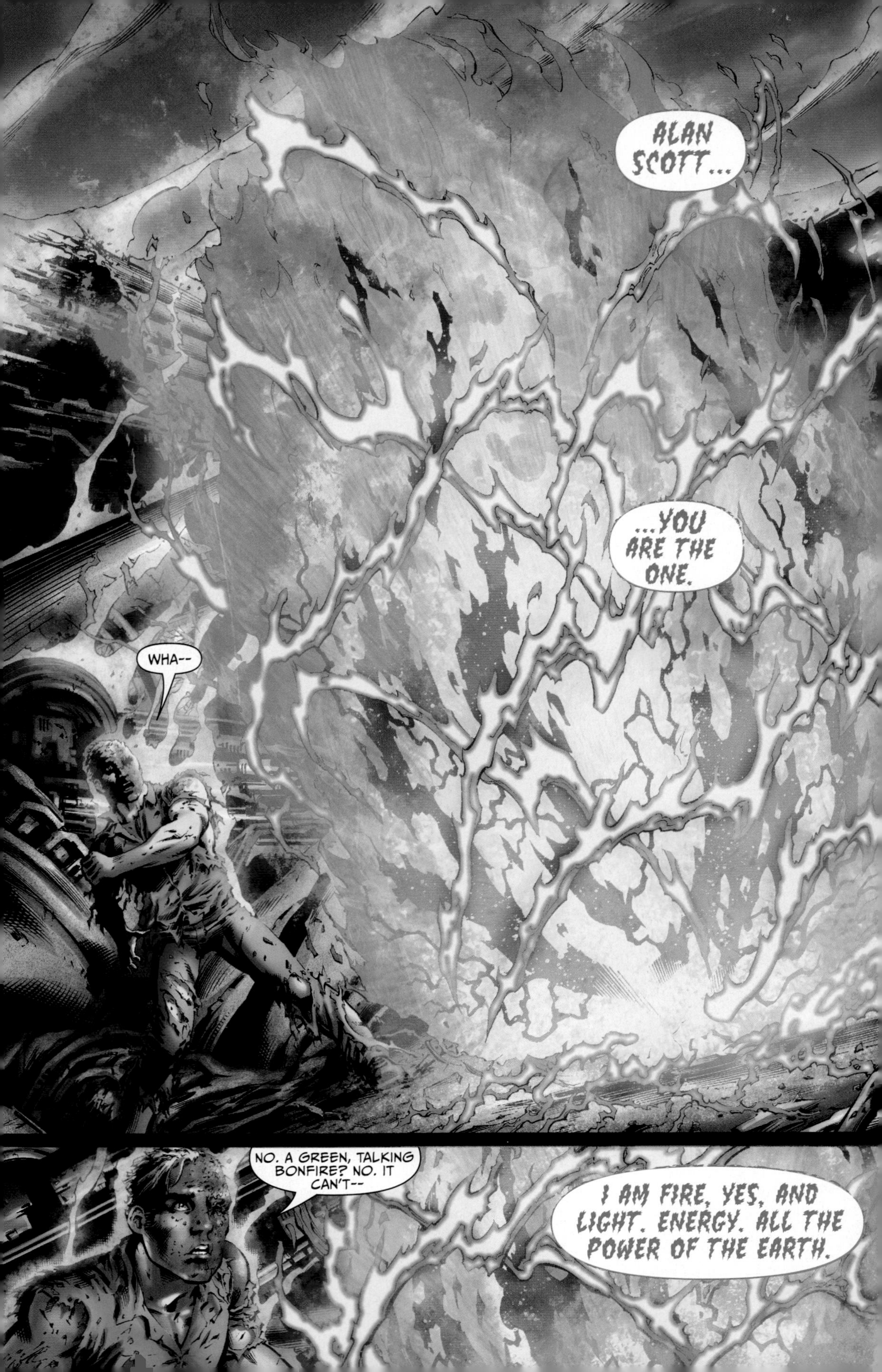
ALAN SCOTT...
...YOU ARE THE ONE.
WHA--
NO. A GREEN, TALKING BONFIRE? NO. IT CAN'T--
I AM FIRE, YES, AND LIGHT. ENERGY. ALL THE POWER OF THE EARTH.

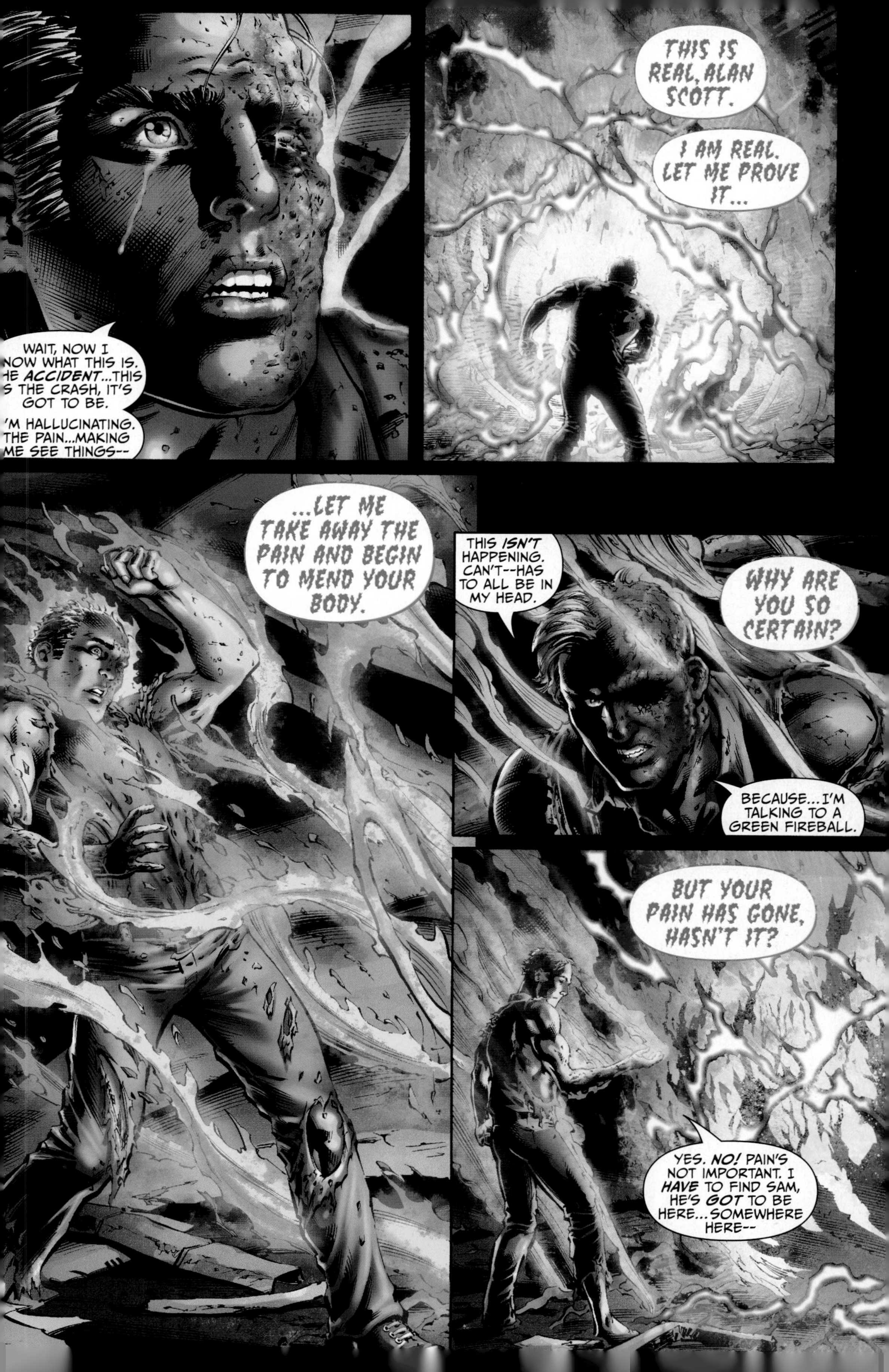

WAIT, NOW I
NOW WHAT THIS IS.
HE *ACCIDENT*...THIS
S THE CRASH, IT'S
GOT TO BE.
'M HALLUCINATING.
THE PAIN...MAKING
ME SEE THINGS--
THIS IS REAL, ALAN SCOTT.
I AM REAL. LET ME PROVE IT...
...LET ME TAKE AWAY THE PAIN AND BEGIN TO MEND YOUR BODY.
THIS *ISN'T* HAPPENING. CAN'T--HAS TO ALL BE IN MY HEAD.
WHY ARE YOU SO CERTAIN?
BECAUSE...I'M TALKING TO A GREEN FIREBALL.
BUT YOUR PAIN HAS GONE, HASN'T IT?
YES. *NO!* PAIN'S NOT IMPORTANT. I *HAVE* TO FIND SAM, HE'S *GOT* TO BE HERE...SOMEWHERE HERE--

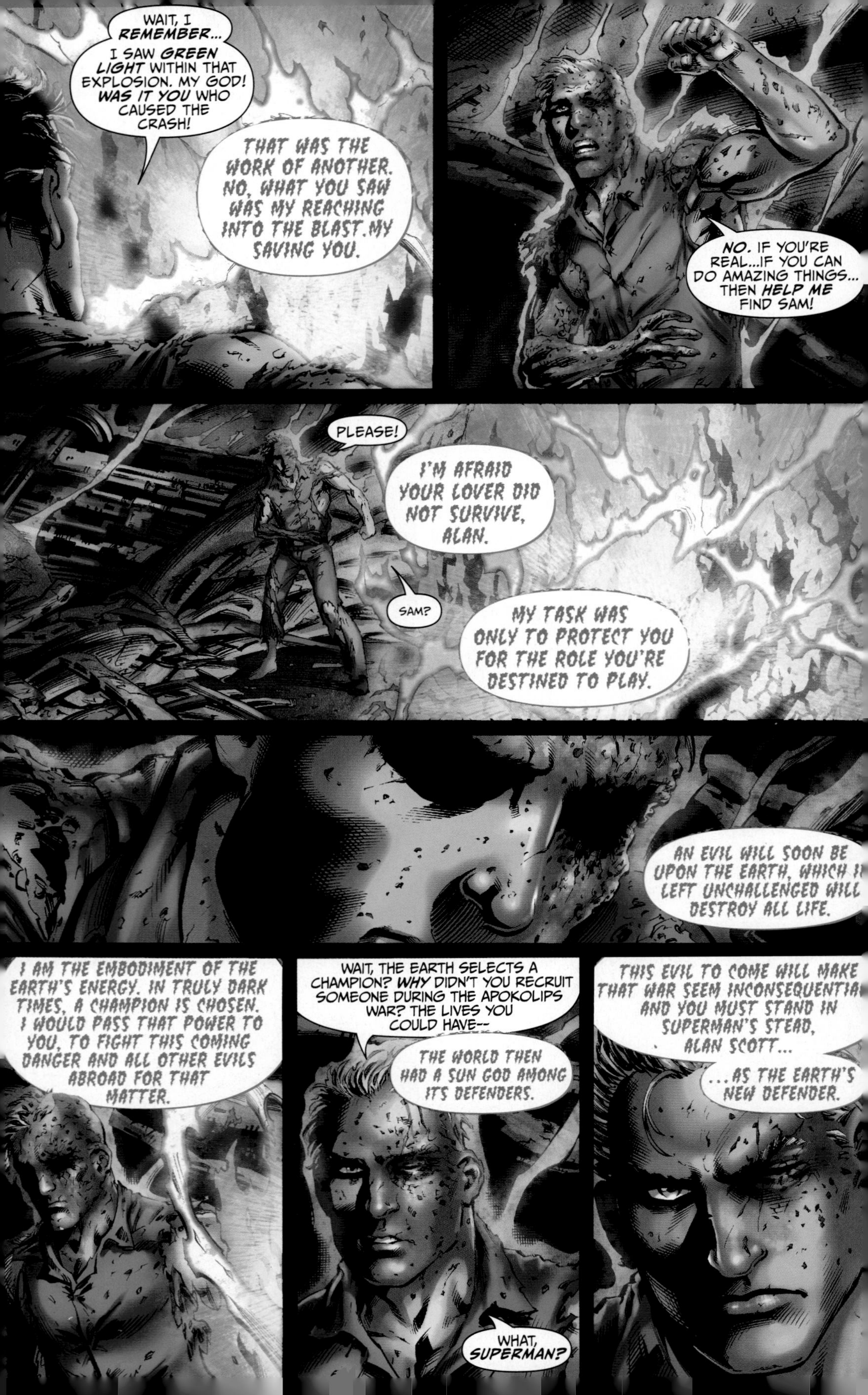
WAIT, I REMEMBER... I SAW GREEN LIGHT WITHIN THAT EXPLOSION. MY GOD! WAS IT YOU WHO CAUSED THE CRASH!
THAT WAS THE WORK OF ANOTHER. NO, WHAT YOU SAW WAS MY REACHING INTO THE BLAST. MY SAVING YOU.
NO. IF YOU'RE REAL...IF YOU CAN DO AMAZING THINGS... THEN HELP ME FIND SAM!
PLEASE!
I'M AFRAID YOUR LOVER DID NOT SURVIVE, ALAN.
SAM?
MY TASK WAS ONLY TO PROTECT YOU FOR THE ROLE YOU'RE DESTINED TO PLAY.
AN EVIL WILL SOON BE UPON THE EARTH, WHICH IF LEFT UNCHALLENGED WILL DESTROY ALL LIFE.
I AM THE EMBODIMENT OF THE EARTH'S ENERGY. IN TRULY DARK TIMES, A CHAMPION IS CHOSEN. I WOULD PASS THAT POWER TO YOU, TO FIGHT THIS COMING DANGER AND ALL OTHER EVILS ABROAD FOR THAT MATTER.
WAIT, THE EARTH SELECTS A CHAMPION? WHY DIDN'T YOU RECRUIT SOMEONE DURING THE APOKOLIPS WAR? THE LIVES YOU COULD HAVE--
THE WORLD THEN HAD A SUN GOD AMONG ITS DEFENDERS.
WHAT, SUPERMAN?
THIS EVIL TO COME WILL MAKE THAT WAR SEEM INCONSEQUENTIAL AND YOU MUST STAND IN SUPERMAN'S STEAD, ALAN SCOTT...
...AS THE EARTH'S NEW DEFENDER.

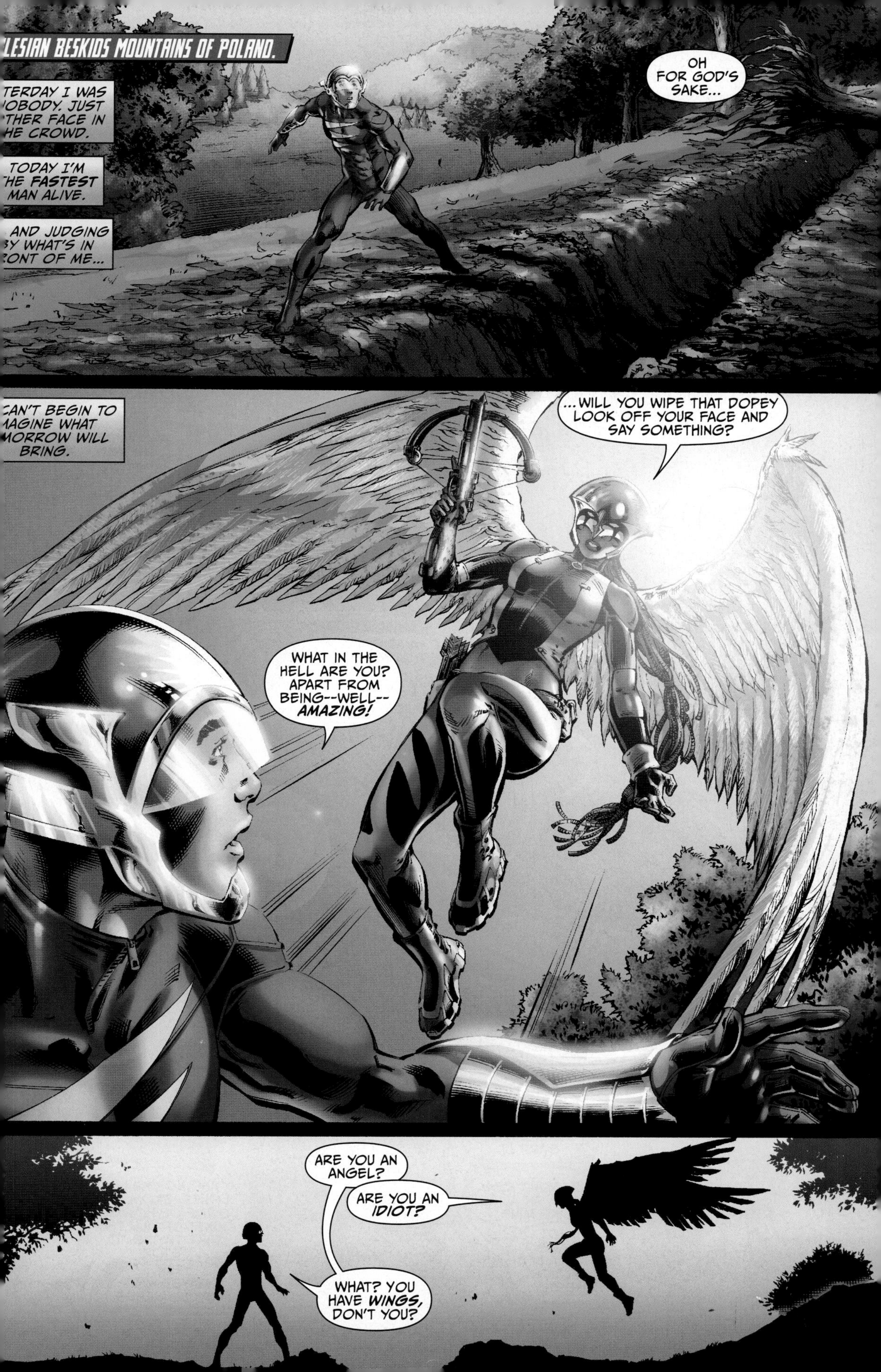
LESIAN BESKIDS MOUNTAINS OF POLAND.
TERDAY I WAS OBODY. JUST THER FACE IN HE CROWD.
TODAY I'M HE FASTEST MAN ALIVE.
AND JUDGING BY WHAT'S IN ONT OF ME...
OH FOR GOD'S SAKE...
CAN'T BEGIN TO AGINE WHAT MORROW WILL BRING.
...WILL YOU WIPE THAT DOPEY LOOK OFF YOUR FACE AND SAY SOMETHING?
WHAT IN THE HELL ARE YOU? APART FROM BEING--WELL--AMAZING!
ARE YOU AN ANGEL?
ARE YOU AN IDIOT?
WHAT? YOU HAVE WINGS, DON'T YOU?

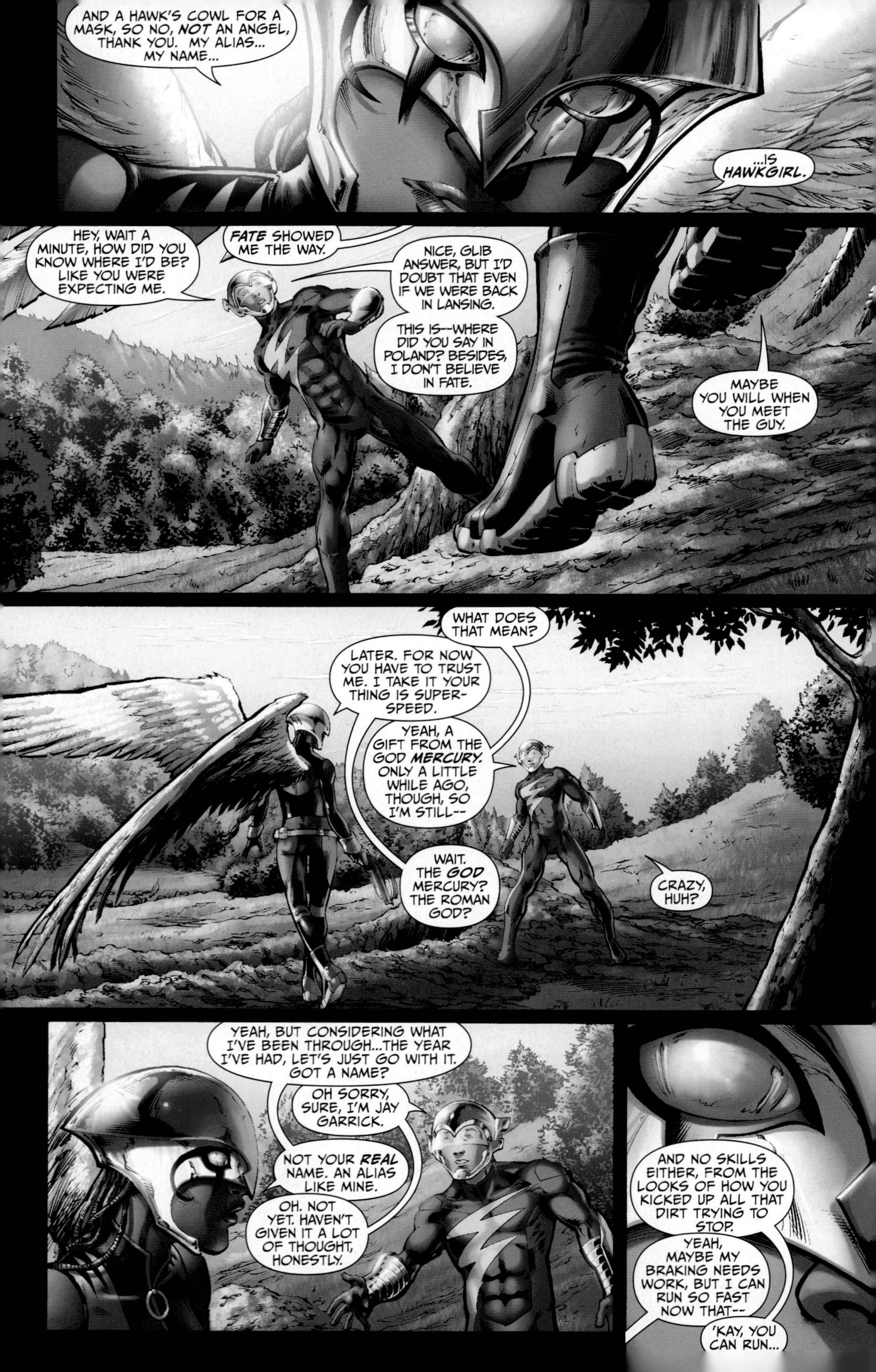

AND A HAWK'S COWL FOR A MASK, SO NO, *NOT* AN ANGEL, THANK YOU. MY ALIAS... MY NAME...
...IS *HAWKGIRL.*
HEY, WAIT A MINUTE, HOW DID YOU KNOW WHERE I'D BE? LIKE YOU WERE EXPECTING ME.
FATE SHOWED ME THE WAY.
NICE, GLIB ANSWER, BUT I'D DOUBT THAT EVEN IF WE WERE BACK IN LANSING.
THIS IS--WHERE DID YOU SAY IN POLAND? BESIDES, I DON'T BELIEVE IN FATE.
MAYBE YOU WILL WHEN YOU MEET THE GUY.
WHAT DOES THAT MEAN?
LATER. FOR NOW YOU HAVE TO TRUST ME. I TAKE IT YOUR THING IS SUPER-SPEED.
YEAH, A GIFT FROM THE GOD *MERCURY.* ONLY A LITTLE WHILE AGO, THOUGH, SO I'M STILL--
WAIT. THE *GOD* MERCURY? THE ROMAN GOD?
CRAZY, HUH?
YEAH, BUT CONSIDERING WHAT I'VE BEEN THROUGH...THE YEAR I'VE HAD, LET'S JUST GO WITH IT. GOT A NAME?
OH SORRY, SURE, I'M JAY GARRICK.
NOT YOUR *REAL* NAME. AN ALIAS LIKE MINE.
OH. NOT YET. HAVEN'T GIVEN IT A LOT OF THOUGHT, HONESTLY.
AND NO SKILLS EITHER, FROM THE LOOKS OF HOW YOU KICKED UP ALL THAT DIRT TRYING TO STOP.
YEAH, MAYBE MY BRAKING NEEDS WORK, BUT I CAN RUN SO FAST NOW THAT--
'KAY, YOU CAN RUN...

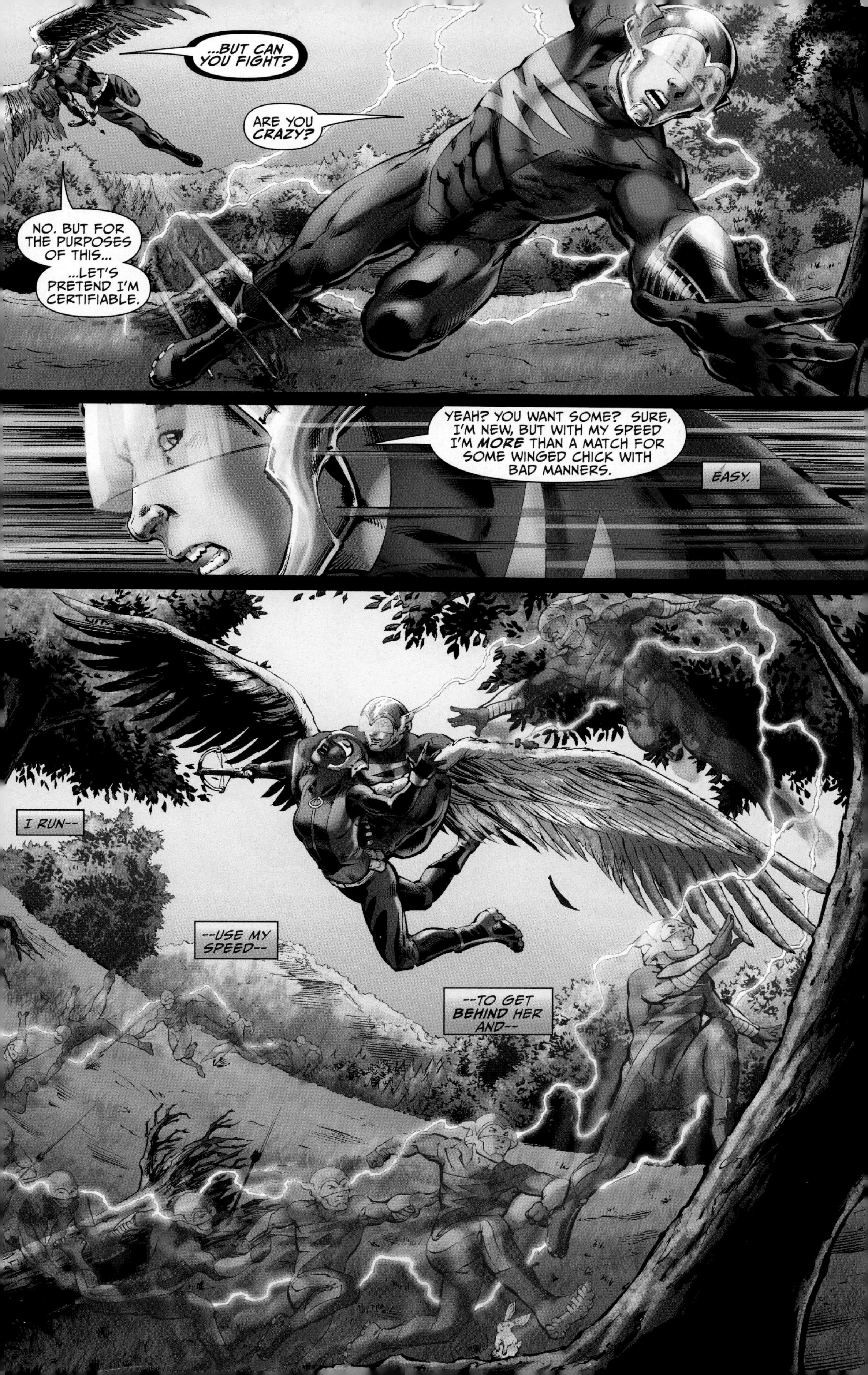
...BUT CAN YOU FIGHT?
ARE YOU CRAZY?
NO. BUT FOR THE PURPOSES OF THIS...
...LET'S PRETEND I'M CERTIFIABLE.
YEAH? YOU WANT SOME? SURE, I'M NEW, BUT WITH MY SPEED I'M MORE THAN A MATCH FOR SOME WINGED CHICK WITH BAD MANNERS.
EASY.
I RUN--
--USE MY SPEED--
--TO GET BEHIND HER AND--

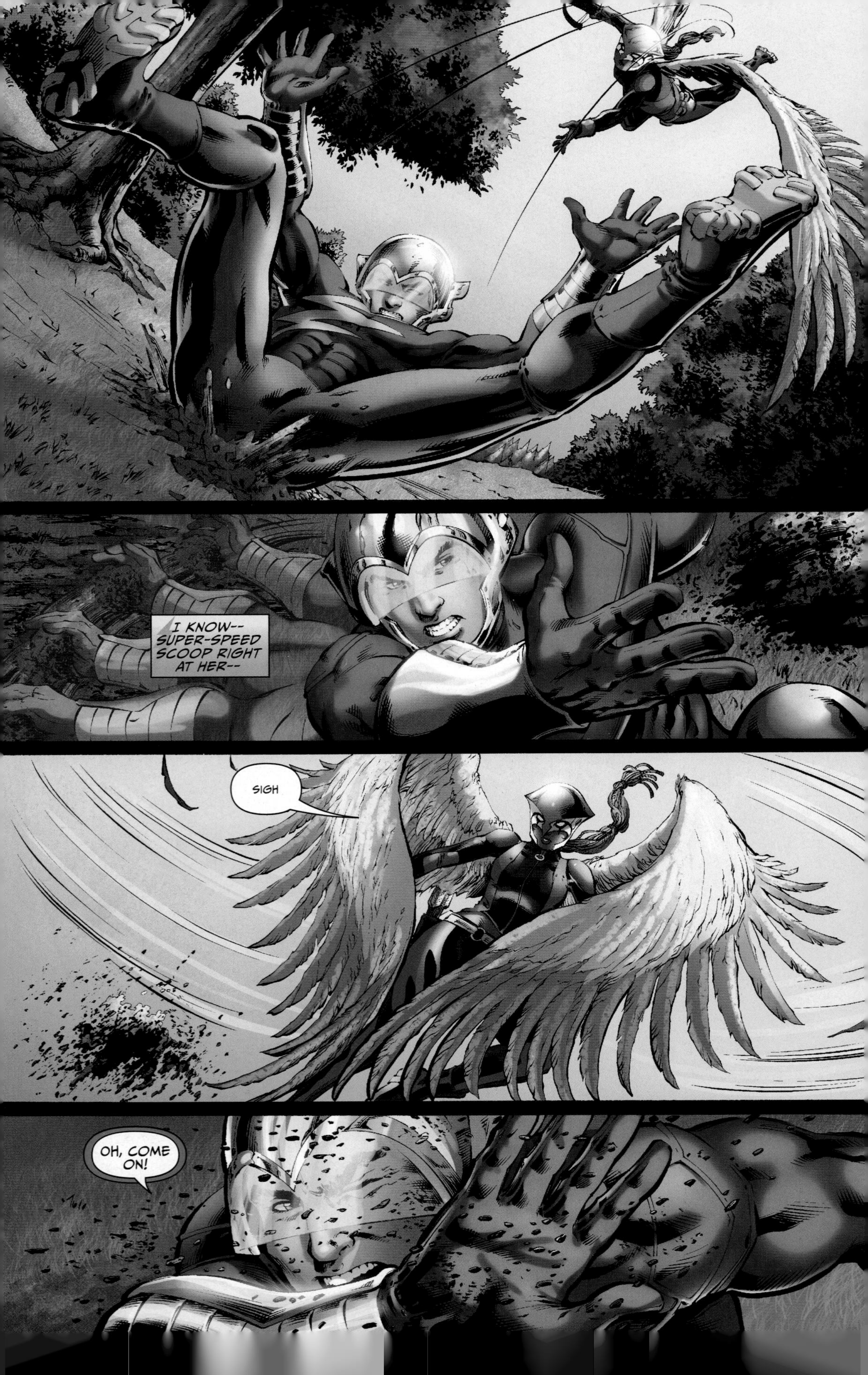
I KNOW--
SUPER-SPEED
SCOOP RIGHT
AT HER--
SIGH
OH, COME ON!

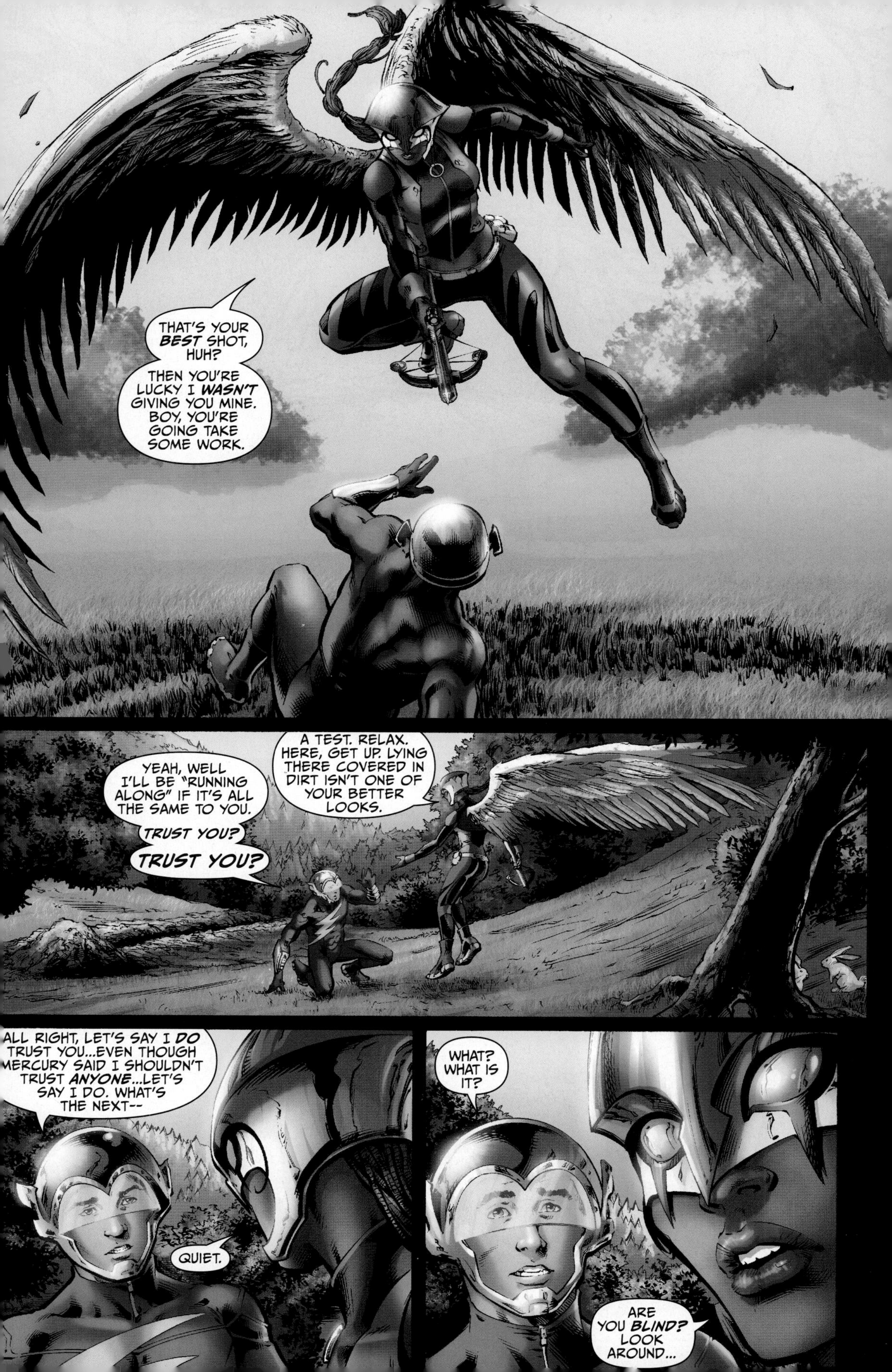
THAT'S YOUR *BEST* SHOT, HUH?
THEN YOU'RE LUCKY I *WASN'T* GIVING YOU MINE. BOY, YOU'RE GOING TAKE SOME WORK.
YEAH, WELL I'LL BE "RUNNING ALONG" IF IT'S ALL THE SAME TO YOU.
A TEST. RELAX. HERE, GET UP. LYING THERE COVERED IN DIRT ISN'T ONE OF YOUR BETTER LOOKS.
TRUST YOU?
TRUST YOU?
ALL RIGHT, LET'S SAY I *DO* TRUST YOU...EVEN THOUGH MERCURY SAID I SHOULDN'T TRUST *ANYONE*...LET'S SAY I DO. WHAT'S THE NEXT--
QUIET.
WHAT? WHAT IS IT?
ARE YOU *BLIND?* LOOK AROUND...

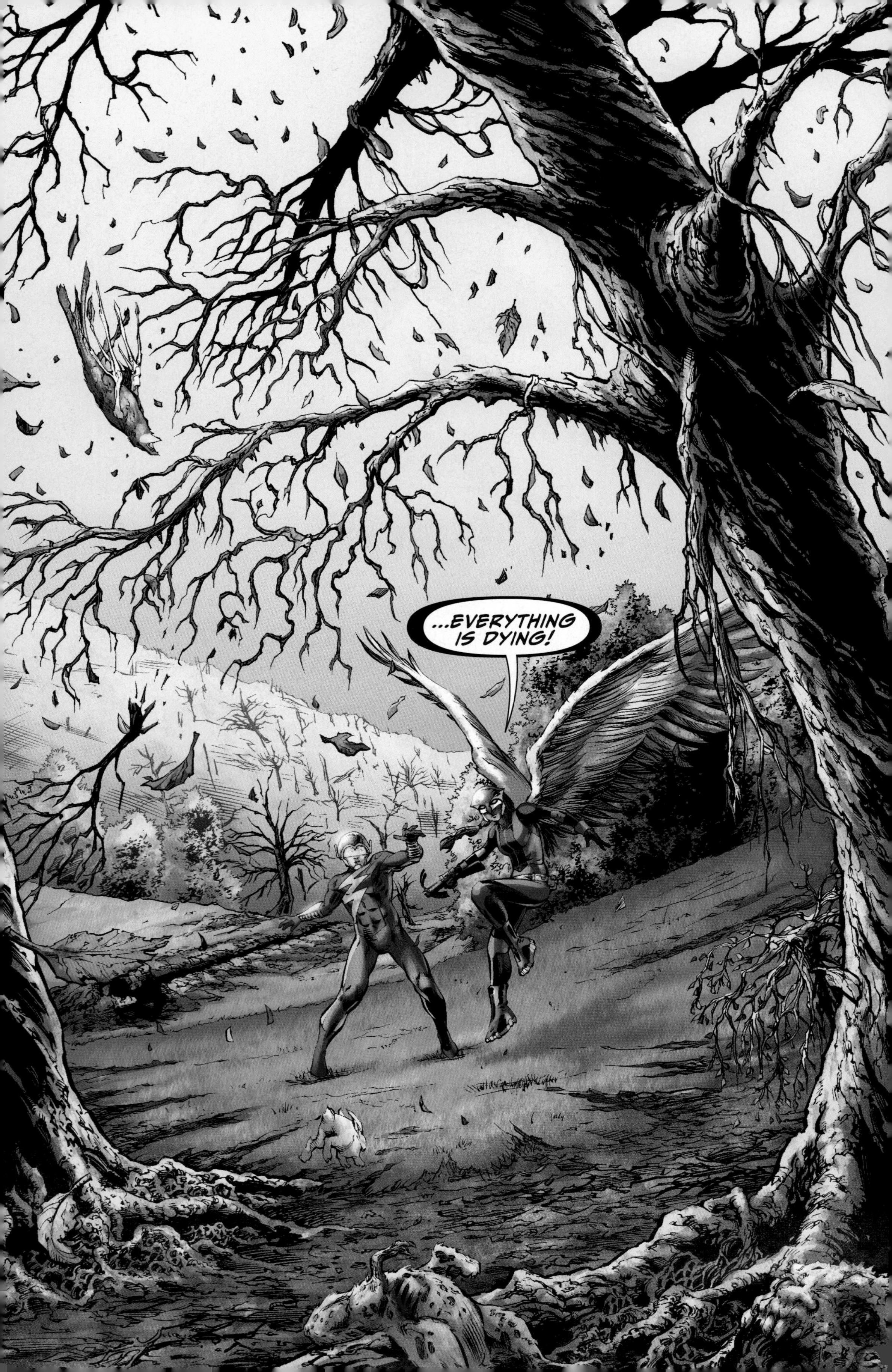
...EVERYTHING IS DYING!

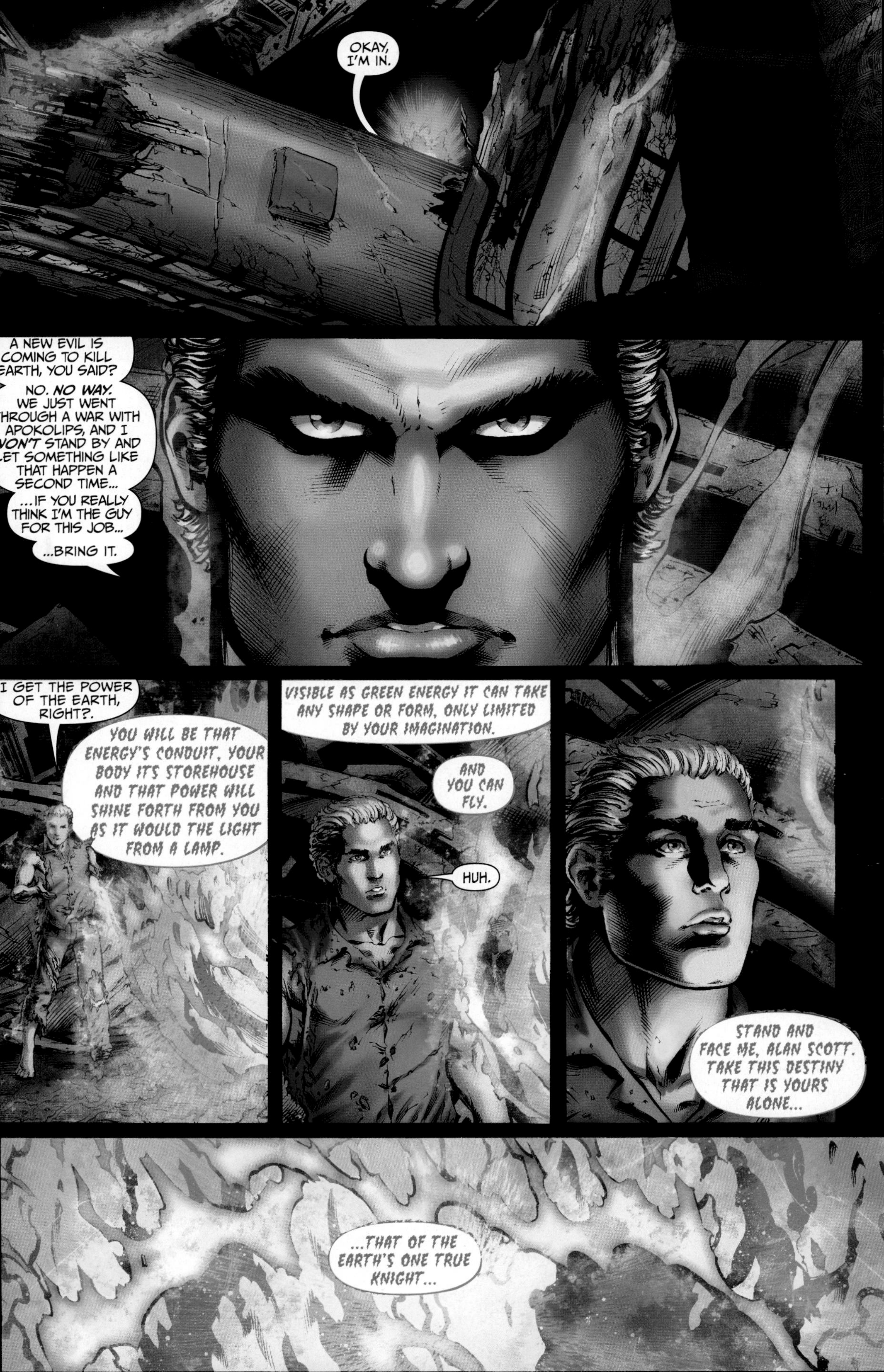
OKAY, I'M IN.
A NEW EVIL IS COMING TO KILL EARTH, YOU SAID?
NO. NO WAY. WE JUST WENT THROUGH A WAR WITH APOKOLIPS, AND I WON'T STAND BY AND LET SOMETHING LIKE THAT HAPPEN A SECOND TIME...
...IF YOU REALLY THINK I'M THE GUY FOR THIS JOB...
...BRING IT.
I GET THE POWER OF THE EARTH, RIGHT?.
YOU WILL BE THAT ENERGY'S CONDUIT, YOUR BODY ITS STOREHOUSE AND THAT POWER WILL SHINE FORTH FROM YOU AS IT WOULD THE LIGHT FROM A LAMP.
VISIBLE AS GREEN ENERGY IT CAN TAKE ANY SHAPE OR FORM, ONLY LIMITED BY YOUR IMAGINATION.
AND YOU CAN FLY.
HUH.
STAND AND FACE ME, ALAN SCOTT. TAKE THIS DESTINY THAT IS YOURS ALONE...
...THAT OF THE EARTH'S ONE TRUE KNIGHT...

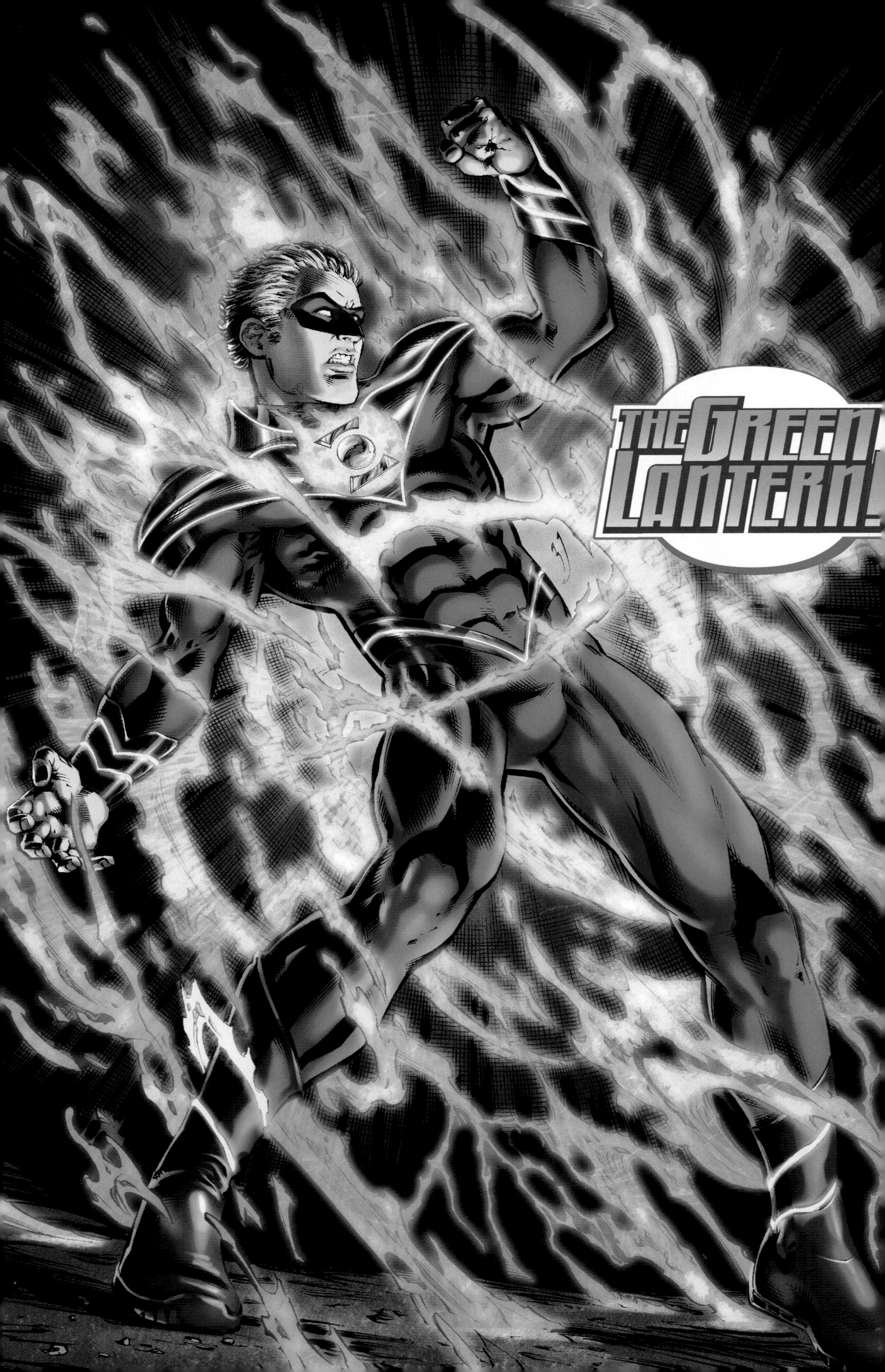
THE GREEN LANTERN!

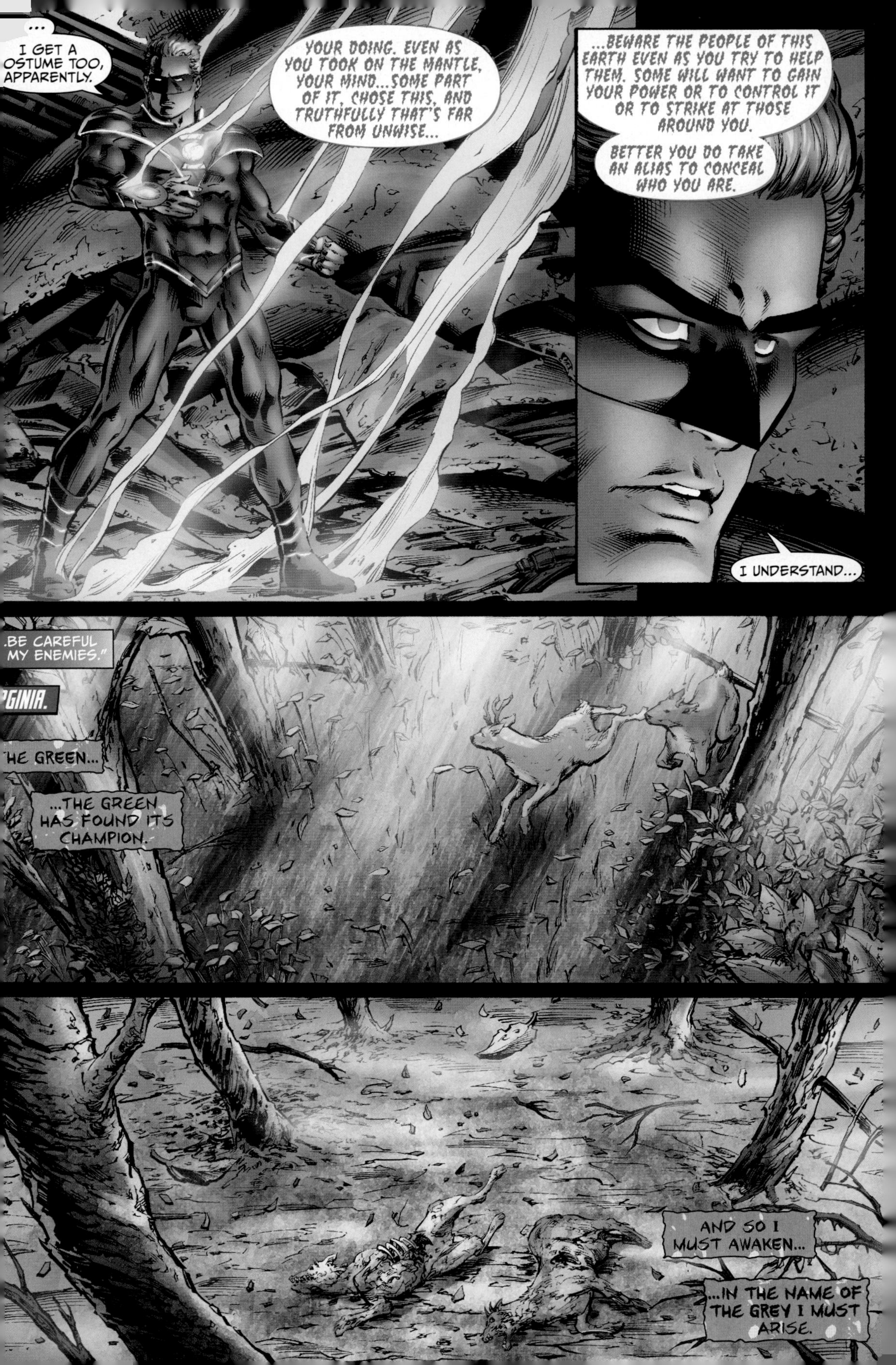
...
I GET A
OSTUME TOO,
APPARENTLY.
YOUR DOING. EVEN AS YOU TOOK ON THE MANTLE, YOUR MIND...SOME PART OF IT, CHOSE THIS, AND TRUTHFULLY THAT'S FAR FROM UNWISE...
...BEWARE THE PEOPLE OF THIS EARTH EVEN AS YOU TRY TO HELP THEM. SOME WILL WANT TO GAIN YOUR POWER OR TO CONTROL IT OR TO STRIKE AT THOSE AROUND YOU.
BETTER YOU DO TAKE AN ALIAS TO CONCEAL WHO YOU ARE.
I UNDERSTAND...
.BE CAREFUL
MY ENEMIES."
GINIA.
HE GREEN...
...THE GREEN HAS FOUND ITS CHAMPION.
AND SO I MUST AWAKEN...
...IN THE NAME OF THE GREY I MUST ARISE.

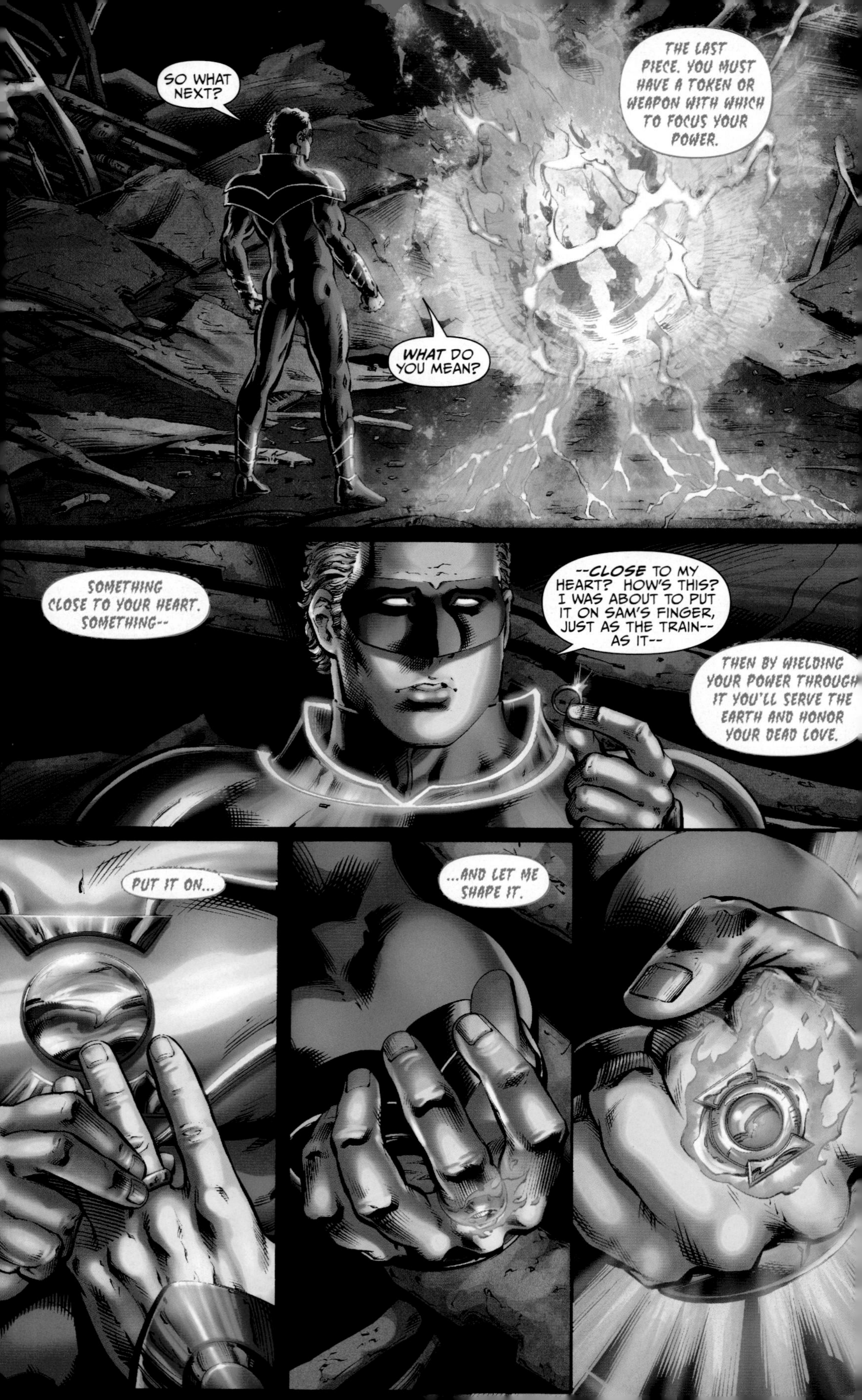
SO WHAT NEXT?
THE LAST PIECE. YOU MUST HAVE A TOKEN OR WEAPON WITH WHICH TO FOCUS YOUR POWER.
WHAT DO YOU MEAN?
SOMETHING CLOSE TO YOUR HEART. SOMETHING--
--CLOSE TO MY HEART? HOW'S THIS? I WAS ABOUT TO PUT IT ON SAM'S FINGER, JUST AS THE TRAIN-- AS IT--
THEN BY WIELDING YOUR POWER THROUGH IT YOU'LL SERVE THE EARTH AND HONOR YOUR DEAD LOVE.
PUT IT ON...
...AND LET ME SHAPE IT.

AND SO A NEW CHAMPION IS BORN.

THE WAY YOU TALK..."NEW CHAMPION"...AND THE SENSE THIS IS A PART OF SOME SORT OF *RITE* THAT I'M PERFORMING.

HAS THIS HAPPENED BEFORE? HAVE *OTHER* MEN...WOMEN...HAVE THERE BEEN "EARTH'S" PROTECTORS IN THE PAST?

YOU'LL UNDERSTAND EVERYTHING WHEN THE TIME IS RIGHT, I PROMISE.

THEN WHAT'S NEXT? UNCOVER WHO CAUSED THE CRASH, RIGHT? FOR SAM AND THE OTHERS.

THAT'S ONE OF COUNTLESS CHALLENGES YOU'LL FACE. WHILE YOU AWAIT THE GREAT EVIL, THERE ARE STILL OTHER THREATS WALKING THE EARTH. YOUR HEART WILL TELL YOU WHERE THEY ARE.

NOT YOU?

MY TIME IS OVER, MY TASK IS DONE.

AGAIN, THE WAY YOU SPEAK. WERE YOU...AT ONE TIME...WERE YOU HUMAN?

GOOD LUCK, ALAN SCOTT...

...AND GOODBYE.

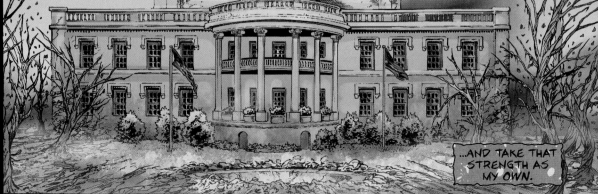

_HINGTON, DC. THE WHITE HOUSE.

SEIZE LIFE, KILL LIFE, SUCK IT DRY, SUCK IT CLEAN...

...AND TAKE THAT STRENGTH AS MY OWN.

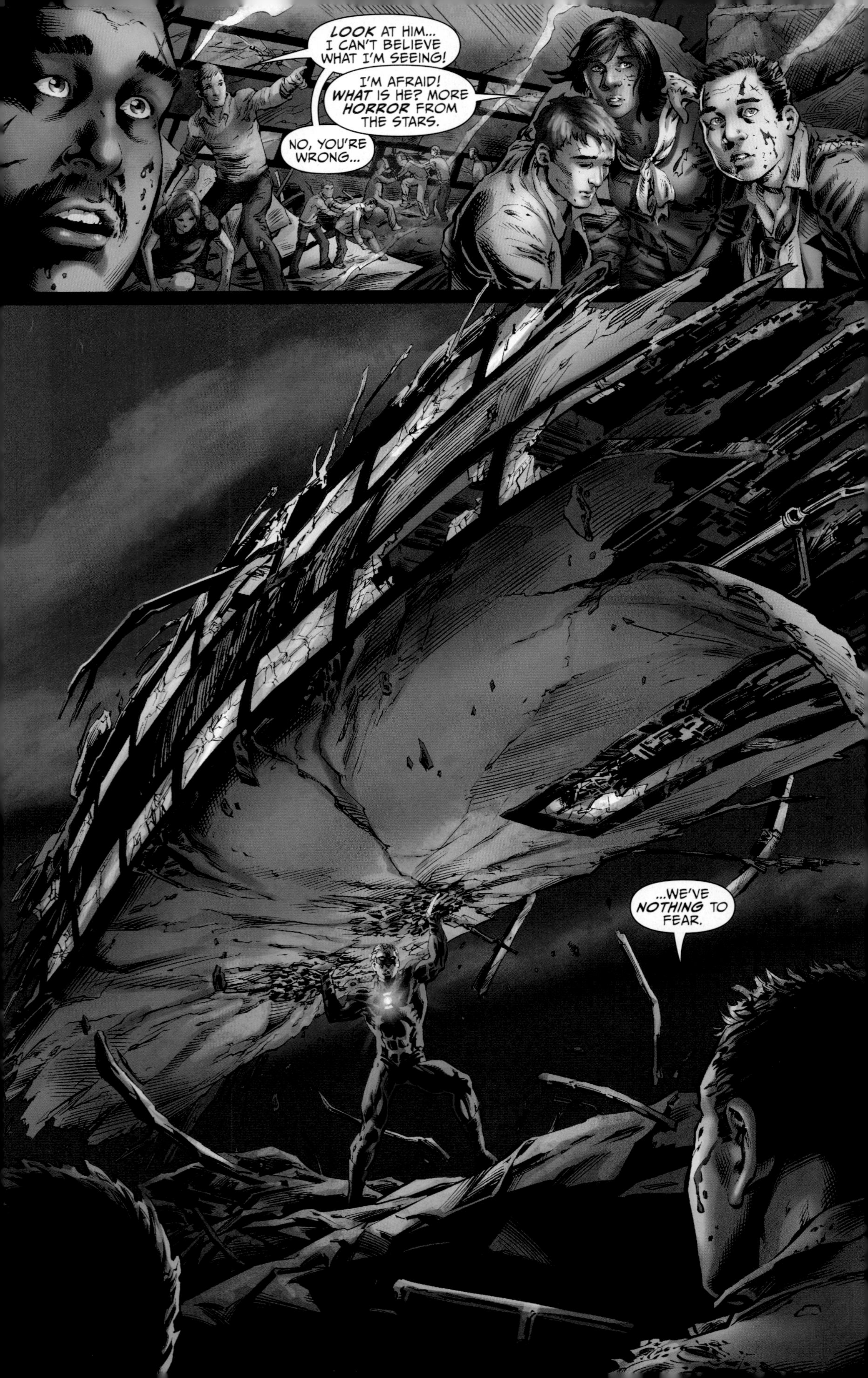
LOOK AT HIM... I CAN'T BELIEVE WHAT I'M SEEING!
I'M AFRAID! WHAT IS HE? MORE HORROR FROM THE STARS.
NO, YOU'RE WRONG...
...WE'VE NOTHING TO FEAR.

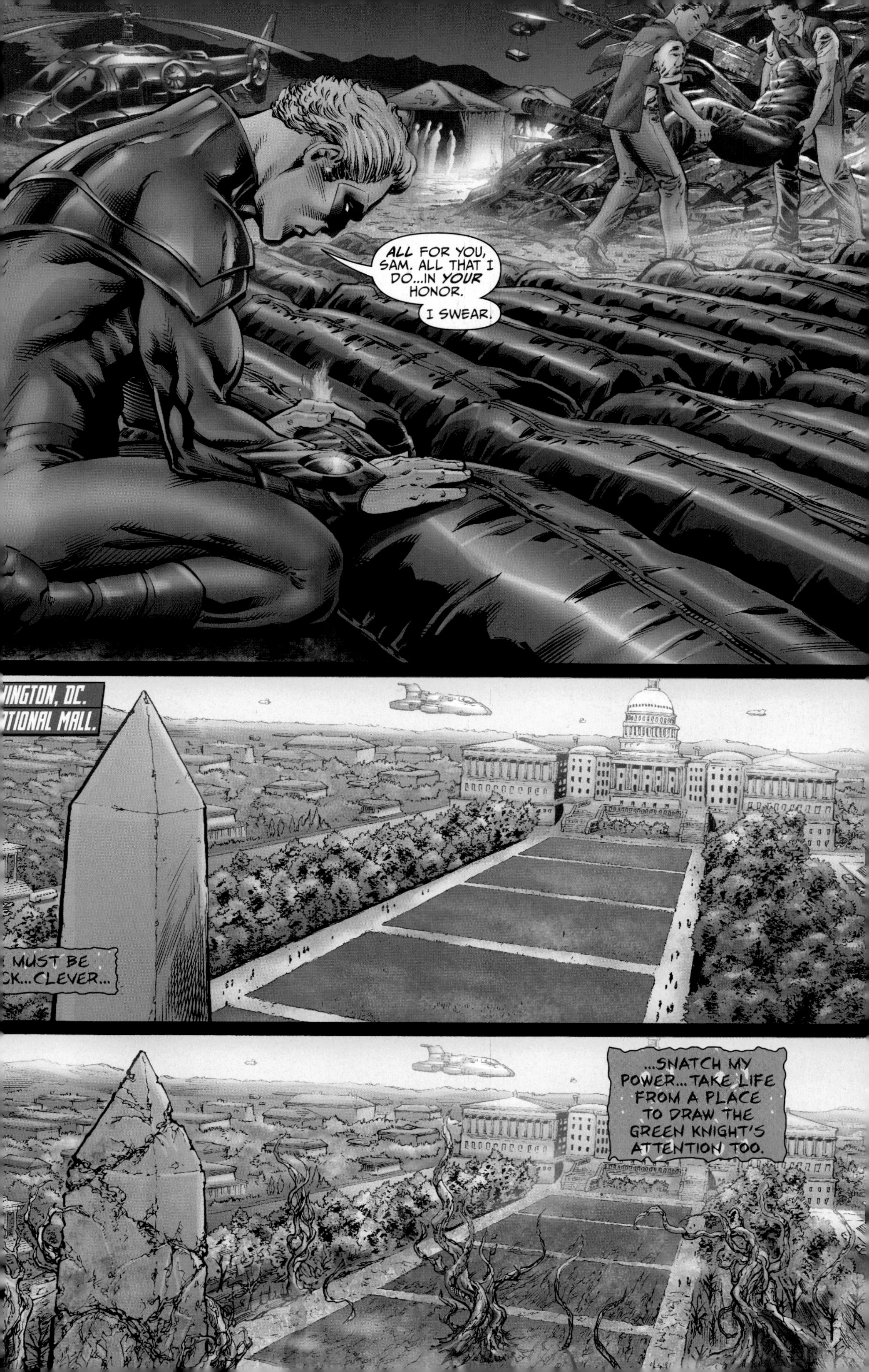
ALL FOR YOU, SAM. ALL THAT I DO...IN YOUR HONOR.
I SWEAR.
INGTON, DC.
TIONAL MALL.
MUST BE
CK...CLEVER...
...SNATCH MY POWER...TAKE LIFE FROM A PLACE TO DRAW THE GREEN KNIGHT'S ATTENTION TOO.

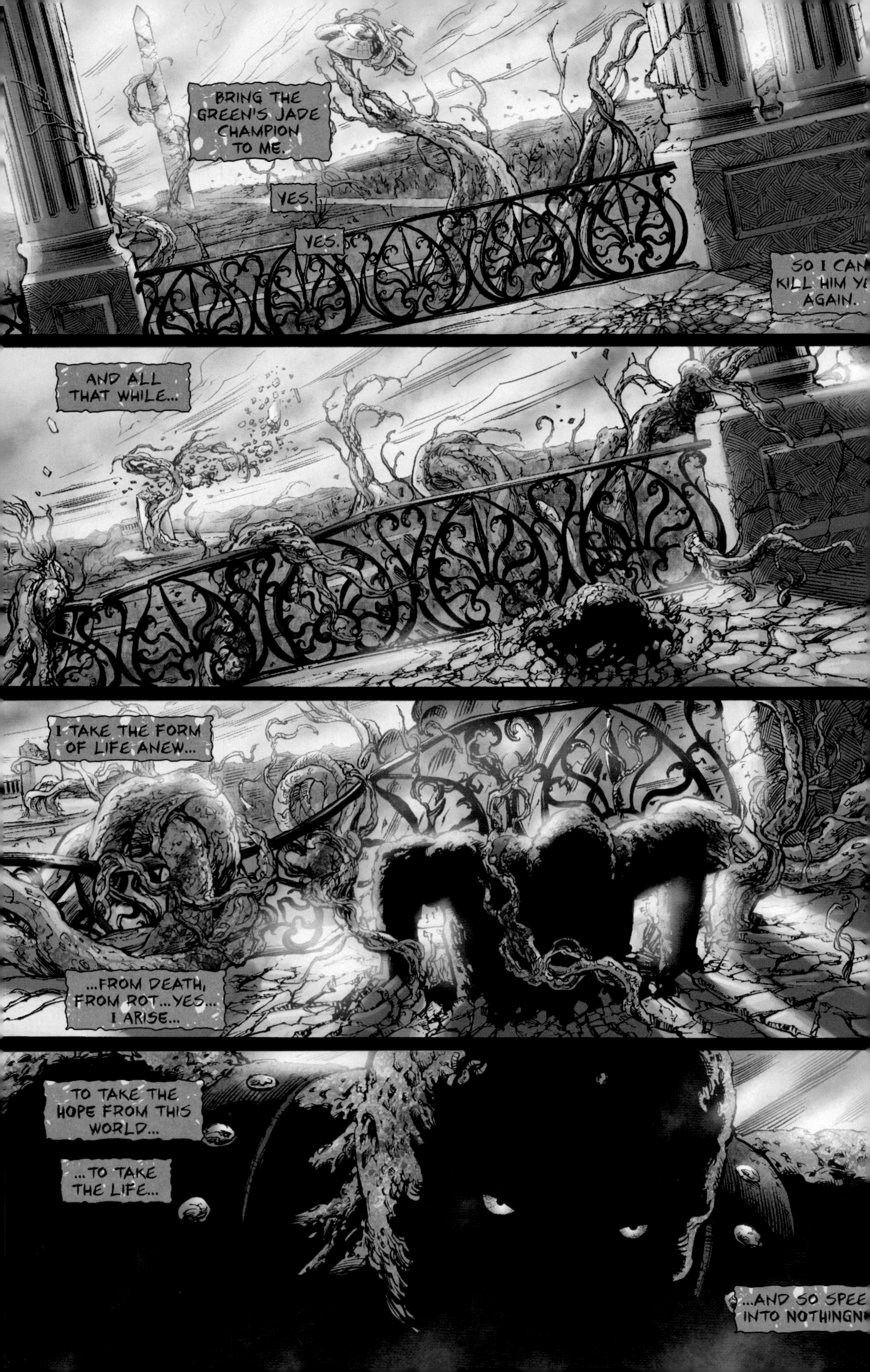
BRING THE GREEN'S JADE CHAMPION TO ME.
YES.
YES.
SO I CAN KILL HIM YE AGAIN.
AND ALL THAT WHILE...
I TAKE THE FORM OF LIFE ANEW...
...FROM DEATH, FROM ROT...YES... I ARISE...
TO TAKE THE HOPE FROM THIS WORLD...
...TO TAKE THE LIFE...
...AND SO SPEE INTO NOTHINGN

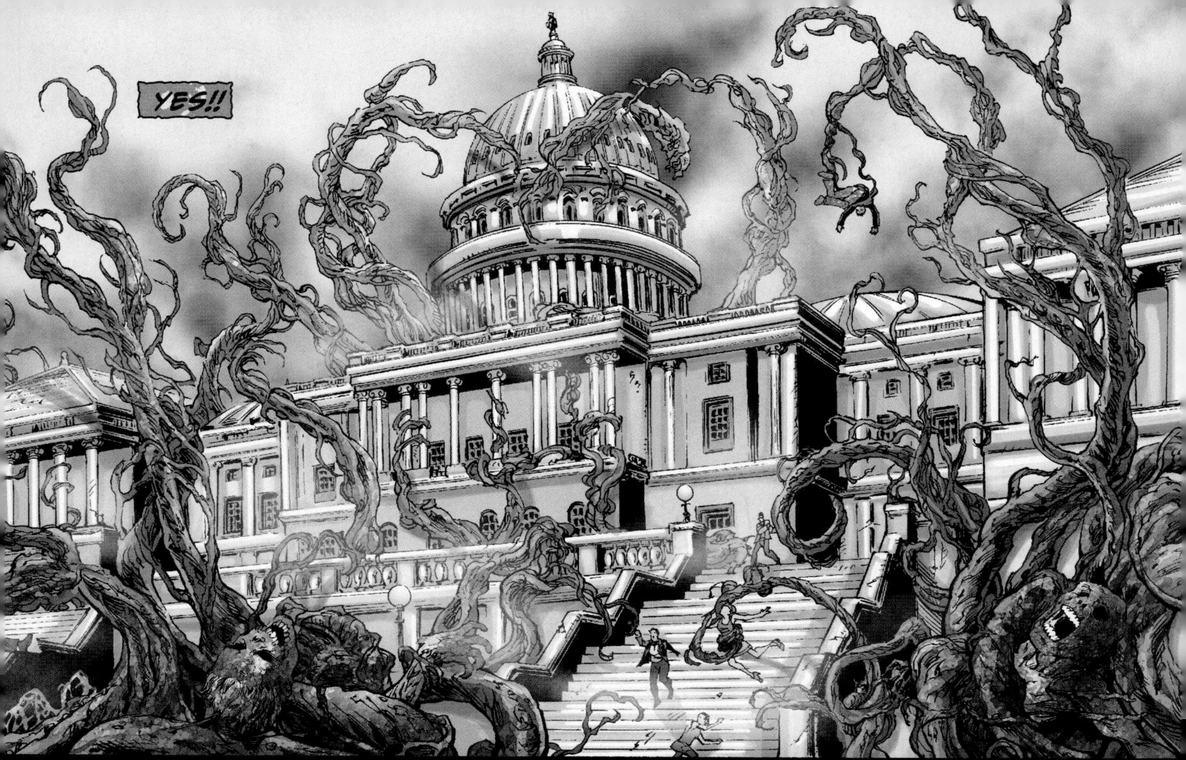
YES!!

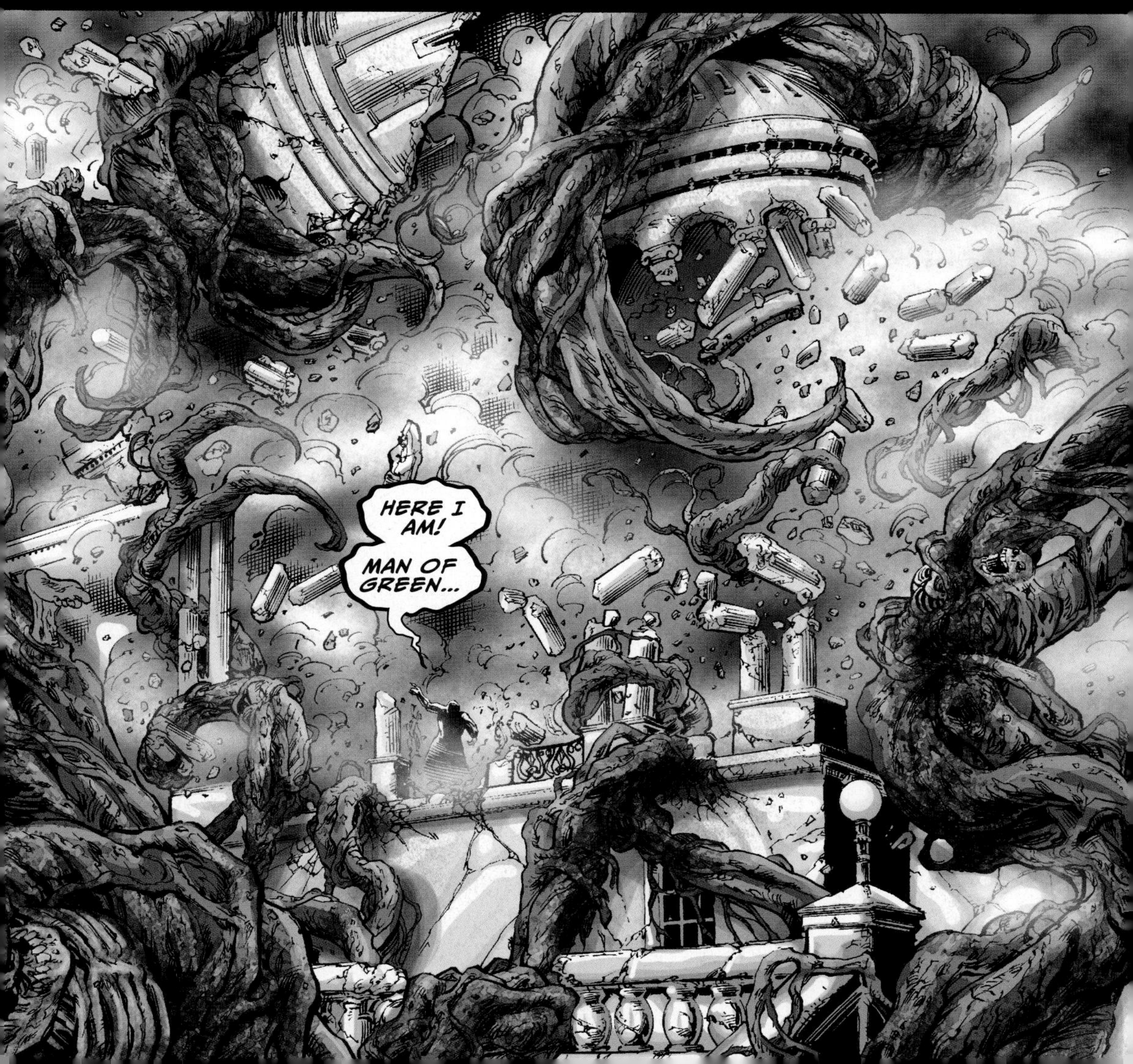
HERE I AM!
MAN OF GREEN...

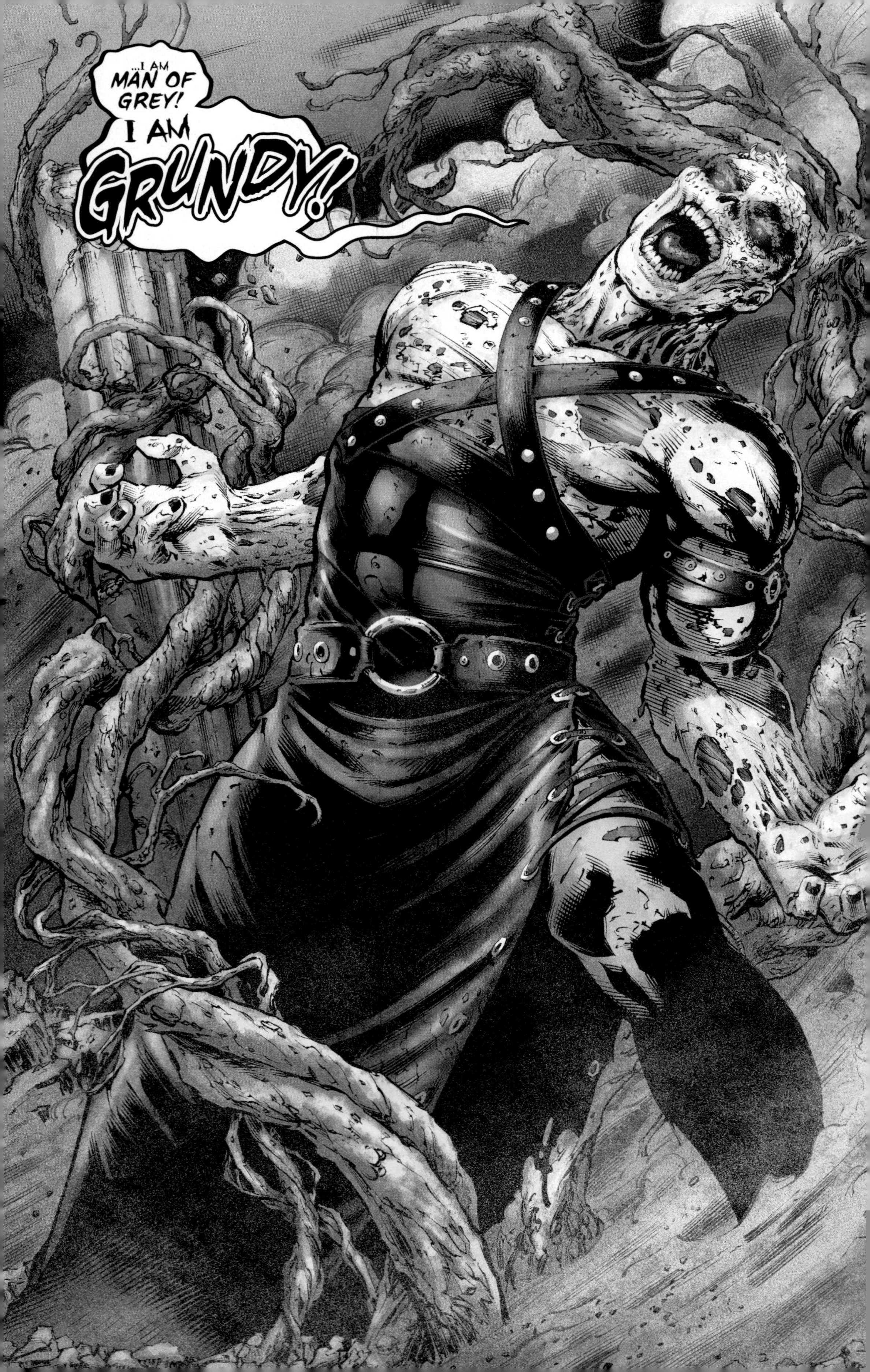
...I AM MAN OF GREY! I AM GRUNDY!

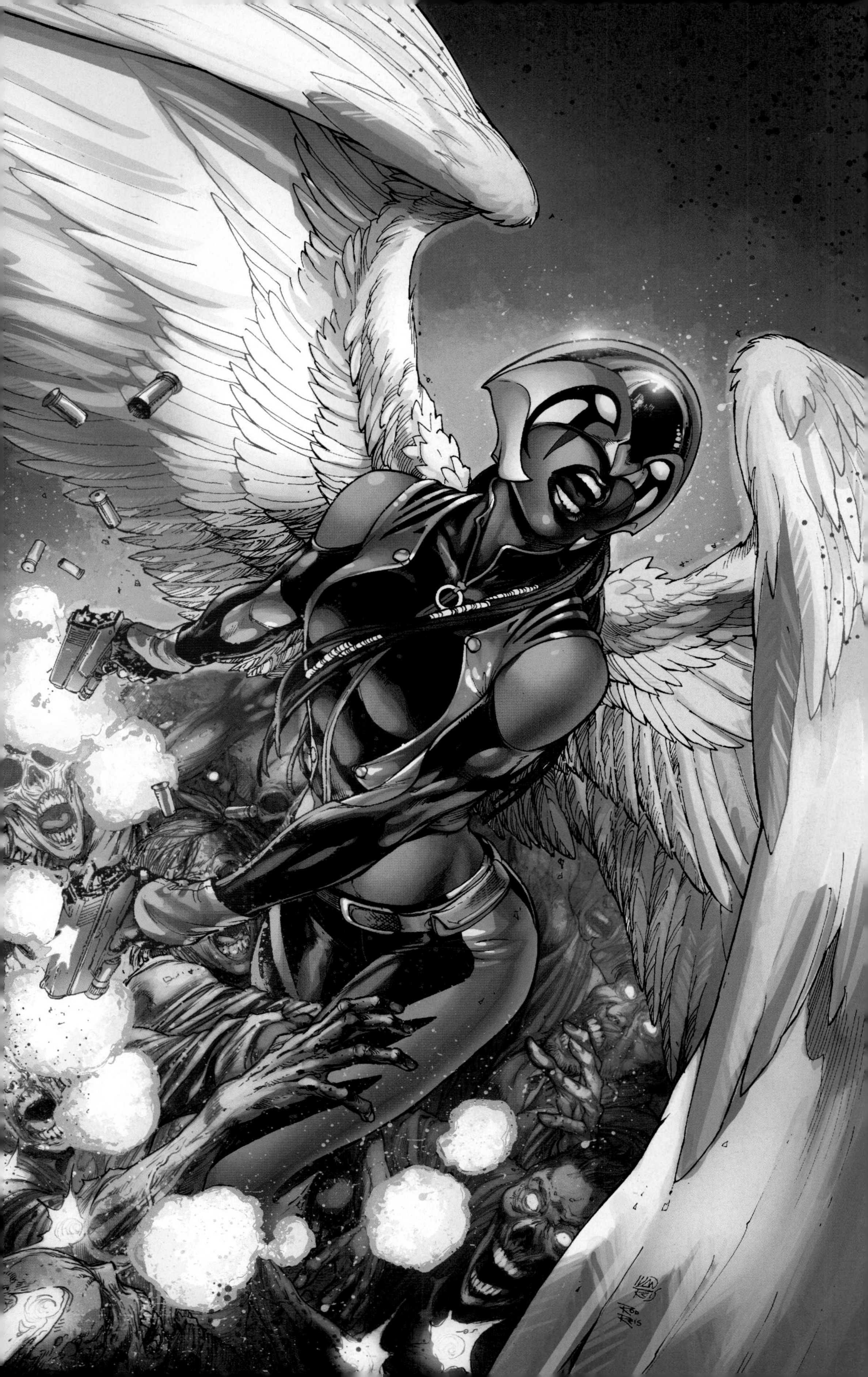

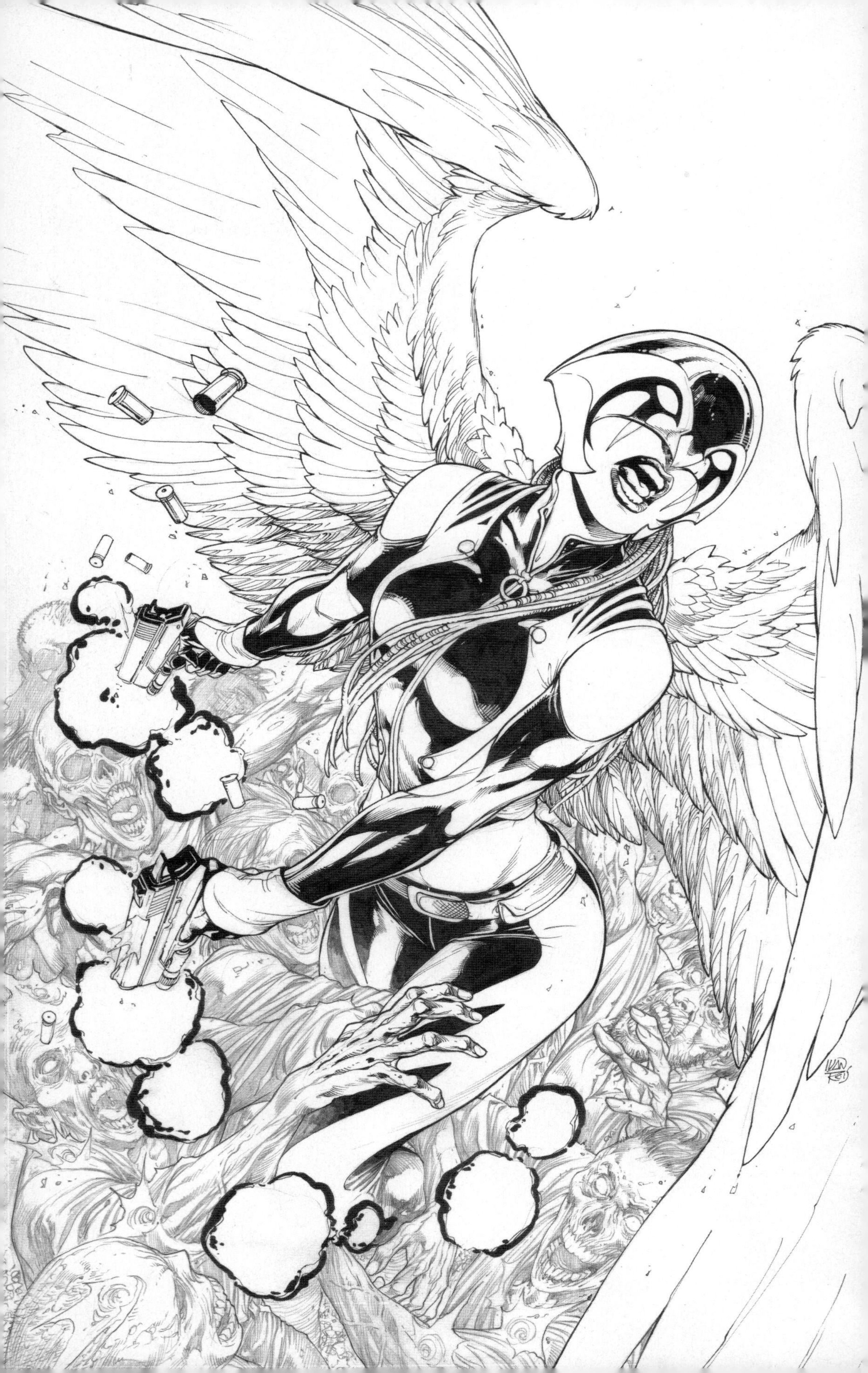

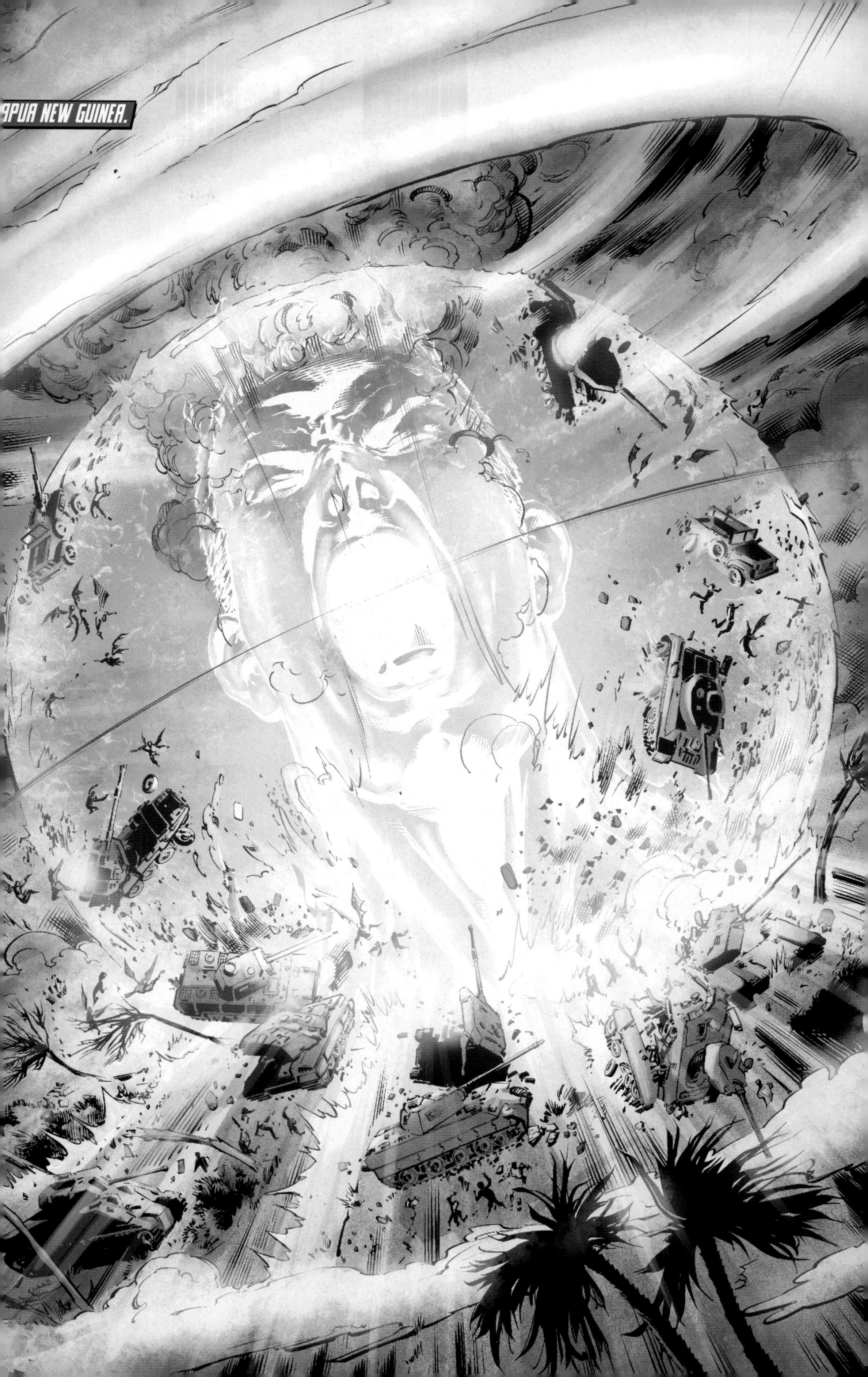
APUA NEW GUINEA.

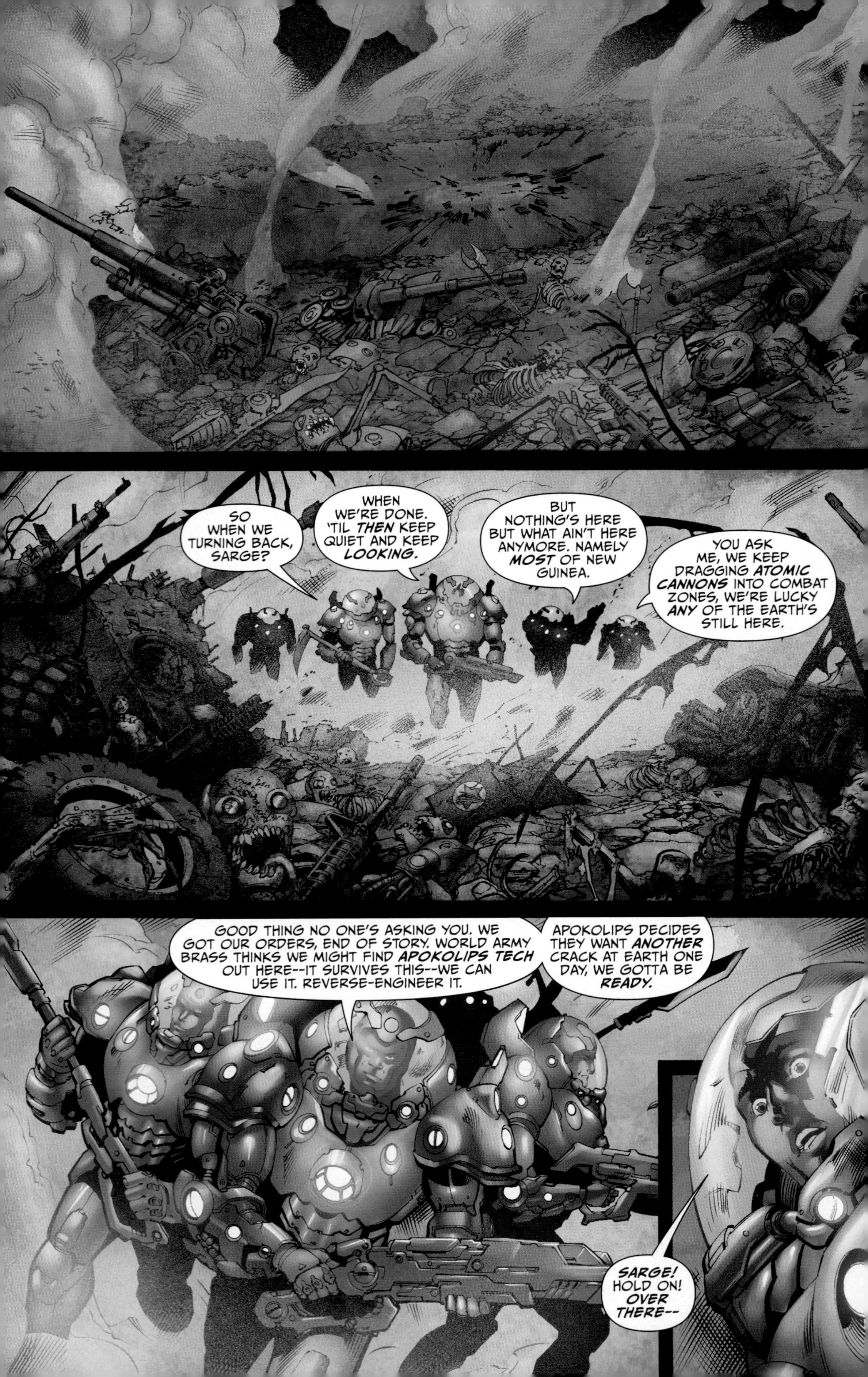
SO WHEN WE TURNING BACK, SARGE?
WHEN WE'RE DONE. 'TIL THEN KEEP QUIET AND KEEP LOOKING.
BUT NOTHING'S HERE BUT WHAT AIN'T HERE ANYMORE. NAMELY MOST OF NEW GUINEA.
YOU ASK ME, WE KEEP DRAGGING ATOMIC CANNONS INTO COMBAT ZONES, WE'RE LUCKY ANY OF THE EARTH'S STILL HERE.
GOOD THING NO ONE'S ASKING YOU. WE GOT OUR ORDERS, END OF STORY. WORLD ARMY BRASS THINKS WE MIGHT FIND APOKOLIPS TECH OUT HERE--IT SURVIVES THIS--WE CAN USE IT. REVERSE-ENGINEER IT.
APOKOLIPS DECIDES THEY WANT ANOTHER CRACK AT EARTH ONE DAY, WE GOTTA BE READY.
SARGE! HOLD ON! OVER THERE--

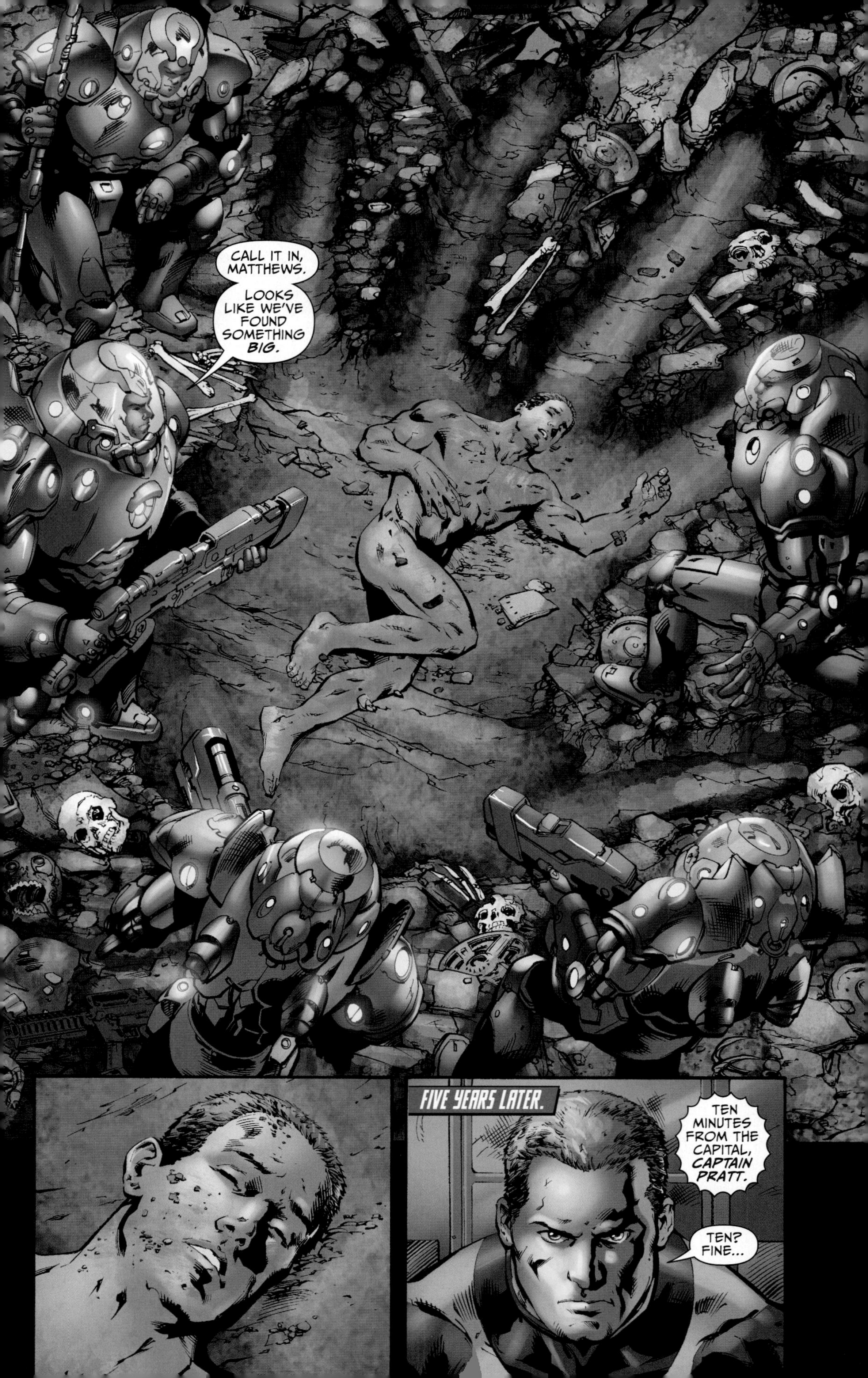
CALL IT IN, MATTHEWS.
LOOKS LIKE WE'VE FOUND SOMETHING BIG.
FIVE YEARS LATER.
TEN MINUTES FROM THE CAPITAL, CAPTAIN PRATT.
TEN? FINE...

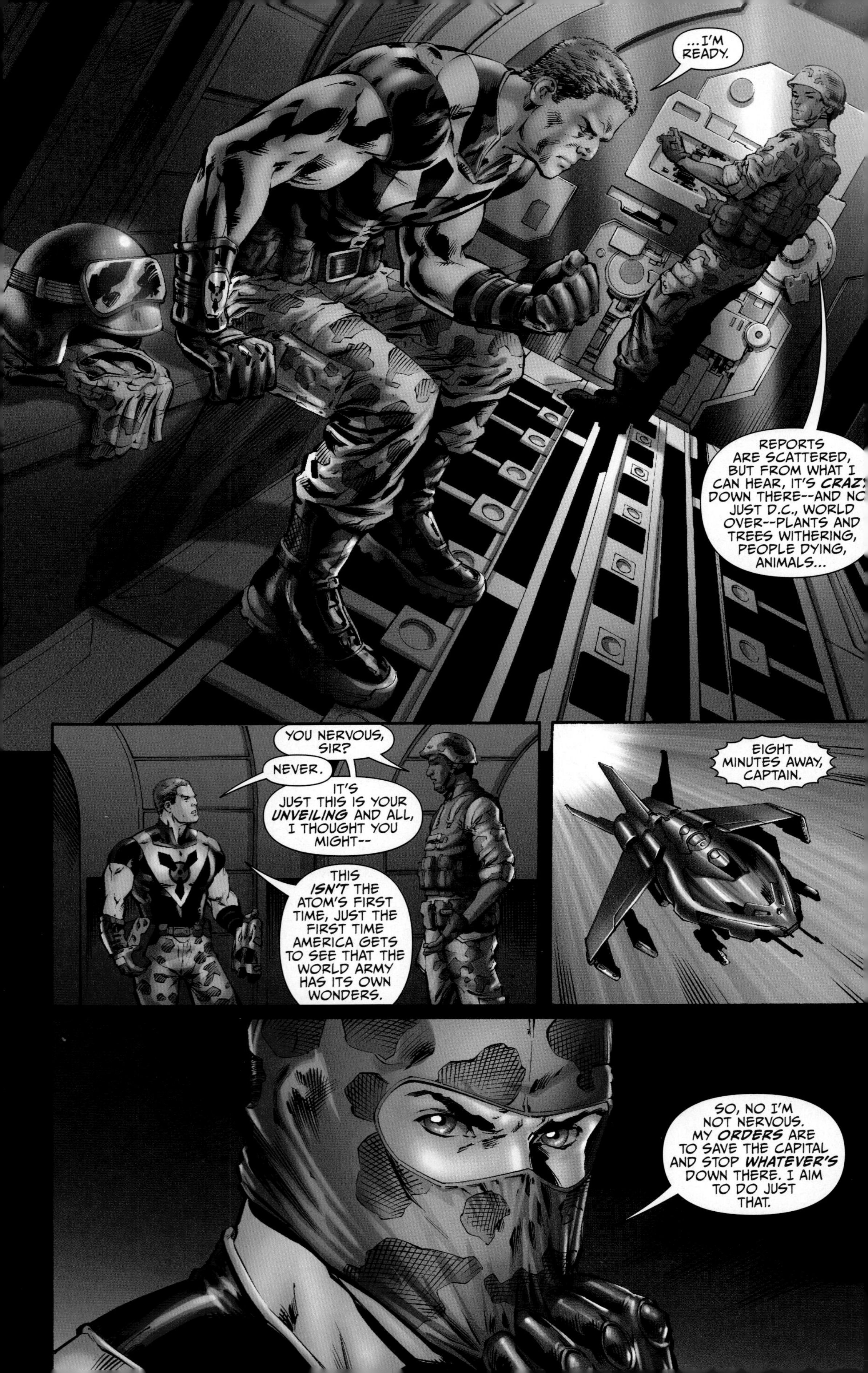
...I'M READY.
REPORTS ARE SCATTERED, BUT FROM WHAT I CAN HEAR, IT'S CRAZ DOWN THERE--AND NO JUST D.C., WORLD OVER--PLANTS AND TREES WITHERING, PEOPLE DYING, ANIMALS...
YOU NERVOUS, SIR?
NEVER.
IT'S JUST THIS IS YOUR UNVEILING AND ALL, I THOUGHT YOU MIGHT--
THIS ISN'T THE ATOM'S FIRST TIME, JUST THE FIRST TIME AMERICA GETS TO SEE THAT THE WORLD ARMY HAS ITS OWN WONDERS.
EIGHT MINUTES AWAY, CAPTAIN.
SO, NO I'M NOT NERVOUS. MY ORDERS ARE TO SAVE THE CAPITAL AND STOP WHATEVER'S DOWN THERE. I AIM TO DO JUST THAT.

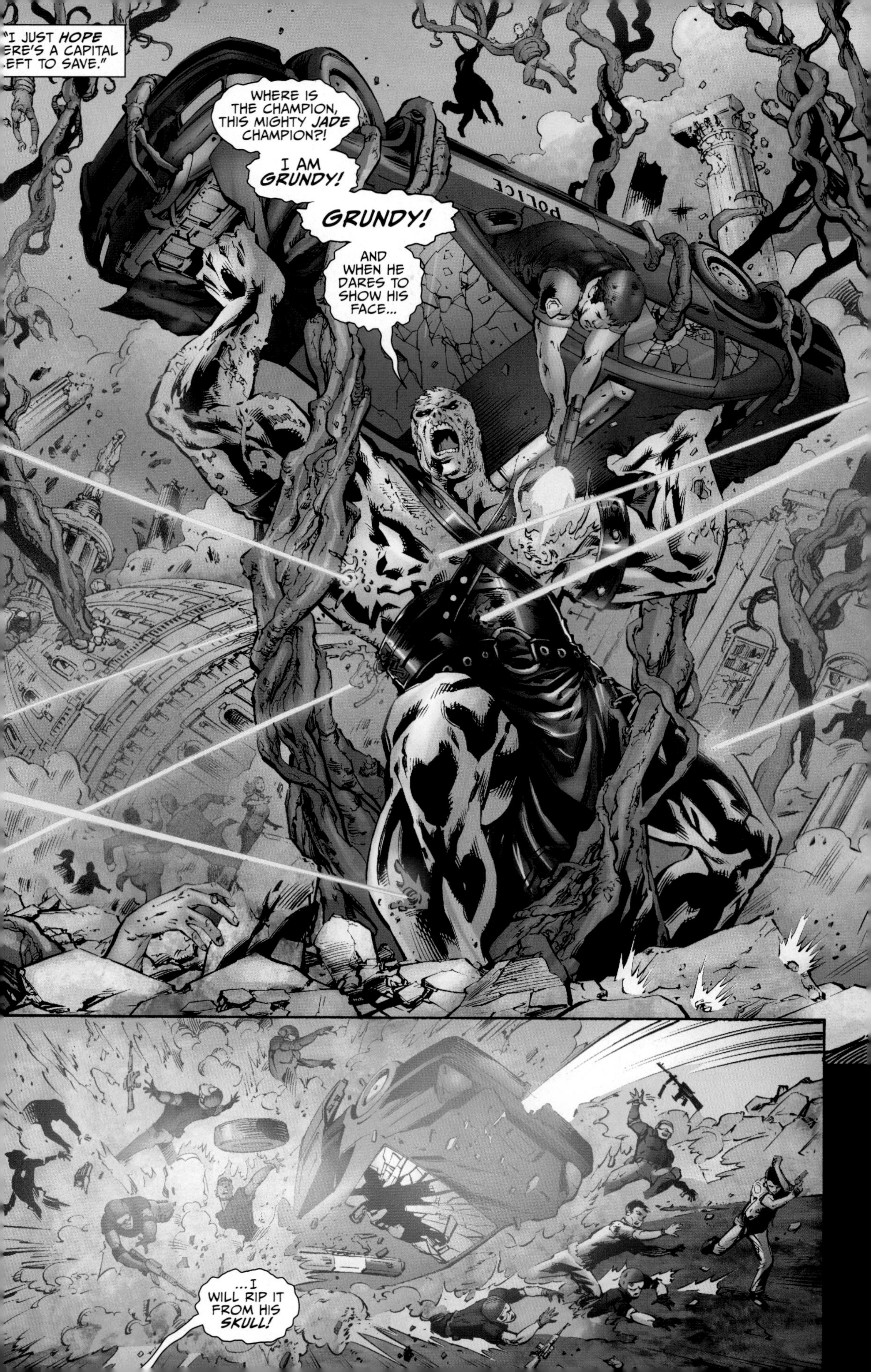
"I JUST HOPE
ERE'S A CAPITAL
LEFT TO SAVE."
WHERE IS THE CHAMPION, THIS MIGHTY JADE CHAMPION?!
I AM GRUNDY!
GRUNDY!
POLICE
AND WHEN HE DARES TO SHOW HIS FACE...
...I WILL RIP IT FROM HIS SKULL!

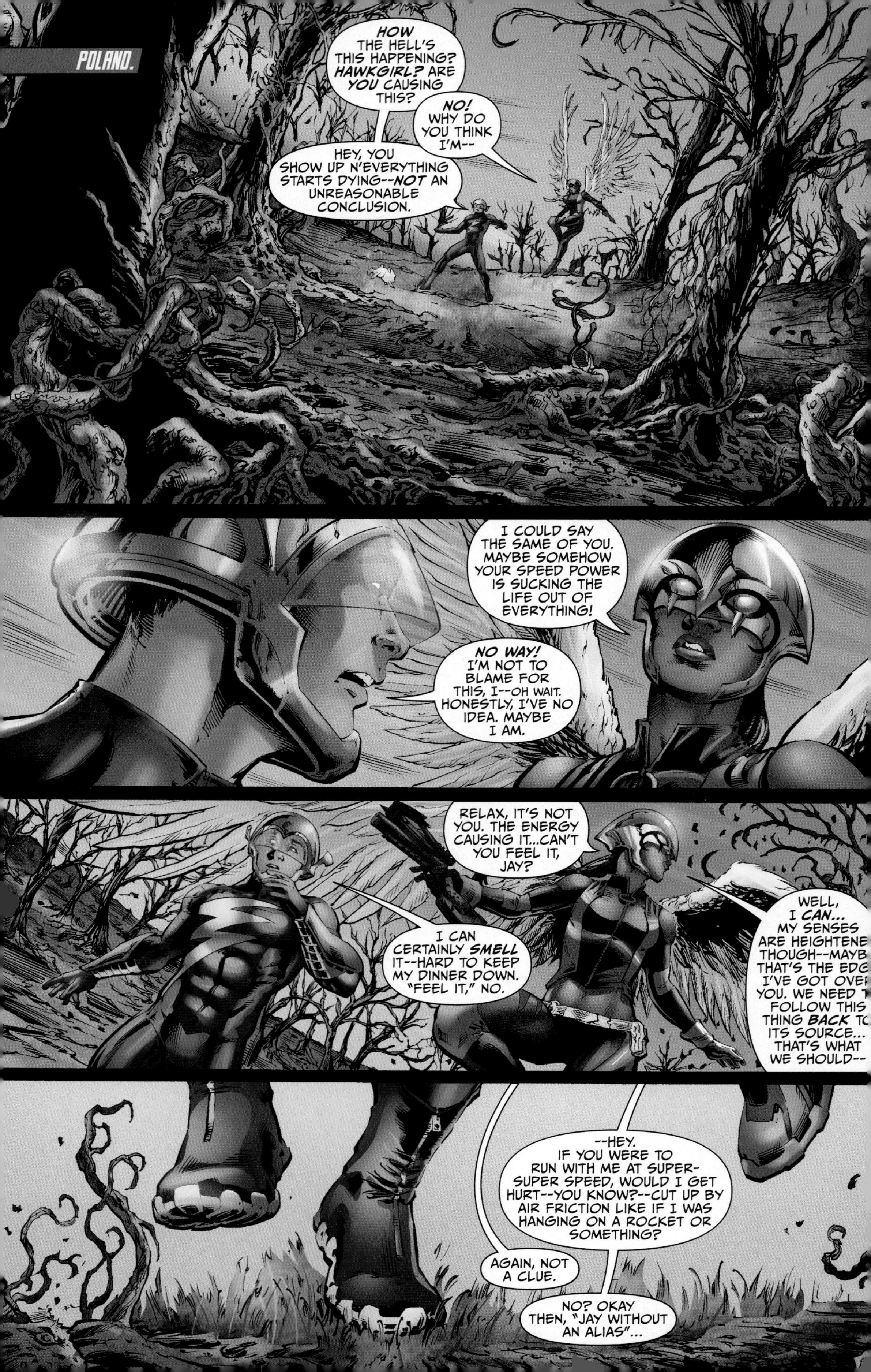
POLAND.
HOW THE HELL'S THIS HAPPENING? HAWKGIRL? ARE YOU CAUSING THIS?
NO! WHY DO YOU THINK I'M--
HEY, YOU SHOW UP N'EVERYTHING STARTS DYING--NOT AN UNREASONABLE CONCLUSION.
I COULD SAY THE SAME OF YOU. MAYBE SOMEHOW YOUR SPEED POWER IS SUCKING THE LIFE OUT OF EVERYTHING!
NO WAY! I'M NOT TO BLAME FOR THIS, I--OH WAIT. HONESTLY, I'VE NO IDEA. MAYBE I AM.
RELAX, IT'S NOT YOU. THE ENERGY CAUSING IT...CAN'T YOU FEEL IT, JAY?
I CAN CERTAINLY SMELL IT--HARD TO KEEP MY DINNER DOWN. "FEEL IT," NO.
WELL, I CAN... MY SENSES ARE HEIGHTENE THOUGH--MAYB THAT'S THE EDG I'VE GOT OVE YOU. WE NEED FOLLOW THIS THING BACK T ITS SOURCE... THAT'S WHAT WE SHOULD--
--HEY. IF YOU WERE TO RUN WITH ME AT SUPER-SUPER SPEED, WOULD I GET HURT--YOU KNOW?--CUT UP BY AIR FRICTION LIKE IF I WAS HANGING ON A ROCKET OR SOMETHING?
AGAIN, NOT A CLUE.
NO? OKAY THEN, "JAY WITHOUT AN ALIAS"...

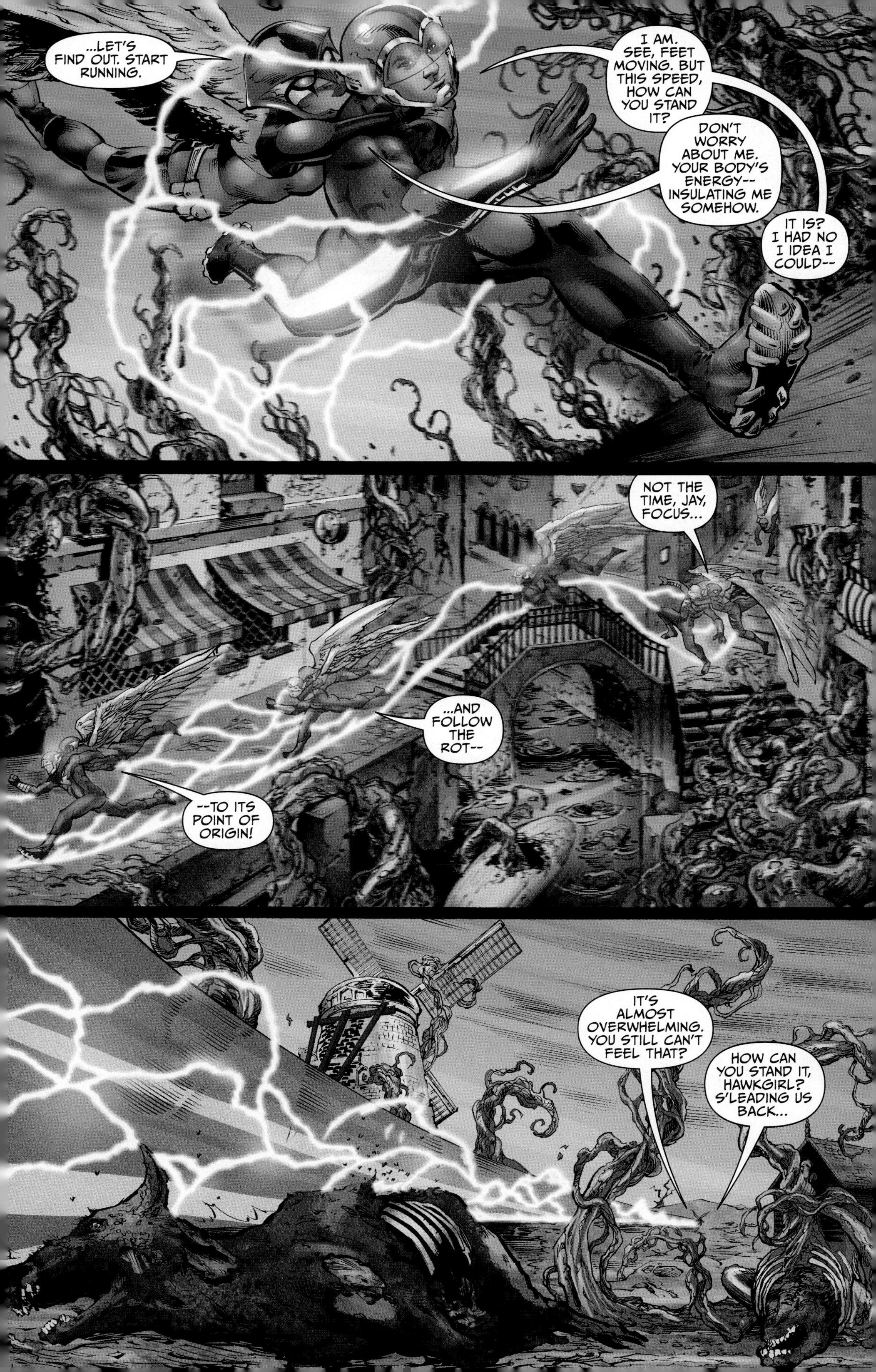
...LET'S FIND OUT. START RUNNING.
I AM. SEE, FEET MOVING. BUT THIS SPEED, HOW CAN YOU STAND IT?
DON'T WORRY ABOUT ME. YOUR BODY'S ENERGY-- INSULATING ME SOMEHOW.
IT IS? I HAD NO I IDEA I COULD--
NOT THE TIME, JAY, FOCUS...
...AND FOLLOW THE ROT--
--TO ITS POINT OF ORIGIN!
IT'S ALMOST OVERWHELMING. YOU STILL CAN'T FEEL THAT?
HOW CAN YOU STAND IT, HAWKGIRL? S'LEADING US BACK...

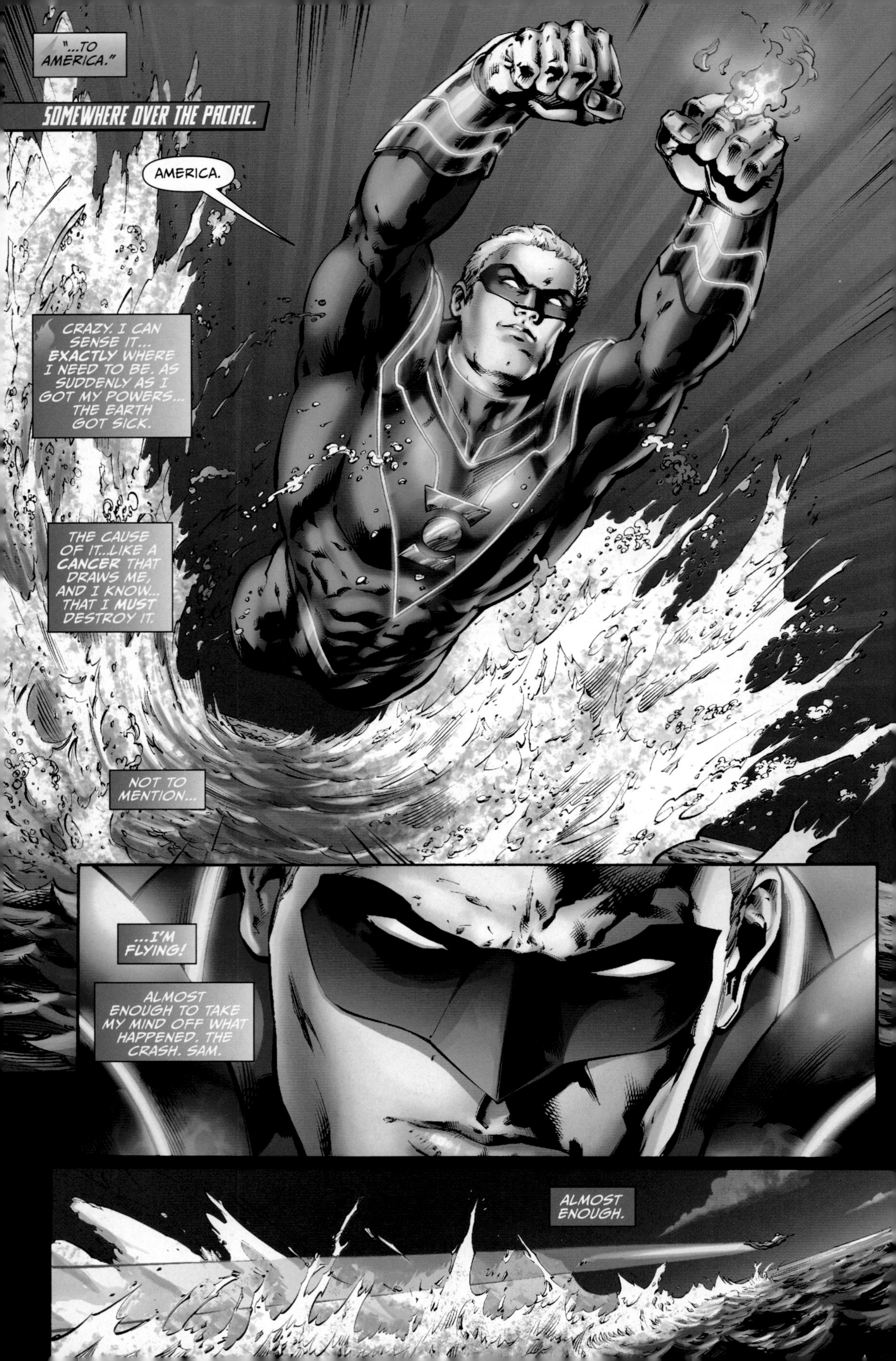
"...TO AMERICA."
SOMEWHERE OVER THE PACIFIC.
AMERICA.
CRAZY. I CAN SENSE IT... EXACTLY WHERE I NEED TO BE. AS SUDDENLY AS I GOT MY POWERS... THE EARTH GOT SICK.
THE CAUSE OF IT...LIKE A CANCER THAT DRAWS ME, AND I KNOW... THAT I MUST DESTROY IT.
NOT TO MENTION...
...I'M FLYING!
ALMOST ENOUGH TO TAKE MY MIND OFF WHAT HAPPENED. THE CRASH. SAM.
ALMOST ENOUGH.

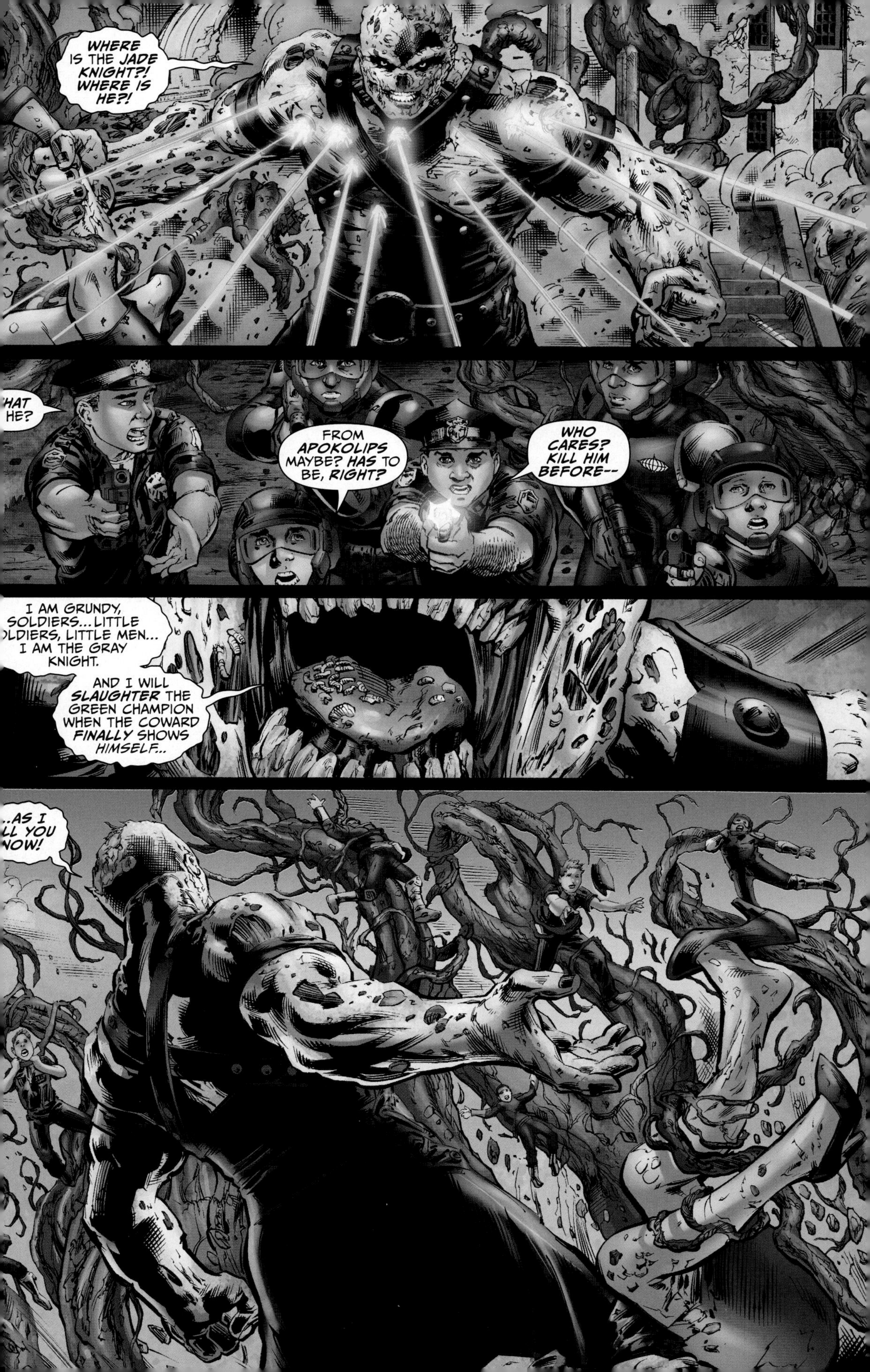
WHERE IS THE JADE KNIGHT?! WHERE IS HE?!
HAT HE?
FROM APOKOLIPS MAYBE? HAS TO BE, RIGHT?
WHO CARES? KILL HIM BEFORE--
I AM GRUNDY, SOLDIERS... LITTLE OLDIERS, LITTLE MEN... I AM THE GRAY KNIGHT.
AND I WILL SLAUGHTER THE GREEN CHAMPION WHEN THE COWARD FINALLY SHOWS HIMSELF...
..AS I LL YOU NOW!

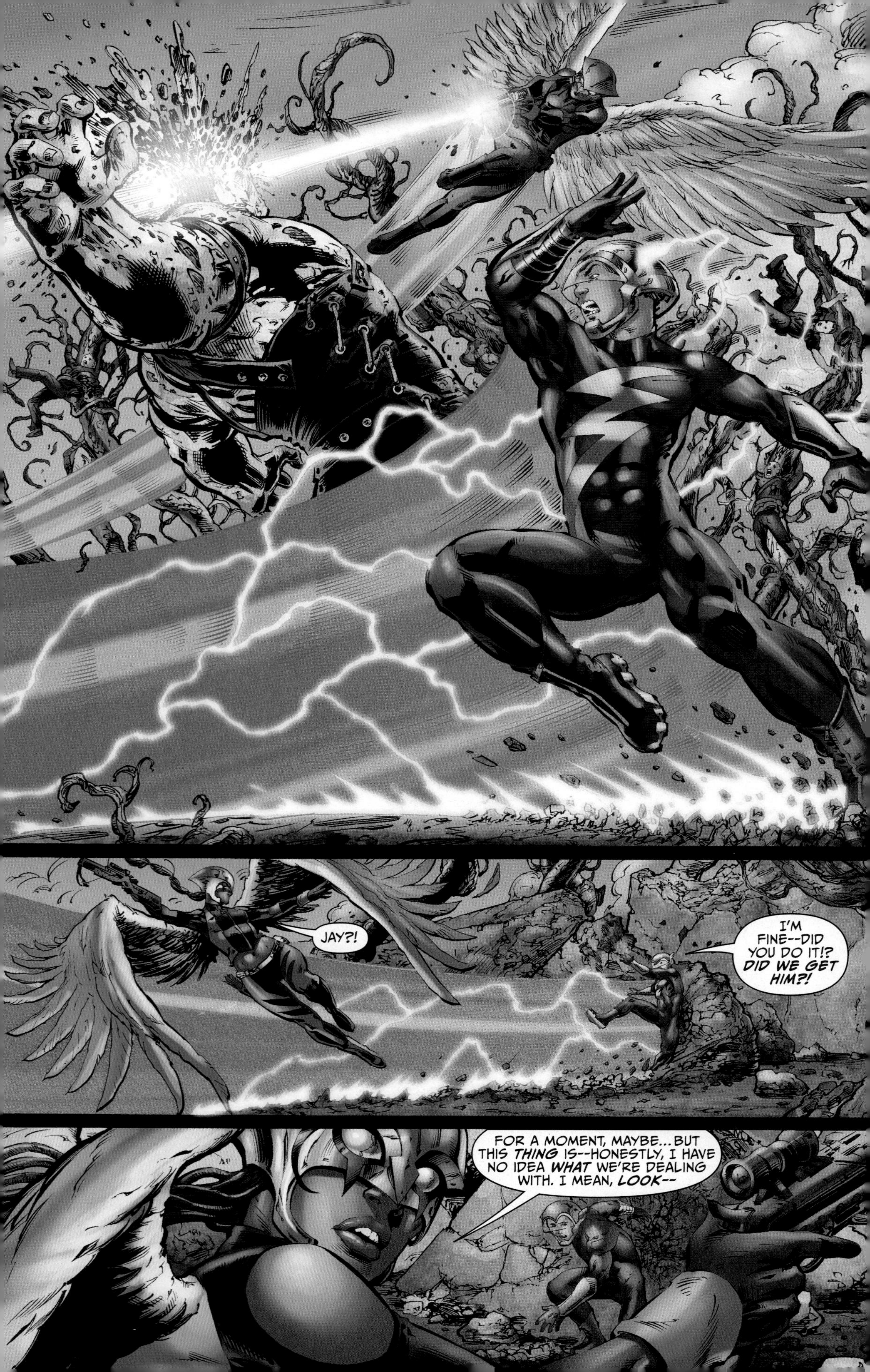
JAY?!
I'M FINE--DID YOU DO IT!? DID WE GET HIM?!
FOR A MOMENT, MAYBE... BUT THIS THING IS--HONESTLY, I HAVE NO IDEA WHAT WE'RE DEALING WITH. I MEAN, LOOK--

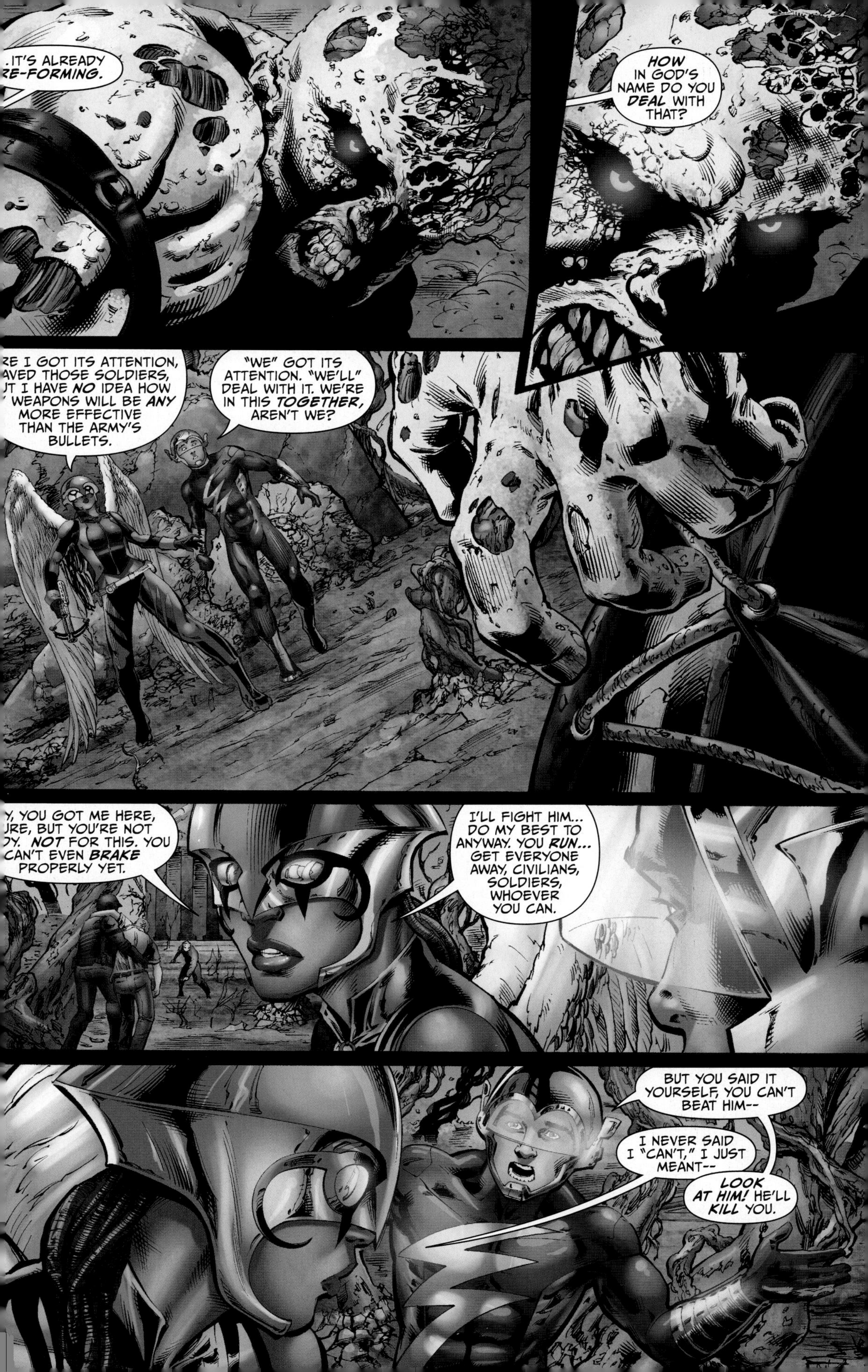

. IT'S ALREADY RE-FORMING.
HOW IN GOD'S NAME DO YOU DEAL WITH THAT?
RE I GOT ITS ATTENTION, AVED THOSE SOLDIERS, JT I HAVE NO IDEA HOW WEAPONS WILL BE ANY MORE EFFECTIVE THAN THE ARMY'S BULLETS.
"WE" GOT ITS ATTENTION. "WE'LL" DEAL WITH IT. WE'RE IN THIS TOGETHER, AREN'T WE?
Y, YOU GOT ME HERE, JRE, BUT YOU'RE NOT DY. NOT FOR THIS. YOU CAN'T EVEN BRAKE PROPERLY YET.
I'LL FIGHT HIM... DO MY BEST TO ANYWAY. YOU RUN... GET EVERYONE AWAY, CIVILIANS, SOLDIERS, WHOEVER YOU CAN.
BUT YOU SAID IT YOURSELF, YOU CAN'T BEAT HIM--
I NEVER SAID I "CAN'T," I JUST MEANT--
LOOK AT HIM! HE'LL KILL YOU.

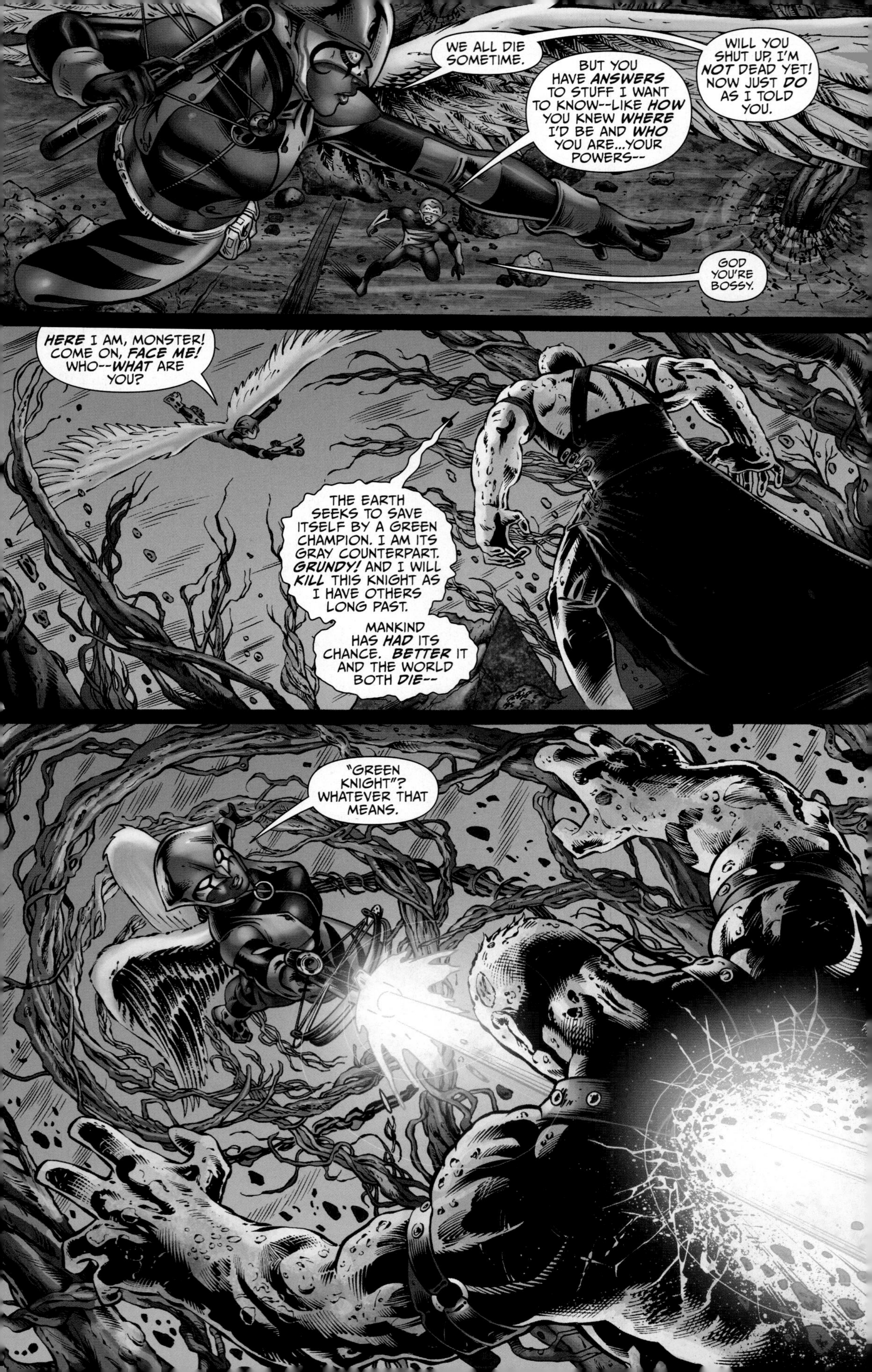
WE ALL DIE SOMETIME.
BUT YOU HAVE ANSWERS TO STUFF I WANT TO KNOW--LIKE HOW YOU KNEW WHERE I'D BE AND WHO YOU ARE...YOUR POWERS--
WILL YOU SHUT UP, I'M NOT DEAD YET! NOW JUST DO AS I TOLD YOU.
GOD YOU'RE BOSSY.
HERE I AM, MONSTER! COME ON, FACE ME! WHO--WHAT ARE YOU?
THE EARTH SEEKS TO SAVE ITSELF BY A GREEN CHAMPION. I AM ITS GRAY COUNTERPART. GRUNDY! AND I WILL KILL THIS KNIGHT AS I HAVE OTHERS LONG PAST.
MANKIND HAS HAD ITS CHANCE. BETTER IT AND THE WORLD BOTH DIE--
"GREEN KNIGHT"? WHATEVER THAT MEANS.

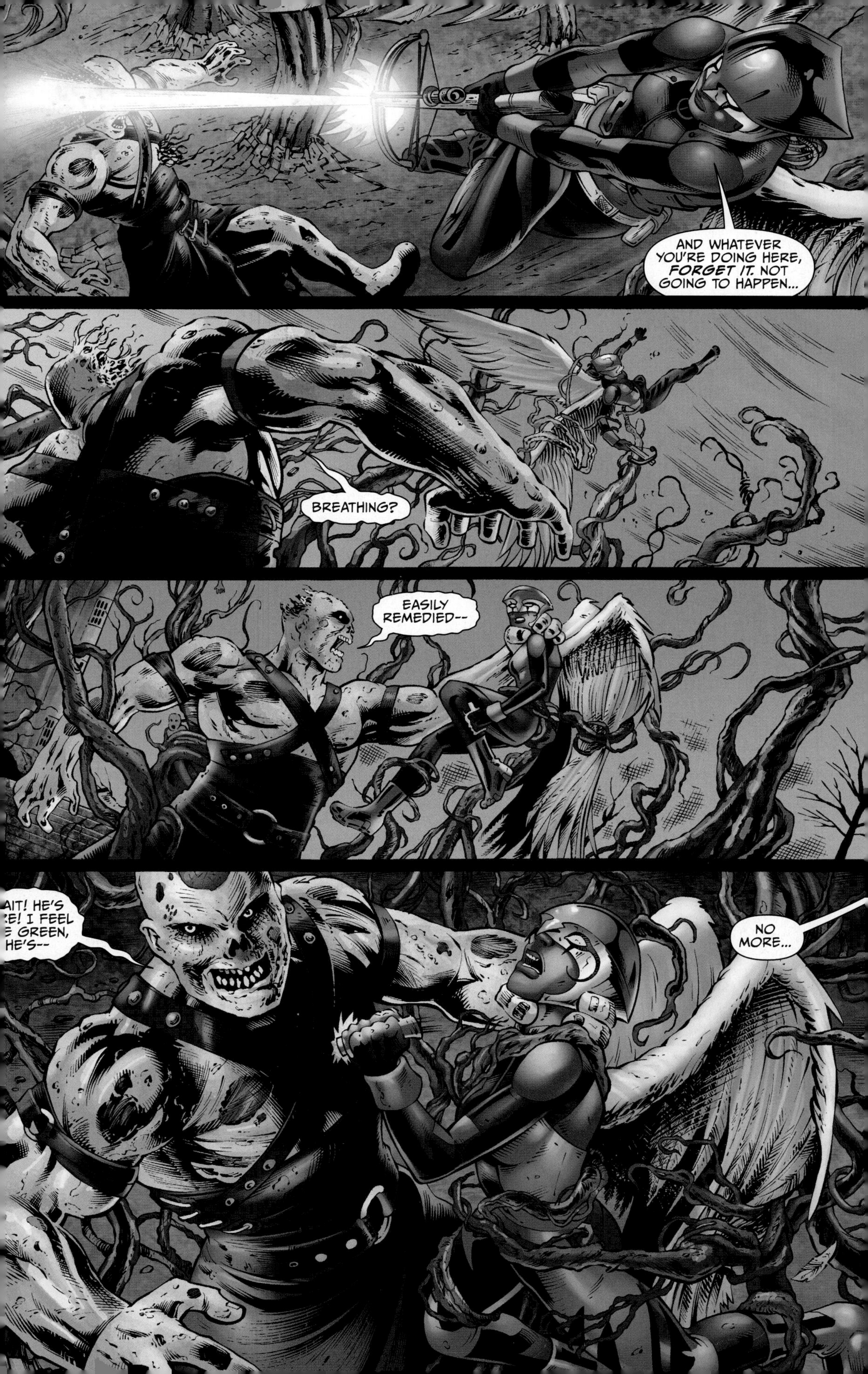
AND WHATEVER YOU'RE DOING HERE, FORGET IT. NOT GOING TO HAPPEN...
BREATHING?
EASILY REMEDIED--
AIT! HE'S
E! I FEEL
E GREEN,
HE'S--
NO MORE...

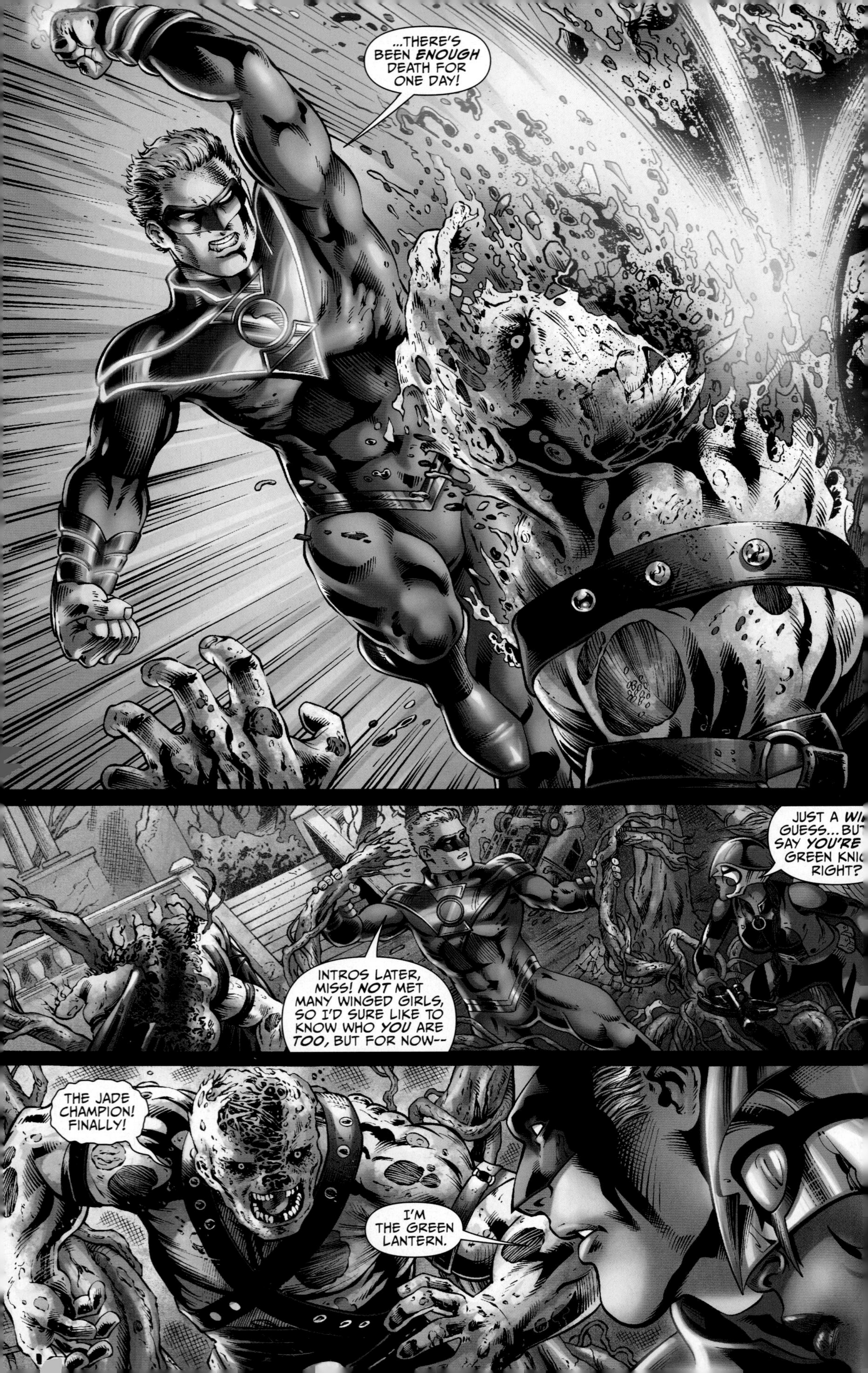
...THERE'S BEEN ENOUGH DEATH FOR ONE DAY!
JUST A WI GUESS...BUT SAY YOU'RE GREEN KNIG RIGHT?
INTROS LATER, MISS! NOT MET MANY WINGED GIRLS, SO I'D SURE LIKE TO KNOW WHO YOU ARE TOO, BUT FOR NOW--
THE JADE CHAMPION! FINALLY!
I'M THE GREEN LANTERN.

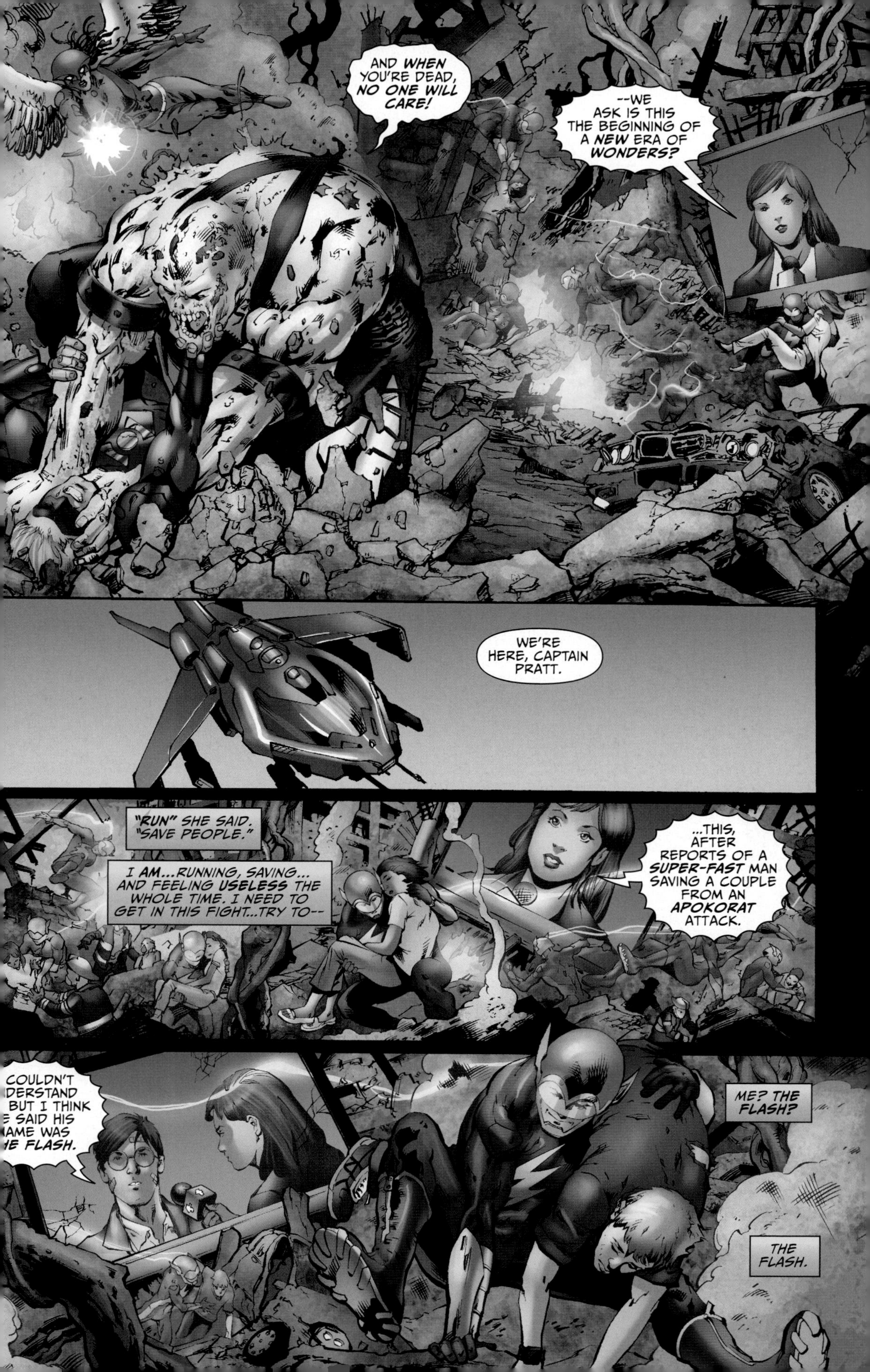
AND WHEN YOU'RE DEAD, NO ONE WILL CARE!
--WE ASK IS THIS THE BEGINNING OF A NEW ERA OF WONDERS?
WE'RE HERE, CAPTAIN PRATT.
"RUN" SHE SAID. "SAVE PEOPLE."
I AM...RUNNING, SAVING... AND FEELING USELESS THE WHOLE TIME. I NEED TO GET IN THIS FIGHT...TRY TO--
...THIS, AFTER REPORTS OF A SUPER-FAST MAN SAVING A COUPLE FROM AN APOKORAT ATTACK.
COULDN'T
BUT I THINK
SAID HIS
ME? THE FLASH?
THE FLASH.

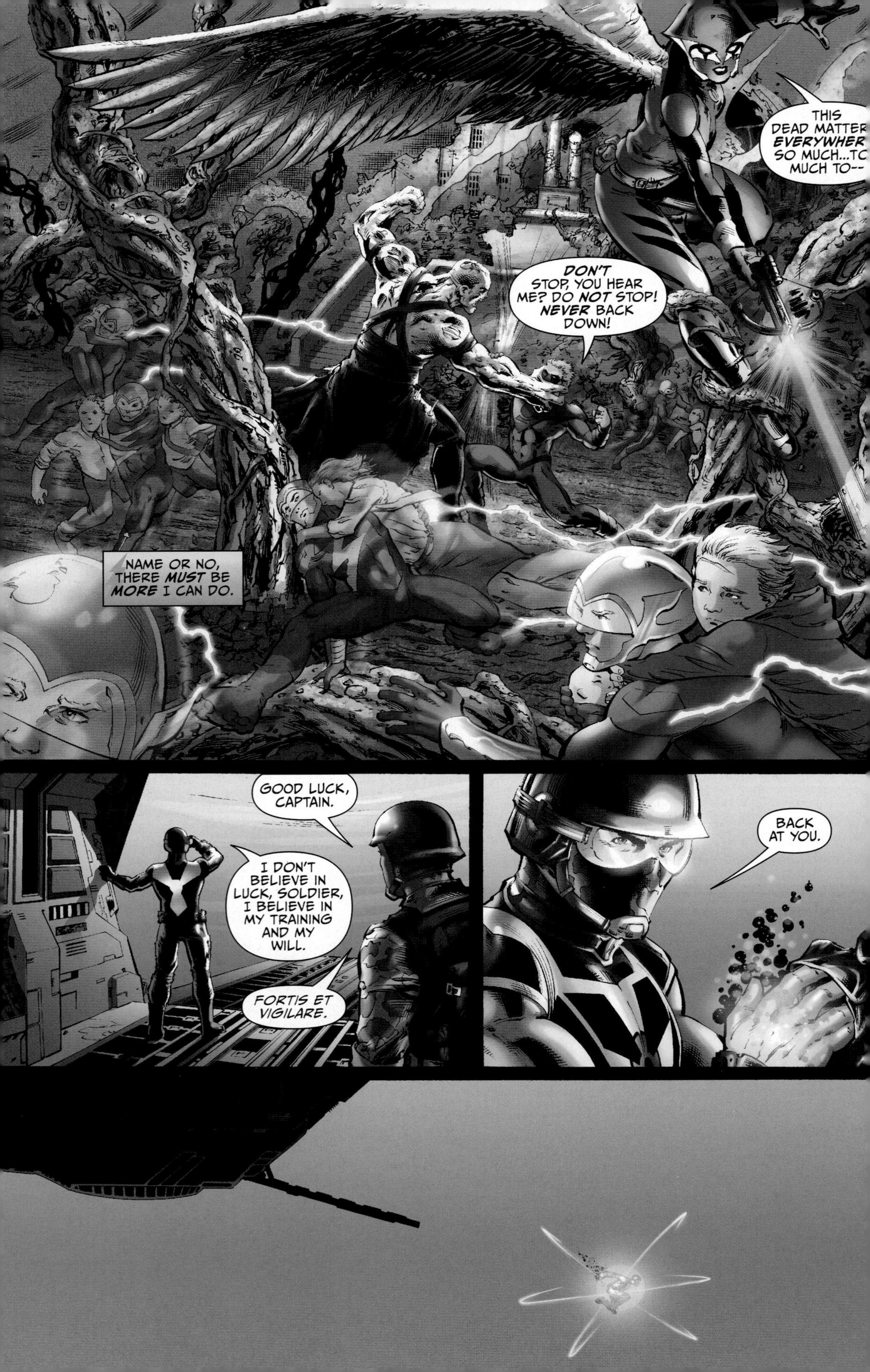
THIS DEAD MATTER EVERYWHER SO MUCH...TO MUCH TO--
DON'T STOP, YOU HEAR ME? DO NOT STOP! NEVER BACK DOWN!
NAME OR NO, THERE MUST BE MORE I CAN DO.
GOOD LUCK, CAPTAIN.
I DON'T BELIEVE IN LUCK, SOLDIER, I BELIEVE IN MY TRAINING AND MY WILL.
FORTIS ET VIGILARE.
BACK AT YOU.

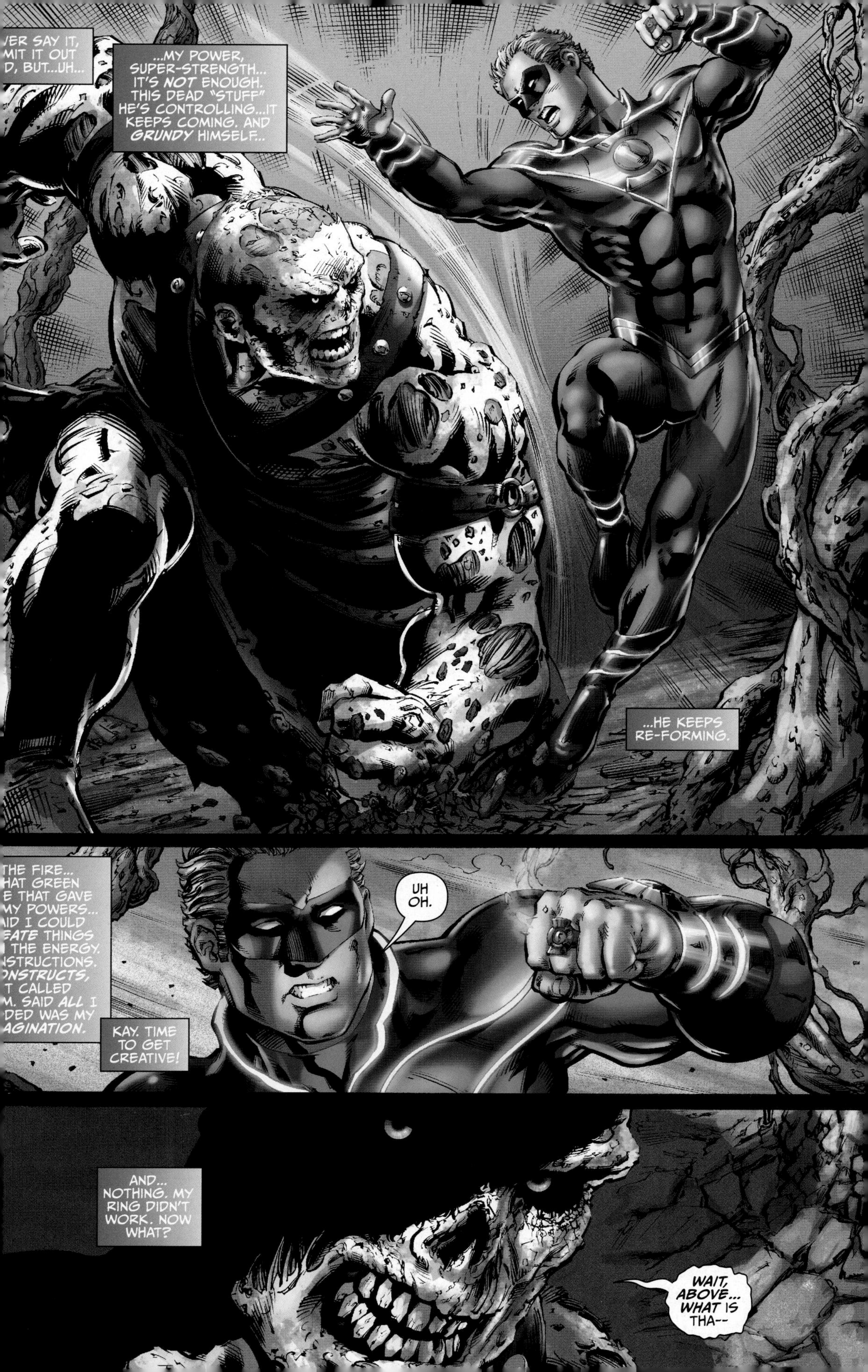

VER SAY IT, MIT IT OUT D, BUT...UH...
...MY POWER, SUPER-STRENGTH... IT'S NOT ENOUGH. THIS DEAD "STUFF" HE'S CONTROLLING...IT KEEPS COMING. AND GRUNDY HIMSELF...
...HE KEEPS RE-FORMING.
THE FIRE... HAT GREEN E THAT GAVE MY POWERS... AID I COULD EATE THINGS THE ENERGY. NSTRUCTIONS. ONSTRUCTS, T CALLED M. SAID ALL I DED WAS MY AGINATION.
UH OH.
KAY. TIME TO GET CREATIVE!
AND... NOTHING. MY RING DIDN'T WORK. NOW WHAT?
WAIT, ABOVE... WHAT IS THA--

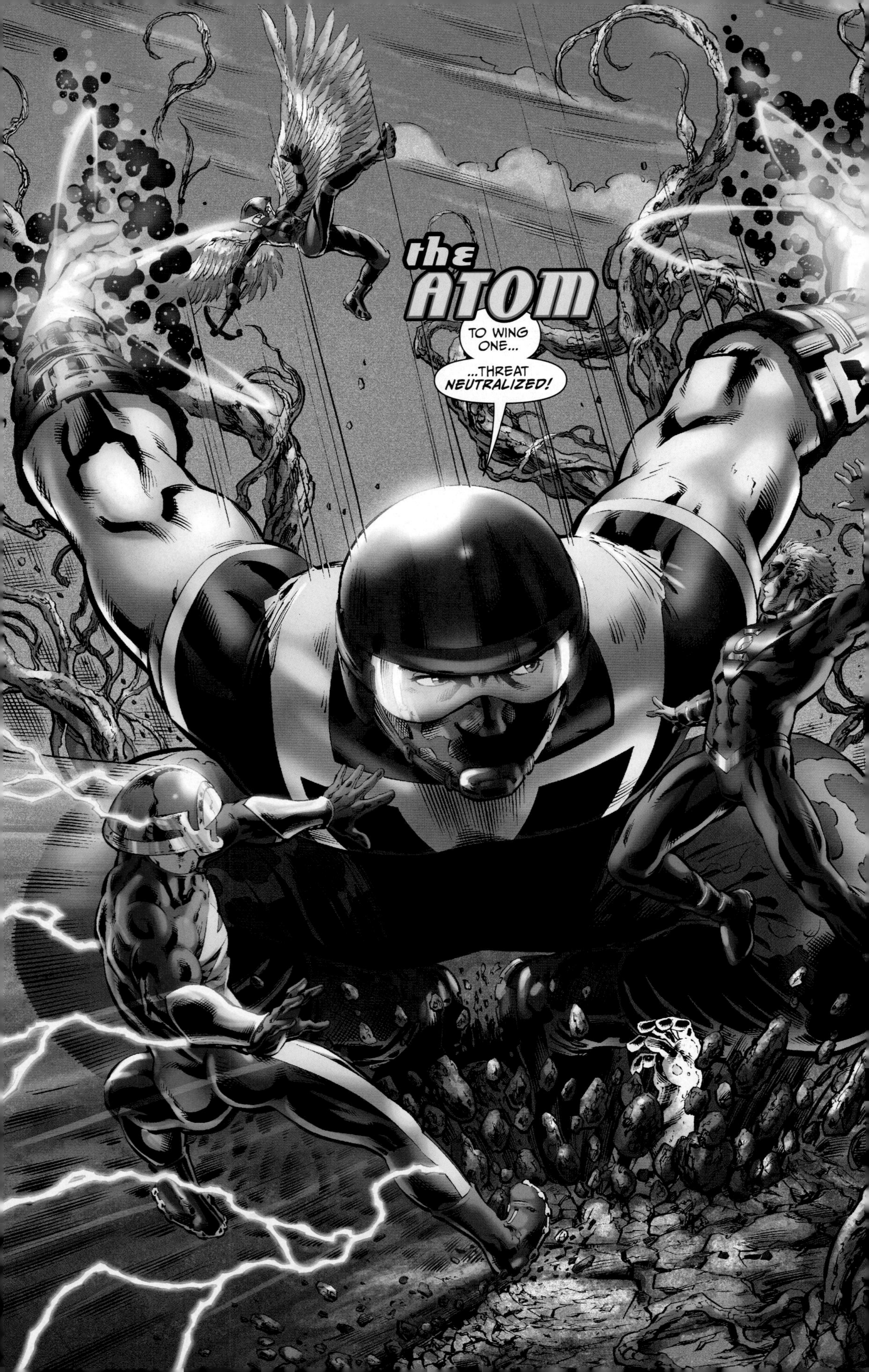
the ATOM
TO WING ONE...
...THREAT NEÜTRALIZED!

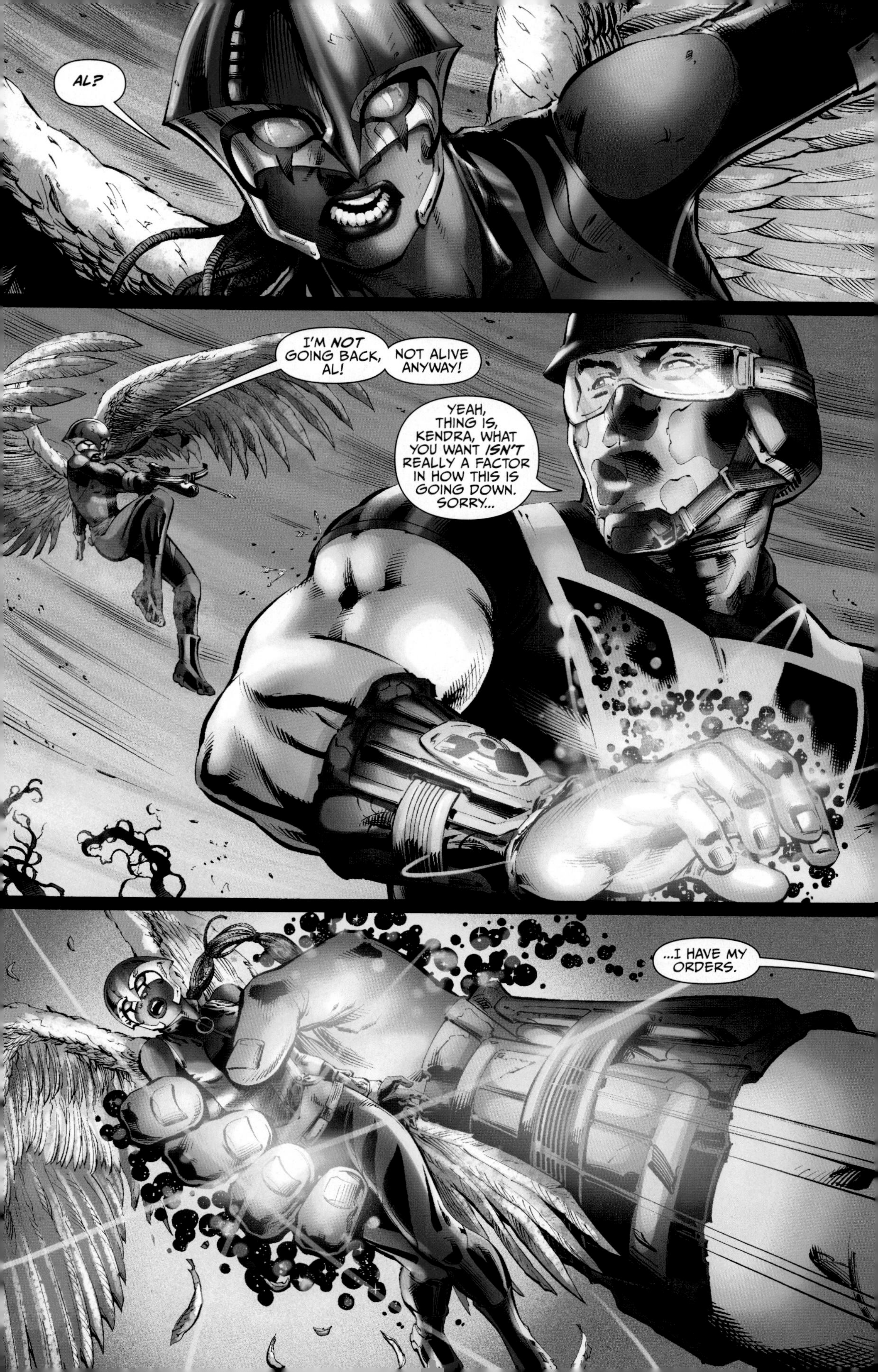
AL?
I'M NOT GOING BACK, AL!
NOT ALIVE ANYWAY!
YEAH, THING IS, KENDRA, WHAT YOU WANT ISN'T REALLY A FACTOR IN HOW THIS IS GOING DOWN. SORRY...
...I HAVE MY ORDERS.

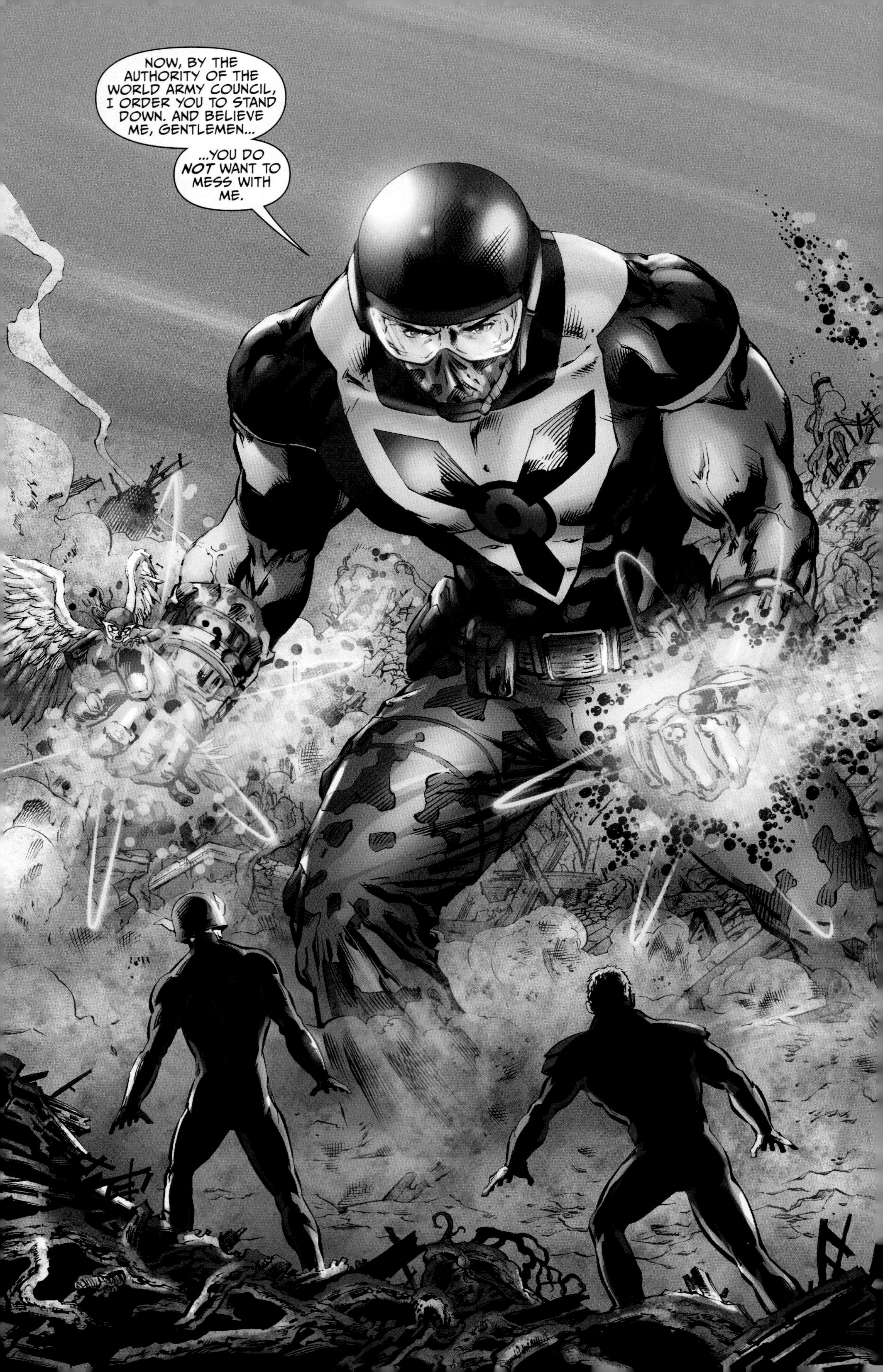
NOW, BY THE AUTHORITY OF THE WORLD ARMY COUNCIL, I ORDER YOU TO STAND DOWN. AND BELIEVE ME, GENTLEMEN...
...YOU DO NOT WANT TO MESS WITH ME.

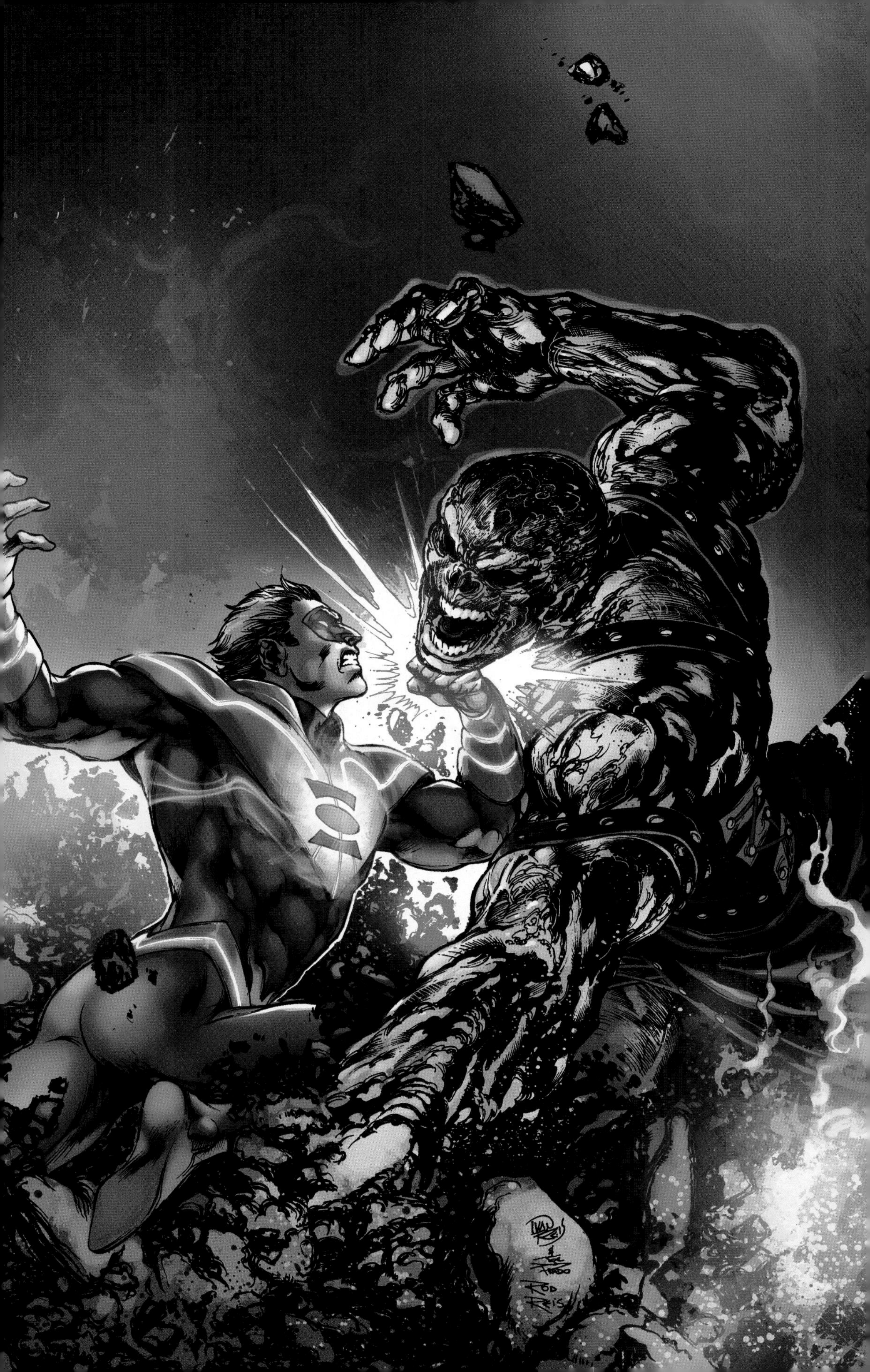

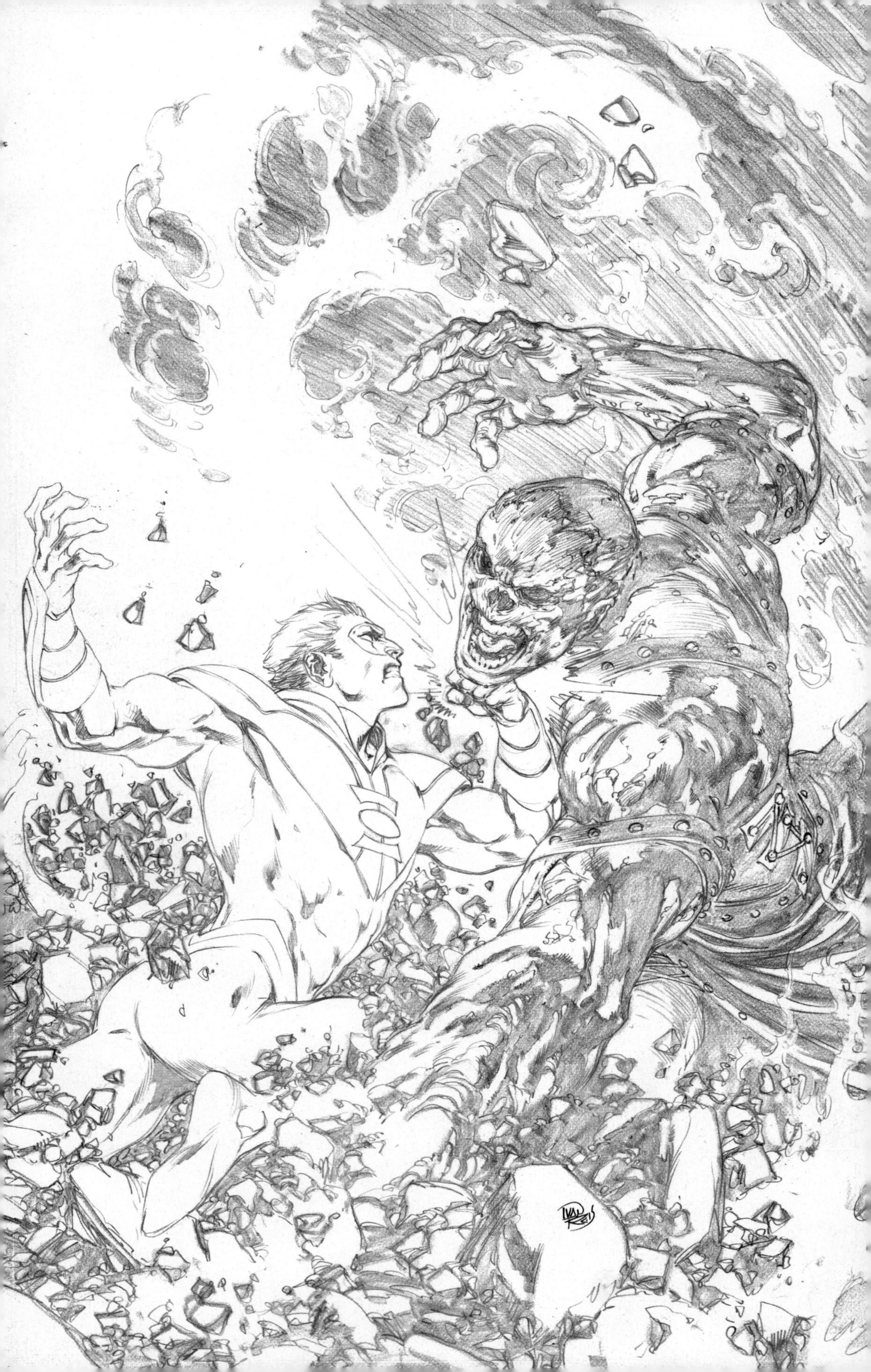

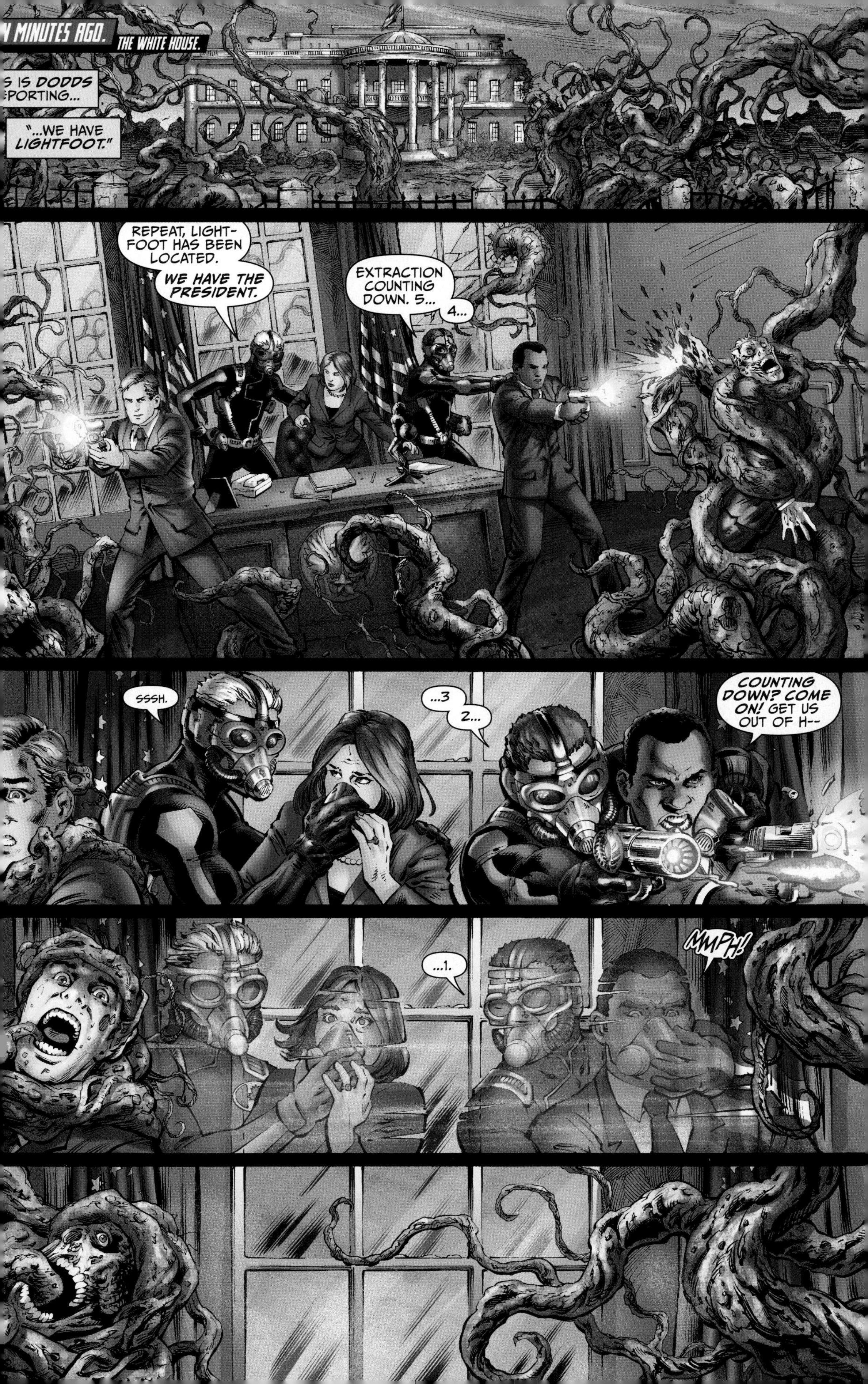
N MINUTES AGO.
THE WHITE HOUSE.
S IS DODDS
EPORTING...
"...WE HAVE LIGHTFOOT."
REPEAT, LIGHT-FOOT HAS BEEN LOCATED. WE HAVE THE PRESIDENT.
EXTRACTION COUNTING DOWN. 5...
4...
SSSH.
...3
2...
COUNTING DOWN? COME ON! GET US OUT OF H--
...1.
MMPH!

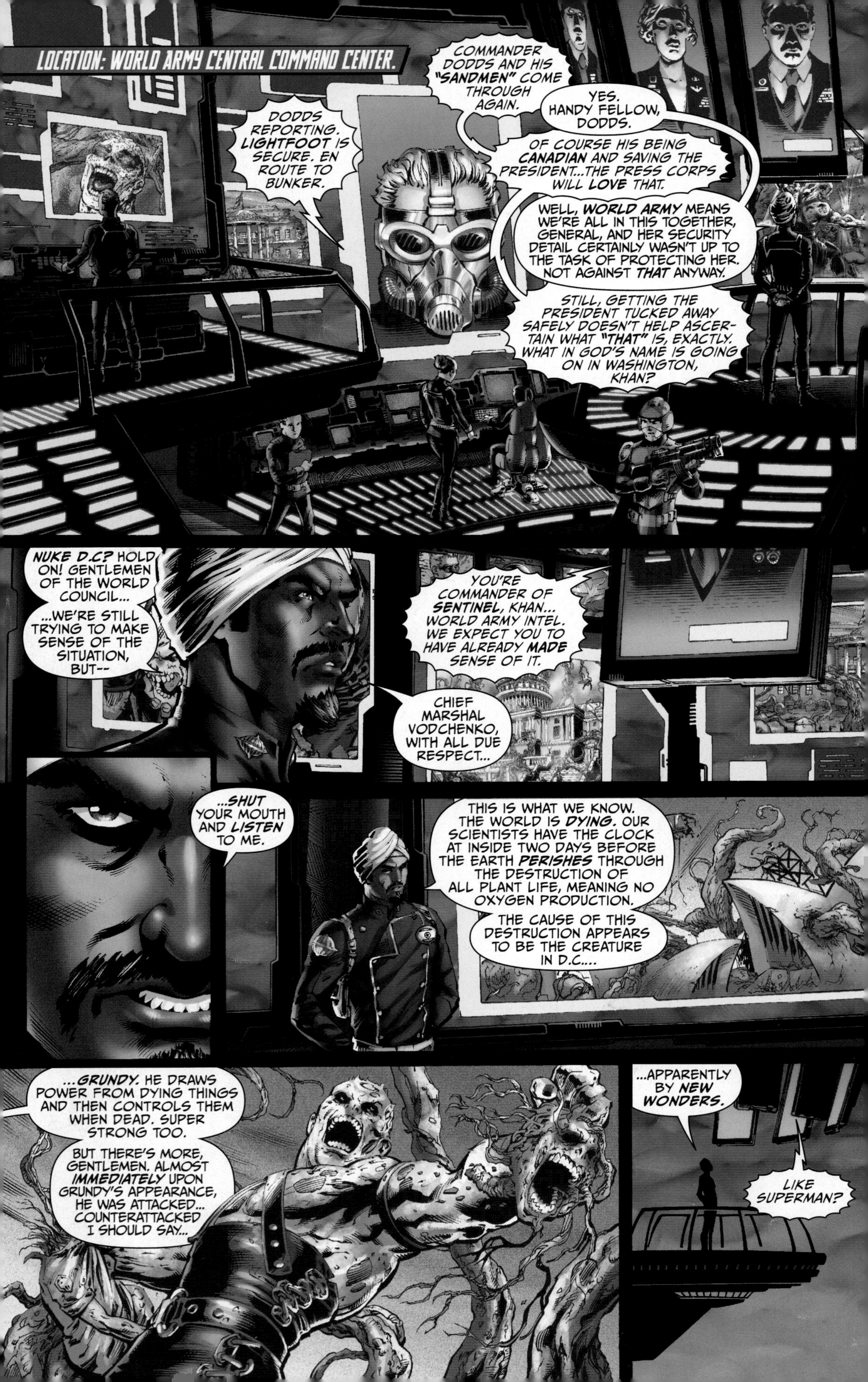
LOCATION: WORLD ARMY CENTRAL COMMAND CENTER.
DODDS REPORTING. LIGHTFOOT IS SECURE. EN ROUTE TO BUNKER.
COMMANDER DODDS AND HIS "SANDMEN" COME THROUGH AGAIN.
YES. HANDY FELLOW, DODDS.
OF COURSE HIS BEING CANADIAN AND SAVING THE PRESIDENT...THE PRESS CORPS WILL LOVE THAT.
WELL, WORLD ARMY MEANS WE'RE ALL IN THIS TOGETHER, GENERAL, AND HER SECURITY DETAIL CERTAINLY WASN'T UP TO THE TASK OF PROTECTING HER. NOT AGAINST THAT ANYWAY.
STILL, GETTING THE PRESIDENT TUCKED AWAY SAFELY DOESN'T HELP ASCERTAIN WHAT "THAT" IS, EXACTLY. WHAT IN GOD'S NAME IS GOING ON IN WASHINGTON, KHAN?
NUKE D.C? HOLD ON! GENTLEMEN OF THE WORLD COUNCIL...
...WE'RE STILL TRYING TO MAKE SENSE OF THE SITUATION, BUT--
YOU'RE COMMANDER OF SENTINEL, KHAN... WORLD ARMY INTEL. WE EXPECT YOU TO HAVE ALREADY MADE SENSE OF IT.
CHIEF MARSHAL VODCHENKO, WITH ALL DUE RESPECT...
...SHUT YOUR MOUTH AND LISTEN TO ME.
THIS IS WHAT WE KNOW. THE WORLD IS DYING. OUR SCIENTISTS HAVE THE CLOCK AT INSIDE TWO DAYS BEFORE THE EARTH PERISHES THROUGH THE DESTRUCTION OF ALL PLANT LIFE, MEANING NO OXYGEN PRODUCTION.
THE CAUSE OF THIS DESTRUCTION APPEARS TO BE THE CREATURE IN D.C....
...GRUNDY. HE DRAWS POWER FROM DYING THINGS AND THEN CONTROLS THEM WHEN DEAD. SUPER STRONG TOO.
BUT THERE'S MORE, GENTLEMEN. ALMOST IMMEDIATELY UPON GRUNDY'S APPEARANCE, HE WAS ATTACKED... COUNTERATTACKED I SHOULD SAY...
...APPARENTLY BY NEW WONDERS.
LIKE SUPERMAN?

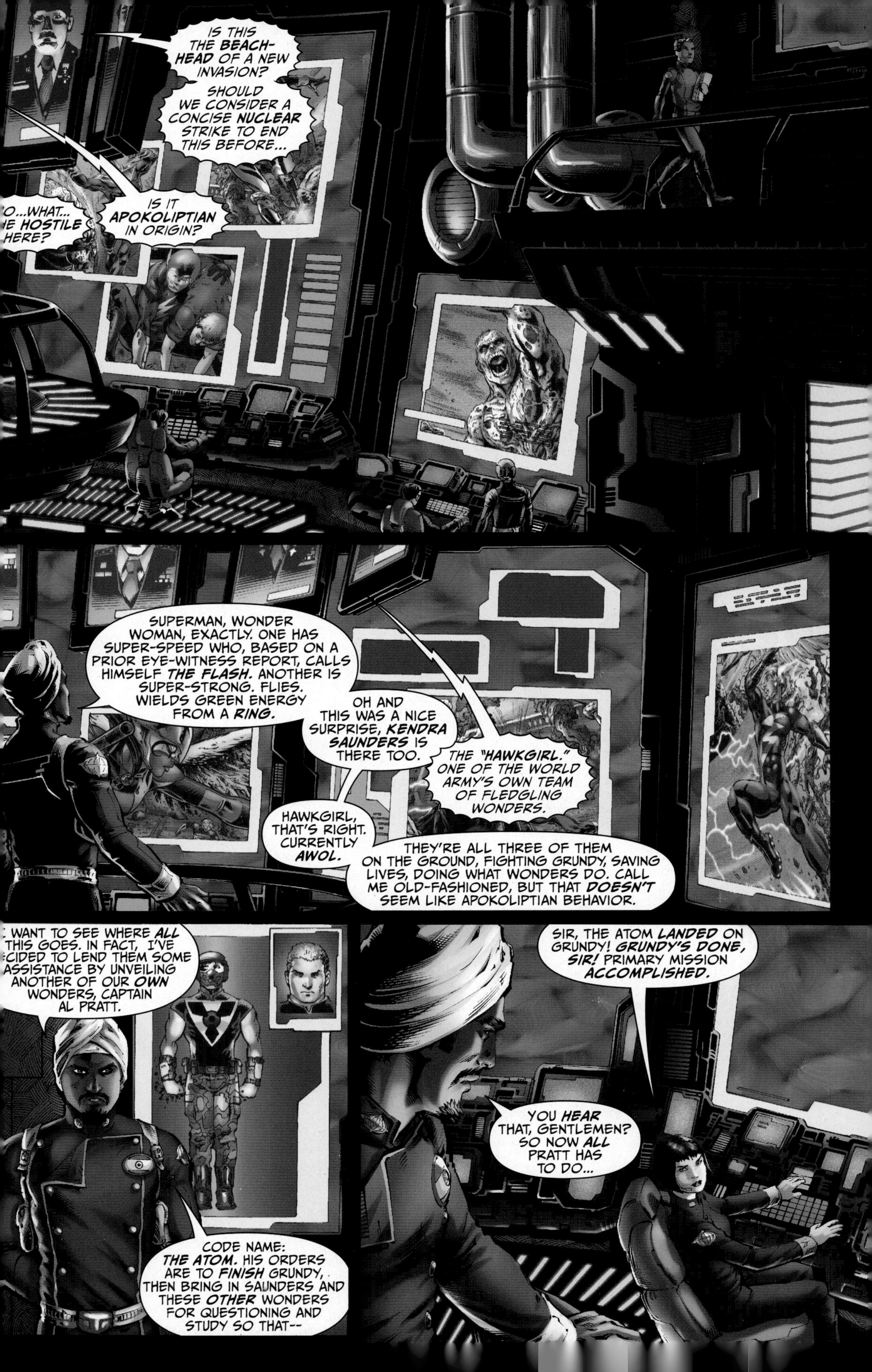

IS THIS THE BEACH-HEAD OF A NEW INVASION?
SHOULD WE CONSIDER A CONCISE NUCLEAR STRIKE TO END THIS BEFORE...
IS IT APOKOLIPTIAN IN ORIGIN?
O...WHAT... HE HOSTILE HERE?
SUPERMAN, WONDER WOMAN, EXACTLY. ONE HAS SUPER-SPEED WHO, BASED ON A PRIOR EYE-WITNESS REPORT, CALLS HIMSELF THE FLASH. ANOTHER IS SUPER-STRONG. FLIES. WIELDS GREEN ENERGY FROM A RING.
OH AND THIS WAS A NICE SURPRISE, KENDRA SAUNDERS IS THERE TOO.
THE "HAWKGIRL." ONE OF THE WORLD ARMY'S OWN TEAM OF FLEDGLING WONDERS.
HAWKGIRL, THAT'S RIGHT. CURRENTLY AWOL.
THEY'RE ALL THREE OF THEM ON THE GROUND, FIGHTING GRUNDY, SAVING LIVES, DOING WHAT WONDERS DO. CALL ME OLD-FASHIONED, BUT THAT DOESN'T SEEM LIKE APOKOLIPTIAN BEHAVIOR.
WANT TO SEE WHERE ALL THIS GOES. IN FACT, I'VE ECIDED TO LEND THEM SOME ASSISTANCE BY UNVEILING ANOTHER OF OUR OWN WONDERS, CAPTAIN AL PRATT.
CODE NAME: THE ATOM. HIS ORDERS ARE TO FINISH GRUNDY, THEN BRING IN SAUNDERS AND THESE OTHER WONDERS FOR QUESTIONING AND STUDY SO THAT--
SIR, THE ATOM LANDED ON GRUNDY! GRUNDY'S DONE, SIR! PRIMARY MISSION ACCOMPLISHED.
YOU HEAR THAT, GENTLEMEN? SO NOW ALL PRATT HAS TO DO...

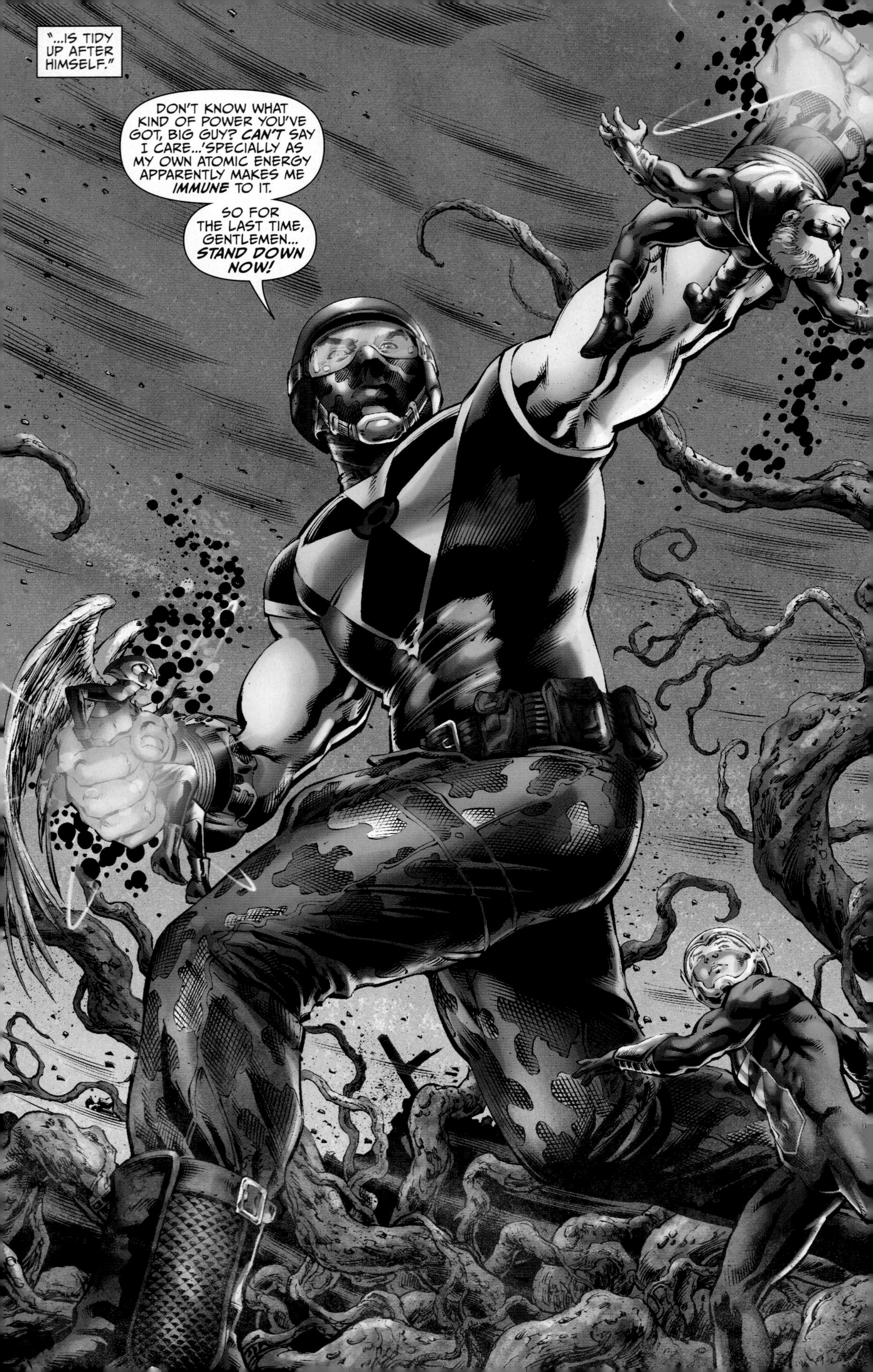
"...IS TIDY UP AFTER HIMSELF."
DON'T KNOW WHAT KIND OF POWER YOU'VE GOT, BIG GUY? CAN'T SAY I CARE...'SPECIALLY AS MY OWN ATOMIC ENERGY APPARENTLY MAKES ME IMMUNE TO IT.
SO FOR THE LAST TIME, GENTLEMEN... STAND DOWN NOW!

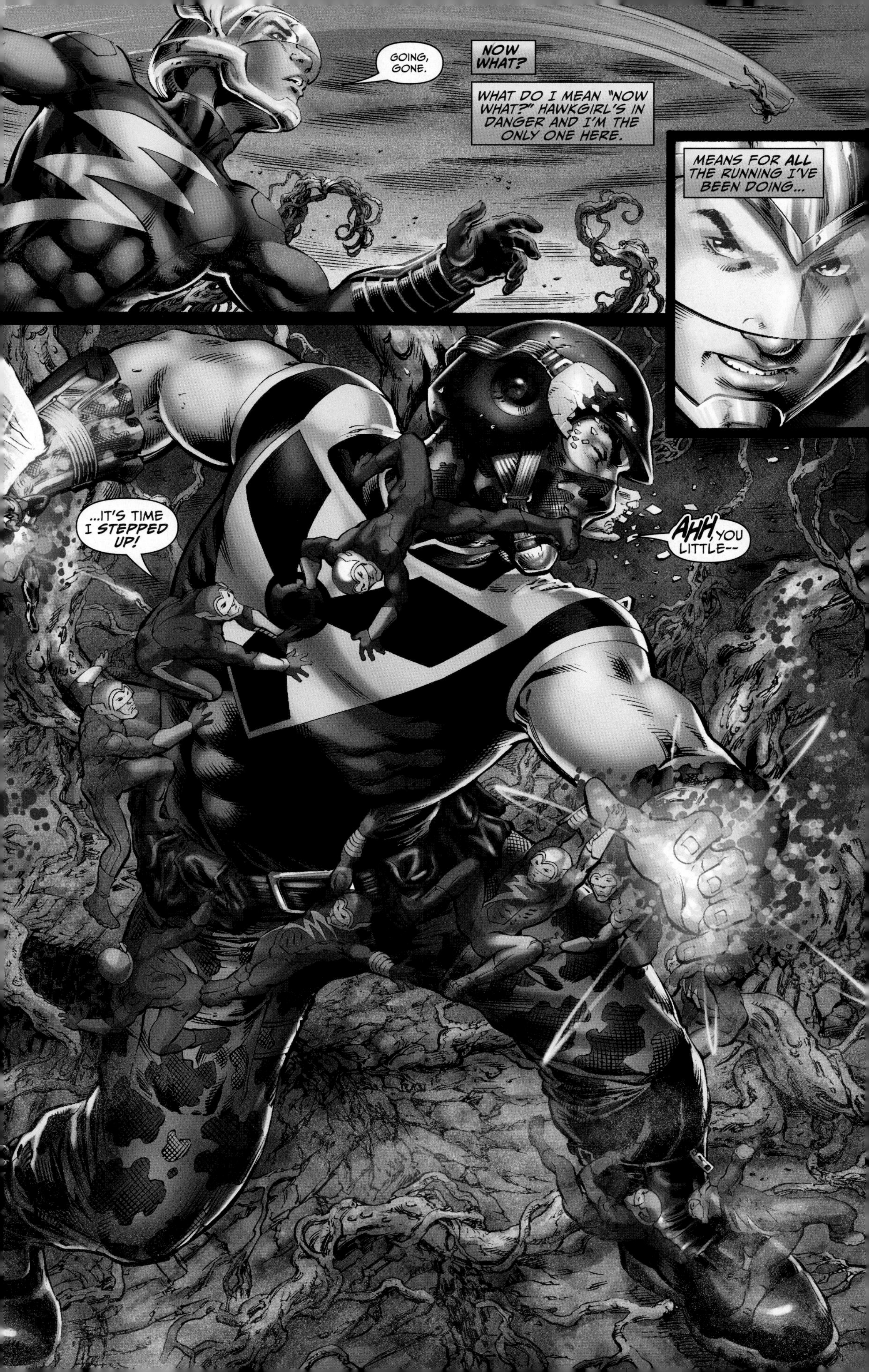
GOING, GONE.
NOW WHAT?
WHAT DO I MEAN "NOW WHAT?" HAWKGIRL'S IN DANGER AND I'M THE ONLY ONE HERE.
MEANS FOR ALL THE RUNNING I'VE BEEN DOING...
...IT'S TIME I STEPPED UP!
AHH, YOU LITTLE--

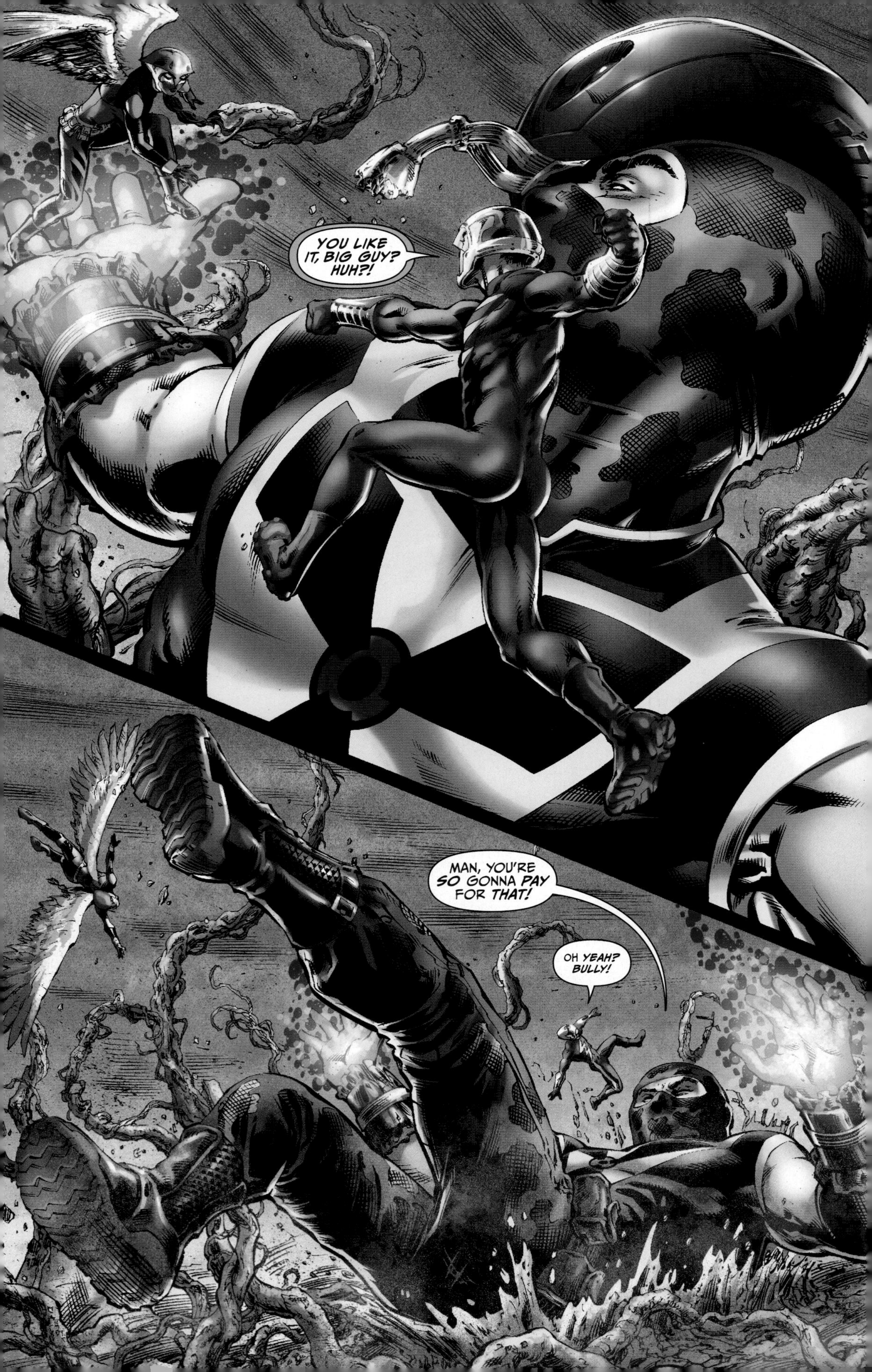

YOU LIKE IT, BIG GUY? HUH?!
MAN, YOU'RE SO GONNA PAY FOR THAT!
OH YEAH? BULLY!

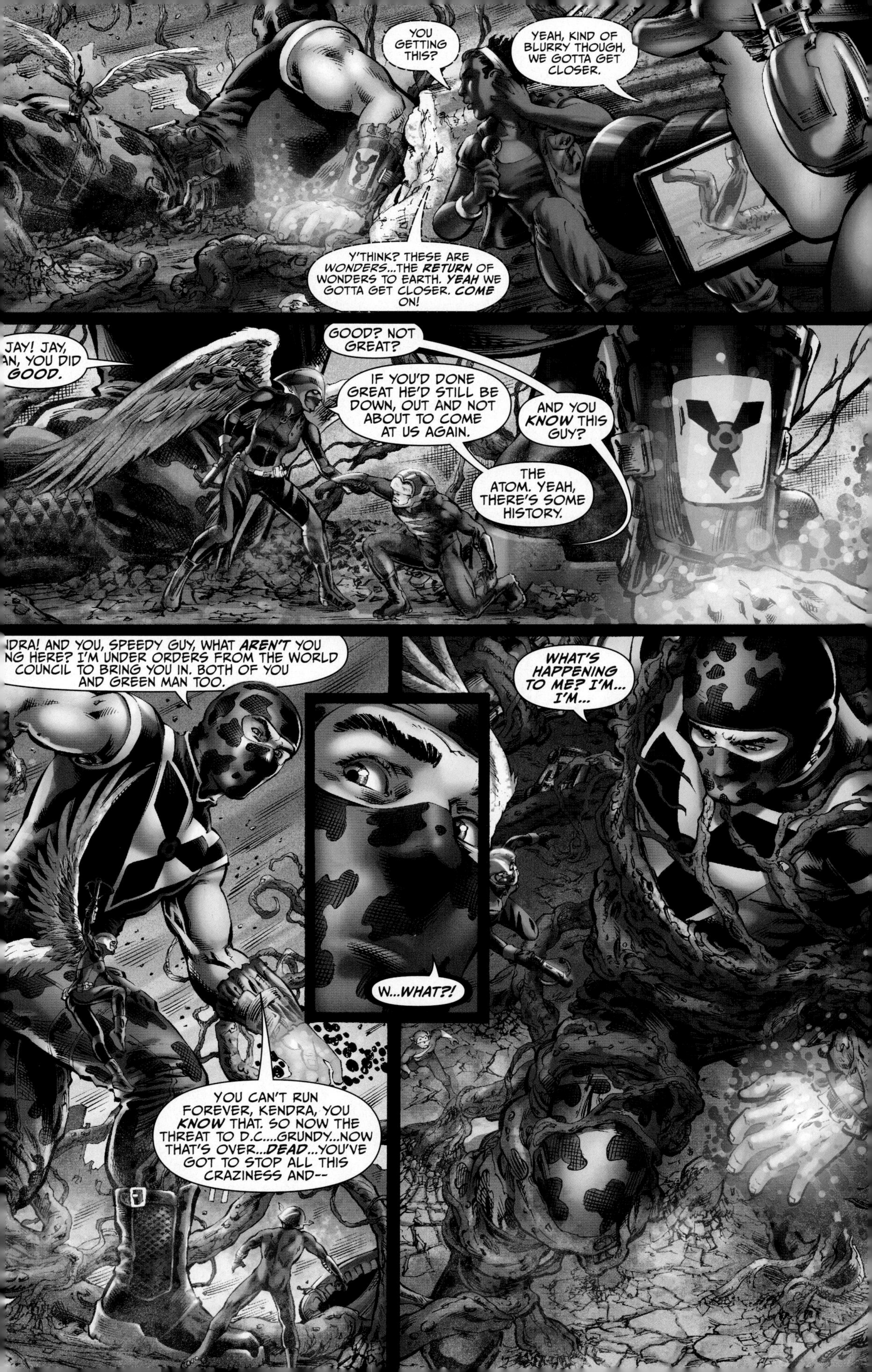

YOU GETTING THIS?
YEAH, KIND OF BLURRY THOUGH, WE GOTTA GET CLOSER.
Y'THINK? THESE ARE WONDERS...THE RETURN OF WONDERS TO EARTH. YEAH WE GOTTA GET CLOSER. COME ON!
JAY! JAY, AN, YOU DID GOOD.
GOOD? NOT GREAT?
IF YOU'D DONE GREAT HE'D STILL BE DOWN, OUT AND NOT ABOUT TO COME AT US AGAIN.
AND YOU KNOW THIS GUY?
THE ATOM. YEAH, THERE'S SOME HISTORY.
IDRA! AND YOU, SPEEDY GUY, WHAT AREN'T YOU NG HERE? I'M UNDER ORDERS FROM THE WORLD COUNCIL TO BRING YOU IN. BOTH OF YOU AND GREEN MAN TOO.
W...WHAT?!
YOU CAN'T RUN FOREVER, KENDRA, YOU KNOW THAT. SO NOW THE THREAT TO D.C....GRUNDY...NOW THAT'S OVER...DEAD...YOU'VE GOT TO STOP ALL THIS CRAZINESS AND--
WHAT'S HAPPENING TO ME? I'M... I'M...

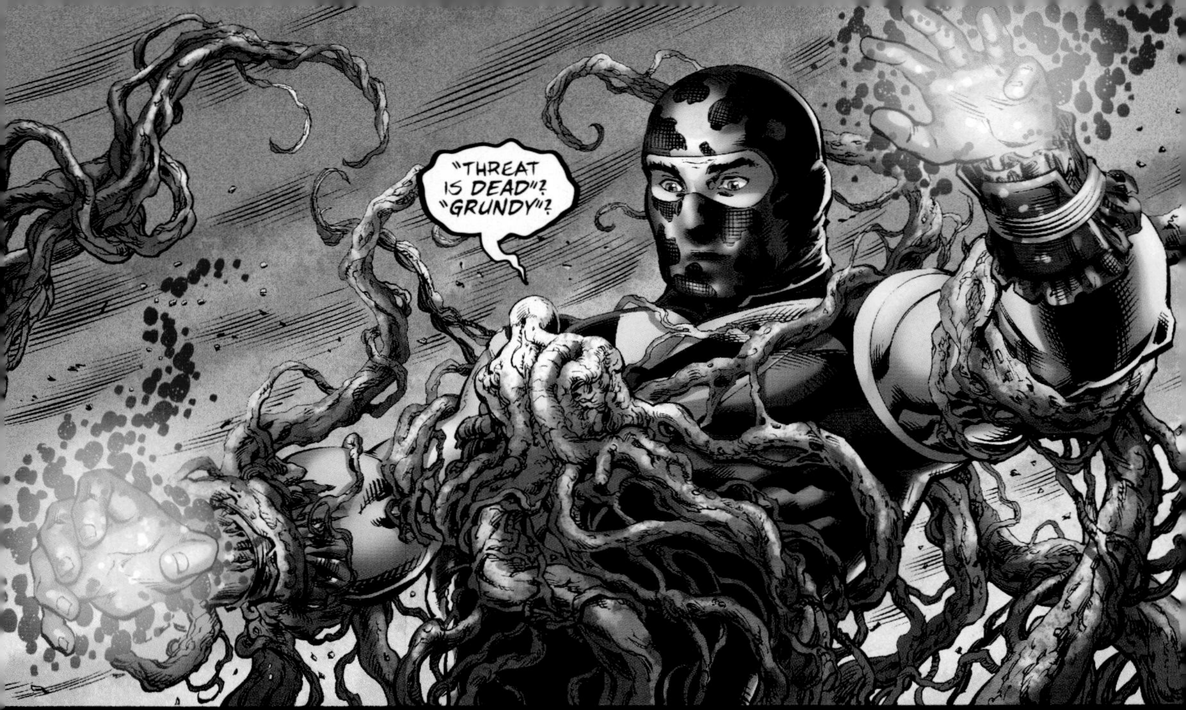
"THREAT IS DEAD"? "GRUNDY"?
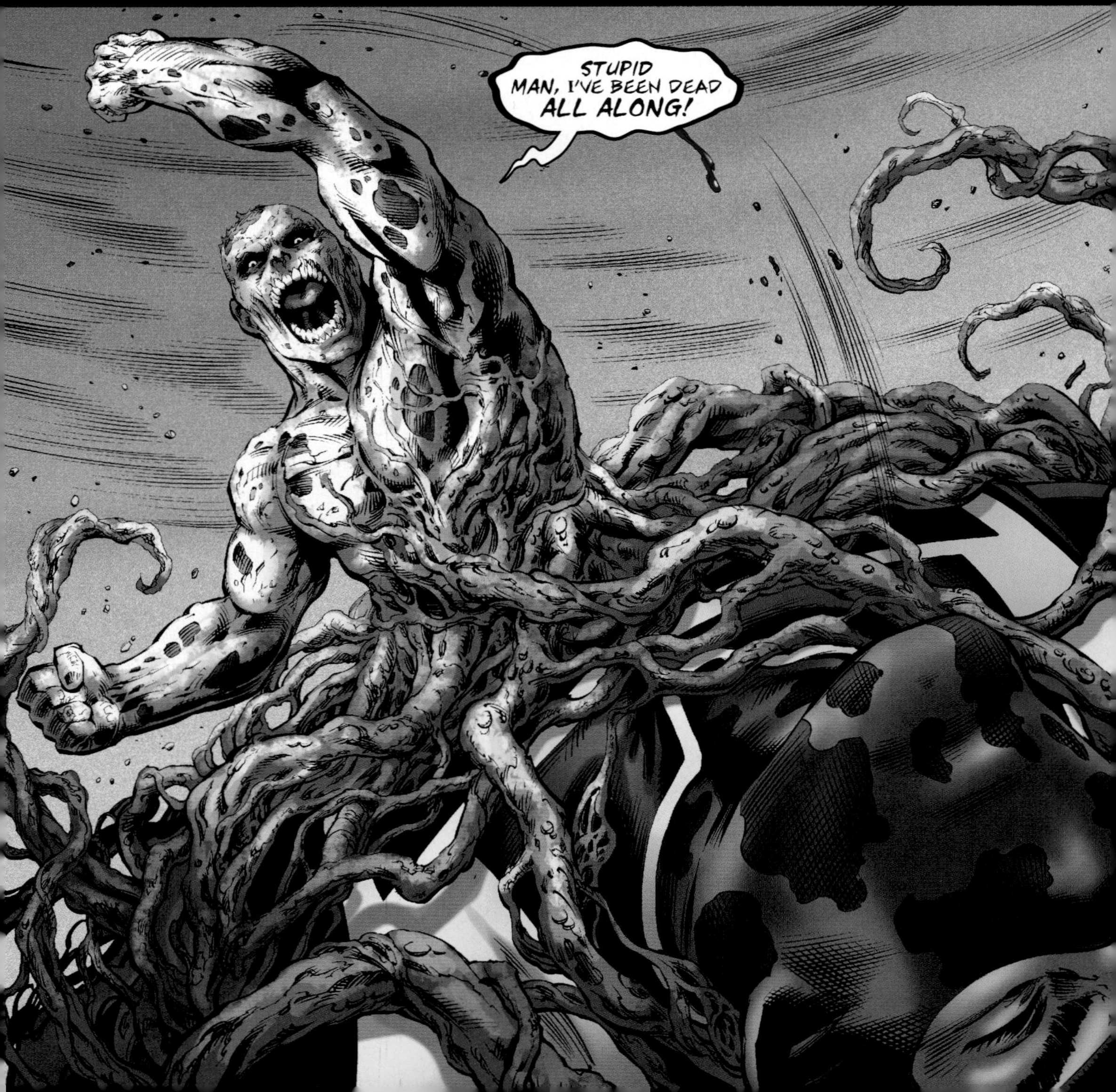
STUPID MAN, I'VE BEEN DEAD ALL ALONG!

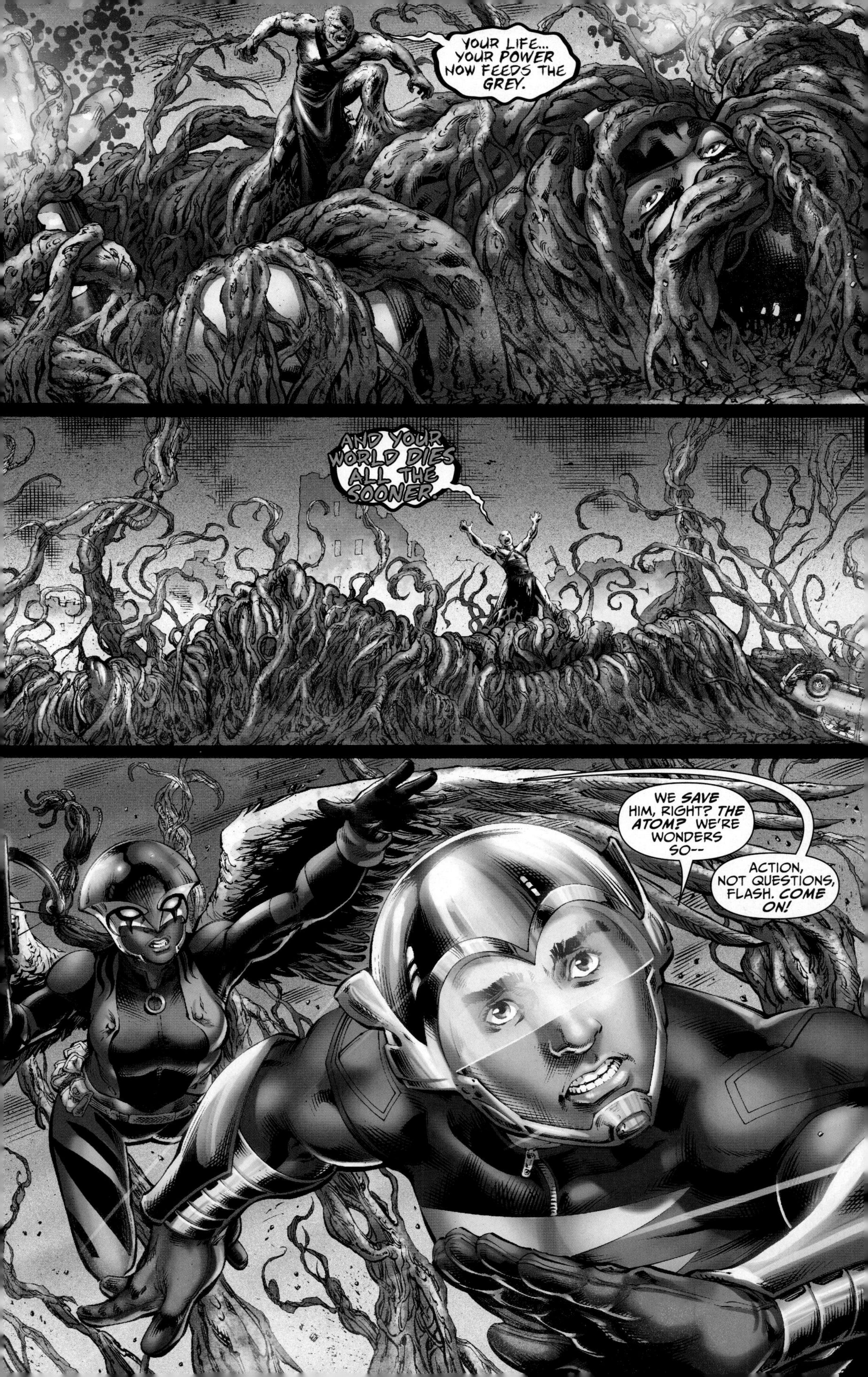
YOUR LIFE... YOUR POWER NOW FEEDS THE GREY.
AND YOUR WORLD DIES ALL THE SOONER.
WE SAVE HIM, RIGHT? THE ATOM? WE'RE WONDERS SO--
ACTION, NOT QUESTIONS, FLASH. COME ON!

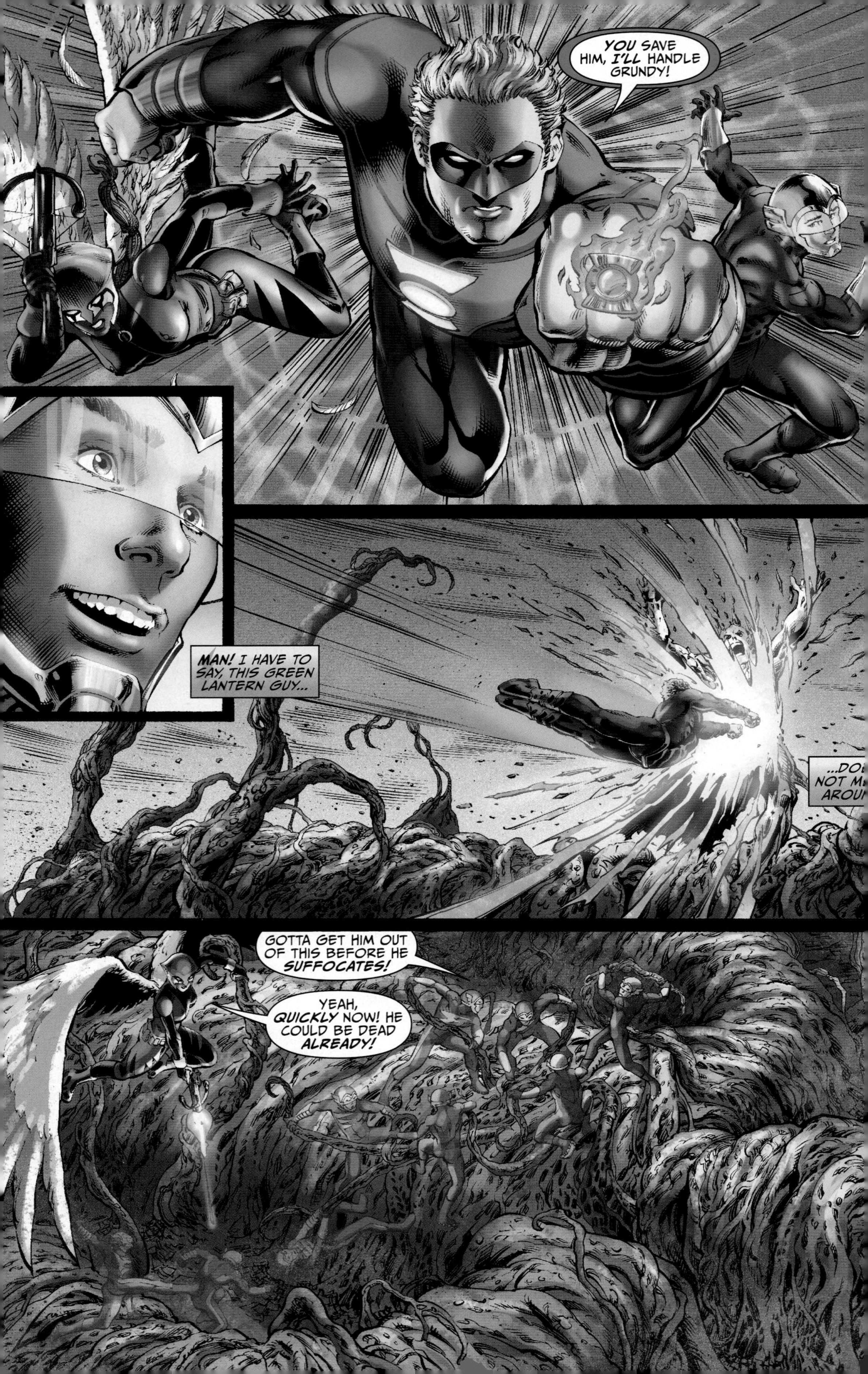
YOU SAVE HIM, I'LL HANDLE GRUNDY!
MAN! I HAVE TO SAY, THIS GREEN LANTERN GUY...
GOTTA GET HIM OUT OF THIS BEFORE HE SUFFOCATES!
YEAH, QUICKLY NOW! HE COULD BE DEAD ALREADY!

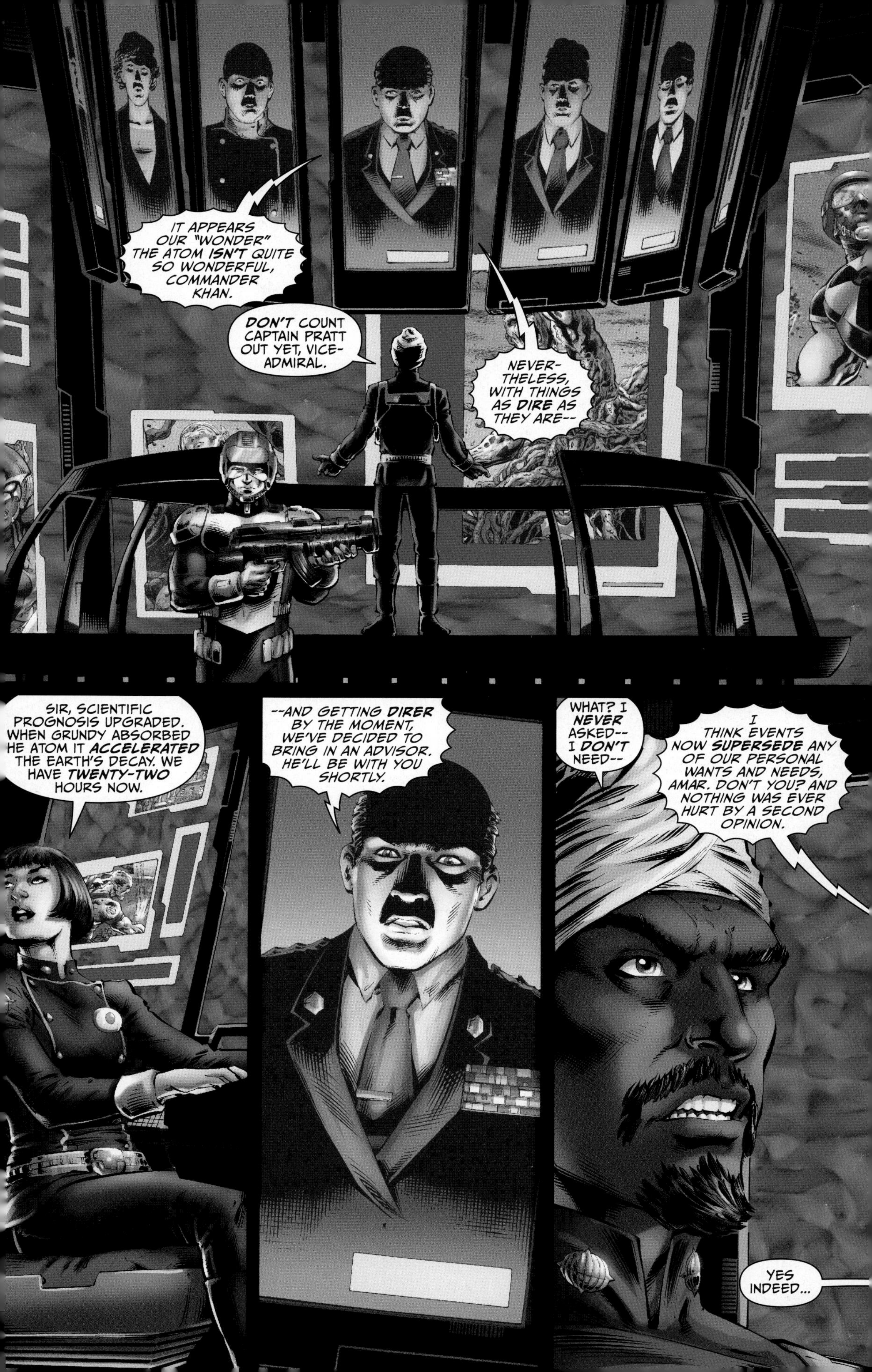
IT APPEARS OUR "WONDER" THE ATOM ISN'T QUITE SO WONDERFUL, COMMANDER KHAN.
DON'T COUNT CAPTAIN PRATT OUT YET, VICE-ADMIRAL.
NEVER-THELESS, WITH THINGS AS DIRE AS THEY ARE--
SIR, SCIENTIFIC PROGNOSIS UPGRADED. WHEN GRUNDY ABSORBED HE ATOM IT ACCELERATED THE EARTH'S DECAY. WE HAVE TWENTY-TWO HOURS NOW.
--AND GETTING DIRER BY THE MOMENT, WE'VE DECIDED TO BRING IN AN ADVISOR. HE'LL BE WITH YOU SHORTLY.
WHAT? I NEVER ASKED-- I DON'T NEED--
I THINK EVENTS NOW SUPERSEDE ANY OF OUR PERSONAL WANTS AND NEEDS, AMAR. DON'T YOU? AND NOTHING WAS EVER HURT BY A SECOND OPINION.
YES INDEED...

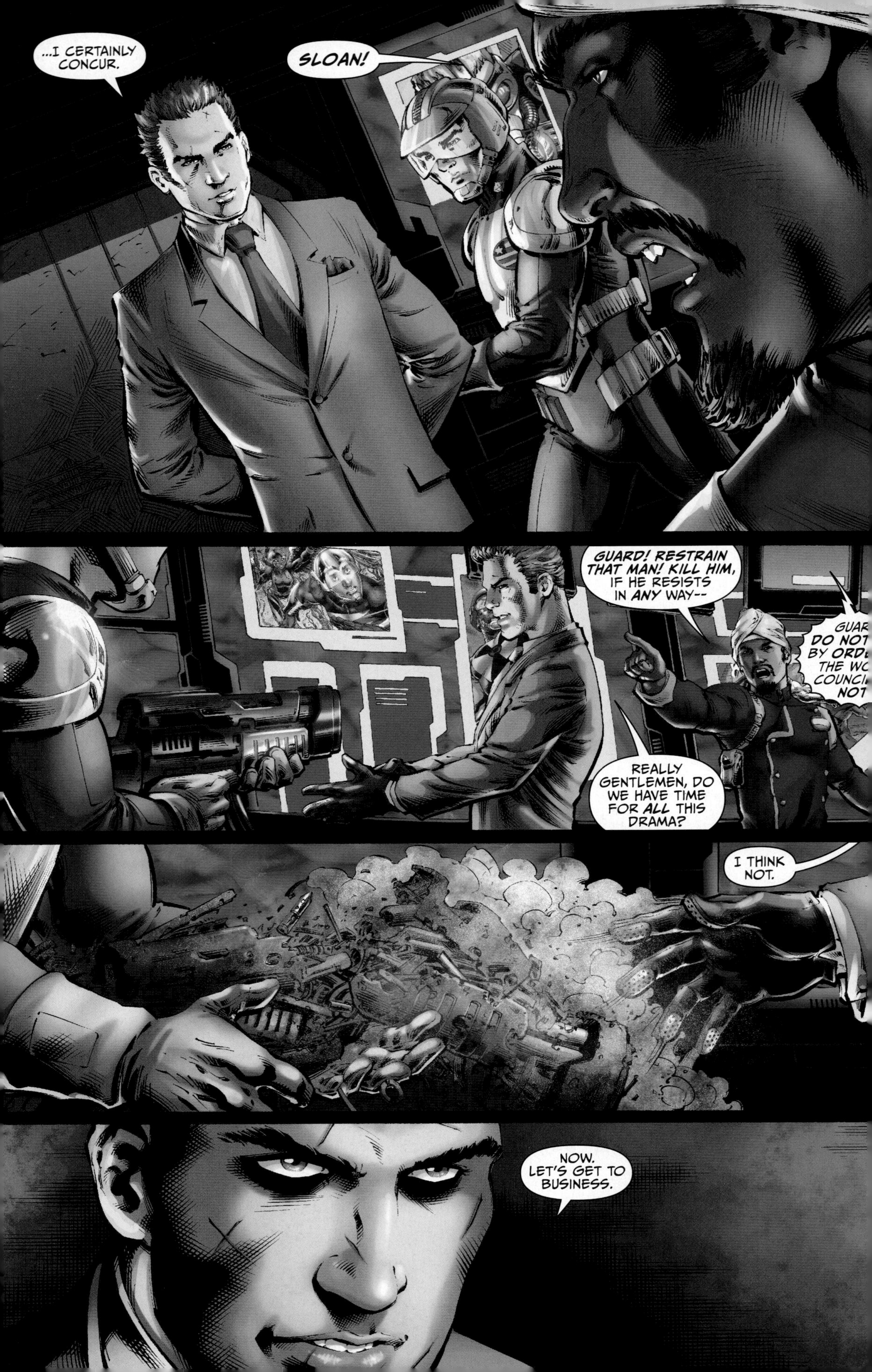
...I CERTAINLY CONCUR.
SLOAN!
GUARD! RESTRAIN THAT MAN! KILL HIM, IF HE RESISTS IN ANY WAY--
REALLY GENTLEMEN, DO WE HAVE TIME FOR ALL THIS DRAMA?
I THINK NOT.
NOW. LET'S GET TO BUSINESS.

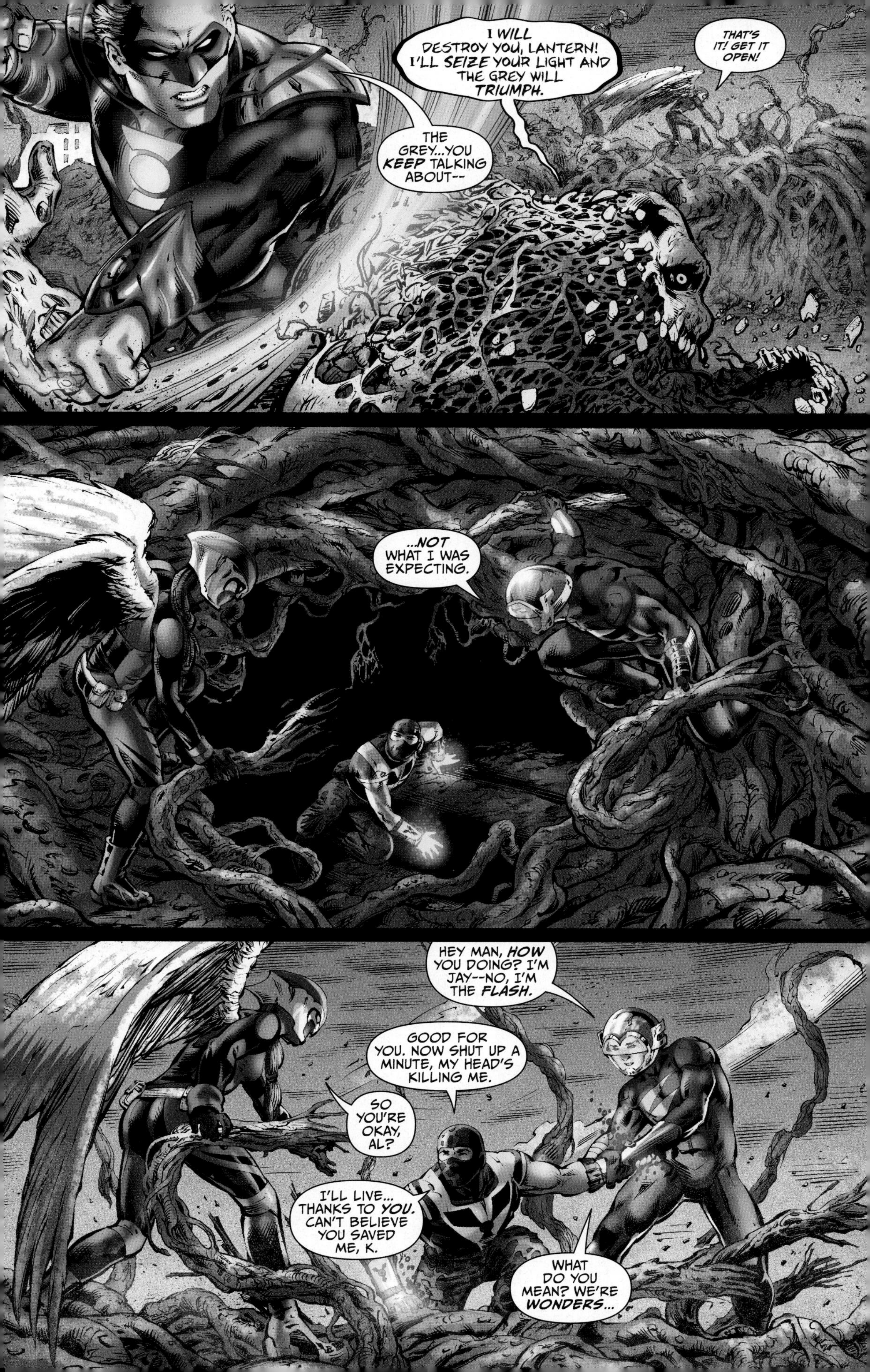
I WILL DESTROY YOU, LANTERN! I'LL SEIZE YOUR LIGHT AND THE GREY WILL TRIUMPH.
THE GREY...YOU KEEP TALKING ABOUT--
THAT'S IT! GET IT OPEN!
...NOT WHAT I WAS EXPECTING.
HEY MAN, HOW YOU DOING? I'M JAY--NO, I'M THE FLASH.
GOOD FOR YOU. NOW SHUT UP A MINUTE, MY HEAD'S KILLING ME.
SO YOU'RE OKAY, AL?
I'LL LIVE... THANKS TO YOU. CAN'T BELIEVE YOU SAVED ME, K.
WHAT DO YOU MEAN? WE'RE WONDERS...

...THAT MAKES US *HEROES,* RIGHT? WE DO THE *RIGHT* THING.

OH BROTHER, WHERE DID THEY FIND *YOU?*

EVERYONE *LISTEN!* I SMASHED GRUNDY APART AGAIN, BUT HE'LL *RE-FORM* IN MOMENTS LIKE HE *ALWAYS* DOES.

THING IS, *THIS* TIME I KNOW WHAT I HAVE TO DO...THINK I DO ANYWAY. IT'S THE *ONLY* CHANCE TO END THIS, BUT IT INVOLVES ALL OF YOU AS WELL, SO LISTEN--

OH, YOU'RE GIVING *ME* ORDERS? *NO.* HAWKGIRL'S A WANTED FUGITIVE... AND YOU AND *SPEEDY GONZALES* ARE *WHAT?* VIGILANTES?

I'M THE *ONLY* ONE HERE WITH *ANY* AUTHORITY, AND I KNOCKED YOU RIGHT ACROSS TOWN, SO DON'T--

YES, LITTLE BIG M AND *WE* CAN GO AG IF YOU WANT BUT N *ISN'T* THE TIME. WE TO WORK *TOGETH* ON THIS.

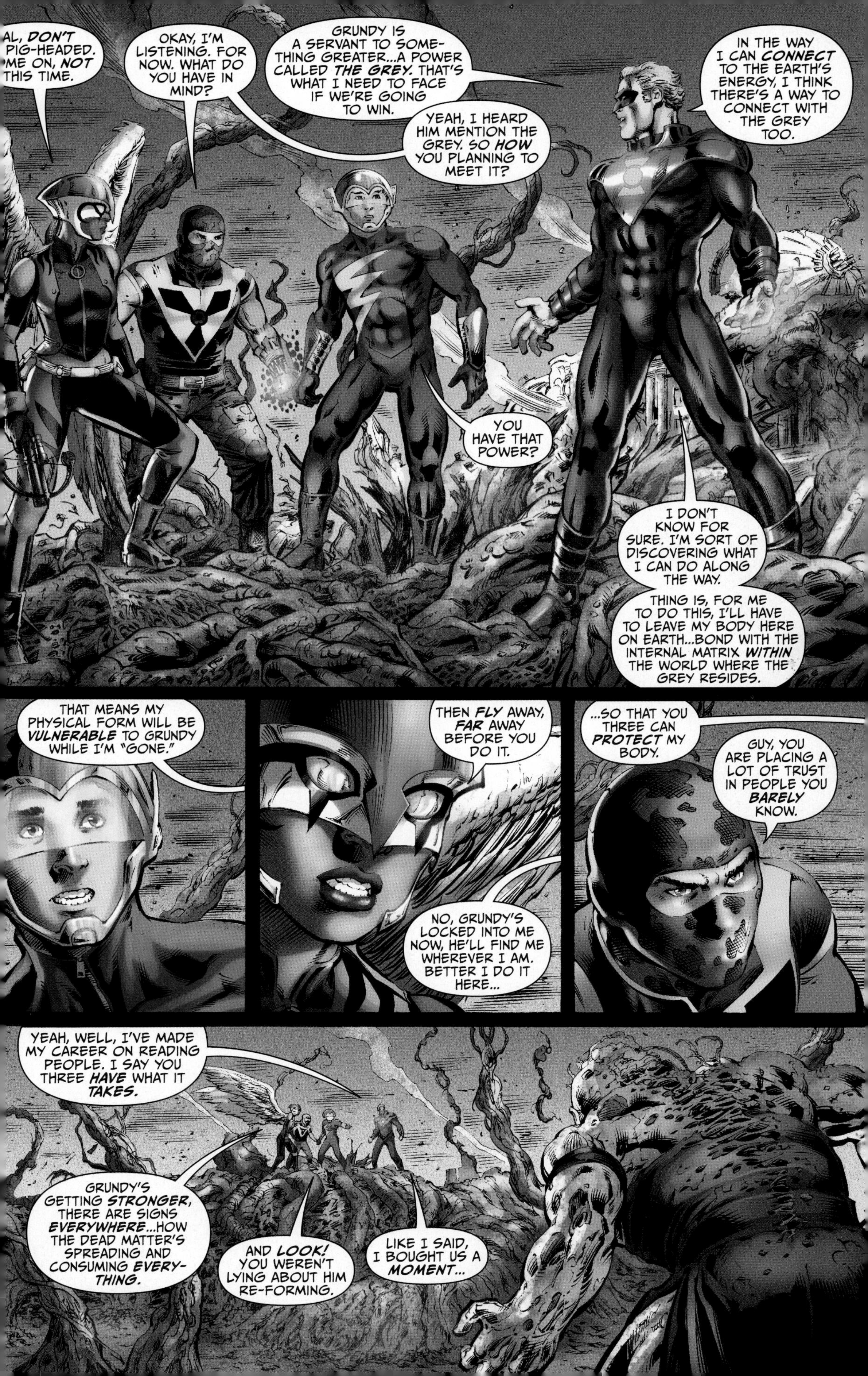
AL, DON'T PIG-HEADED. ME ON, NOT THIS TIME.
OKAY, I'M LISTENING. FOR NOW. WHAT DO YOU HAVE IN MIND?
GRUNDY IS A SERVANT TO SOMETHING GREATER...A POWER CALLED THE GREY. THAT'S WHAT I NEED TO FACE IF WE'RE GOING TO WIN.
YEAH, I HEARD HIM MENTION THE GREY. SO HOW YOU PLANNING TO MEET IT?
IN THE WAY I CAN CONNECT TO THE EARTH'S ENERGY, I THINK THERE'S A WAY TO CONNECT WITH THE GREY TOO.
YOU HAVE THAT POWER?
I DON'T KNOW FOR SURE. I'M SORT OF DISCOVERING WHAT I CAN DO ALONG THE WAY.
THING IS, FOR ME TO DO THIS, I'LL HAVE TO LEAVE MY BODY HERE ON EARTH...BOND WITH THE INTERNAL MATRIX WITHIN THE WORLD WHERE THE GREY RESIDES.
THAT MEANS MY PHYSICAL FORM WILL BE VULNERABLE TO GRUNDY WHILE I'M "GONE."
THEN FLY AWAY, FAR AWAY BEFORE YOU DO IT.
NO, GRUNDY'S LOCKED INTO ME NOW, HE'LL FIND ME WHEREVER I AM. BETTER I DO IT HERE...
...SO THAT YOU THREE CAN PROTECT MY BODY.
GUY, YOU ARE PLACING A LOT OF TRUST IN PEOPLE YOU BARELY KNOW.
YEAH, WELL, I'VE MADE MY CAREER ON READING PEOPLE. I SAY YOU THREE HAVE WHAT IT TAKES.
GRUNDY'S GETTING STRONGER, THERE ARE SIGNS EVERYWHERE...HOW THE DEAD MATTER'S SPREADING AND CONSUMING EVERYTHING.
AND LOOK! YOU WEREN'T LYING ABOUT HIM RE-FORMING.
LIKE I SAID, I BOUGHT US A MOMENT...

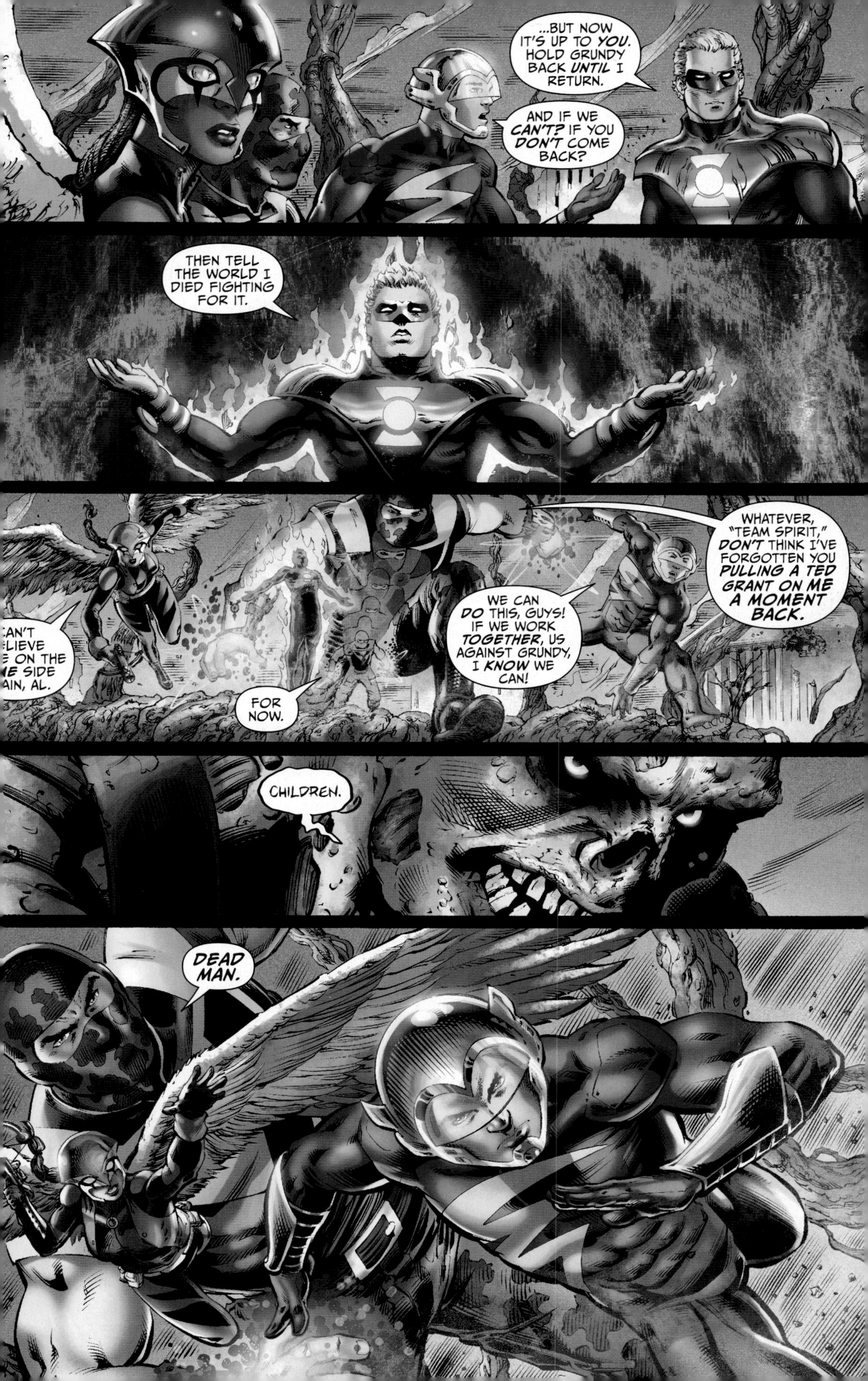

...BUT NOW IT'S UP TO YOU. HOLD GRUNDY BACK UNTIL I RETURN.
AND IF WE CAN'T? IF YOU DON'T COME BACK?
THEN TELL THE WORLD I DIED FIGHTING FOR IT.
WHATEVER, "TEAM SPIRIT," DON'T THINK I'VE FORGOTTEN YOU PULLING A TED GRANT ON ME A MOMENT BACK.
WE CAN DO THIS, GUYS! IF WE WORK TOGETHER, US AGAINST GRUNDY, I KNOW WE CAN!
FOR NOW.
CHILDREN.
DEAD MAN.

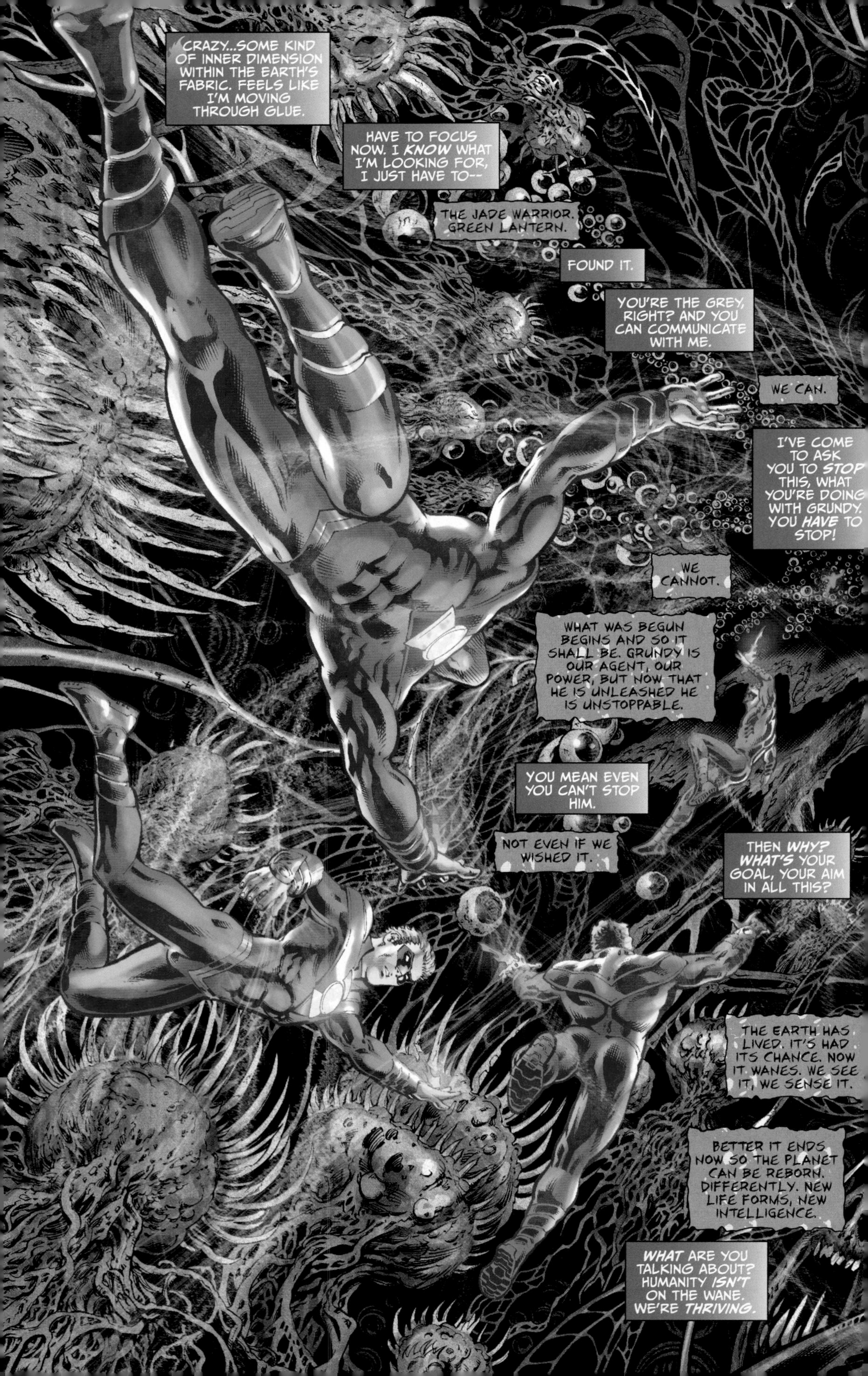
CRAZY...SOME KIND OF INNER DIMENSION WITHIN THE EARTH'S FABRIC. FEELS LIKE I'M MOVING THROUGH GLUE.
HAVE TO FOCUS NOW. I KNOW WHAT I'M LOOKING FOR, I JUST HAVE TO--
THE JADE WARRIOR. GREEN LANTERN.
FOUND IT.
YOU'RE THE GREY, RIGHT? AND YOU CAN COMMUNICATE WITH ME.
WE CAN.
I'VE COME TO ASK YOU TO STOP THIS, WHAT YOU'RE DOING WITH GRUNDY. YOU HAVE TO STOP!
WE CANNOT.
WHAT WAS BEGUN BEGINS AND SO IT SHALL BE. GRUNDY IS OUR AGENT, OUR POWER, BUT NOW THAT HE IS UNLEASHED HE IS UNSTOPPABLE.
YOU MEAN EVEN YOU CAN'T STOP HIM.
NOT EVEN IF WE WISHED IT.
THEN WHY? WHAT'S YOUR GOAL, YOUR AIM IN ALL THIS?
THE EARTH HAS LIVED. IT'S HAD ITS CHANCE. NOW IT WANES. WE SEE IT, WE SENSE IT.
BETTER IT ENDS NOW SO THE PLANET CAN BE REBORN. DIFFERENTLY. NEW LIFE FORMS, NEW INTELLIGENCE.
WHAT ARE YOU TALKING ABOUT? HUMANITY ISN'T ON THE WANE. WE'RE THRIVING.

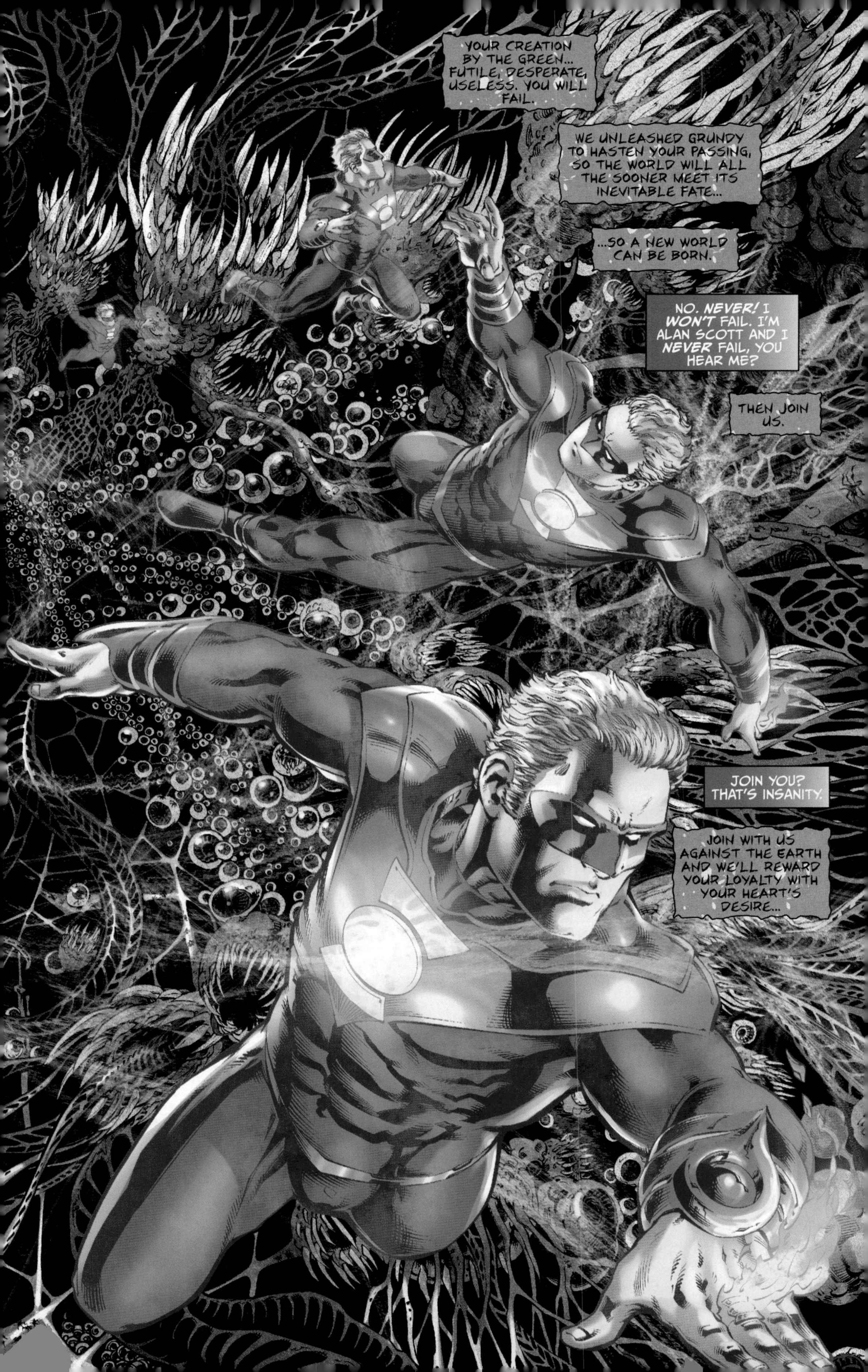
YOUR CREATION BY THE GREEN... FUTILE, DESPERATE, USELESS. YOU WILL FAIL.
WE UNLEASHED GRUNDY TO HASTEN YOUR PASSING, SO THE WORLD WILL ALL THE SOONER MEET ITS INEVITABLE FATE...
...SO A NEW WORLD CAN BE BORN.
NO. NEVER! I WON'T FAIL. I'M ALAN SCOTT AND I NEVER FAIL, YOU HEAR ME?
THEN JOIN US.
JOIN YOU? THAT'S INSANITY.
JOIN WITH US AGAINST THE EARTH AND WE'LL REWARD YOUR LOYALTY WITH YOUR HEART'S DESIRE...

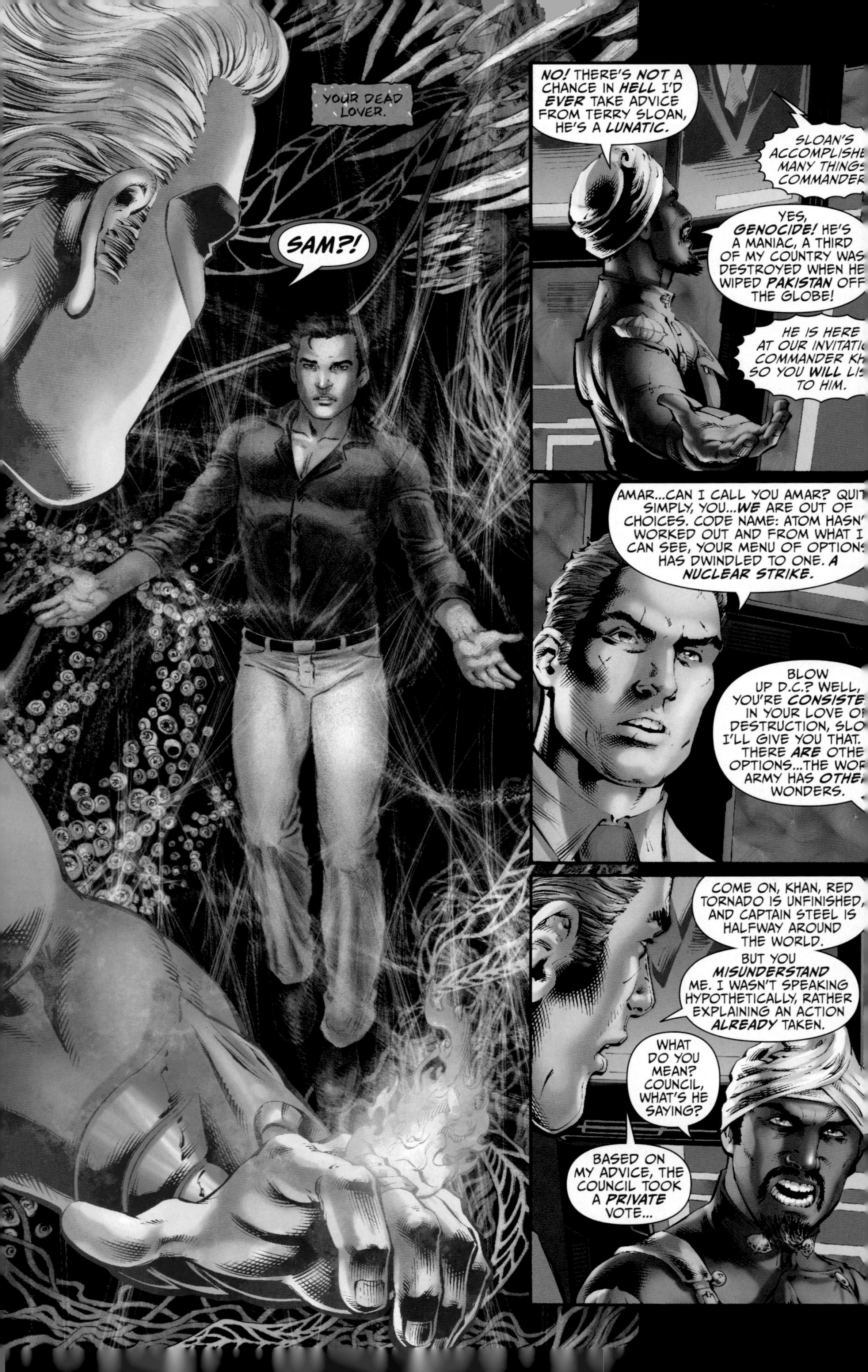
YOUR DEAD LOVER.
SAM?!
NO! THERE'S NOT A CHANCE IN HELL I'D EVER TAKE ADVICE FROM TERRY SLOAN, HE'S A LUNATIC.
SLOAN'S ACCOMPLISHE MANY THINGS COMMANDER
YES, GENOCIDE! HE'S A MANIAC, A THIRD OF MY COUNTRY WAS DESTROYED WHEN HE WIPED PAKISTAN OFF THE GLOBE!
HE IS HERE AT OUR INVITATI COMMANDER KH SO YOU WILL LIS TO HIM.
AMAR...CAN I CALL YOU AMAR? QUIT SIMPLY, YOU...WE ARE OUT OF CHOICES. CODE NAME: ATOM HASN' WORKED OUT AND FROM WHAT I CAN SEE, YOUR MENU OF OPTION HAS DWINDLED TO ONE. A NUCLEAR STRIKE.
BLOW UP D.C.? WELL, YOU'RE CONSISTE IN YOUR LOVE O DESTRUCTION, SLO I'LL GIVE YOU THAT. THERE ARE OTHE OPTIONS...THE WOR ARMY HAS OTHE WONDERS.
COME ON, KHAN, RED TORNADO IS UNFINISHED, AND CAPTAIN STEEL IS HALFWAY AROUND THE WORLD.
BUT YOU MISUNDERSTAND ME. I WASN'T SPEAKING HYPOTHETICALLY, RATHER EXPLAINING AN ACTION ALREADY TAKEN.
WHAT DO YOU MEAN? COUNCIL, WHAT'S HE SAYING?
BASED ON MY ADVICE, THE COUNCIL TOOK A PRIVATE VOTE...

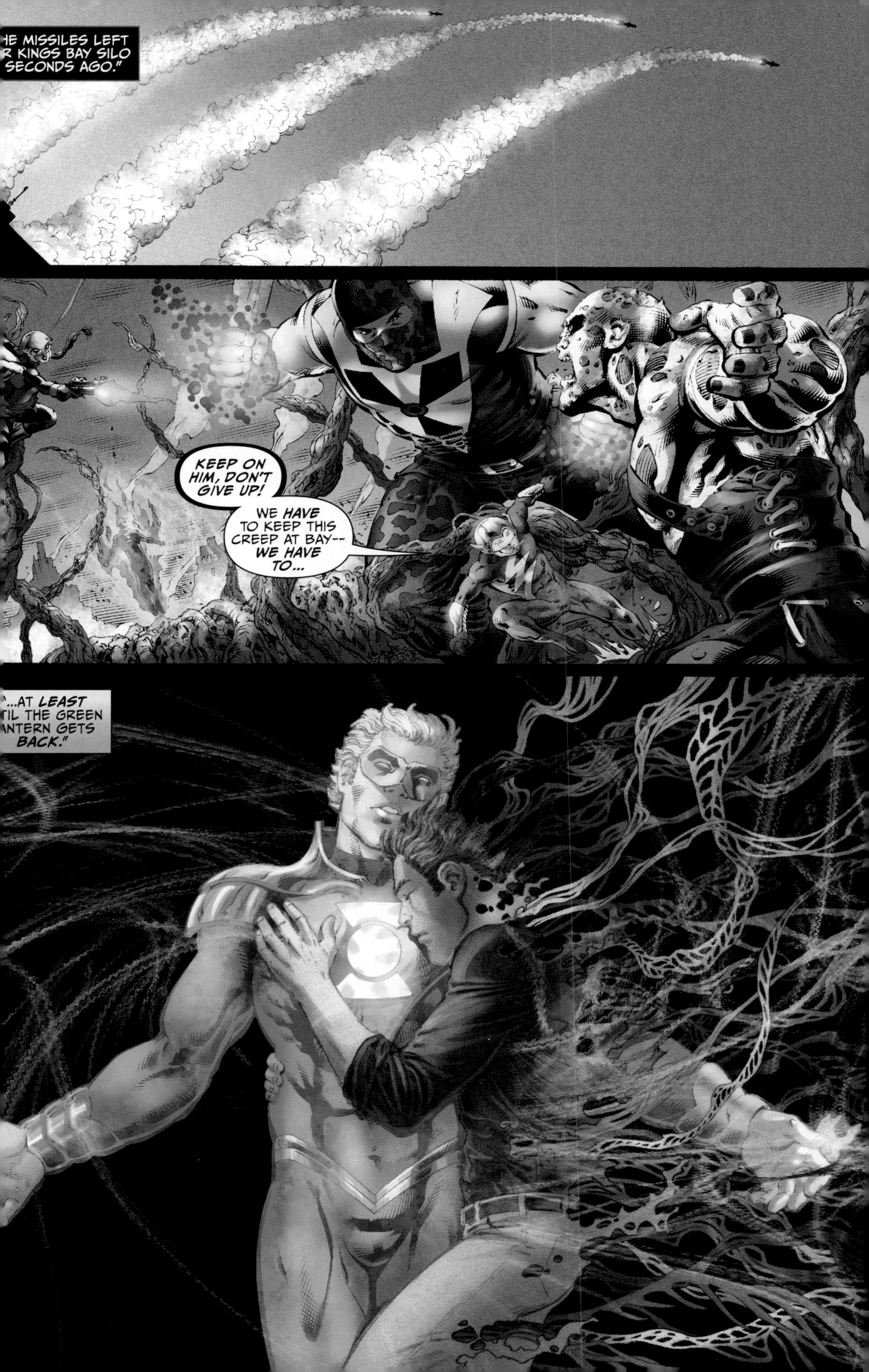

HE MISSILES LEFT R KINGS BAY SILO SECONDS AGO."
KEEP ON HIM, DON'T GIVE UP!
WE HAVE TO KEEP THIS CREEP AT BAY-- WE HAVE TO...
"...AT LEAST TIL THE GREEN ANTERN GETS BACK."

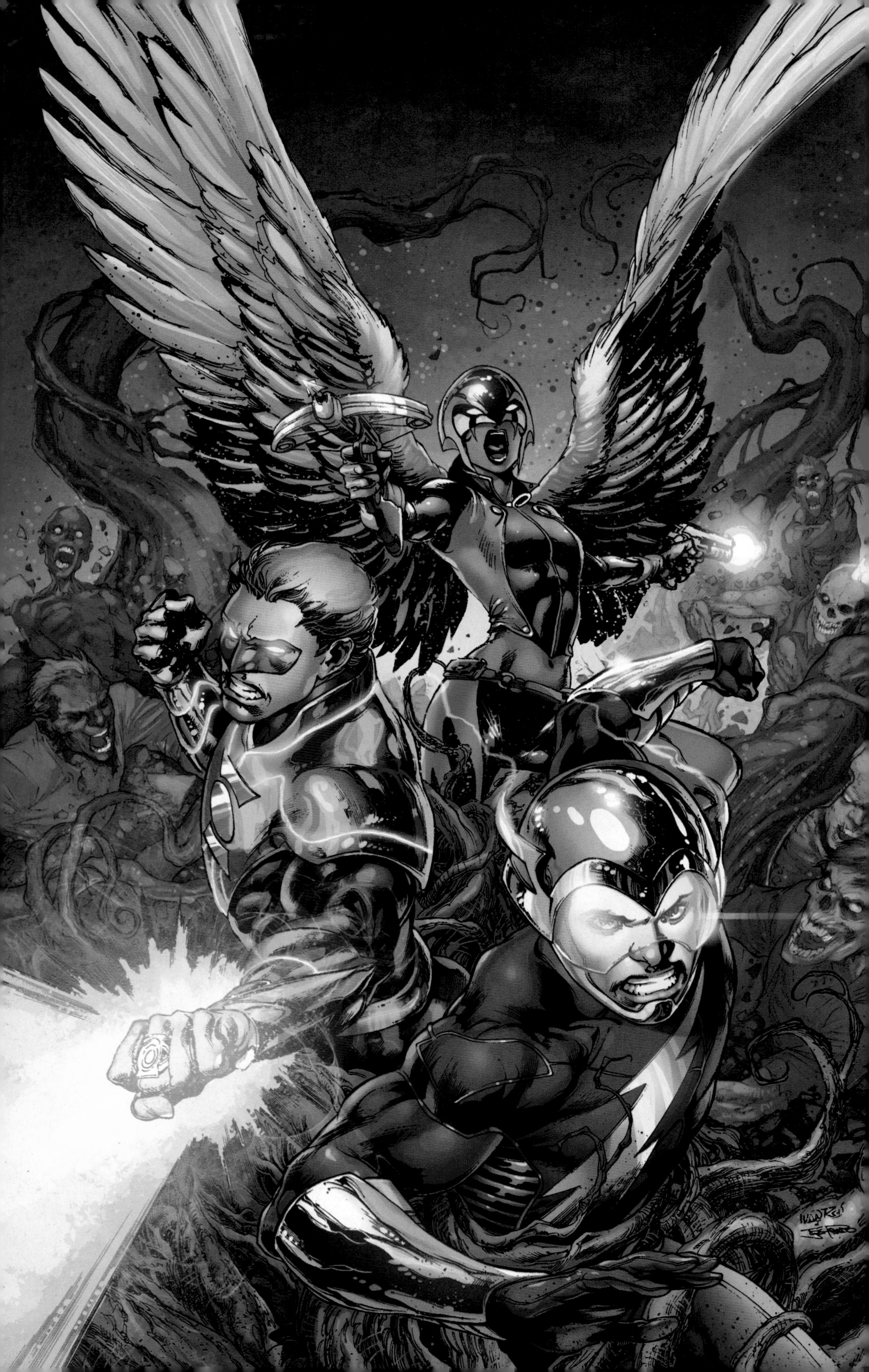

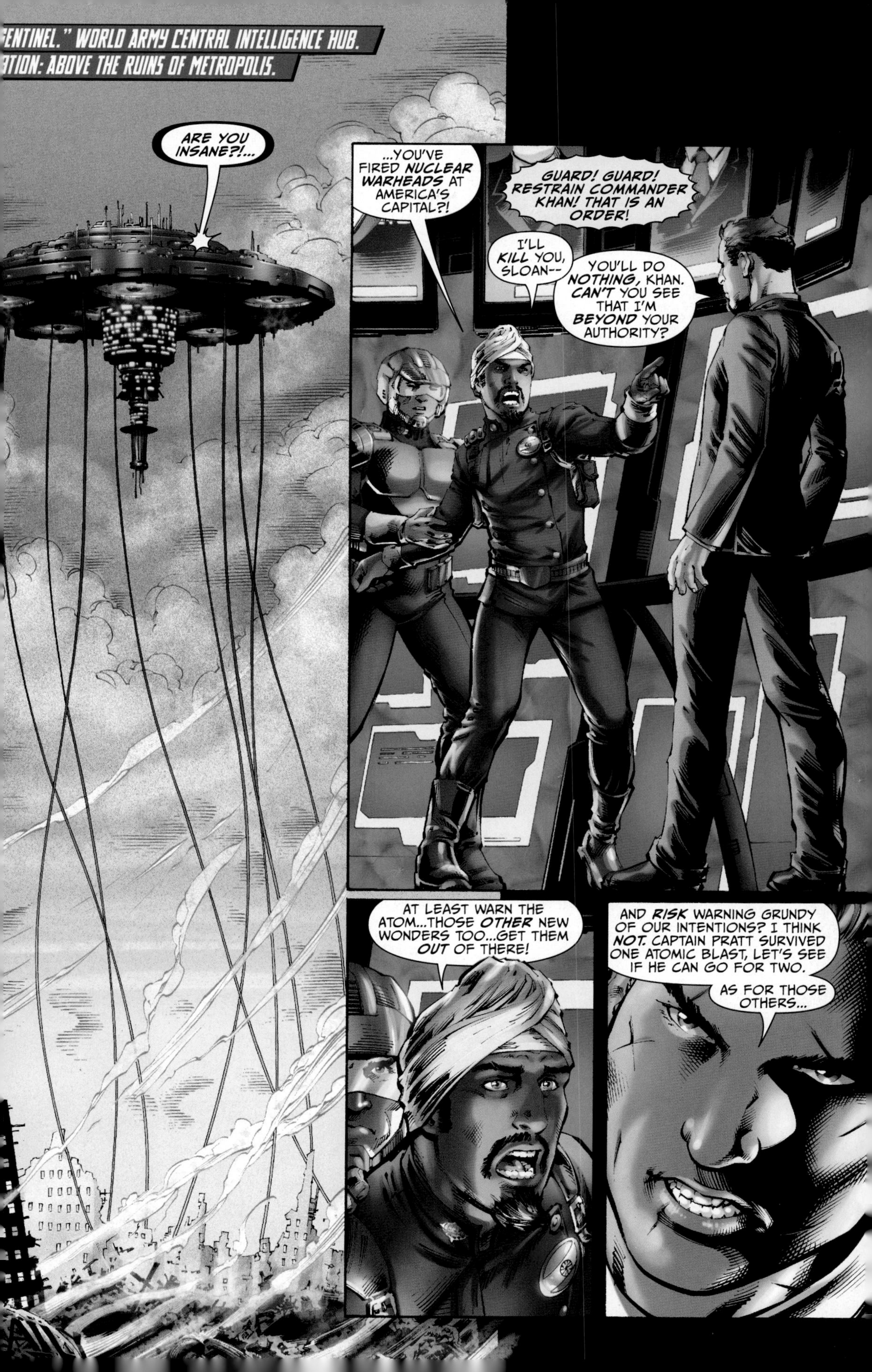

"SENTINEL." WORLD ARMY CENTRAL INTELLIGENCE HUB.
ATION: ABOVE THE RUINS OF METROPOLIS.
ARE YOU INSANE?!...
...YOU'VE FIRED NUCLEAR WARHEADS AT AMERICA'S CAPITAL?!
GUARD! GUARD! RESTRAIN COMMANDER KHAN! THAT IS AN ORDER!
I'LL KILL YOU, SLOAN--
YOU'LL DO NOTHING, KHAN. CAN'T YOU SEE THAT I'M BEYOND YOUR AUTHORITY?
AT LEAST WARN THE ATOM...THOSE OTHER NEW WONDERS TOO...GET THEM OUT OF THERE!
AND RISK WARNING GRUNDY OF OUR INTENTIONS? I THINK NOT. CAPTAIN PRATT SURVIVED ONE ATOMIC BLAST, LET'S SEE IF HE CAN GO FOR TWO.
AS FOR THOSE OTHERS...

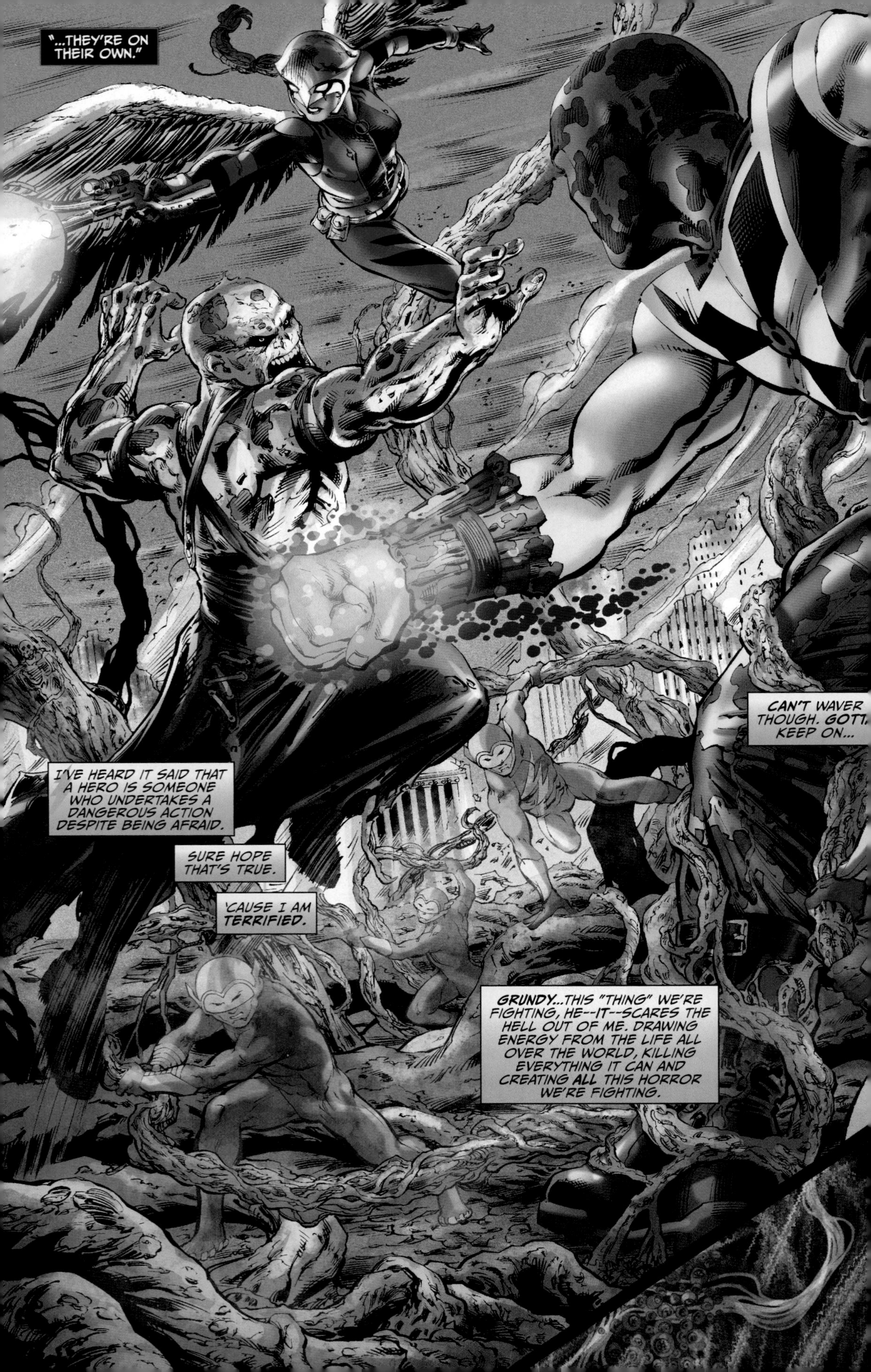
"...THEY'RE ON THEIR OWN."
I'VE HEARD IT SAID THAT A HERO IS SOMEONE WHO UNDERTAKES A DANGEROUS ACTION DESPITE BEING AFRAID.
SURE HOPE THAT'S TRUE.
'CAUSE I AM TERRIFIED.
GRUNDY...THIS "THING" WE'RE FIGHTING, HE--IT--SCARES THE HELL OUT OF ME. DRAWING ENERGY FROM THE LIFE ALL OVER THE WORLD, KILLING EVERYTHING IT CAN AND CREATING ALL THIS HORROR WE'RE FIGHTING.
CAN'T WAVER THOUGH. GOTT KEEP ON...

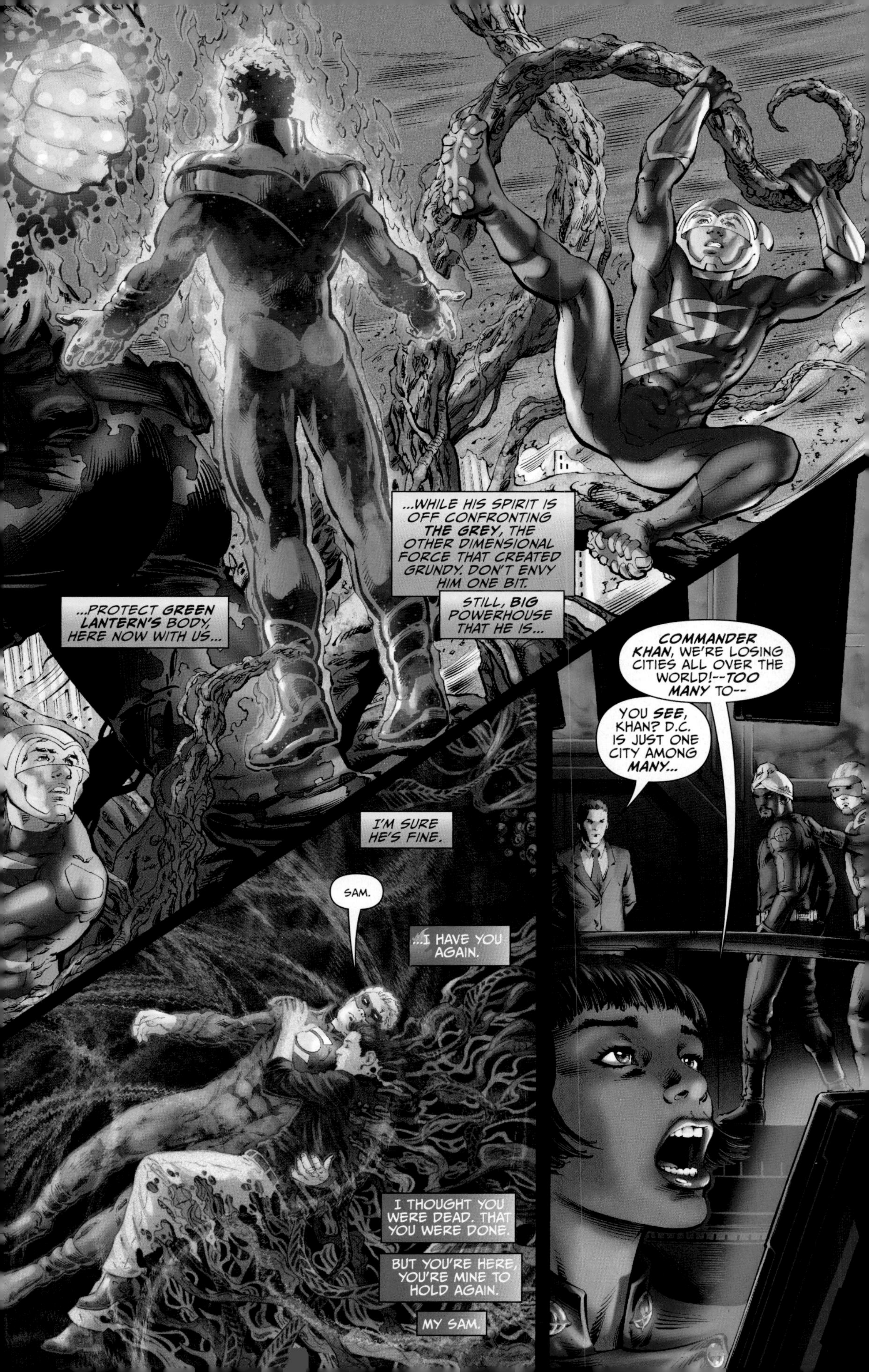
...PROTECT GREEN LANTERN'S BODY, HERE NOW WITH US...
...WHILE HIS SPIRIT IS OFF CONFRONTING THE GREY, THE OTHER DIMENSIONAL FORCE THAT CREATED GRUNDY. DON'T ENVY HIM ONE BIT.
STILL, BIG POWERHOUSE THAT HE IS...
I'M SURE HE'S FINE.
SAM.
...I HAVE YOU AGAIN.
I THOUGHT YOU WERE DEAD. THAT YOU WERE DONE.
BUT YOU'RE HERE, YOU'RE MINE TO HOLD AGAIN.
MY SAM.
COMMANDER KHAN, WE'RE LOSING CITIES ALL OVER THE WORLD!--TOO MANY TO--
YOU SEE, KHAN? D.C. IS JUST ONE CITY AMONG MANY...

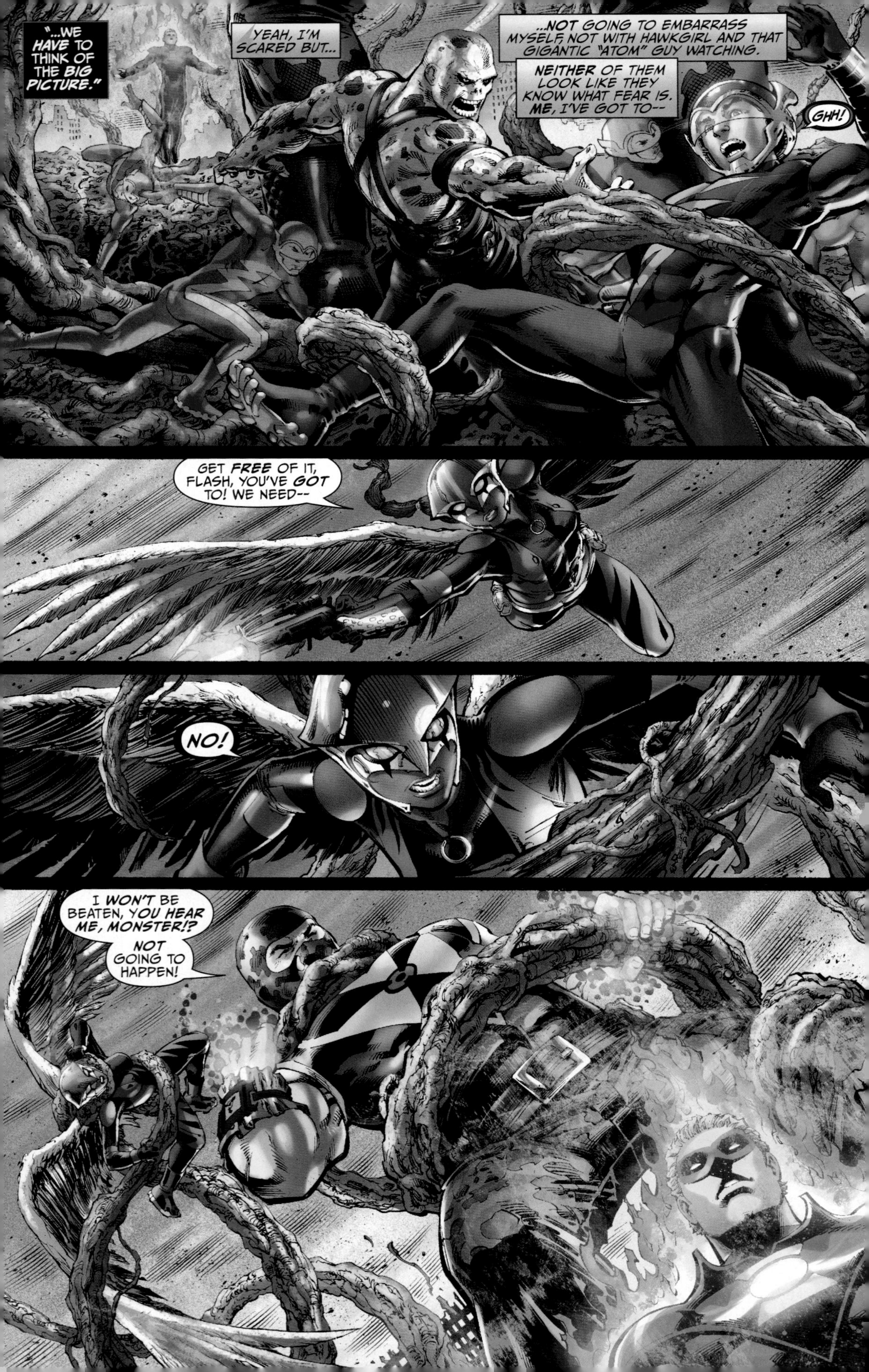
"...WE HAVE TO THINK OF THE BIG PICTURE."
YEAH, I'M SCARED BUT...
...NOT GOING TO EMBARRASS MYSELF, NOT WITH HAWKGIRL AND THAT GIGANTIC "ATOM" GUY WATCHING.
NEITHER OF THEM LOOK LIKE THEY KNOW WHAT FEAR IS. ME, I'VE GOT TO--
GHH!
GET FREE OF IT, FLASH, YOU'VE GOT TO! WE NEED--
NO!
I WON'T BE BEATEN, YOU HEAR ME, MONSTER!? NOT GOING TO HAPPEN!

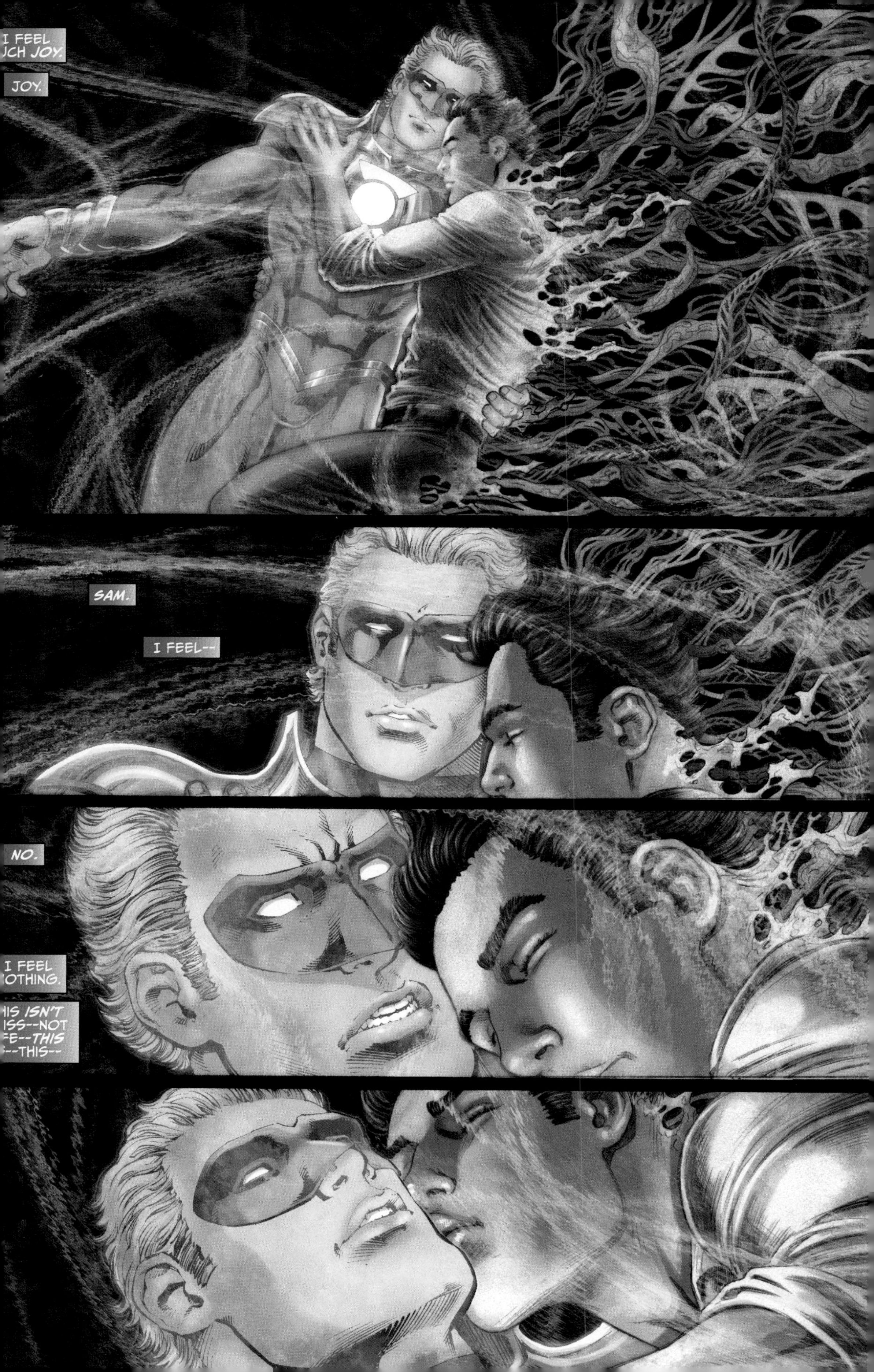
I FEEL
ICH JOY.
JOY.
SAM.
I FEEL--
NO.
I FEEL
OTHING.
HIS ISN'T
ISS--NOT
FE--THIS
--THIS--

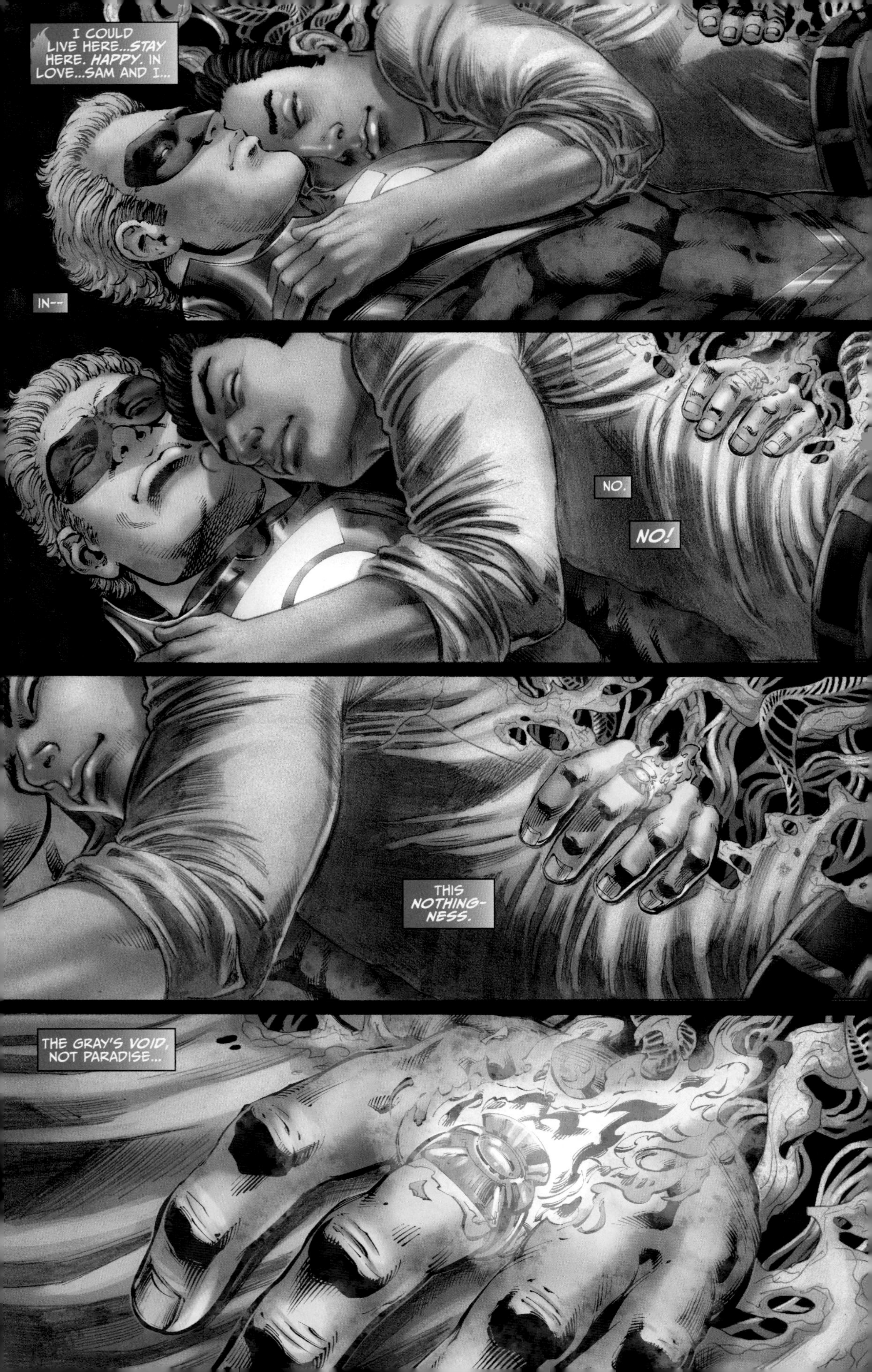
I COULD LIVE HERE...*STAY* HERE. *HAPPY.* IN LOVE...SAM AND I...
IN--
NO.
NO!
THIS *NOTHING-NESS.*
THE GRAY'S *VOID,* NOT PARADISE...

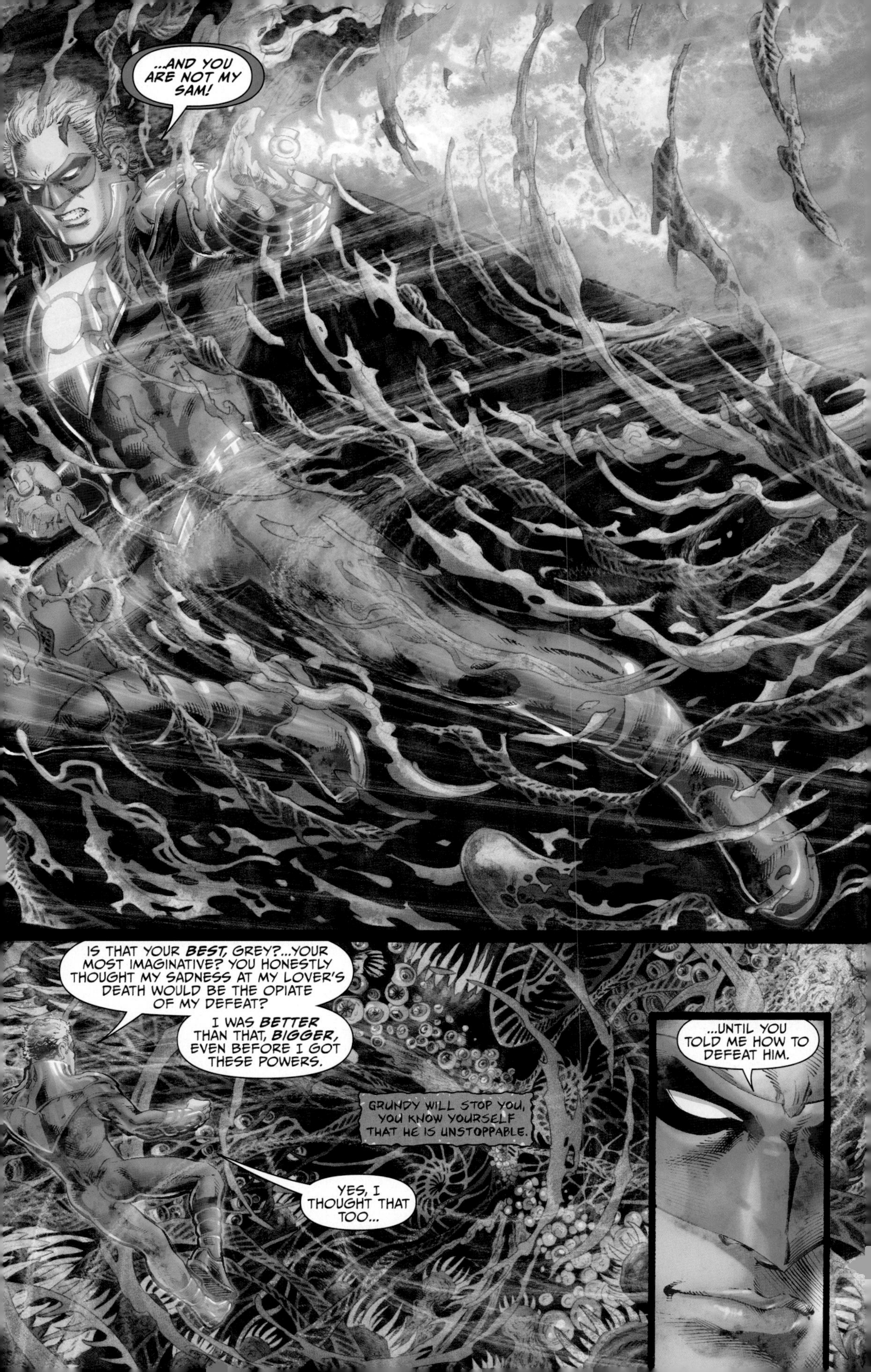
...AND YOU ARE NOT MY SAM!
IS THAT YOUR BEST, GREY?...YOUR MOST IMAGINATIVE? YOU HONESTLY THOUGHT MY SADNESS AT MY LOVER'S DEATH WOULD BE THE OPIATE OF MY DEFEAT?
I WAS BETTER THAN THAT, BIGGER, EVEN BEFORE I GOT THESE POWERS.
GRUNDY WILL STOP YOU, YOU KNOW YOURSELF THAT HE IS UNSTOPPABLE.
YES, I THOUGHT THAT TOO...
...UNTIL YOU TOLD ME HOW TO DEFEAT HIM.

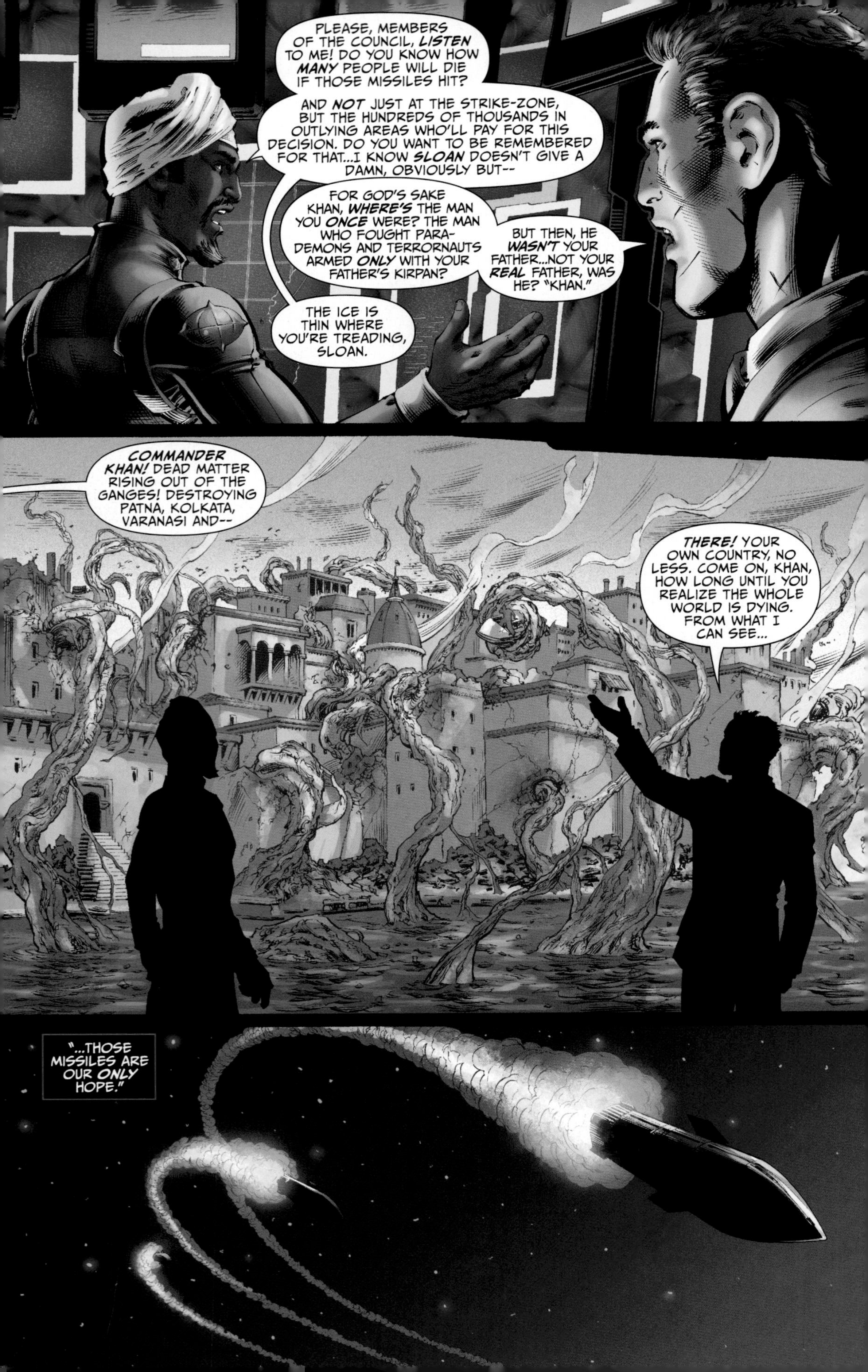
PLEASE, MEMBERS OF THE COUNCIL, LISTEN TO ME! DO YOU KNOW HOW MANY PEOPLE WILL DIE IF THOSE MISSILES HIT?
AND NOT JUST AT THE STRIKE-ZONE, BUT THE HUNDREDS OF THOUSANDS IN OUTLYING AREAS WHO'LL PAY FOR THIS DECISION. DO YOU WANT TO BE REMEMBERED FOR THAT...I KNOW SLOAN DOESN'T GIVE A DAMN, OBVIOUSLY BUT--
FOR GOD'S SAKE KHAN, WHERE'S THE MAN YOU ONCE WERE? THE MAN WHO FOUGHT PARA-DEMONS AND TERRORNAUTS ARMED ONLY WITH YOUR FATHER'S KIRPAN?
BUT THEN, HE WASN'T YOUR FATHER...NOT YOUR REAL FATHER, WAS HE? "KHAN."
THE ICE IS THIN WHERE YOU'RE TREADING, SLOAN.
COMMANDER KHAN! DEAD MATTER RISING OUT OF THE GANGES! DESTROYING PATNA, KOLKATA, VARANASI AND--
THERE! YOUR OWN COUNTRY, NO LESS. COME ON, KHAN, HOW LONG UNTIL YOU REALIZE THE WHOLE WORLD IS DYING. FROM WHAT I CAN SEE...
"...THOSE MISSILES ARE OUR ONLY HOPE."

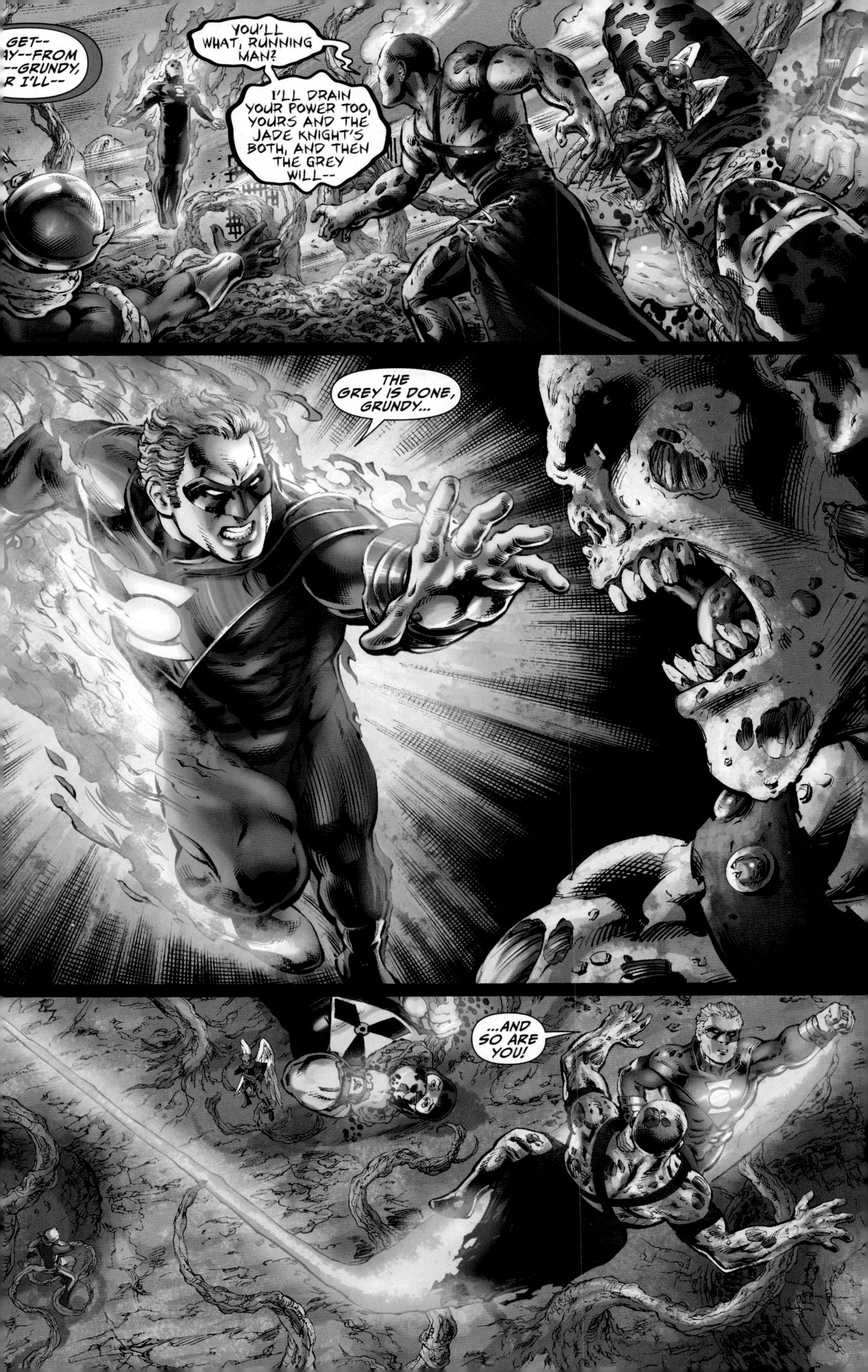
GET--
AY--FROM
--GRUNDY,
R I'LL--
YOU'LL WHAT, RUNNING MAN?
I'LL DRAIN YOUR POWER TOO, YOURS AND THE JADE KNIGHT'S BOTH, AND THEN THE GREY WILL--
THE GREY IS DONE, GRUNDY...
...AND SO ARE YOU!

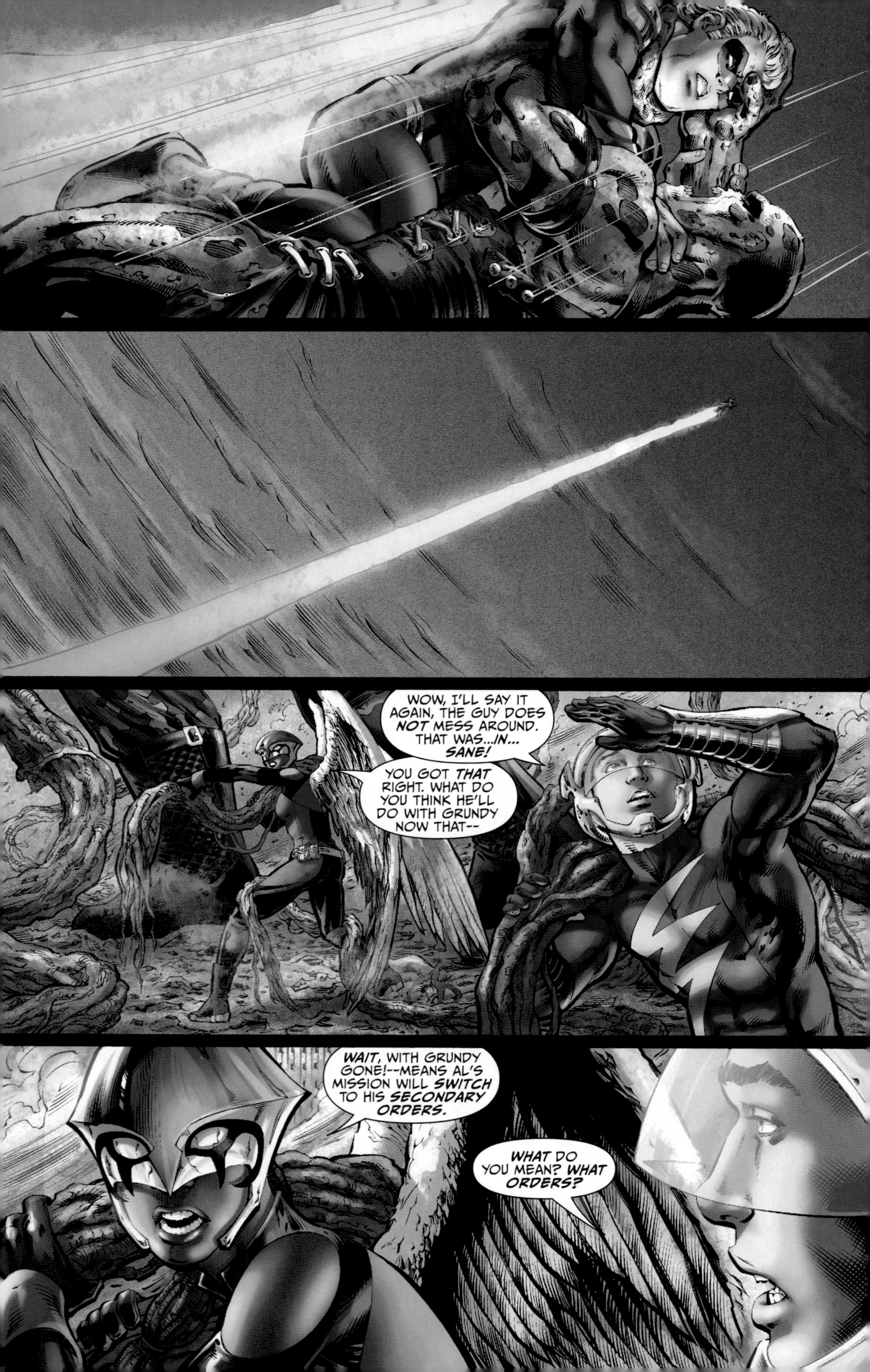
WOW, I'LL SAY IT AGAIN, THE GUY DOES NOT MESS AROUND. THAT WAS...IN... SANE!
YOU GOT THAT RIGHT. WHAT DO YOU THINK HE'LL DO WITH GRUNDY NOW THAT--
WAIT, WITH GRUNDY GONE!--MEANS AL'S MISSION WILL SWITCH TO HIS SECONDARY ORDERS.
WHAT DO YOU MEAN? WHAT ORDERS?

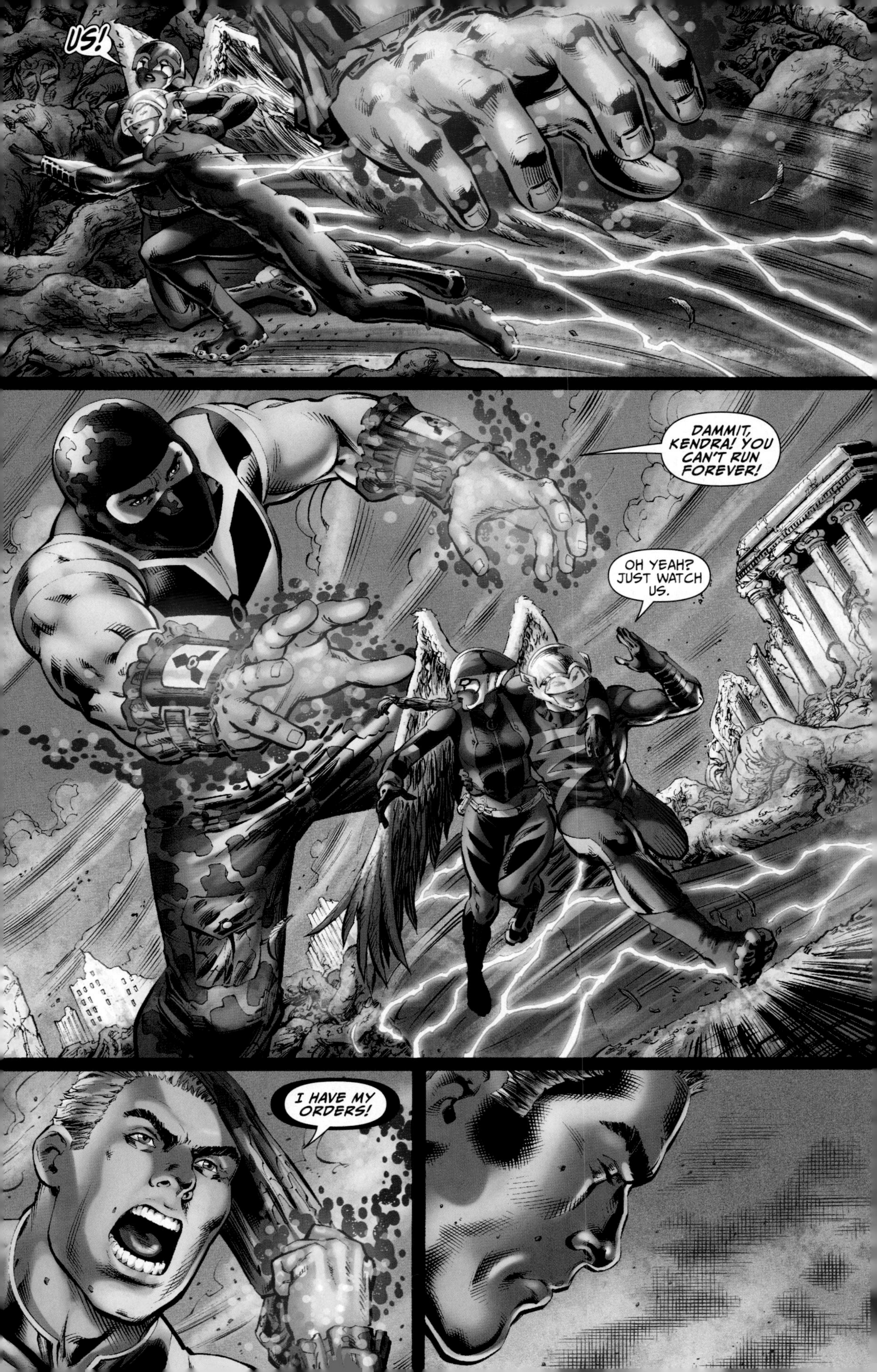
US!
DAMMIT, KENDRA! YOU CAN'T RUN FOREVER!
OH YEAH? JUST WATCH US.
I HAVE MY ORDERS!

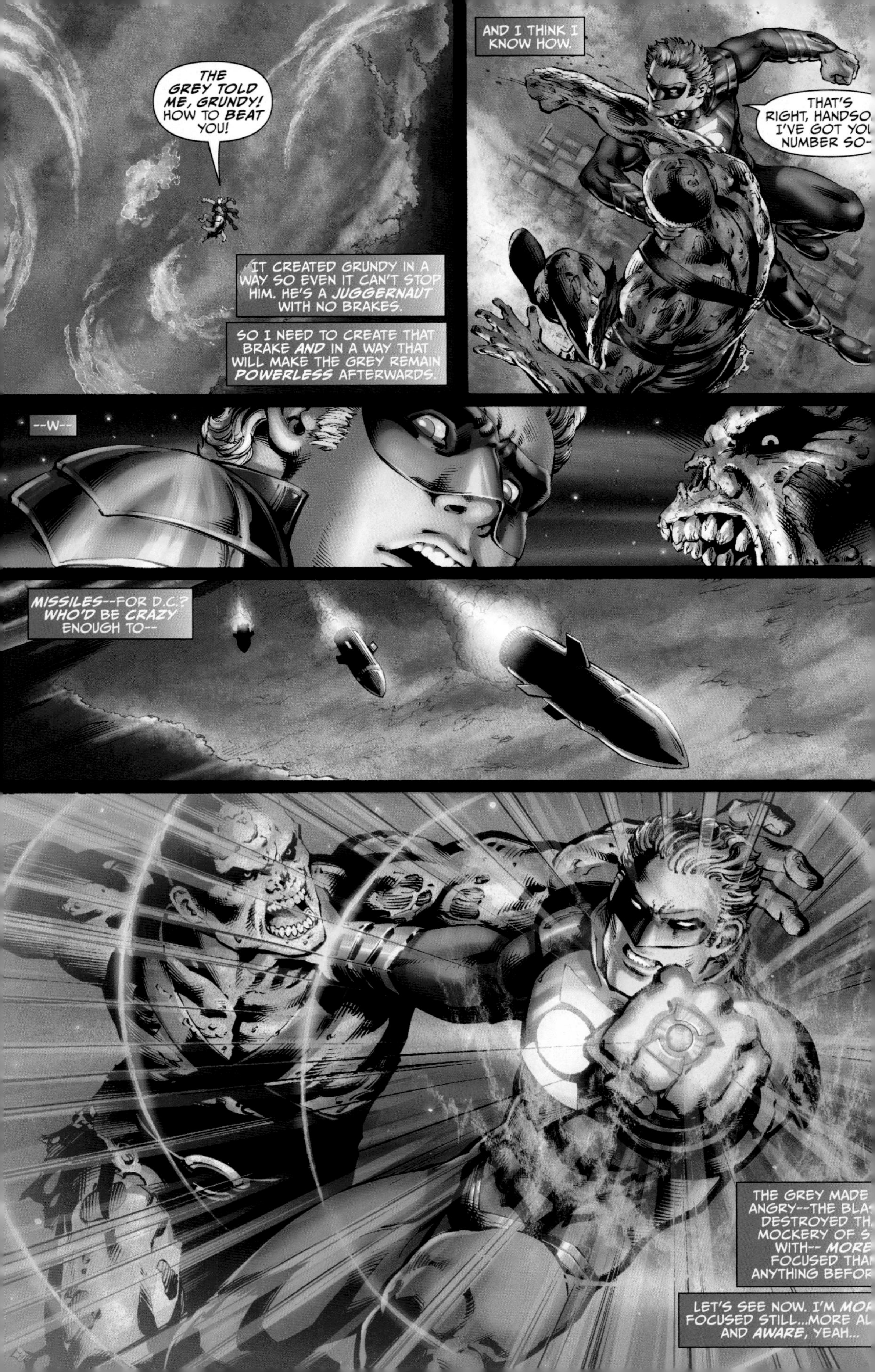
THE GREY TOLD ME, GRUNDY! HOW TO BEAT YOU!
IT CREATED GRUNDY IN A WAY SO EVEN IT CAN'T STOP HIM. HE'S A JUGGERNAUT WITH NO BRAKES.
SO I NEED TO CREATE THAT BRAKE AND IN A WAY THAT WILL MAKE THE GREY REMAIN POWERLESS AFTERWARDS.
AND I THINK I KNOW HOW.
THAT'S RIGHT, HANDSO I'VE GOT YO NUMBER SO-
--W--
MISSILES--FOR D.C.? WHO'D BE CRAZY ENOUGH TO--
THE GREY MADE ANGRY--THE BLA DESTROYED TH MOCKERY OF S WITH-- MORE FOCUSED THA ANYTHING BEFOR
LET'S SEE NOW. I'M MO FOCUSED STILL...MORE AL AND AWARE, YEAH...

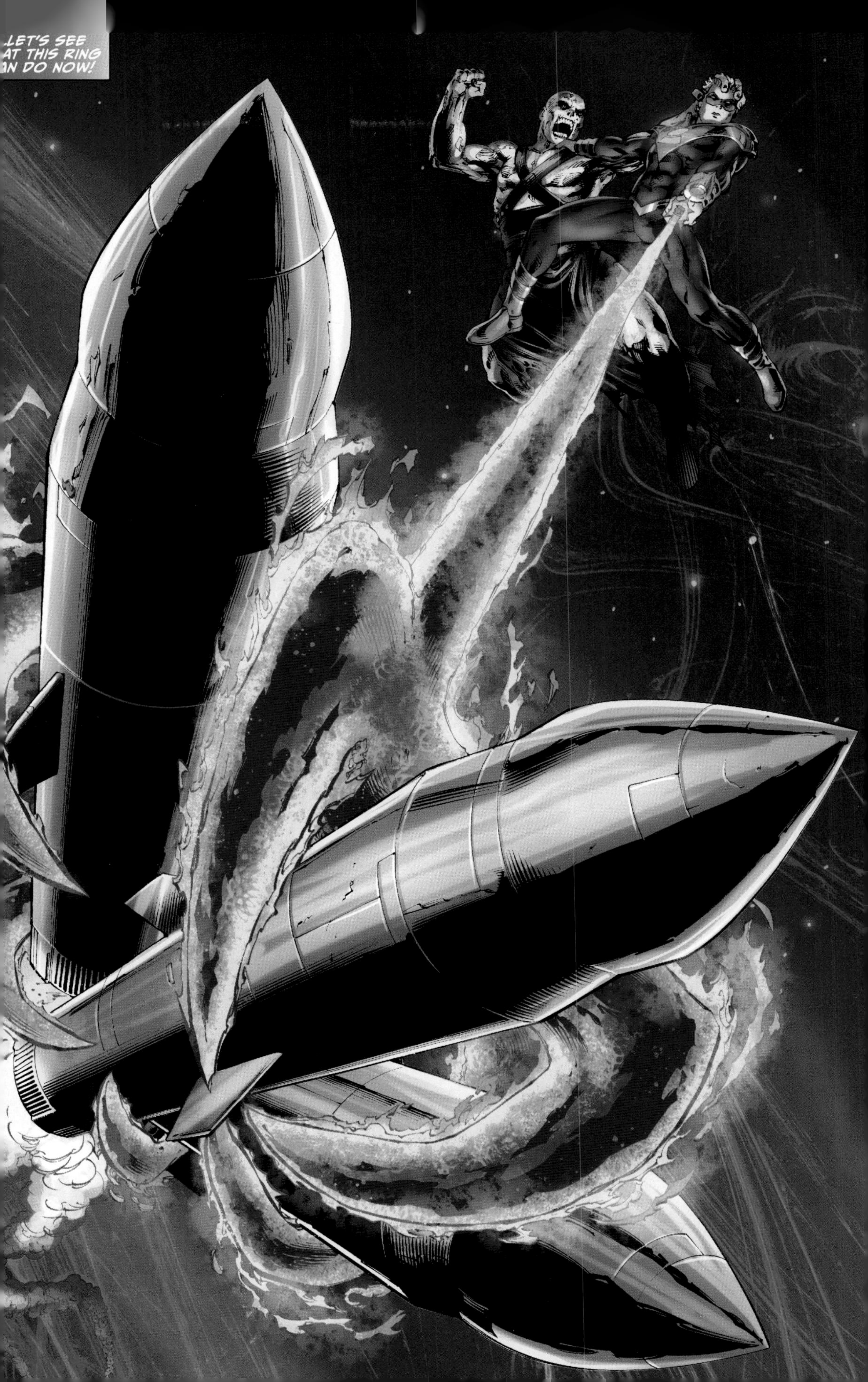
.LET'S SEE
AT THIS RING
AN DO NOW!

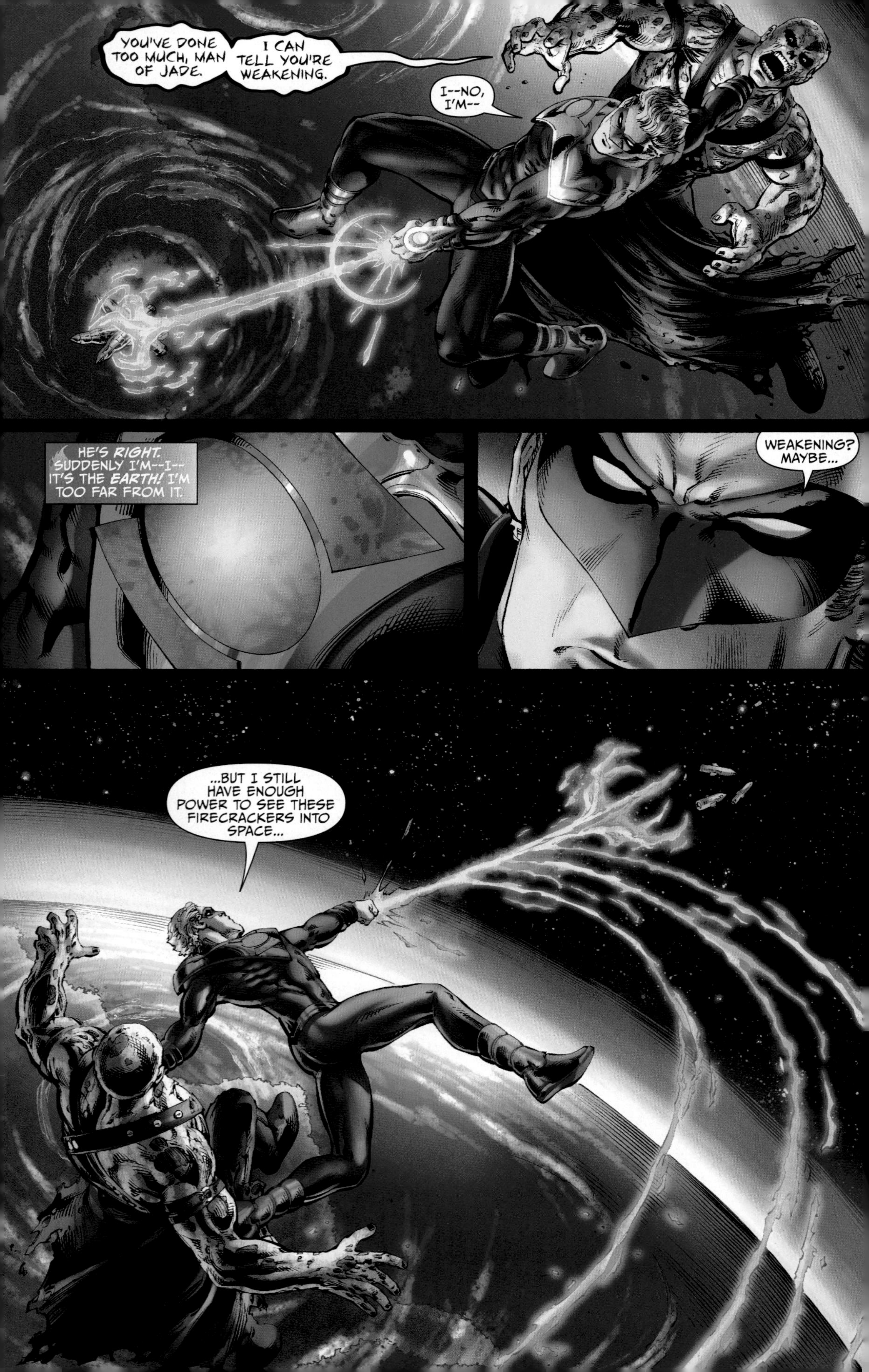
YOU'VE DONE TOO MUCH, MAN OF JADE.
I CAN TELL YOU'RE WEAKENING.
I--NO, I'M--
HE'S RIGHT. SUDDENLY I'M--I--IT'S THE EARTH! I'M TOO FAR FROM IT.
WEAKENING? MAYBE...
...BUT I STILL HAVE ENOUGH POWER TO SEE THESE FIRECRACKERS INTO SPACE...

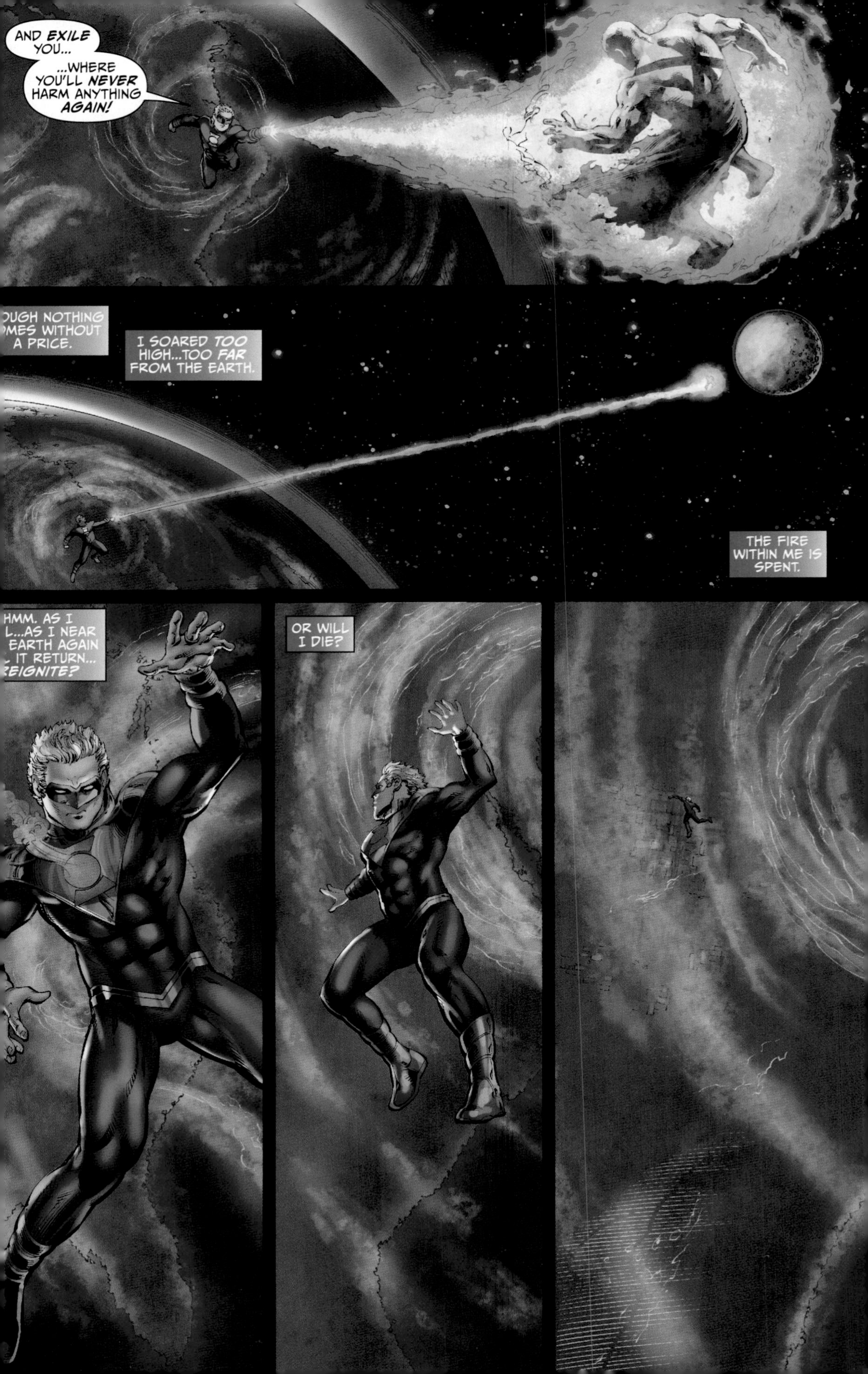
AND EXILE YOU...
...WHERE YOU'LL NEVER HARM ANYTHING AGAIN!
OUGH NOTHING OMES WITHOUT A PRICE.
I SOARED TOO HIGH...TOO FAR FROM THE EARTH.
THE FIRE WITHIN ME IS SPENT.
HMM. AS I L...AS I NEAR EARTH AGAIN IT RETURN... REIGNITE?
OR WILL I DIE?

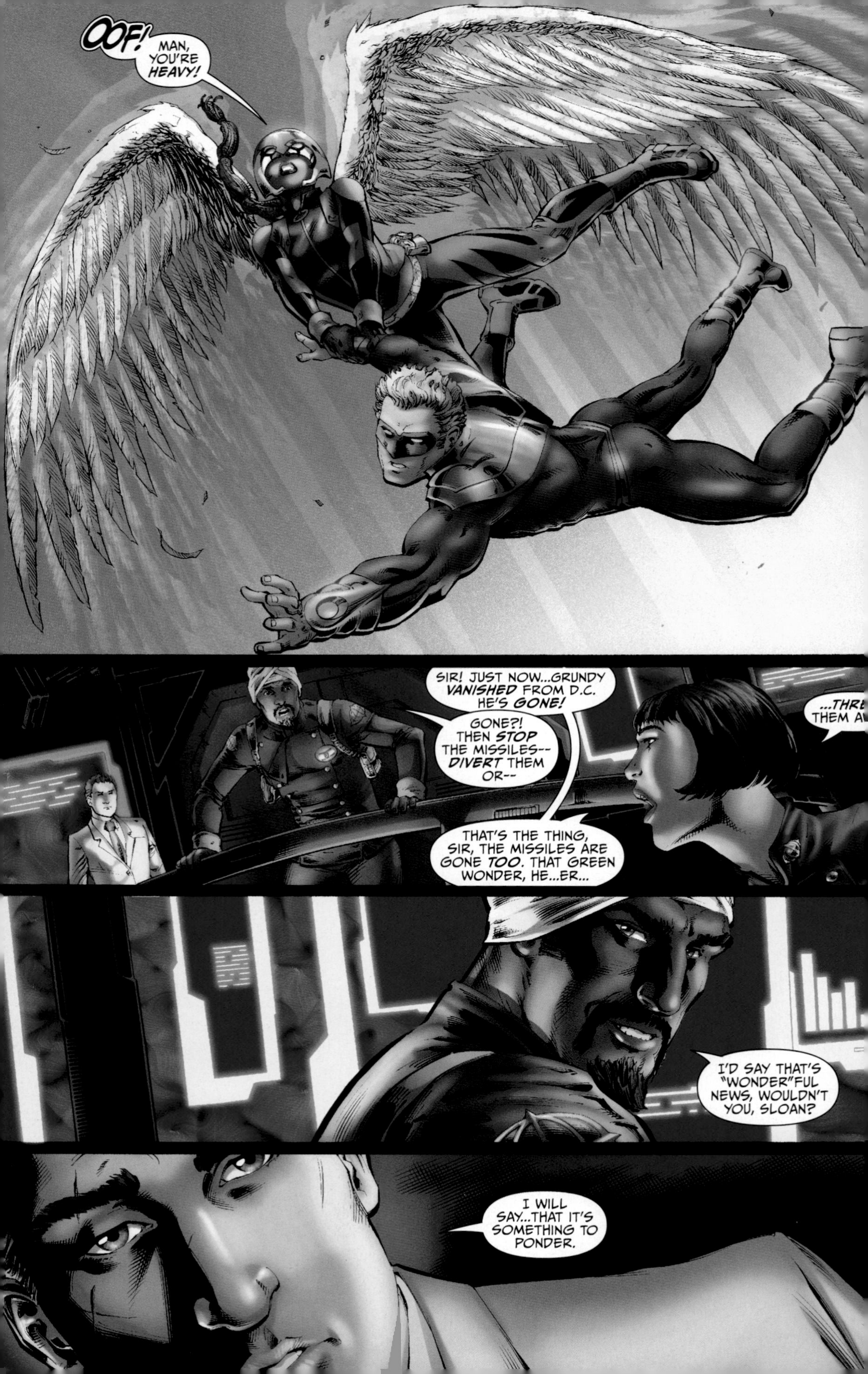
OOF!
MAN, YOU'RE HEAVY!
SIR! JUST NOW...GRUNDY VANISHED FROM D.C. HE'S GONE!
GONE?! THEN STOP THE MISSILES-- DIVERT THEM OR--
THAT'S THE THING, SIR, THE MISSILES ARE GONE TOO. THAT GREEN WONDER, HE...ER...
I'D SAY THAT'S "WONDER"FUL NEWS, WOULDN'T YOU, SLOAN?
I WILL SAY...THAT IT'S SOMETHING TO PONDER.

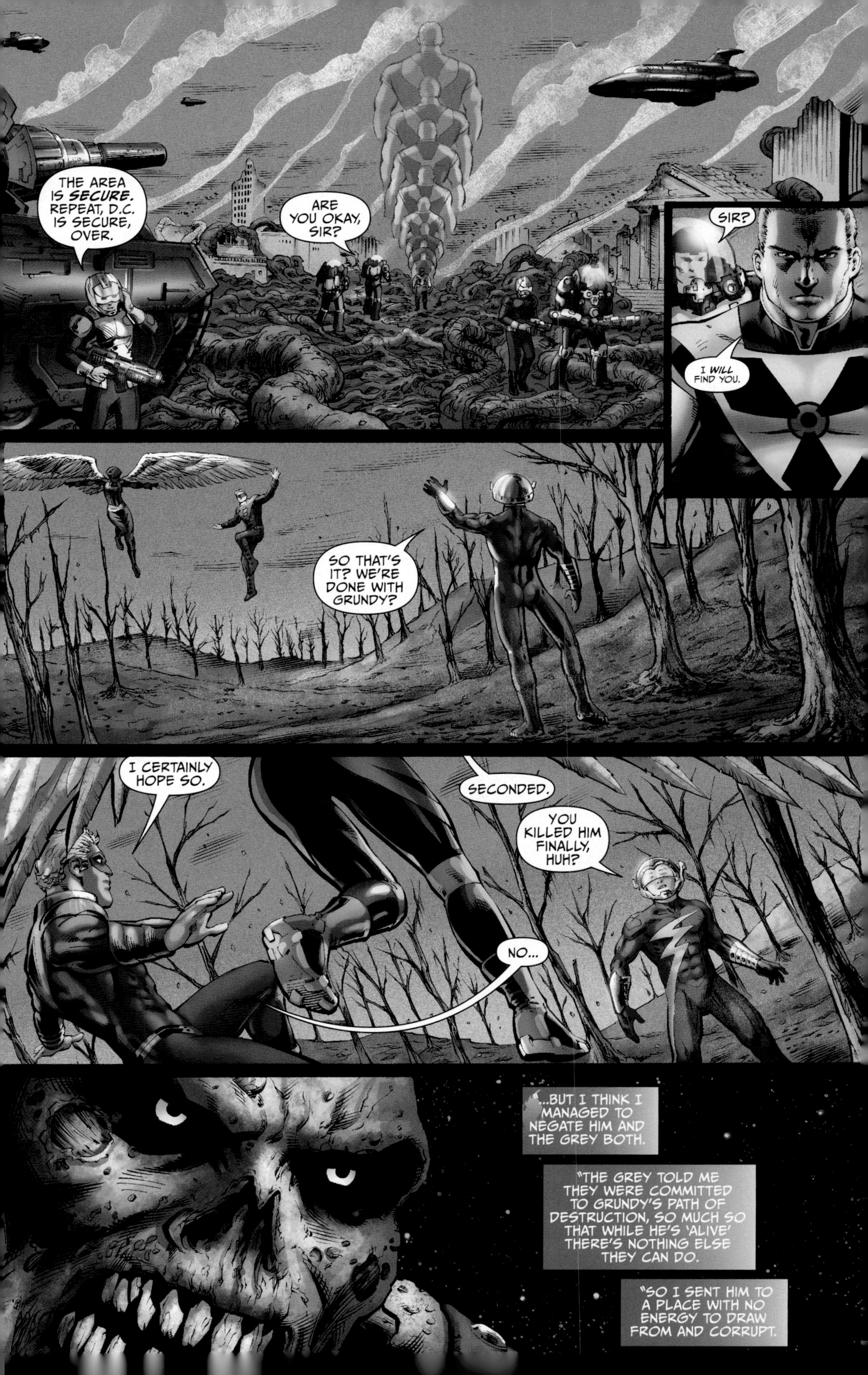
THE AREA IS SECURE. REPEAT, D.C. IS SECURE, OVER.
ARE YOU OKAY, SIR?
SIR?
I WILL FIND YOU.
SO THAT'S IT? WE'RE DONE WITH GRUNDY?
I CERTAINLY HOPE SO.
SECONDED.
YOU KILLED HIM FINALLY, HUH?
NO...
"...BUT I THINK I MANAGED TO NEGATE HIM AND THE GREY BOTH.
"THE GREY TOLD ME THEY WERE COMMITTED TO GRUNDY'S PATH OF DESTRUCTION, SO MUCH SO THAT WHILE HE'S 'ALIVE' THERE'S NOTHING ELSE THEY CAN DO.
"SO I SENT HIM TO A PLACE WITH NO ENERGY TO DRAW FROM AND CORRUPT.

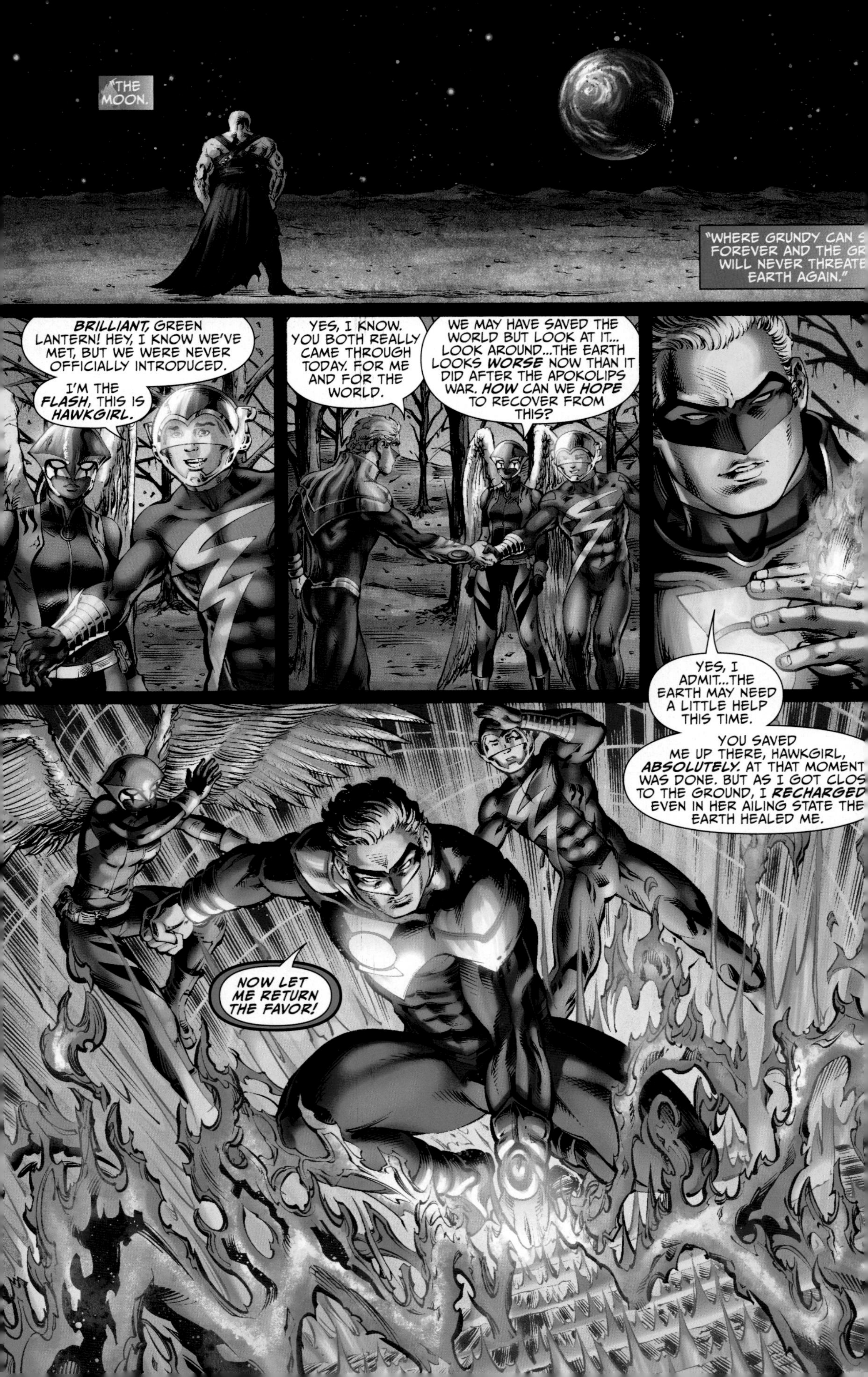
"THE MOON.
"WHERE GRUNDY CAN S
FOREVER AND THE GR
WILL NEVER THREATE
EARTH AGAIN."
BRILLIANT, GREEN LANTERN! HEY, I KNOW WE'VE MET, BUT WE WERE NEVER OFFICIALLY INTRODUCED.
I'M THE FLASH, THIS IS HAWKGIRL.
YES, I KNOW. YOU BOTH REALLY CAME THROUGH TODAY. FOR ME AND FOR THE WORLD.
WE MAY HAVE SAVED THE WORLD BUT LOOK AT IT... LOOK AROUND...THE EARTH LOOKS WORSE NOW THAN IT DID AFTER THE APOKOLIPS WAR. HOW CAN WE HOPE TO RECOVER FROM THIS?
YES, I ADMIT...THE EARTH MAY NEED A LITTLE HELP THIS TIME.
YOU SAVED ME UP THERE, HAWKGIRL, ABSOLUTELY. AT THAT MOMENT WAS DONE. BUT AS I GOT CLOS TO THE GROUND, I RECHARGED EVEN IN HER AILING STATE THE EARTH HEALED ME.
NOW LET ME RETURN THE FAVOR!

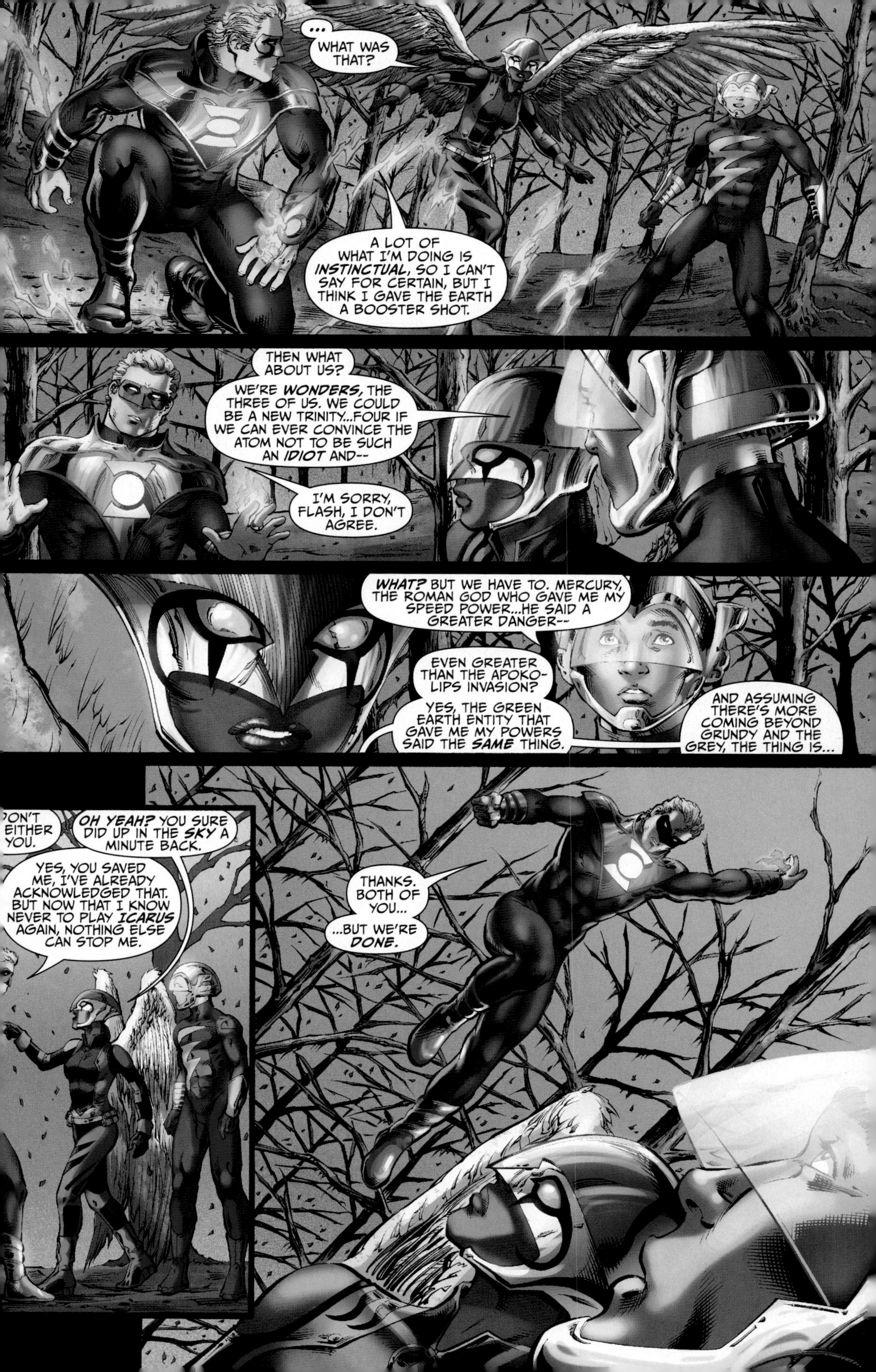

...
WHAT WAS THAT?
A LOT OF WHAT I'M DOING IS *INSTINCTUAL*, SO I CAN'T SAY FOR CERTAIN, BUT I THINK I GAVE THE EARTH A BOOSTER SHOT.
THEN WHAT ABOUT US?
WE'RE *WONDERS*, THE THREE OF US. WE COULD BE A NEW TRINITY...FOUR IF WE CAN EVER CONVINCE THE ATOM NOT TO BE SUCH AN *IDIOT* AND--
I'M SORRY, FLASH, I DON'T AGREE.
WHAT? BUT WE HAVE TO. MERCURY, THE ROMAN GOD WHO GAVE ME MY SPEED POWER...HE SAID A GREATER DANGER--
EVEN GREATER THAN THE APOKOLIPS INVASION?
YES, THE GREEN EARTH ENTITY THAT GAVE ME MY POWERS SAID THE *SAME* THING.
AND ASSUMING THERE'S MORE COMING BEYOND GRUNDY AND THE GREY, THE THING IS...
EITHER YOU.
OH YEAH? YOU SURE DID UP IN THE *SKY* A MINUTE BACK.
YES, YOU SAVED ME, I'VE ALREADY ACKNOWLEDGED THAT. BUT NOW THAT I KNOW NEVER TO PLAY *ICARUS* AGAIN, NOTHING ELSE CAN STOP ME.
THANKS. BOTH OF YOU...
...BUT WE'RE *DONE.*

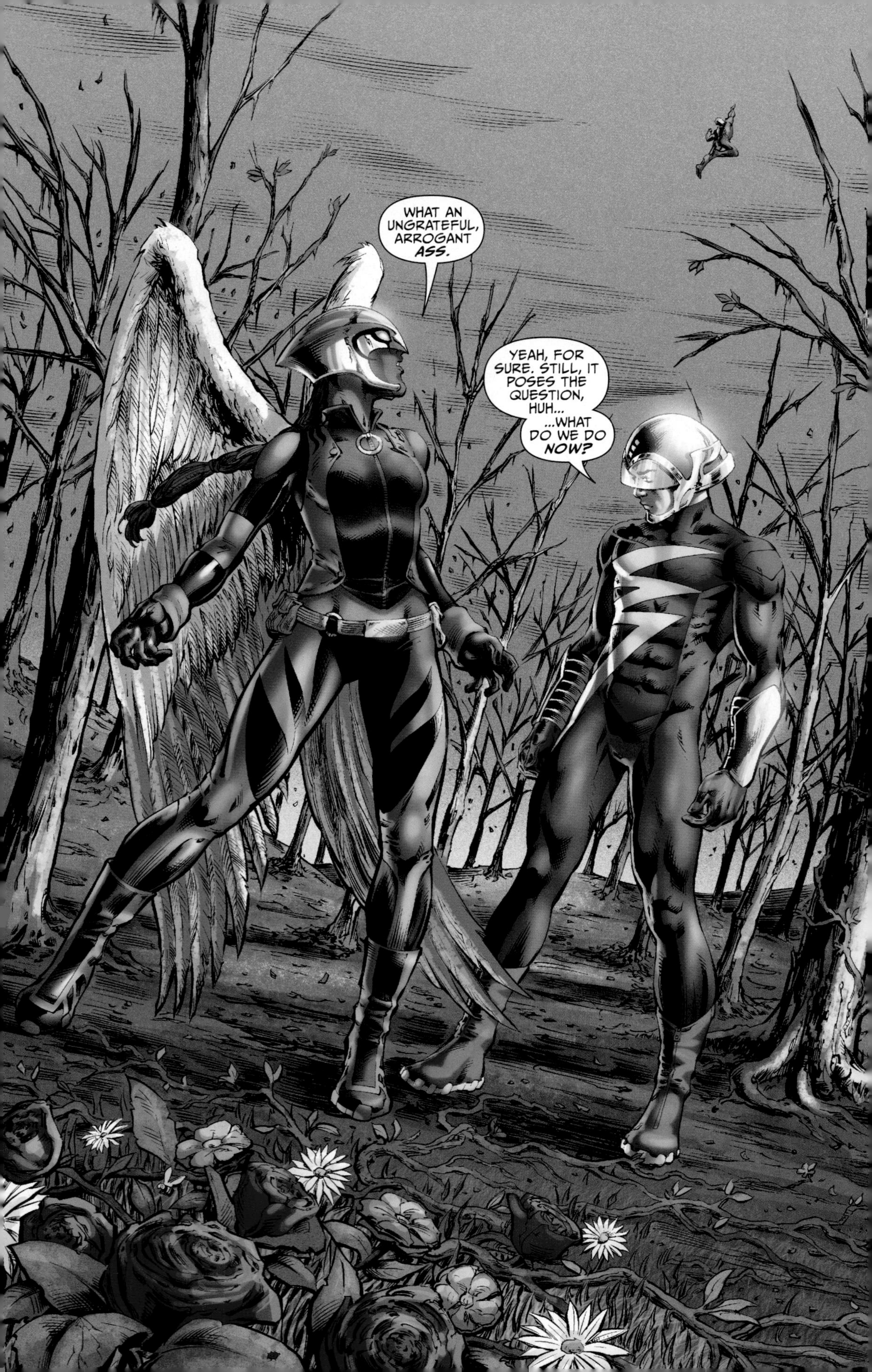
WHAT AN UNGRATEFUL, ARROGANT ASS.
YEAH, FOR SURE. STILL, IT POSES THE QUESTION, HUH...
...WHAT DO WE DO NOW?

EARTH 2 #1 variant cover art by Bryan Hitch & Paul Mounts

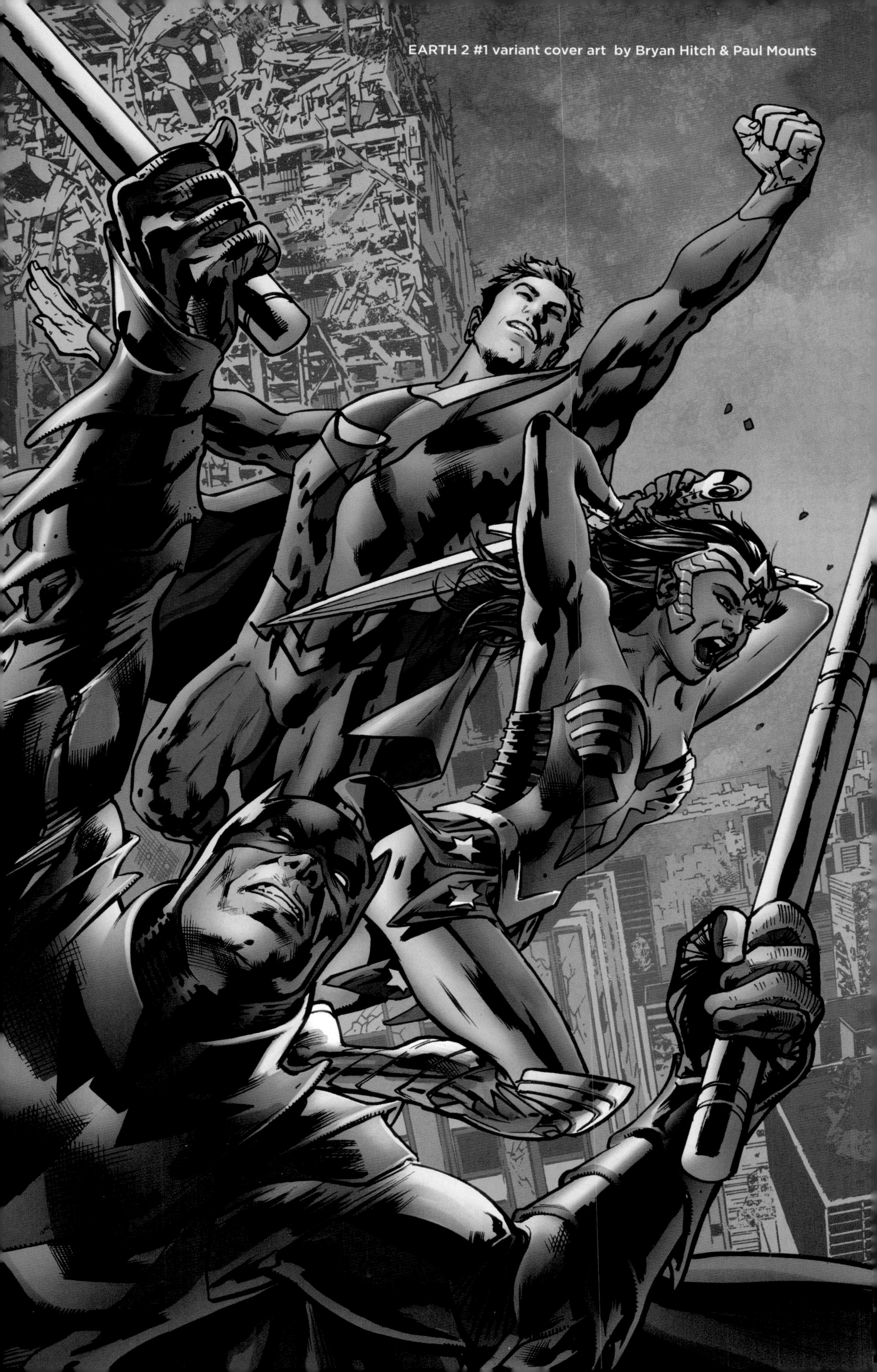

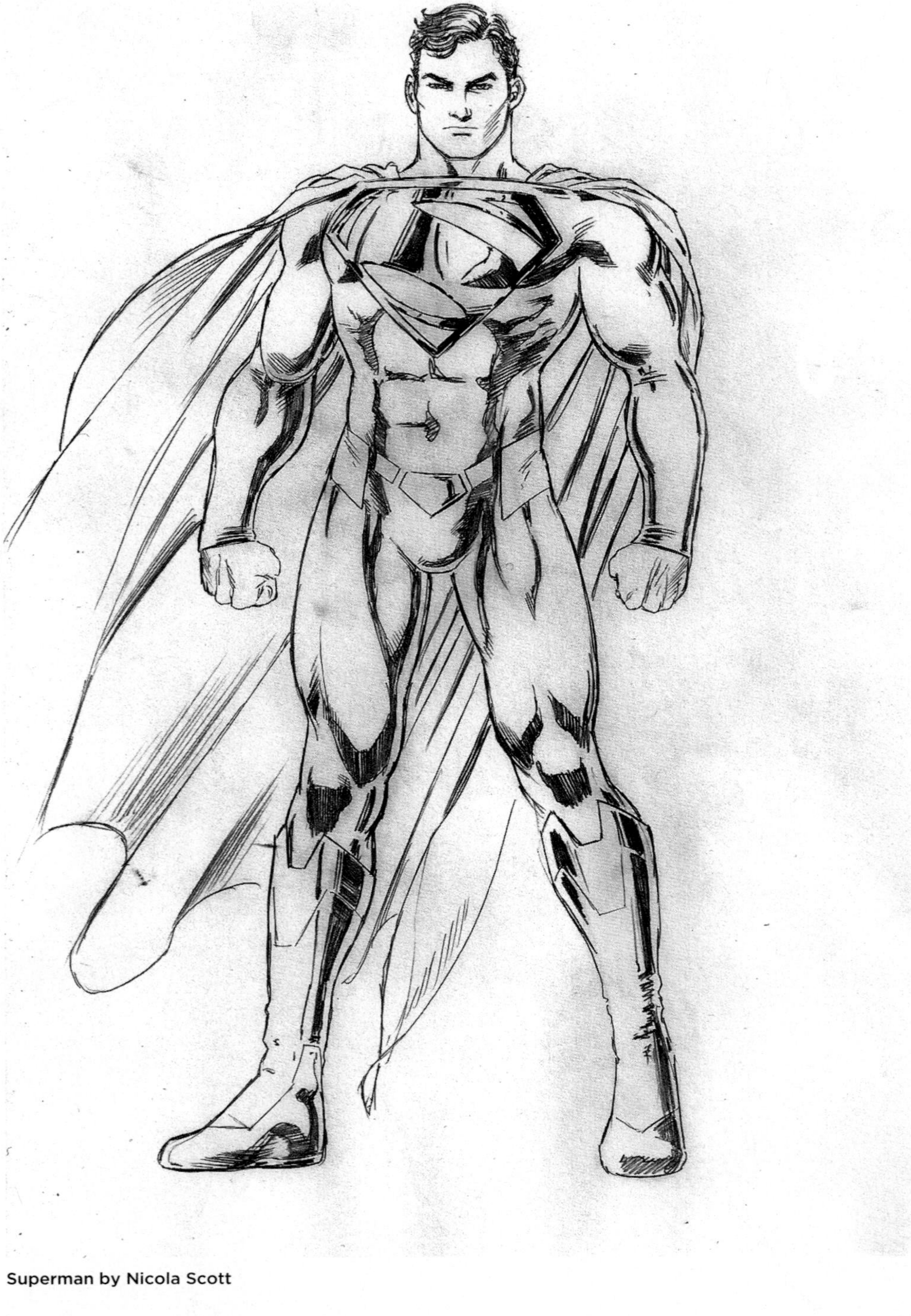

Superman by Nicola Scott

Vonder Woman by Nicola Scott

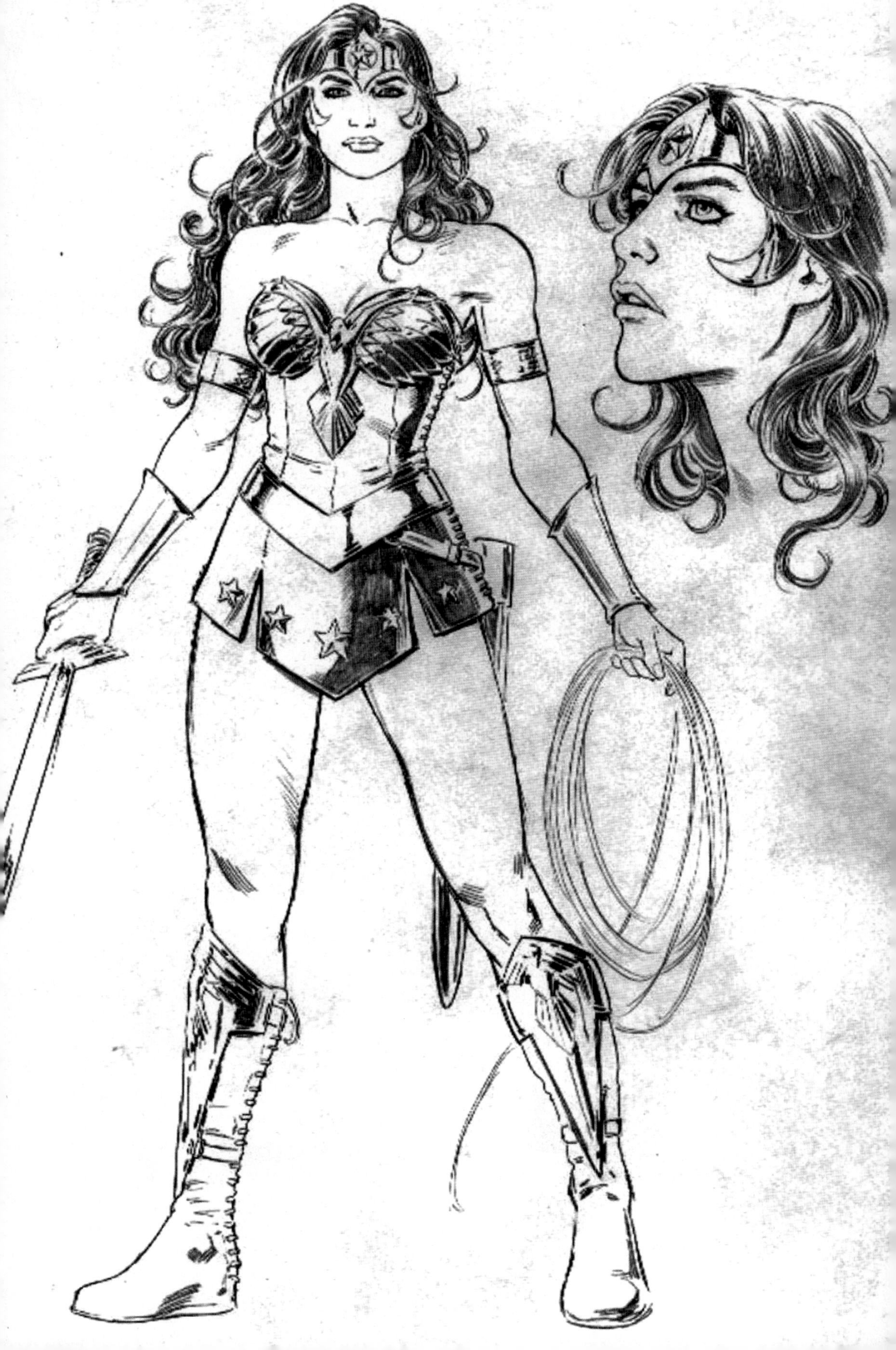

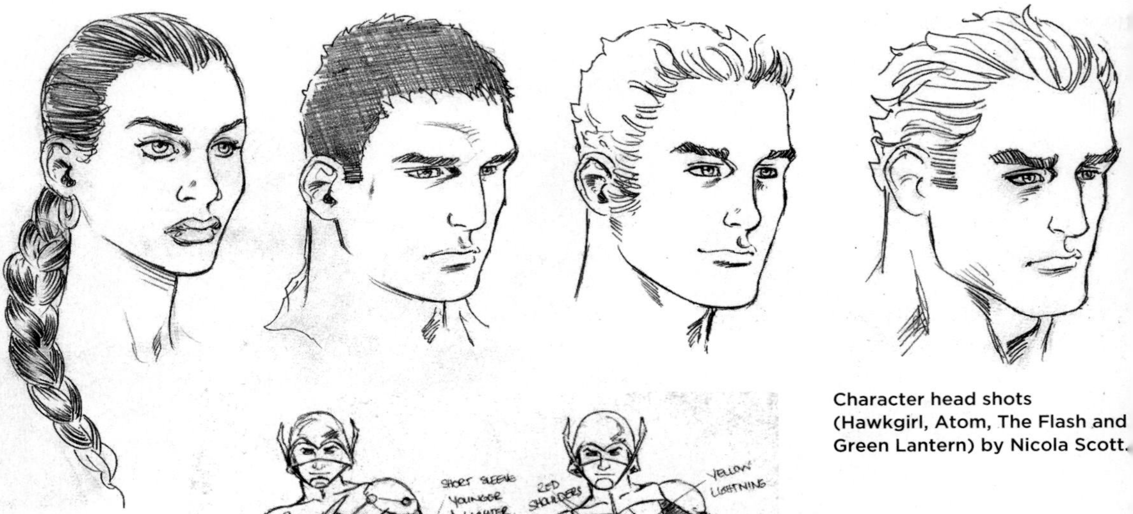

Character head shots (Hawkgirl, Atom, The Flash and Green Lantern) by Nicola Scott.

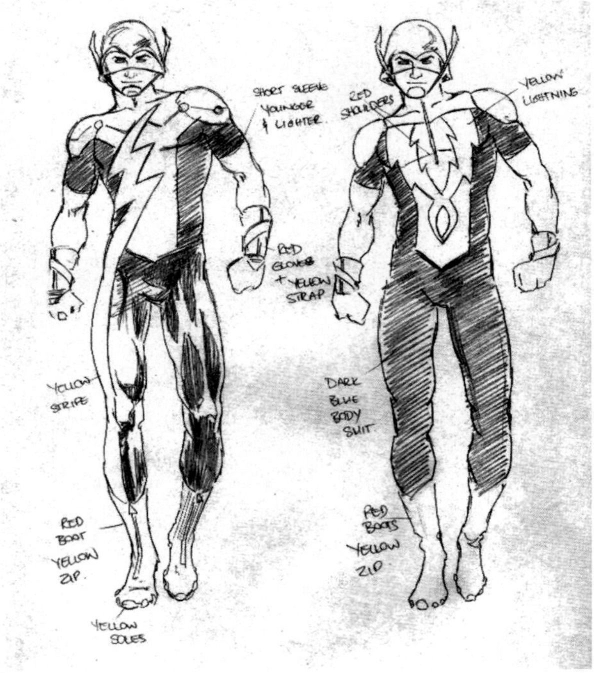
SHORT SLEEVE
YOUNGER & LIGHTER
RED GLOVES + YELLOW STRAP
YELLOW STRIPE
RED BOOT
YELLOW ZIP.
YELLOW SOLES
RED SHOULDERS
YELLOW LIGHTNING
DARK BLUE BODY SUIT
RED BOOTS
YELLOW ZIP

The Flash by Nicola Scott

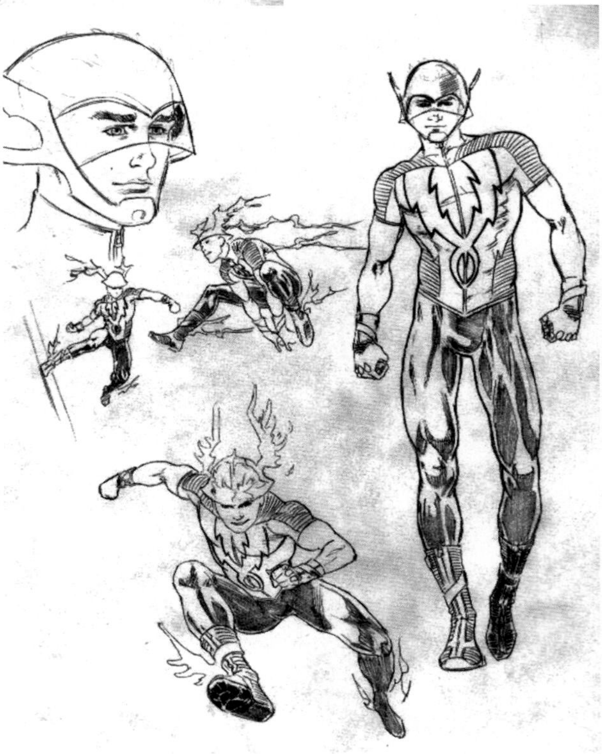

The Sandmen by Nicola Scott

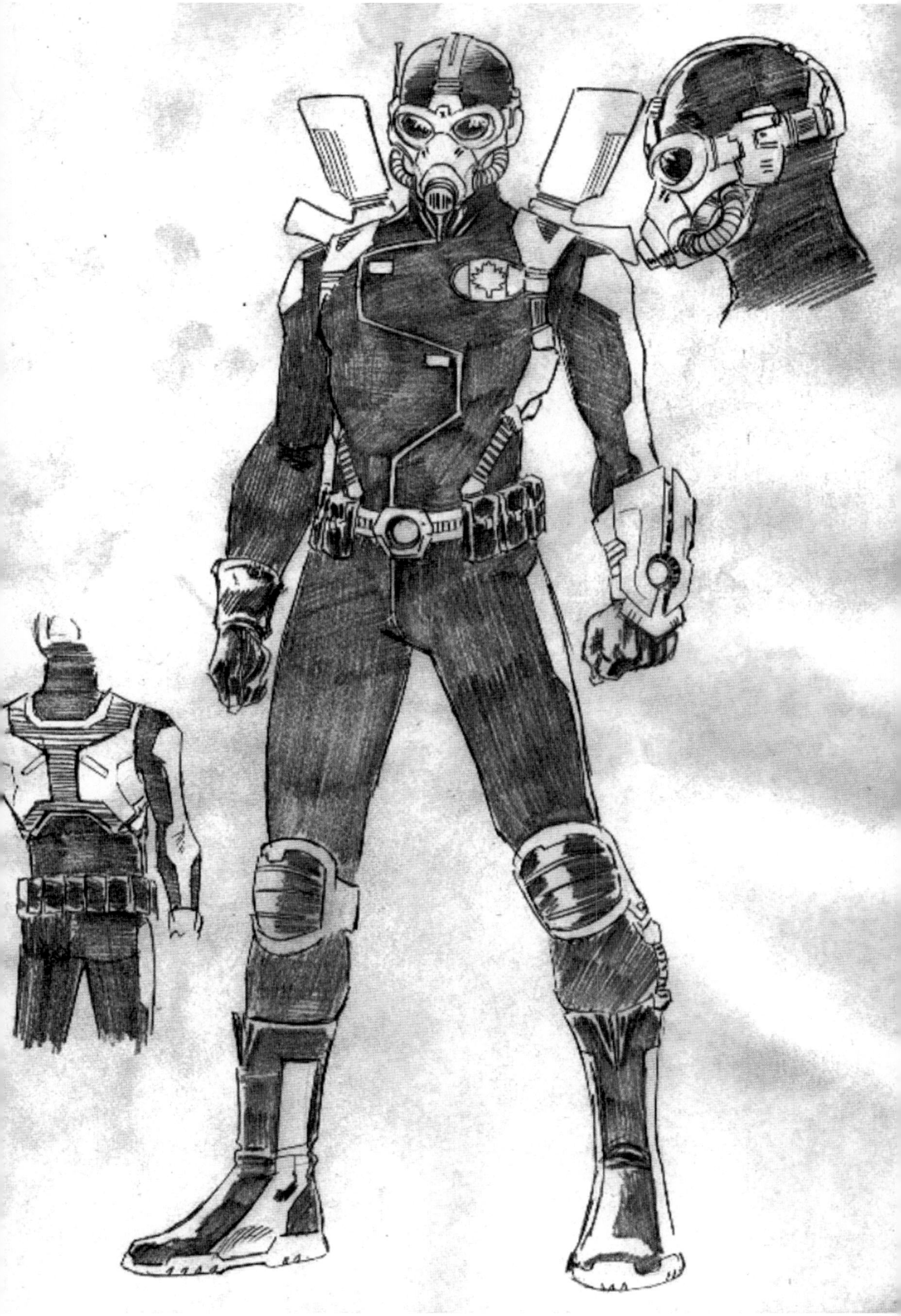

Batman sketch by Jim Lee

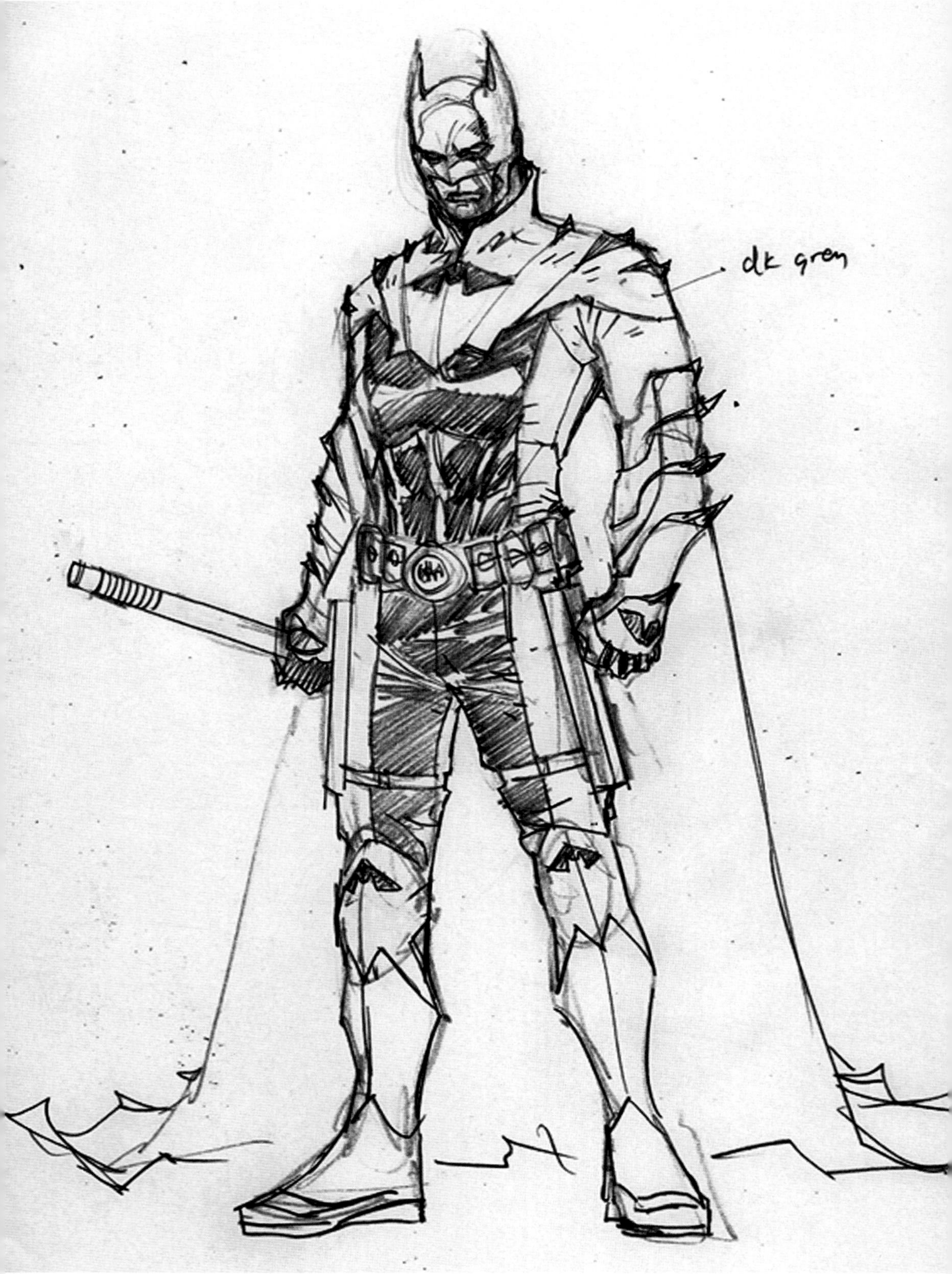
dk grey

reen Lantern by Joe Prado

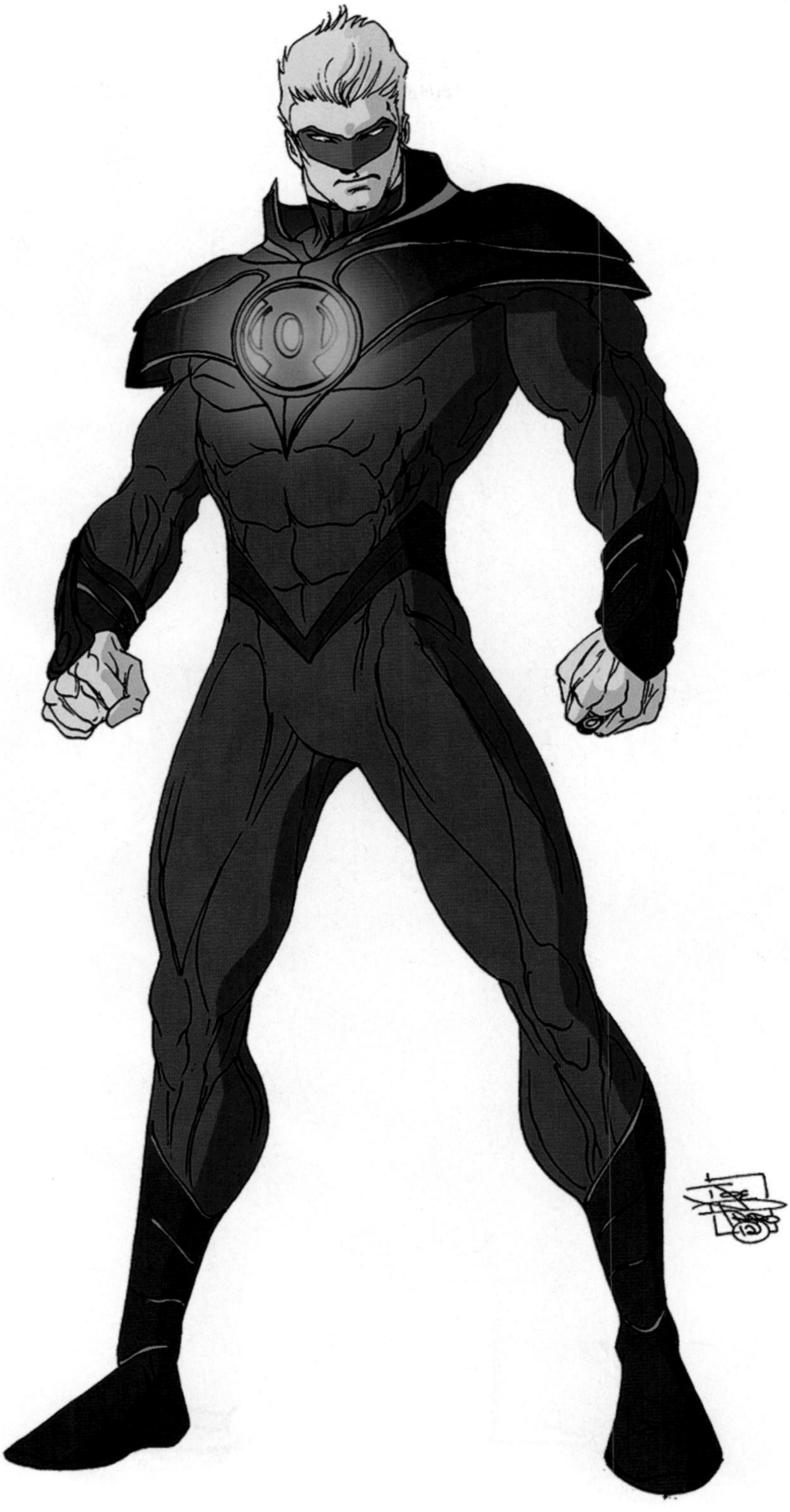

The Atom by Jim Lee

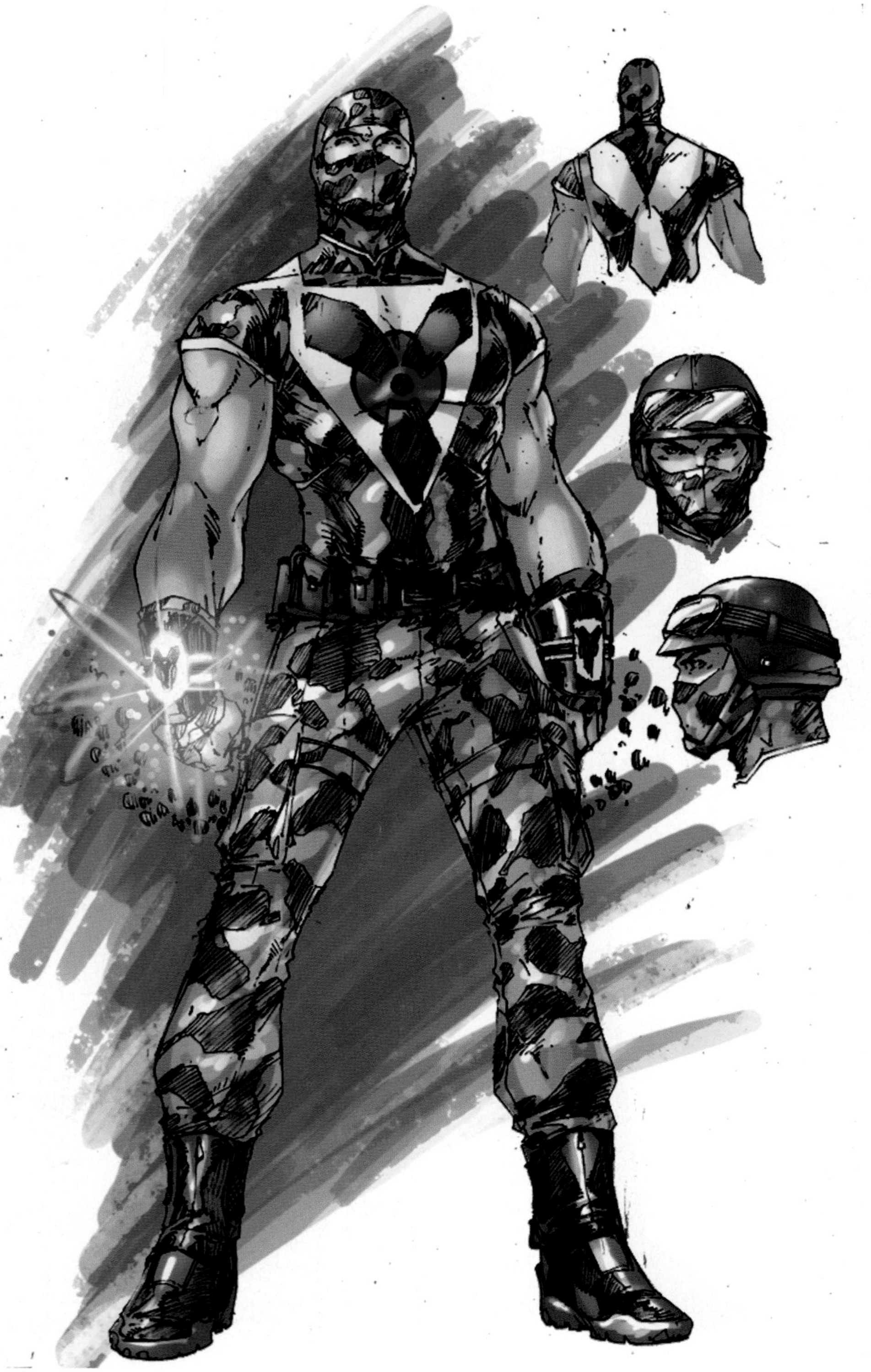

teppenwolf by Jim Lee

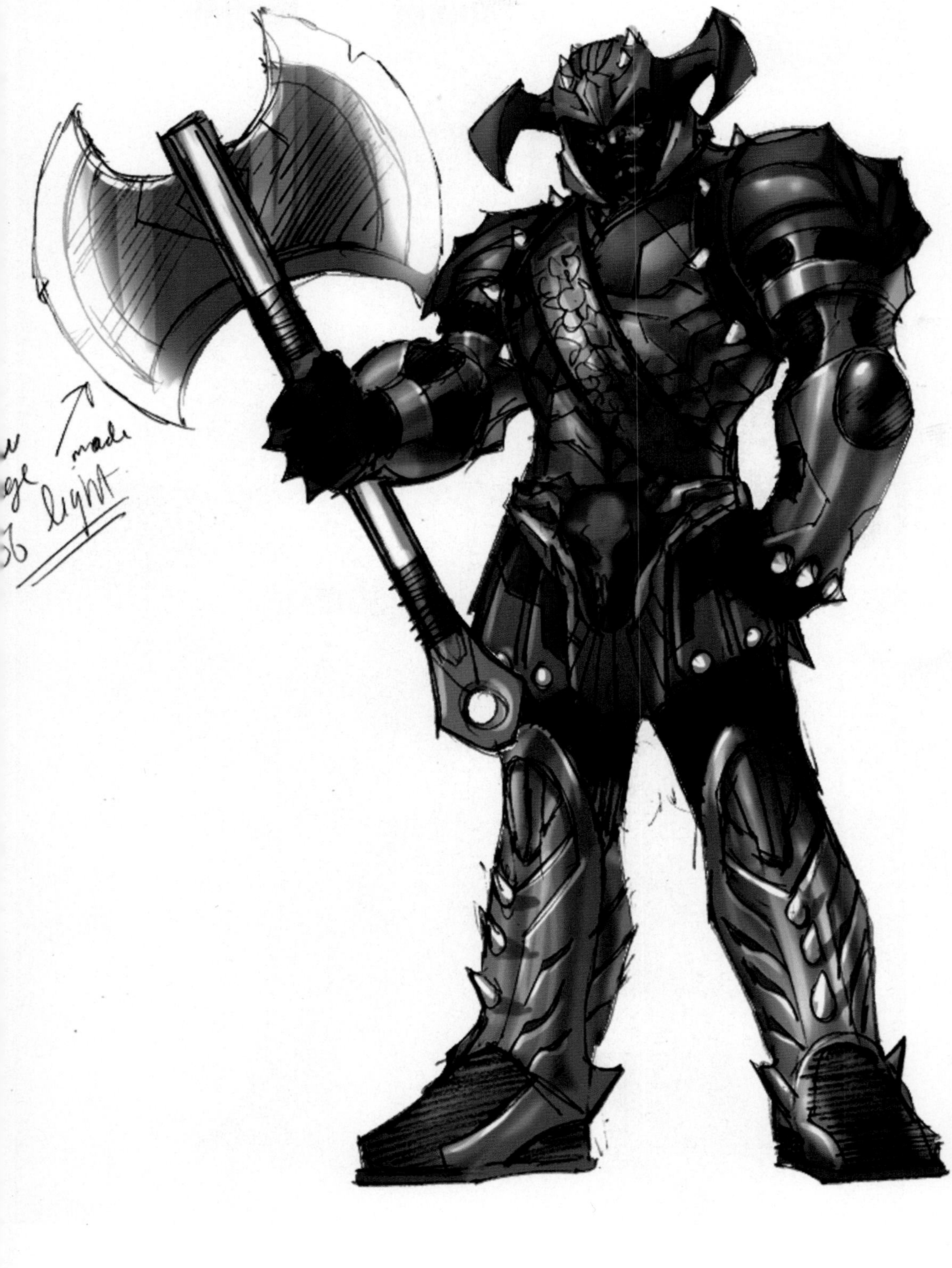
made
light

Solomon Grundy by Jim Lee

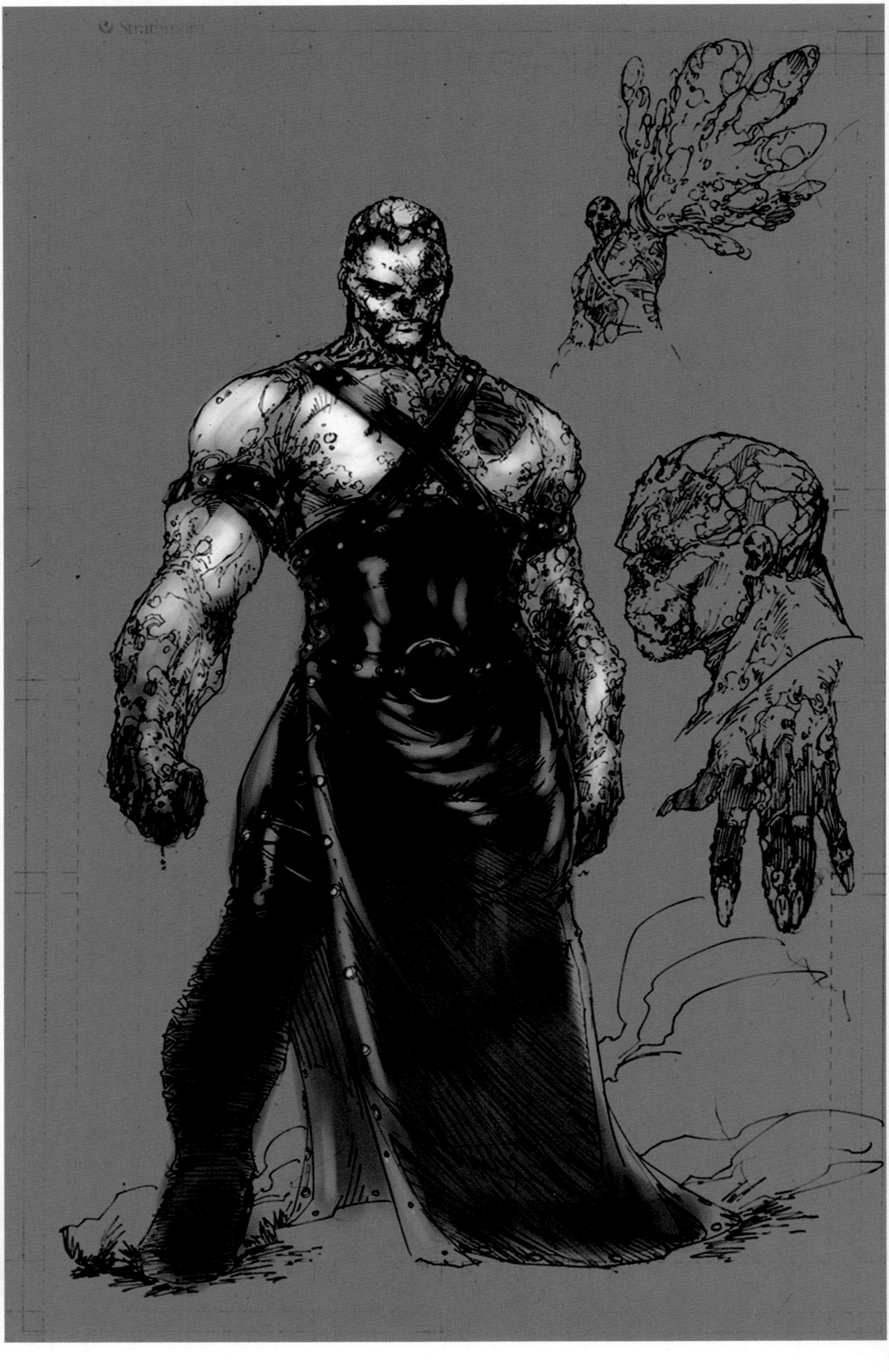

EARTH 2

PENCILLED PAGES FROM EARTH 2 #1 BY NICOLA SCOTT

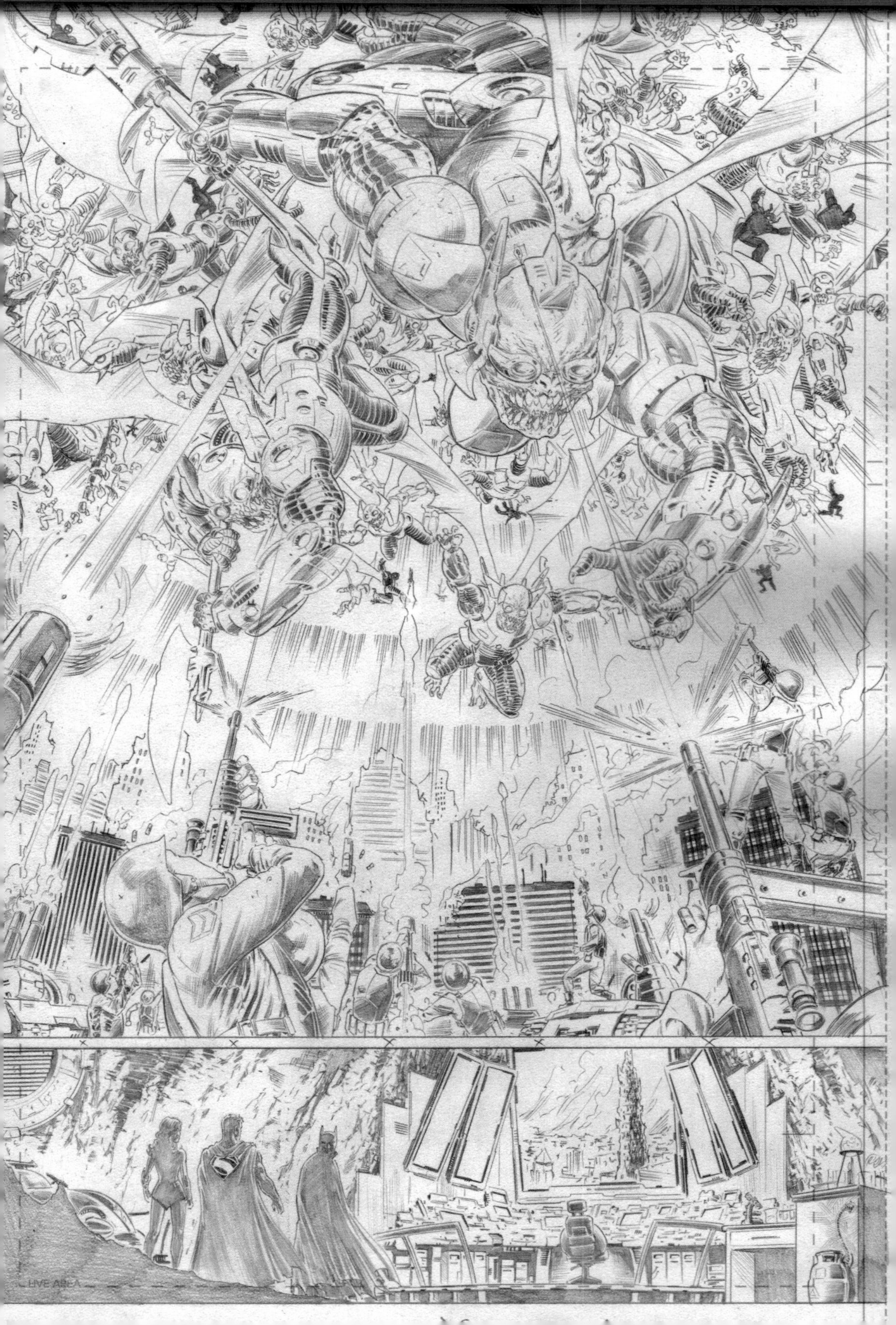

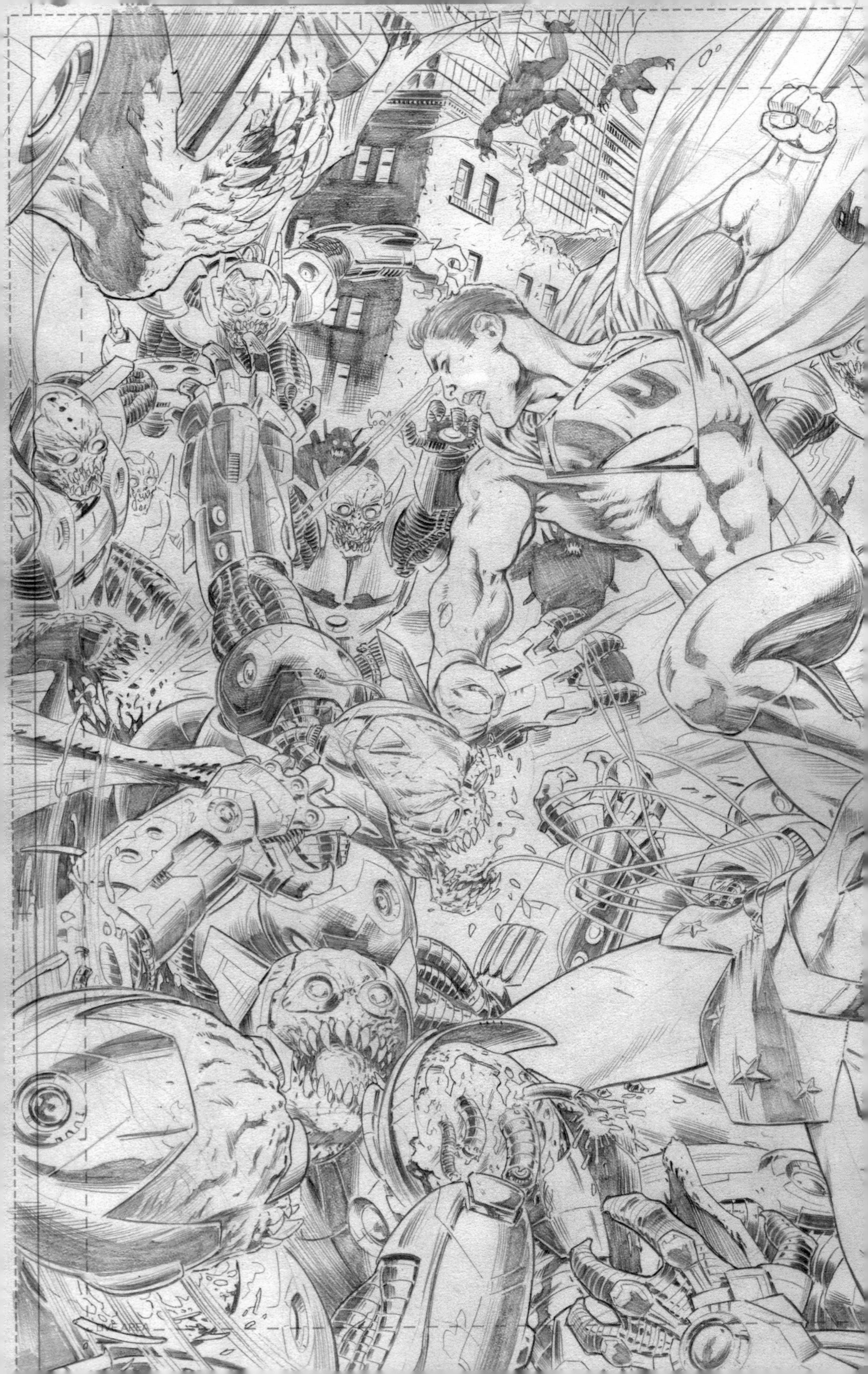

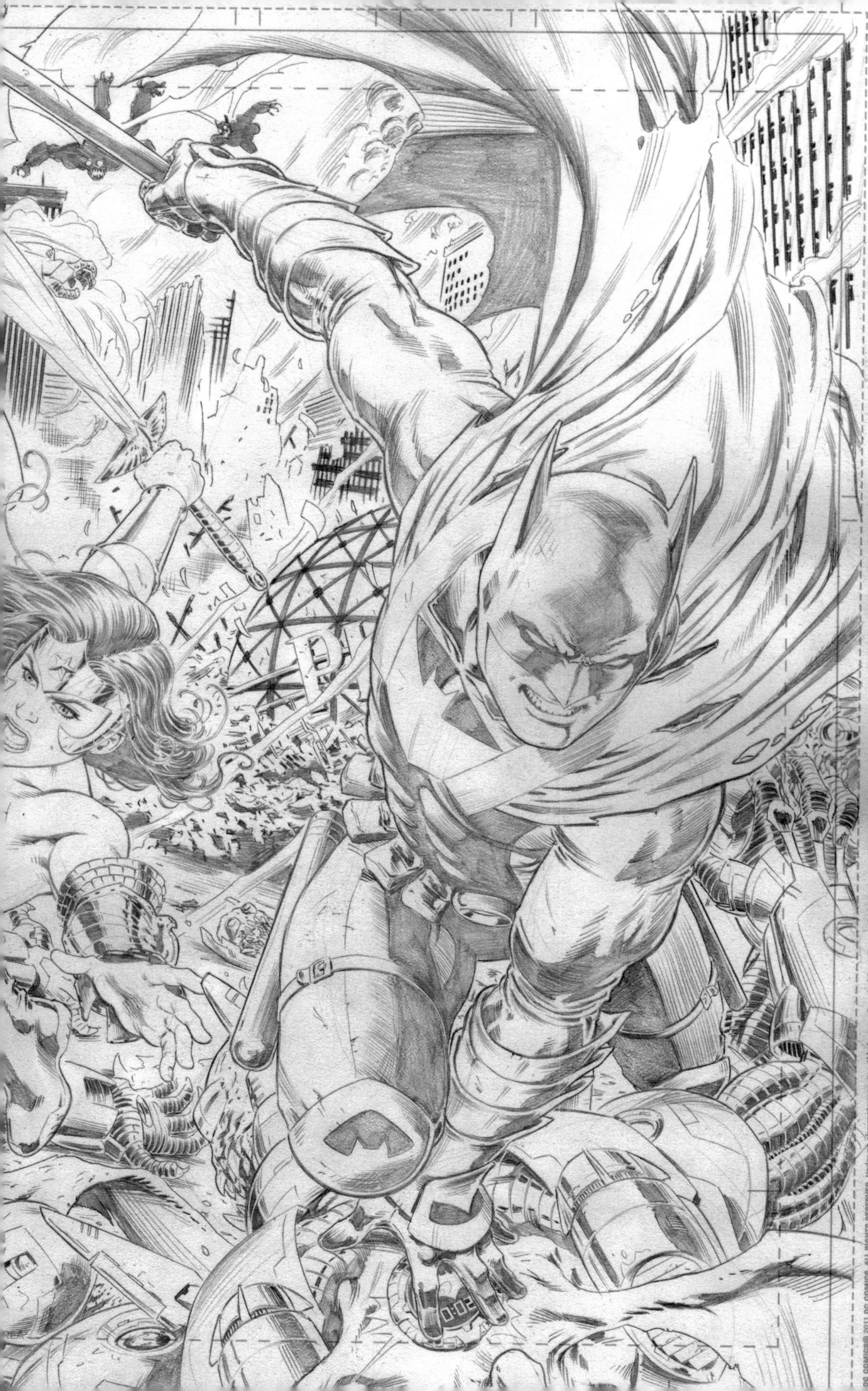
0:02

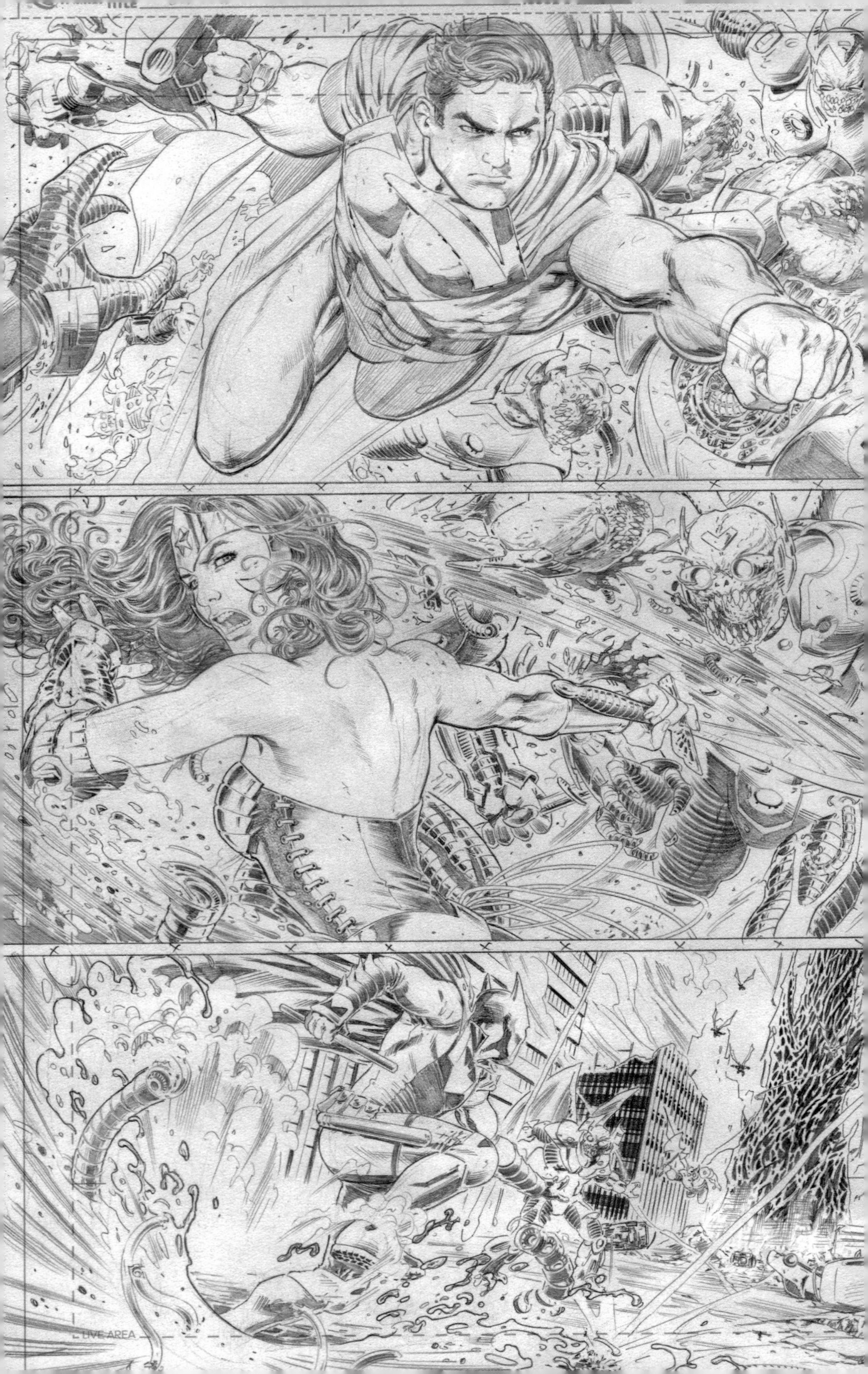
LIVE AREA